Topics in Mathematics for the Eleventh Grade
Based on teaching practices in Waldorf schools

Topics in Mathematics for the Eleventh Grade

Based on teaching practices in Waldorf schools

Analytical Geometry
Projective Geometry
Spherical Geometry
Sequences and Limits

Peter Baum, Karl-F. Georg, Uwe Hansen, Markus Hünig,
Klaus Labudde, Rolf Rosbigalle, Stephan Sigler
Editor: Robert Neumann

Published by the Lesson Plan Initiative of the Pedagogical Research Center in Kassel in cooperation with Waldorf Publications and the Research Institute for Waldorf Education.
Printed with the support of the Waldorf Curriculum Fund

www.lehrerseminar-forschung.de
www.waldorfbuch.de
www.waldorfpublications.org

Impressum

All portions of this book are protected by copyright. All rights reserved, in particular the rights to translate the material, and the rights to any form of reproduction or even partial reproduction in any way. The translation has not been revised by the authors.

© Bildungswerk Beruf und Umwelt

1. Edition 1-15-2011
Reprinted 6-30-2014
Typesetting: Robert Neumann, Freiburg
Printed by Waldorf Publications

Contents

Analytic Geometry as an Example of Efficiency in Teaching
    (Uwe Hansen) 7

Introduction to Analytical Geometry
    (Karl-Friedrich Georg) 21

A Characterization of Analytic Geometry
    (Uwe Hansen) 35

Stepping-Stones in a Projective Geometry Block
    (Stephan Sigler) 49

Projective Geometry – the main lesson block in the 11th grade
    (Karl-Friedrich Georg) 71

Projective Geometry
    (Markus Hünig) 149

A Path to Projective Geometry
    (Rolf Rosbigalle) 175

From Ratio to Cross-Ratio
    (Uwe Hansen) 201

Spherical Geometry
    (Klaus Labudde) 211

The Inner Symmetry of Spherical Geometry
    (Uwe Hansen) 223

Basic Spherical Trigonometry
    (Peter Baum) 227

The Angle Cosine Rule of Spherical Trigonometry
    (Peter Baum) 229

Constructing and Solving Spherical Triangles
    (Peter Baum) 231

The Conic Section
    (Peter Baum) 239

The Projective Construction of the Conic Section
    (Peter Baum) 243

Orthogonal Pencils of Circles
    (Peter Baum) 255

Creating Regular Solids from the Tetrahedron
    (Uwe Hansen) 265

A Note about Limits
    (Uwe Hansen) 277

Preface

With this volume, Topics in Mathematics for the 11th Grade, the «Math Curriculum Initiative» work-group presents its most substantial production so far.

The focal topic being projective geometry, it seemed reasonable to go into considerable detail here, especially since there is hardly any literature about teaching this topic. The few – but precious – existing texts are referenced in the articles. Aside from this it was a concern of the team to present a broad cross-section of the great variety of possible ways of handling the subject matter especially of this topic in the classroom. Thus one will find very diverse approaches in the various articles devoted to introducing projective geometry in the 11th Grade. They have resulted from the particular teaching situations as well as the personal experiences and leanings of the authors. They represent a broad spectrum of alternatives which should stimulate the reader ultimately to find his or her own way.

In contrast, spherical geometry and trigonometry are frequently dealt with in the technical literature, whether in relation to geodesy, cartography or astronomy, so the emphasis here was on the choice of subject matter and its method of preparation.

Analytic geometry is treated in many textbooks. For instruction in a Waldorf school many considerations arise relating to content or methodology for which there is no provision in these books, however. Thus, even those familiar with analytic geometry as customarily treated in schools will be able to discover in this volume relevant suggestions, interesting cross connections and unexpected approaches.

A few articles containing background knowledge, little insights, or basic pedagogic observations round off the book.

The authors, who have brought together their experiences with such commitment, hope that this book, too, will be able to provide beginners with assistance in getting started and experienced colleagues with stimuli for further work.

I would like to express our warm thanks to Sebastian Labusch, who did a great deal of the word-processing and type-setting.

Markus Hünig Mülheim an der Ruhr, Spring 2006

Preface

Preface to the English Edition

This book is the second in the series of «green books» for mathematics teachers to be translated. It is considerably more extensive than the tenth-grade book, chiefly due to its many articles about projective geometry. Because many teachers may be relatively unfamiliar with this topic, we decided to translate all of these. Each is presented according to its author's unique viewpoint, providing a good opportunity to become acquainted with the topic.

Projective geometry is rarely taught outside of Waldorf Schools. As it offers a wonderful opportunity to exercise the imagination and thinking, extending these to embrace the points at infinity without leaving the secure ground of mathematics, it would be advantageous for this branch of geometry to be more widely taught.

As the book was translated by several different people, the articles might vary at times in expressions and style.

Special thanks go to the translators, Paul Courtney, Brent Daeuble, Harlan Gilbert and Charles Gunn, and to those who funded the translation, the Pädagogische Forschungsstelle in Kassel and the Association of Waldorf Schools of North America.

Robert Neumann

December 2010

Analytic Geometry as an Example of Efficiency in Teaching

UWE HANSEN

Teachers experience daily that the lesson time is insufficient to present subjects in sufficient depth. The following examples will draw on topics from various realms to show how lessons can be given an enlivened form while incorporating brief and cogent presentations of the most significant aspects of a subject.

Example 1

Through tasks in transformational geometry, students can practice the mapping of points using the coordinate system.

A 90° clockwise rotation around the point Z(2, 1) can be defined by:

$$P(x, y) \rightarrow P'(y+1, -x+3)$$

By applying this transformation recursively, triangle ABC gives rise to three further triangles:

$$
\begin{array}{ccccccccc}
A(3, 2) & \rightarrow & A'(3, 0) & \rightarrow & A''(1, 0) & \rightarrow & A'''(1, 2) & \rightarrow & A \\
B(5, 1) & \rightarrow & B'(2, -2) & \rightarrow & B''(-1, 1) & \rightarrow & B'''(2, 4) & \rightarrow & B \\
C(4, 4) & \rightarrow & C'(5, -1) & \rightarrow & C''(0, -2) & \rightarrow & C'''(-1, 3) & \rightarrow & C
\end{array}
$$

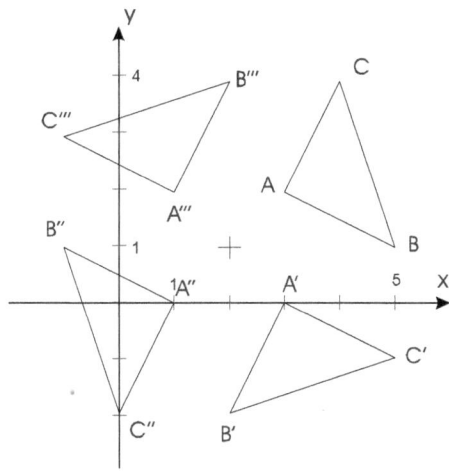

Figure 1

If the center of rotation has coordinates Z(a, b), then a 90° clockwise rotation is given by

$$P(x, y) \rightarrow P'(y+a-b, -x+a+b)$$

While a 90° counter-clockwise rotation around $Z(a, b)$ is given by:

$$P(x, y) \to P'(-y+a+b, x-a+b)$$

Example 2

Triangle ABC with $A(4, 3)$, $B(7, 1)$, $C(10, 2)$ is transformed through the following seven transformations:

a) $P(x, y) \to P'(x, 4-y)$ reflection across axis $y = 2$
b) $P(x, y) \to P'(6-x, y)$ reflection across axis $x = 3$
c) $P(x, y) \to P'(y+1, x-1)$ reflection across axis $y = x - 1$
d) $P(x, y) \to P'(-y+5, -x+5)$ reflection across axis $y = -x+5$
e) $P(x, y) \to P'(y+1, -x+5)$ 90° clockwise rotation around $Z(3 \mid 2)$
f) $P(x, y) \to P'(-y+5, x-1)$ 90° clockwise rotation around $Z(3 \mid 2)$
g) $P(x, y) \to P'(-x+6, -y+4)$ reflection across axis $Z(3 \mid 2)$

All the figures should be constructed in the same diagram, giving figure 2.

Together with the identity operation these transformations compose a non-commutative group of order 8.

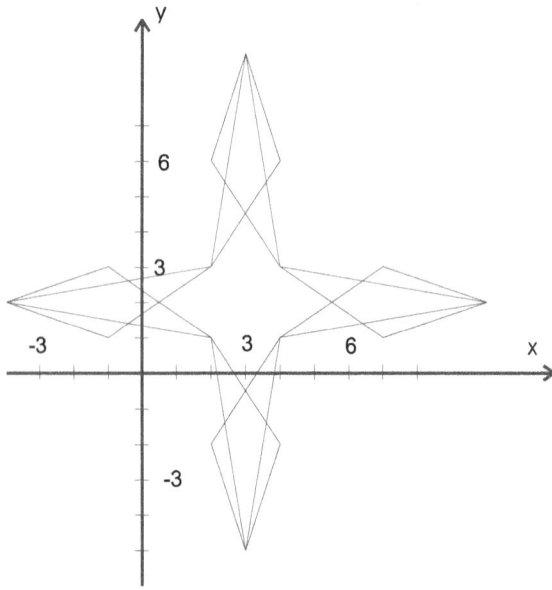

Figure 2

Example 3

Reflecting a point successively across two mutually-intersecting lines results in a rotation around the point of intersection, with the angle of rotation equal to twice the angle of intersection.

If we choose the x-axis as the first axis of reflection $P(x, y) \to P'(x, -y)$ and the angle-bisector $y = x$ as the second axis of reflection $P(x, y) \to P'(y, x)$, then we arrive at a 90° counter-clockwise rotation around the origin. The image point P should then be put through these same two reflections repeatedly.

Using a starting point $P(2, 1)$ gives figure 3 below.

The reflection across the line $y = x + k$ can be described by the transformation:

$$P(x, y) \to P'(y - k, x + k)$$

The reflection across the line $y = -x + k$ can be described by the transformation:

$$P(x, y) \to P'(-y + k, -x + k)$$

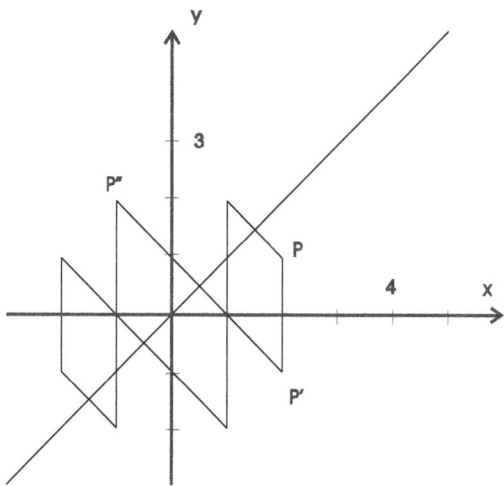

Figure 3

Example 4

By joining the reflection across the axis $y = x + 2$, describable by $P(x, y) \to P'(y - 2, x + 2)$ with the reflection across the axis $y = -x - 2$, describable by $P(x, y) \to P'(-y - 2, -x - 2)$, gives a reflection through the point $Z(-2, 0)$, describable by:

$$P(x, y) \to P'(-x - 4, -y)$$

To generalize this process: a mirroring through (or 180° rotation around) a center $Z(a, b)$ is describable by

$$P(x, y) \to P'(-x + 2, -y + 2b)$$

9

Example 5

By joining the two reflections through a point:

$P(x, y) \to P'(-x+4, -y-2)$, center $Z_1(2, -1)$

$P(x, y) \to P'(-x+8, -y+4)$, center $Z_2(-2, 0)$

gives the translation $\overrightarrow{Z_1 Z_2}$:
$$P(x, y) \to P'(x+2, y+3)$$

To practice this students can transform a simple triangle twice.

Example 6

If we combine a 90° counter-clockwise rotation around the origin with the translation $P(x, y) \to P'(x-1, y+3)$, we get the 90° counter-clockwise rotation around the point $Z(-2, 1)$. This can be confirmed using a few points.

Example 7

If we combine a reflection and a translation, we get a glide reflection, also known simply as a glide.

The reflection across the line $y = x - 1$ and the translation $P(x, y) \to P'(x+1, y+1)$ results in the glide reflection
$$P(x, y) \to P'(y+2, x)$$

Thus, for example, the series of images arise (fig. 4)

$P_1(0, 0) \quad \to \quad P_2(2, 0) \quad \to \quad P_3(2, 2) \quad \to \quad P_4(4, 2) \quad \to \quad P_5(4, 4) \quad \to \quad ...$
$P_1(1, 0) \quad \to \quad P_2(2, 1) \quad \to \quad P_3(3, 2) \quad \to \quad P_4(4, 3) \quad \to \quad P_5(5, 4) \quad \to \quad ...$
$P_1(-1, 1) \quad \to \quad P_2(3, -1) \quad \to \quad P_3(1, 3) \quad \to \quad P_4(5, 1) \quad \to \quad P_5(3, 5) \quad \to \quad ...$

On the basis of these examples pupils can see that combinations of reflections can produce the other transformations, particularly rotations (and especially reflections through a point as well as translations taken as rotations around infinitely distant points considered as the intersections of parallel lines).

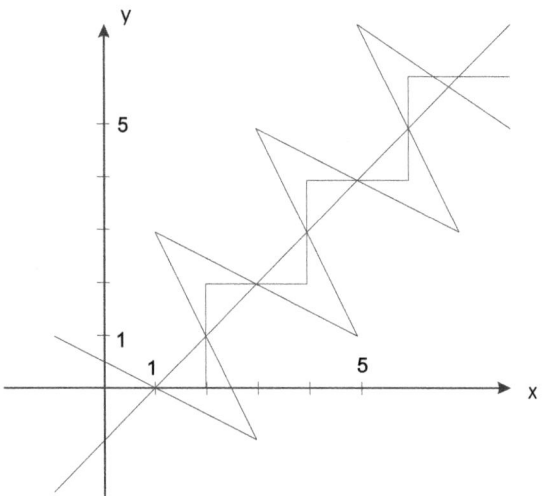

Figure 4

Example 8

In this example, we perform three successive point reflections. After six point reflections, we thus must return to our starting point; this gives students a good way to check their calculations.

The three transformations are given by

$A_1 : P(x, y) \to P'(2-x, 4-y)$, Zentrum $(1, 2)$

$A_2 : P(x, y) \to P'(-x, -y)$, Zentrum $(0, 0)$

$A_3 : P(x, y) \to P'(-2-x, 4-y)$, Zentrum $(-1, 2)$

In figure 5 the two starting points $P_1 (0, 3)$ and $P_2 (3,5, 4)$ have been chosen.

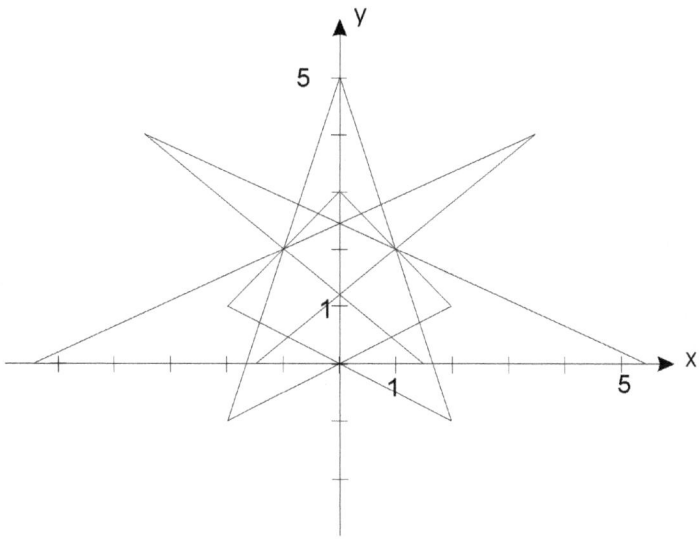

Figure 5

Example 9

Through the transformation $P(x, y) \to P'\left(\frac{12-x}{2}, \frac{6-y}{2}\right)$, the point P is reflected across the invariant point $F(4, 2)$, but so that the image point P' is only half as far from F as point P. This gives an infinite series of points tending toward the limit point F.

$$P_0(0, 6) \to P_1(6, 0) \to P_2(3, 3) \to P_3\left(\frac{9}{2}, \frac{3}{2}\right) \to P_4\left(\frac{15}{4}, \frac{9}{4}\right) \to \ldots$$

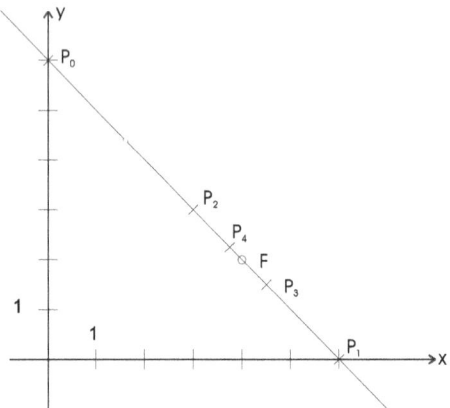

Figure 6

Thus

$$x_n = 4 - 4\left(-\frac{1}{2}\right)^n$$

$$y_n = 2 + 4\left(-\frac{1}{2}\right)^n$$

Point F divides the segment P_0P_1 in a proportion $2:1$. That the limit point creates this relationship is immediately obvious:

In this transformation P_{n+1} is always the middle point of segment $P_{n-1}P_n$. Thus P_0P_2 is twice as long as P_1P_3, P_2P_4 twice as long as P_3P_5. Since each segment to the «left» of F, $P_{2n}P_{2n+2}$ is twice as long as the following segment to the right of F $P_{2n+1}P_{2n+3}$, this must also be the case for the limit point: P_0F is twice as long as FP_1.

Example 10

The transformation $P(x, y) \to P'\left(1 - \frac{x}{2}, 1 + \frac{y}{2}\right)$

illustrates a very similar principle. This is a compressed glide reflection across the line $x = \frac{1}{3}$.

Using the starting point $P_0(0, 0)$ gives the infinite series

$$x_n = \frac{1}{3} - \frac{1}{3}\left(-\frac{1}{2}\right)^n$$

$$y_n = 1 - \frac{1}{2^n}$$

The limit point is $F\left(\frac{1}{3}, 1\right)$.

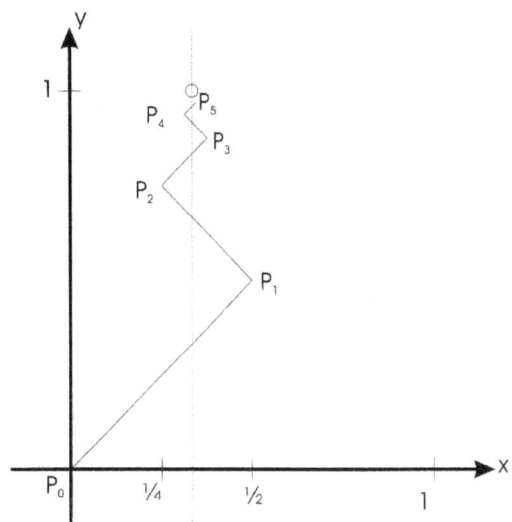

Figure 7

Example 11

Two sequences of points are given: $P_n(n, 0)$, $Q_n(n, 1)$, $n \in \mathbb{N}$

- A_1 is midpoint of P_0Q_1, B_1 the midpoint of A_1P_1
- A_2 is midpoint of B_1Q_2, B_2 the midpoint of A_2P_2
- A_n is midpoint of $B_{n-1}Q_n$, B_n the midpoint of A_nP_n.

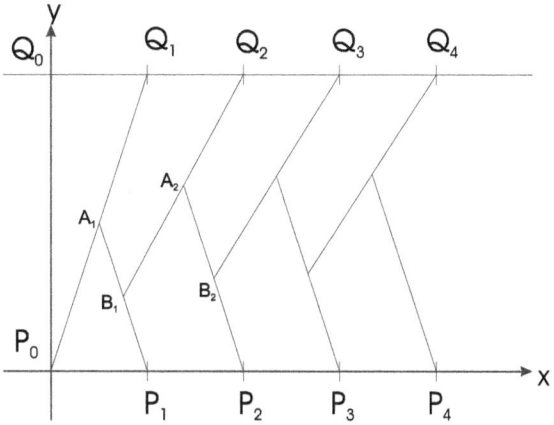

Figure 8

The y-Values of points A_n, B_n rise steadily. What are the limiting values?

Let s be the limit of the sequence of points B_n. s must satisfy the condition:

$$\frac{\frac{s+1}{2}}{2} = s$$

Thus $s = \frac{1}{3}$. The two sought limits are thus $\frac{1}{3}$ and $\frac{2}{3}$. This can also be demonstrated with the following equation. If $B_n(x_n, y_n)$ then

$$y_n = \frac{1}{3} - \frac{1}{3 \cdot 4^n}$$

The limiting points of the sequences A_n, B_n lie on the boundary lines of the plane. To avoid this, the problem can be posed in the following form:

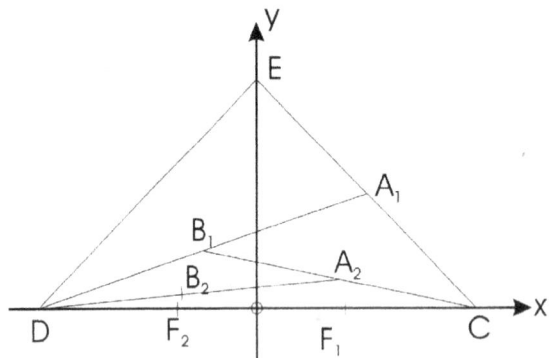

Figure 9

Given three points $C(1, 0)$, $D(-1, 0)$ and $E(0, 1)$: The sequence of points A_n, B_n is established by finding the successive midpoints. The two limiting points now have the coordinates

$$F_1\left(\frac{1}{3}, 0\right), F_2\left(-\frac{1}{3}, 0\right)$$

Example 12

This example shows how finding successive midpoints – in this case cyclic – gives rise to four sequences of points that converge to four limit points.

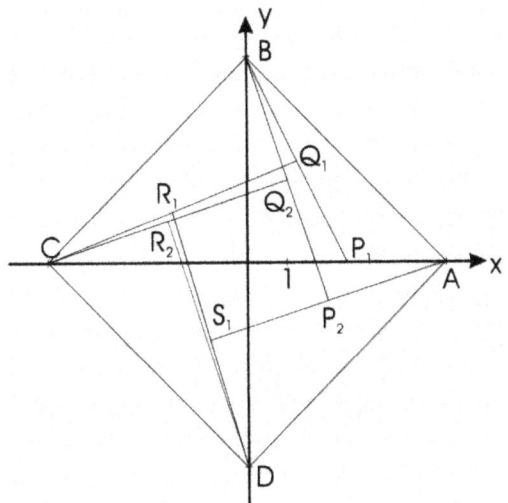

Figure 10

Given the four points $A(5, 0)$, $B(0, 5)$, $C(-5, 0)$, $D(0, -5)$.

- Let P_1 be the midpoint of OA
- Let Q_1 be the midpoint of $P_1 B$
- Let R_1 be the midpoint of $Q_1 C$
- Let S_1 be the midpoint of $R_1 D$
- Let P_2 be the midpoint of $S_1 A$
- Let Q_2 be the midpoint of $P_2 B$ etc.

These four sequences of points P_n, Q_n, R_n, S_n converge on the square $P(2, 1)$, $Q(1, 2)$, $R(2, 1)$, $S(1, 2)$. It's easy to show that the area of this square is one-fifth the area of square ABCD (fig. 11). square is one-fifth the area of square ABCD (fig. 11). This bounding square is independent of the chosen starting point, here the point $O(0, 0)$.

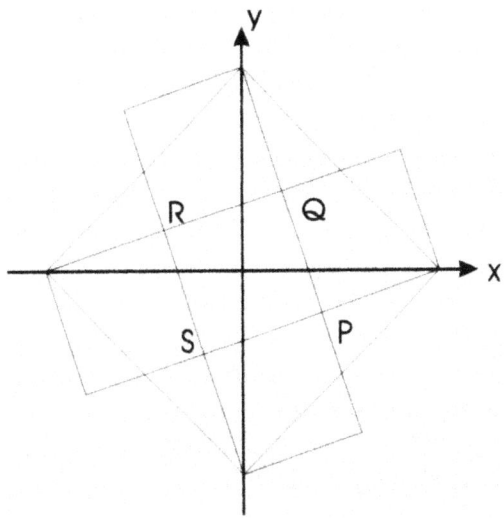

Figure 11

Example 13

This example treats a similar problem: the square is replaced by the triangle $T(7, 0)$, $R(0, 14)$, $S(-7, 0)$.

- Let A_1 be an arbitrary point;
- Let B_1 be the midpoint of $A_1 R$
- Let C_1 be the midpoint of $B_1 S$
- Let A_2 be the midpoint of $C_1 T$
- Let B_2 be the midpoint of $A_2 R$ usw.

Points A_n then converge on limit point $A(2, 2)$, Points B_n on $B(1, 8)$. Points C_n on $C(-3, 4)$.

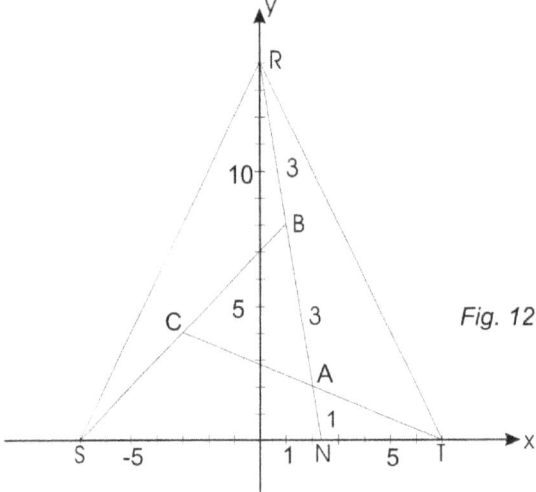

Fig. 12

This figure also shows intriguing numerical proportions:

$$NA : AB : BR = 1 : 3 : 3$$

and

$$SN : NT = 2 : 1$$

Example 14

This example should show how finding the midpoint can be replaced by establishing the center of gravity.

Given four points:
$A(5, -5)$, $B(5, 5)$, $C(-5, 5)$, $D(-5, -5)$.

- Let T be an arbitrary point, e.g. the origin.
- P_1 is the center of gravity of $\triangle TAB$

- Q_1 is the center of gravity of $\Delta P_1 BC$
- R_1 is the center of gravity of $\Delta Q_1 CD$
- S_1 is the center of gravity of $\Delta R_1 DA$
- P_2 is the center of gravity of $\Delta S_1 AB$
- Q_2 is the center of gravity of $\Delta P_2 BC$

etc.

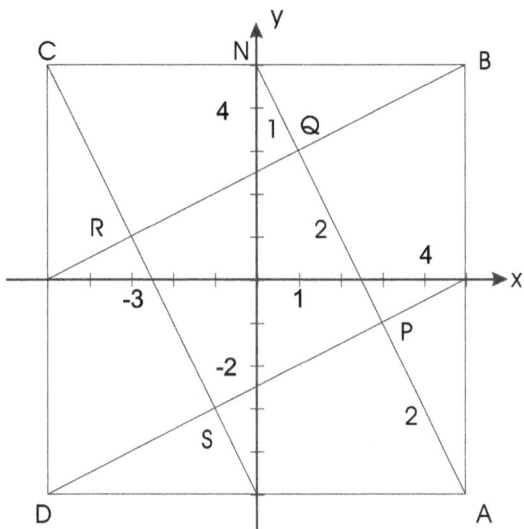

Figure 13

These four sequences of points P_n, Q_n, R_n, S_n then converge on the limiting square with coordinates $P(3, -1)$, $Q(1, 3)$, $R(-3, 1)$, $S(-1, -3)$. This is the same square as in example 12. This is true since, for example, the segment AN is divided by P and Q in a proportion of $2 : 2 : 1$.

Example 15

The transformation

$$P(x, y) \to P'\left(\frac{5+y}{2}, \frac{15-x}{2}\right)$$

produces spiral sequences of points through repeated iterations. In figure 14, we have chosen the four starting points $A_0(-3, -3)$, $B_0(3, -3)$, $C_0(13, 13)$, $D_0(7, 13)$.

These sequences of segments tend toward the limit point $G(5, 5)$. This is the invariant point of the transformation.

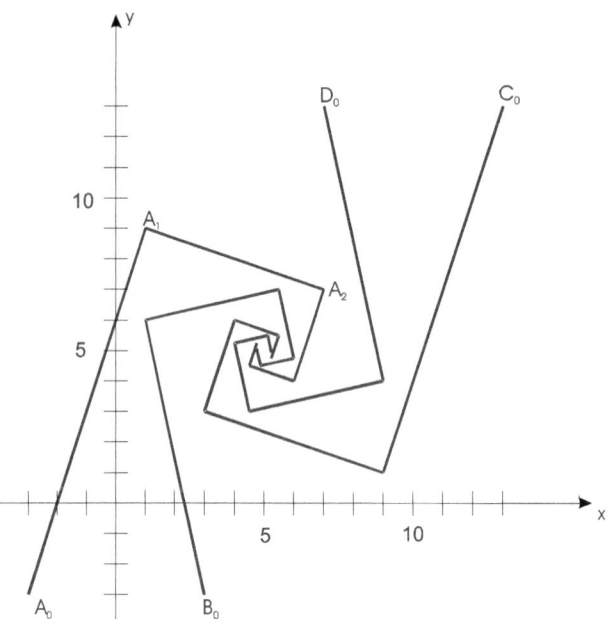

Figure 14

In connection with problems of this kind, interesting questions arise: How can we construct these sequences of segments? How are successive segments diminishing in length? Can we constructe the limit point? Is there a total length of the chain? Is there an equation of the spiral that passes through the corners of the segment chain? Is it even possible to speak of a limit point when it will never be reached?

These questions often lead to intense discussions. If the points of a plane are reflected through a line, this line is then a invariant line, and all lines perpendicular to this line as these are all mutually parallel, they thus meet in a point on the ideal line at infinity of the plane are invariant lines.

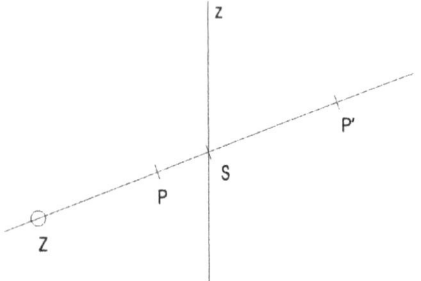

Figure 15

If, on the contrary, the planes points are reflected across an invariant point, then all the lines of this point are invariant lines, while the points of the lines at infinity are invariant points, which means that the line at infinity of the plane is also an invariant line.

Thus, for a conventional reflection, determining elements lie at infinity. For a general harmonic reflection the axis, that is, the line of invariant points, and the center, that is, the inter-section of the invariant lines, can be on the finite plane.

In order to determine the image P' of P, the intersection of line PZ (Z being the center) with the axis z is found; let this intersection be S (figure 15). P' is then the fourth harmonic point, that is ZS. PP' divide one another harmonically.

The image of a triangle is not similar to the original triangle. They are perspective to one another in the sense of Desargues law (figure 16).

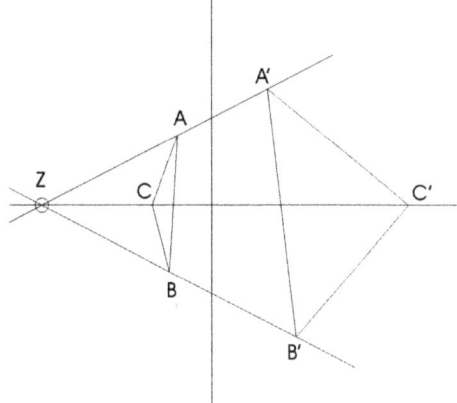

Figure 16

Example 16

The transformation $P(x, y) \to P'\left(\frac{1}{x}, \frac{y}{x}\right)$ is a harmonic reflection. $A(-1, 0)$ is the center and the line $x = 1$ is the axis.

This transformation inverts the unit circle $x^2 + y^2 = 1$ into the hyperbola $x^2 - y^2 = 1$.
The circle $x^2 - x + y^2 = 0$ is transformed into the parabola $y^2 = x - 1$ (Figur 17).

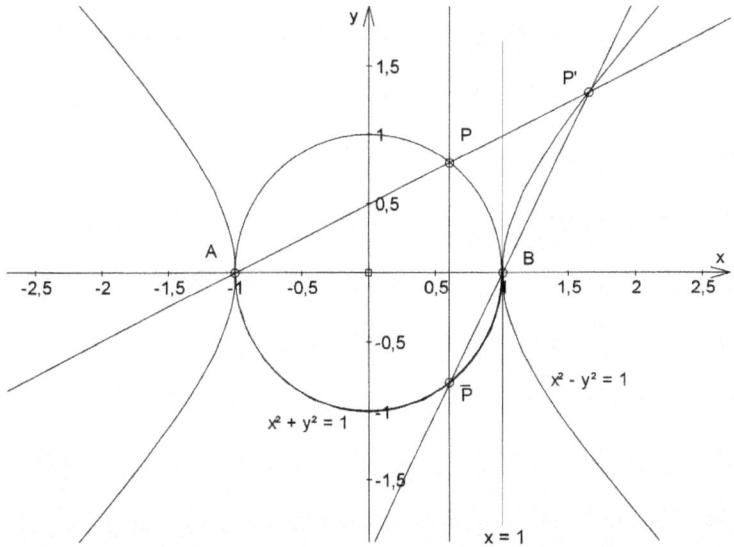

Figure 17

This last example is meant to awaken an interest in projective principles.

Introduction to analytical geometry – a possible start for a main lesson block

KARL-FRIEDRICH GEORG

With the introduction to analytical geometry, the goal is that certain geometric questions be made accessible to computational treatment in the most simple and broad way possible. For this, we will begin with the classical coordinate method. The traditional construction first treats the geometry of linear structures (linear algebra) – later, this is continued with the geometry of structures of the second order. This also ties to the intensification of the algebraic demands. Today, the lesson plans of the cultural ministries include mainly «linear algebra» under analytic geometry- and, as non-plane structures, the cube at best. In comparison to the treatment of conic sections, a strong reduction to formal algebra, to the detriment of a visual geometric endeavor, is connected with this. The skills of practical construction are no longer taught.

If analytical geometry is called for in the Waldorf School's eleventh grade lesson plans, up to the conic sections, it is built on diverse experience of these students with curves: In the ninth grade, the conic sections were introduced as curves of position. In the tenth grade, these conic sections were constructed as intersecting lines of cone and plane. The following step in the eleventh grade shows that these known curves can also be grasped algebraically: an equation in connection with a coordinate system represents a curve and the reverse is true. The place definition of a curve leads to its characteristic equation. Here we are aware that the fundamentals have geometric content.

This main-lesson block clarifies the changing relation of equation and curve – without having to concern oneself just with distances, line equations, and partial ratios. Such an entry into this block can be carried out in the following way. First of all, the student experiences the direct relationship of equation and attendant form (curve). The curves are either known or are constructed additionally. Secondly, for setting up the value tables, an exercise in the practical use of the calculator is provided.

A continuation of the study of curves can take place in the twelfth grade – in the free geometry of plane curves.

The following explanation corresponds to the beginning of a block.

In the further course of the block, for the themes of distance and line, the areas are selected which form the basis for being able to master derivation and problems with conic sections, circle, ellipse, hyperbola, and parabola. When the student achieves confidence with calculation in regard to circles (pole/polar), we need less time with the other curves. If we are not to shortchange the element of construction, a block length of four weeks is necessary.

Introduction

For the equation $x^2 + y^2 = 25$ there is an infinite number of number pairs (x,y) which fulfills it. For purposes of calculation, we have solved this equation for y and made a table

$$y^2 = 25 - x^2; \quad y = \pm\sqrt{25 - x^2}$$

x	3	3	4	0	5	-3	-4	1	2	-1	-2
y	4	-4	±3	±5	0	±4	±3	±4.90	±4.58	±4.90	±4.58

It is clear from the number pairs that this equation conveys a certain relation between the unknowns x and y. Both unknowns can take on different values, but not arbitrarily – rather, they are dependent on each other. Thus, in such equations, we call x and y variables and the equation relationship equation.

In a coordinate system, we can visualize each numeric pair (x, y) as a point. The horizontal axis is the x-axis and the vertical is the y-axis (see below). The intersecting point of both axes is the origin of coordinates.

We call x the abscissa and y the ordinate of the point P. Each number pair arranged (x, y) represents a point $P(x, y)$; we call x and y the coordinates of the point P. We also call the crossing of axes standing vertically to each other a Cartesian coordinate system, named after one of the two founders of analytic geometry, Rene Descartes. He was called Cartesius (1596-1650). We can also visualize the coordinates of the point P as distances on the coordinate axes or on lines parallel to it.

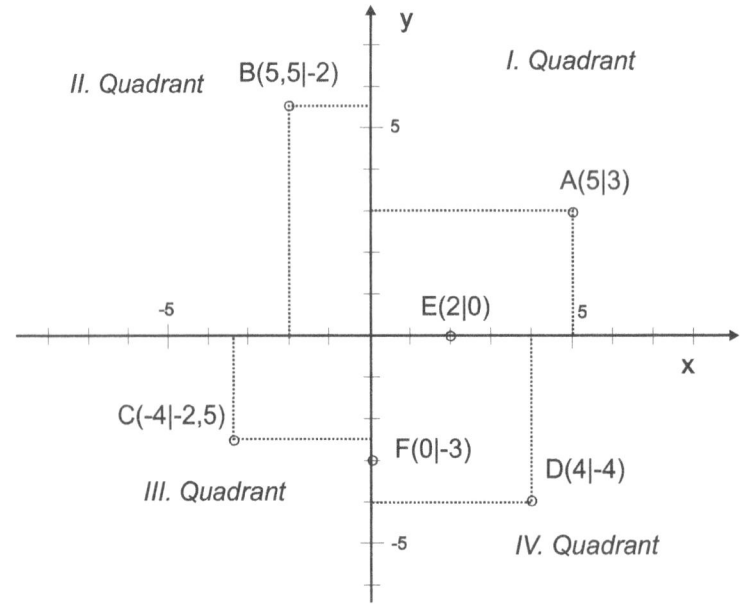

We enter the number pairs of our table into the coordinate system as points.

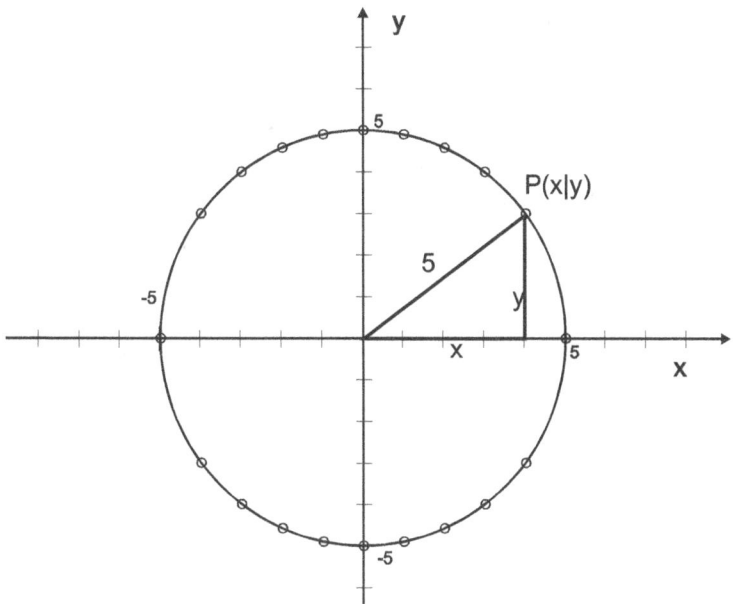

Fig. 2

Since with each point, x and y form the sides of a right angle triangle and the hypotenuse remains a constant 5, all points lie on a curve around the origin. The equation $y = \sqrt{25 - x^2}$ only makes sense when $25 - x^2 \geq 0$, that ist $25 \geq x^2$.

This is only achieved when $x \leq 5$ and $x \geq -5$, as well as: $-5 \leq x \leq 5$.

In the analytical geometry of the plane, we are dealing with equations in which two variables x and y occur. The number of all solutions (x, y) of such equations represents the number of all points $P(x, y)$ of straight lines or curves. Accordingly, there are two basic problems:

1. The determination of the geometric properties of a line, which is provided by an equation.
2. The formation of the equation of a line, proceeding from its geometric properties.

Our introductory example is an example for the basic problem.

Further examples:

Example 1

$16x - 3y^2 = 0$; solving for y, the equation reads: $y = \pm\frac{4}{3}\sqrt{3x}$.

For x, we enter some suitable values and enter the solutions in the table:

x	0	$\frac{1}{3}$	$\frac{4}{3}$	3	$\frac{16}{3}$	$\frac{25}{3}$	12
y	0	$\pm\frac{4}{3}$	$\pm\frac{8}{3}$	± 4	$\pm\frac{16}{3}$	$\pm\frac{20}{3}$	± 8

The resulting curve could be a parabola.

Introduction to Analytical Geometry   Karl-Friedrich Georg

From the equation, we conclude the following:

There are no points with negative abscissa which lie in a curve. For every positive x-value, there are two different y-values, which distinguish themselves only by the sign. So the curve is symmetric in regard to the x-axis. As x increases, the value of y grows – so the curve becomes increasingly distant from the x-axis.

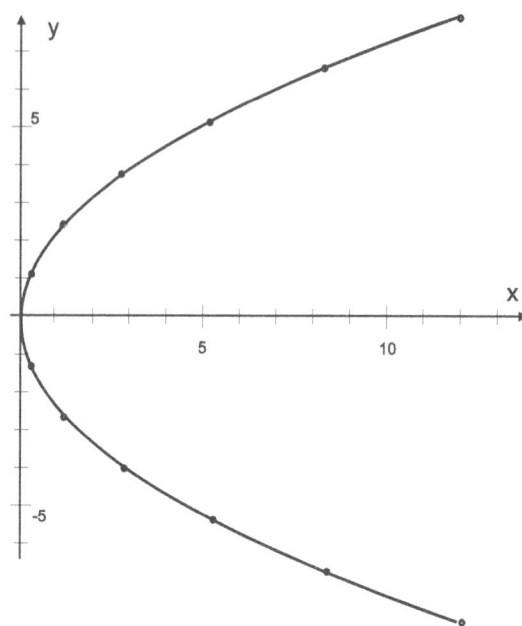

Example 2

$x^2 - y^2 = 4$; for the solution of y, we get this result: $y = \pm\sqrt{x^2 - 4}$.

Here we also set up a table with examples of solution pairs:

x	±2	±2.5	±3	±4	±5	±6	±7
y	0	±1.5	±2.24	±3.64	±4.58	±5.66	±6.71

... and we enter the number pairs as points.

With this example, a curve results, which could be a hyperbola. From the equation, we conclude: there are no points for $-2 < x < 2$, which lie on the curve.

Also here there are two different y-values for each x-value available – the only difference is the sign. So the curve is symmetric in regard to the x-axis. Since, for the positive and negative x-values, the same two y-values result, the curve is also symmetric to the y-axis.

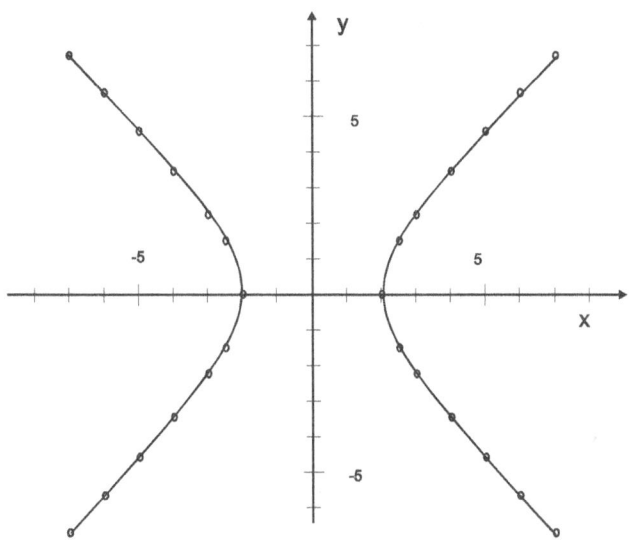

Example 3

$(x^2 + y^2)^2 = 50(x^2 + y^2)$; for the solution of y, we get this result:

$$x^4 + 2x^2y^2 + y^4 = 50x^2 - 50y^2$$
$$y^4 + 2(x^2 + 25)y^2 + x^4 - 50x^2 = 0 \mid \text{with } y^2 = z \text{ follows}$$
$$z^2 + 2(x^2 + 25)z + x^4 - 50x^2 = 0$$

thus

$$z_{1,2} = -(x^2 + 25) \pm \sqrt{(x^2 + 25)^2 - (x^4 - 50x^2)}$$
$$z_{1,2} = -(x^2 + 25) \pm \sqrt{x^4 + 50x^2 + 625 - x^4 + 50x^2}$$
$$z_{1,2} = -(x^2 + 25) \pm \sqrt{25(4x^2 + 25)} \mid \text{because } z = y^2$$
$$y_{1,2}^2 = 5\sqrt{4x^2 + 25} - (x^2 + 25)$$

As y^2 has to be positive, there is only the root with the +-sign allowed. For y we get:

$$y_{1,2} = \pm\sqrt{5\sqrt{4x^2 + 25} - x^2 - 25}$$

Table:

x	0	±1	±2	±3	±4	±4,5
y	0	±0.96	±1.74	±2.25	±2.48	±2.50
x	±5	±6	±6,5	±7	±$\sqrt{50}$	
y	±2.43	±2.00	±1.55	±0.57	0	

Introduction to Analytical Geometry   Karl-Friedrich Georg

In this example, a curve results which represents a lemniskate. In the ninth grade, we became familiar with this as one of the Cassinian curves through construction. We conclude from the equations or number of solutions that the curve must be symmetrical to both coordinate axes. From the drawing, we see that this closed curve exists only within certain x- and y- values. Through calculation, we find the x-limits for $y = 0$:

$$-5 \cdot \sqrt{2} \leqslant x \leqslant 5 \cdot \sqrt{2}$$

From the drawing we conclude: $-\frac{5}{2} \leqslant y \leqslant \frac{5}{2}$

Curve points exist only for these x- or y-values

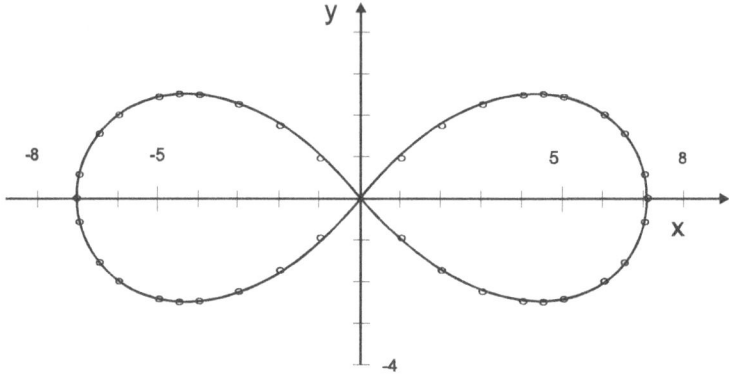

Example 4

$y^2 = x^2 \cdot \frac{5+x}{5-x}$ bzw. $y = \pm x \cdot \sqrt{\frac{5+x}{5-x}}$

From the equation, we conclude that the curve is symmetrical to the x-axis and that not all y-values are possible with the root. In order to obtain y-values, the radicand (root content) may not become negative. This is achieved when numerator and denominator are both positive or negative. So:

Case 1:

$$5+x \geqslant 0 \text{ and } 5-x > 0$$
$$x \geqslant -5 \text{ and } 5 > x$$
$$-5 \leqslant x < 5$$

Case 2:

$$5+x \leqslant 0 \text{ and } 5-x < 0$$
$$x \leqslant -5 \text{ and } 5 < x$$
contradiction!

Result: There are only curve points when : $-5 < x < 5$.

Table:

x	-5	-4.5	-3	-2	-1	0
y	0	± 1.03	± 1.33	± 1.50	± 1.31	± 0.82
x	1	2	2.5	3	3.5	
y	0	± 1.22	± 3.06	± 3.00	± 8.33	

The curve resulting is a strophoid. It can easily be gained through construction.

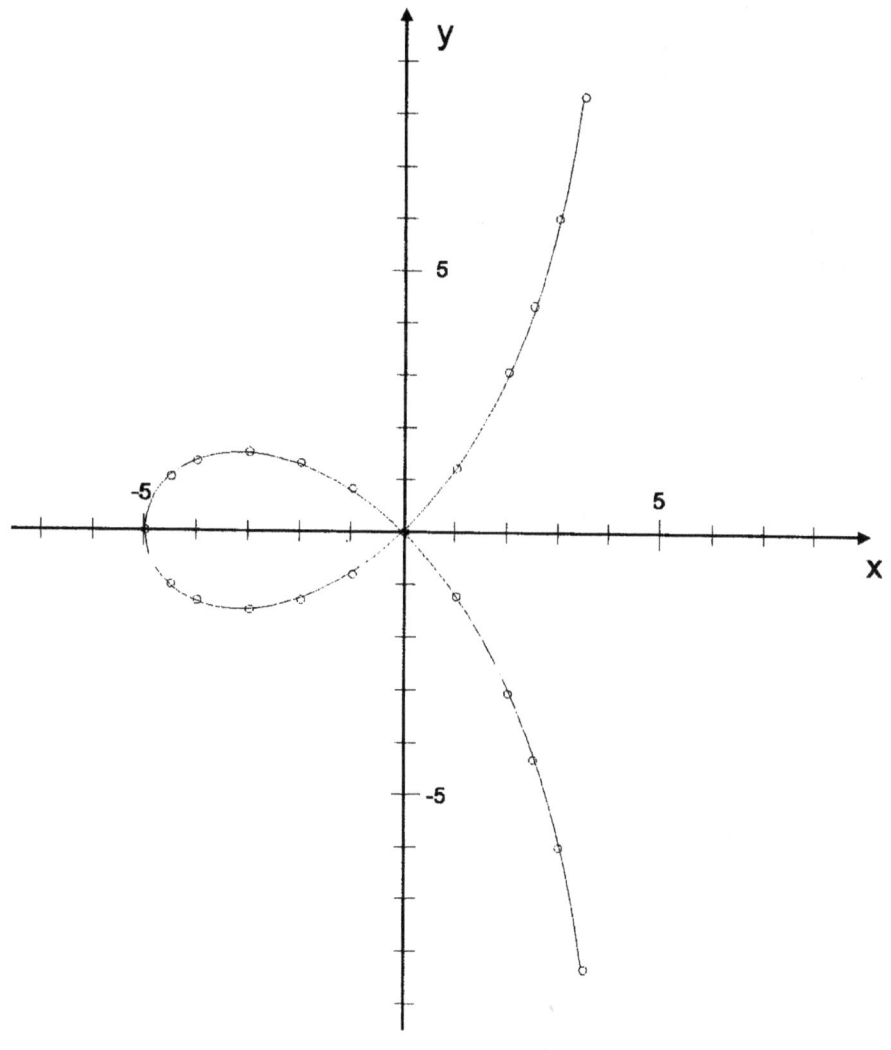

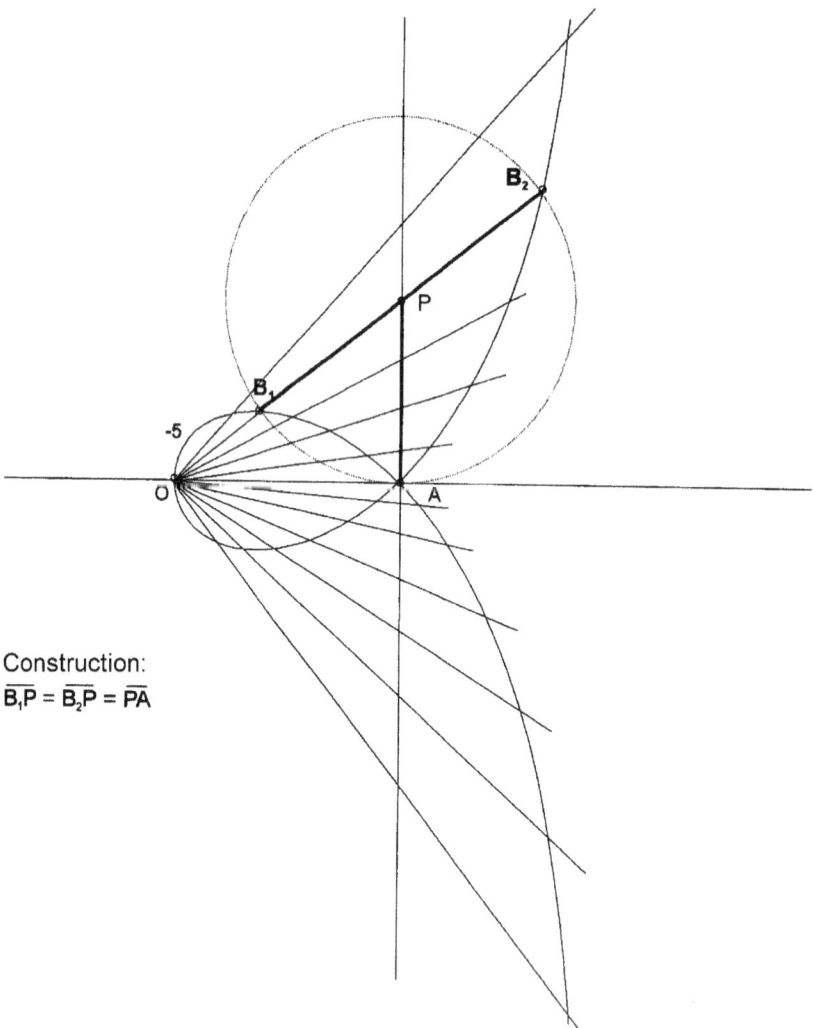

Construction:
$\overline{B_1P} = \overline{B_2P} = \overline{PA}$

Example 5

$$(x-5)^2 \cdot (x^2 + y^2) = 25x^2$$

This equation is developed according to y:

$$x^2 + y^2 = \frac{25x^2}{(x-5)^2} \Leftrightarrow y^2 = x^2 \cdot \left(\frac{25}{(x-5)^2} - 1\right) \Leftrightarrow y^2 = x^2 \cdot \frac{25-(x-5)^2}{(x-5)^2}$$

it follows:

$$y^2 = \frac{x^2}{(x-5)^2}(10x - x^2) \Leftrightarrow y_{1,2} = \pm \frac{x}{x-5} \cdot \sqrt{10x - x^2}$$

We see from the equation that there are no y-values for $x < 0$, and for $x = 5$, y becomes infinitely large. Also, there are no y-values for $x > 10$.

Table:

x	0	0,5	1	1.5	2	2.5	3	3,5
y	0	±0.24	±0.75	±1.53	±2.67	±4.33	±6.87	±11.13
x	3.6	7.5	8	8.5	9	9.5	9.8	10
y	±12.34	±12.99	±10.67	±8.67	±6.75	±4.60	±2.86	0

This curve is called conchoid. It also can be constructed simply.

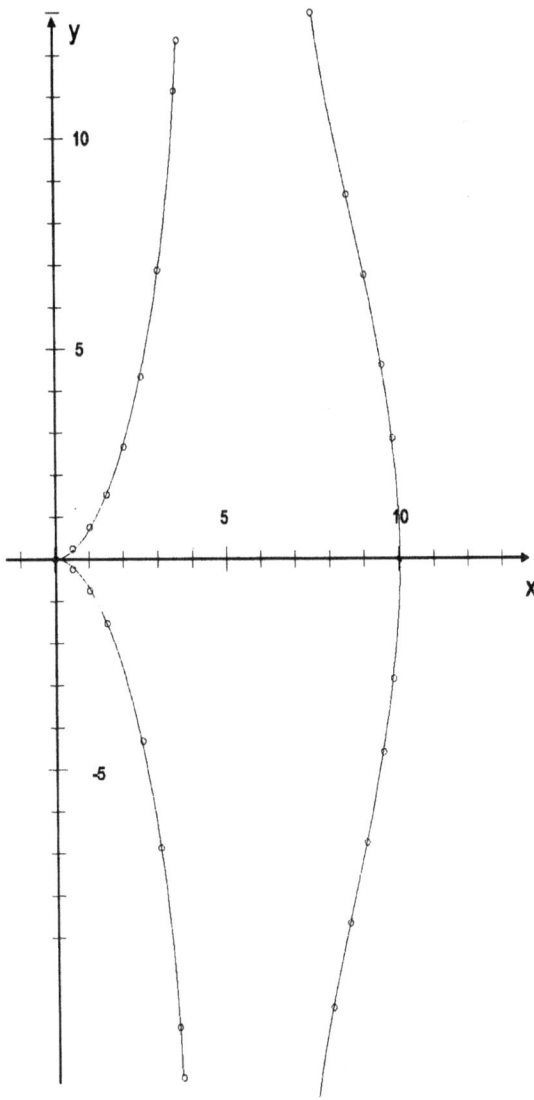

Introduction to Analytical Geometry *Karl-Friedrich Georg*

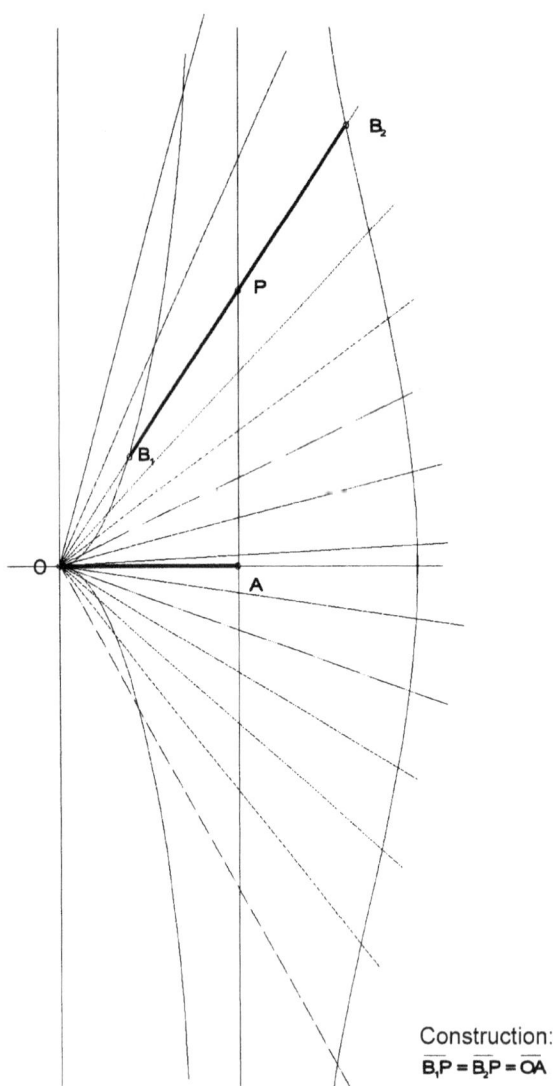

Construction:
$\overline{B_1P} = \overline{B_2P} = \overline{OA}$

Example 6

$$(x^2 + y^2 - 8x)^2 = 16 \cdot (x^2 + y^2)$$

solution for y:

$$x^4 + y^4 + 64x^2 + 2x^2y^2 - 16x^3 - 16xy^2 = 16x^2 + 16y^2$$

Karl-Friedrich Georg   Introduction to Analytical Geometry

$$y^4 + \underbrace{(2x^2 - 16x - 16)}_{p} y^2 + \underbrace{x^4 + 48x^2 - 16x^3}_{q} = 0$$

auxillary computation to determine the radicand in the «p-q-formula»[1] $\left(\frac{p}{2}\right)^2 - q$:

$$(x^2 - 8x - 8)^2 - (x^4 + 48x^2 - 16x^3) = x^4 + 64x^2 + 64 - 16x^3 - 16x^2 + 128x - x^4 - 48x^2 + 16x^3$$
$$= 64 + 128x = 64 \cdot (1 + 2x)$$

Inserting in the pq-formula leads to:

$$y_{1,2}^2 = -(x^2 - 8x - 8) \pm 8\sqrt{1+2x} = 8 + 8x - x^2 \pm 8\sqrt{1+2x} \quad | \sqrt{}$$

$$y_{1,2}^2 = \pm\sqrt{8 + 8x - x^2 + 8\sqrt{1+2x}} \qquad (1)$$

$$y_{3,4}^2 = \pm\sqrt{8 + 8x - x^2 - 8\sqrt{1+2x}} \qquad (2)$$

Table:

For (1):

x	0	1	2	3	4	5	6	7	8
y	±4	±5.37	±6.16	±6.65	±6.93	±7.04	±6.99	±6.78	±6.40
x	9	10	11	11.5	11.9	12	−0.25	0,5	
y	±5.82	±4.97	±3.66	±2.63	±1.20	±0	±3.41	±4.80	

For (2):

x	0	0.5	1	2	3	3.5	3.75	4	−0.25	−0,5
y	0	±0.66	±1.07	±1.45	±1.35	±1.06	0.78	±0	±0.53	±1.94

(drawing on the next page)

It is clear from the drawing that equation (1) defined is for $-0,5 \leqslant x \leqslant 12$ and equation (2) for $-0,5 \leqslant x \leqslant 4$.

The curve obtained is a limaçon (Pascal's limaçon, as well known as «conchoid of the circle»). It can be easily produced through construction as the previous ones.

(Construction: $\overline{PB_1} = \overline{PB_2} = \overline{OA} = \overline{AP}$)

---

[1] In Germany, in order to solve quadratical equations like $x^2 + px + q = 0$ the so called «p-q-Formula» is very popular: $x_{1;2} = -\frac{p}{2} \pm \sqrt{\frac{p^2}{4} - q}$

Introduction to Analytical Geometry   *Karl-Friedrich Georg*

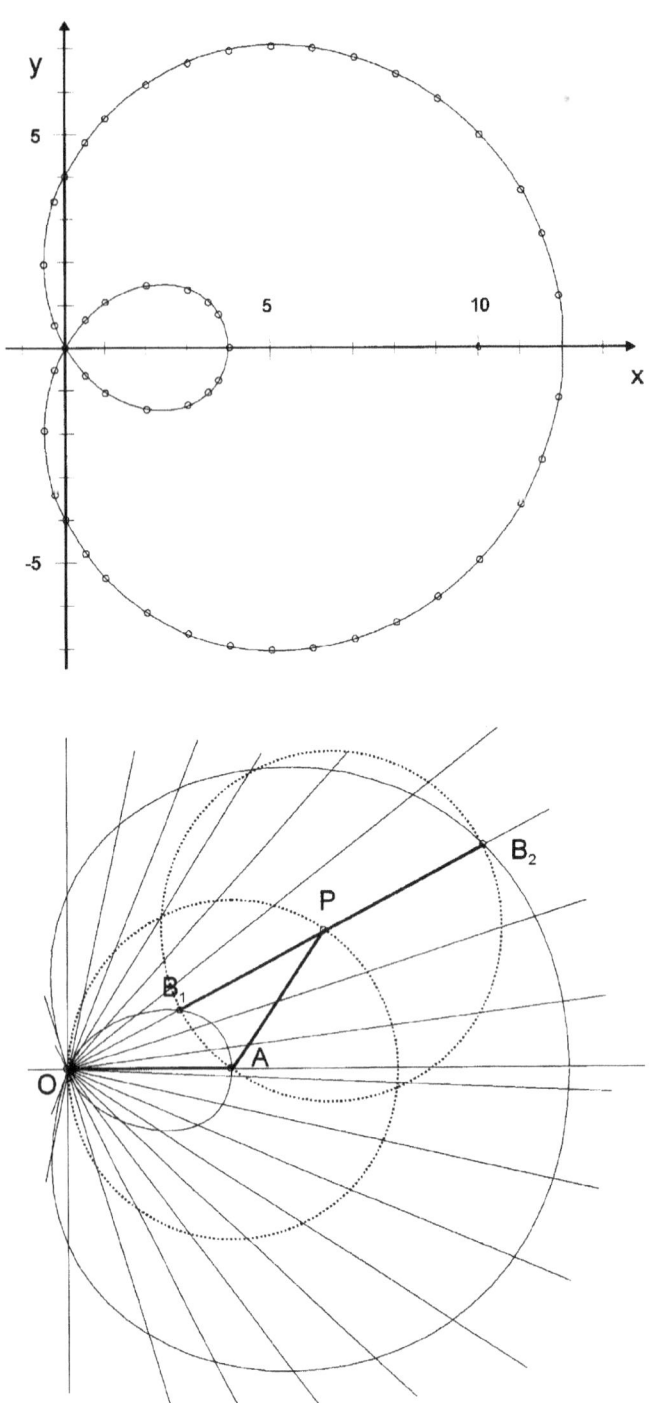

At this point it is possible to refer to another coordinate system, to the polar coordinates:

A point P in the direction φ (as relates to the polar axis), which has the distance of r from the pole O, is designated with these coordinates r and φ, P(r, φ).

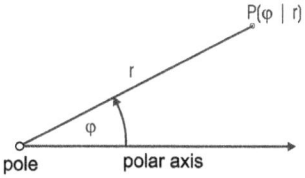

In this system, for instance, a circle around O has an especially simple equation: $r = 4$.

The following is an example of an equation, for which we apply a value table as a basis of the drawing:

$$(r - 8\cos\varphi)^2 = 16$$

solution for r:

$$r_1 = 8\cos\varphi + 4 \quad \text{and} \quad r_2 = 8\cos\varphi - 4$$

Table:

φ	0°	10°	20°	30°	40°	50°	60°	70°	80°	90°
r_1	12.0	11.88	11.52	10.93	10.13	9.14	8.00	6.74	5.39	4.0
r_2	4.0	3.88	3.52	2.93	2.13	1.14	0.00	−1.26	−2.61	−4.0

φ	100°	110°	120°	130°	140°	150°	160°	170°	180°
r_1	2.61	1.23	0.0	−1.14	−2.12	−2.93	−3.252	−3.88	−4.0
r_2	−5.93	−6.74	−8.0	−9.14	−10.13	−10.93	−11.52	−11.88	−12.0

We obtain the same limaçon as in example 6:

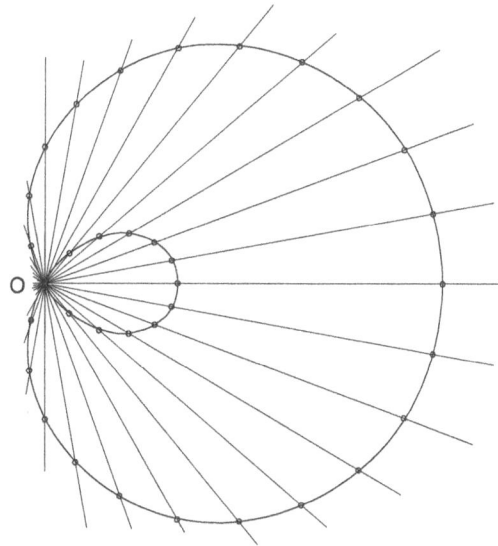

Example 7

$$x + 2y - 6 = 0$$
$$y = -\frac{1}{2}x + 3$$

Table:

x	-3	-2	-1	0	1	2	3	4	5	6	7	8
y	$\frac{9}{2}$	4	$\frac{7}{2}$	3	$\frac{5}{2}$	2	$\frac{3}{2}$	1	$\frac{1}{2}$	0	$-\frac{1}{2}$	-1

In the value table we see: If the abscissa x grows by 1, then the ordinate value y decreases by 0.5. It is an even linear process. The curve is a straight line, in short: a line.

The next chapter should deal with the line, with the distance as a starting point.

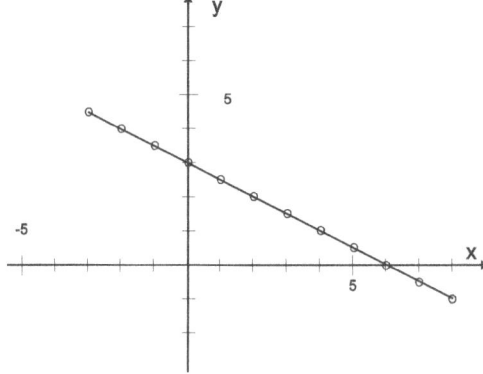

For many of the mentioned curves there exist construction-guides in the internet.

A Characterization of Analytic Geometry

UWE HANSEN

In a significant early work, «Rules for the Direction of the Mind», René Descartes (1596-1650) explaines his explanations of Rule IV:

> We are well aware that the geometers of antiquity employed a sort of analysis which they went on to apply to the solution of every problem, though they begrudged revealing it to posterity. At the present time a sort of arithmetic called «algebra» is flourishing, and this is achieving for numbers what the ancients did for figures [...] I shall have much to say below about figures and numbers [...] But if one attends closely to my meaning, one will readily see that ordinary mathematics is far from my mind here, that it is quite another discipline I am expounding, and that these illustrations are more its outer garments than its inner parts.[1]

Descartes then expresses the thought that the first discoverers of philosophy in ancient times knew a quite different mathematics than that common in our age. This he named Universal Mathematics; from it arise arithmetic and geometry. Analytic geometry arose out of his search for this all-encompassing universal mathematics.

Analytic geometry thus arose out of the conviction that arithmetic and geometry have a common root. This commonality shows itself on the one hand in the fact that geometric laws can be formulated algebraically and on the other hand through the possibility of presenting algebraic relationships geometrically in various ways.

Calculating with equations is characteristic of analytic geometry. The appearance of such equations derives from, however, congruences in geometry. Thus, in the Cartesian coordinate system, the equation of a line is based upon the equal proportions in similar triangles; the equation of a circle is based upon the equality of areas in the Pythagorean Theorem; and the equation of a parabola is derived from the equality of areas of the right-triangle altitude theorem. We must always try to consider an equation in a way that allows us to recognize the underlying principle.

In the following, I have sketched out various possibilities for the beginning of a mainlesson-block.

For example, one can begin with the question: on what curve do the points lie that are twice as far from a fixed point A as from point B, given that A and B are 6 cm. apart?

---

[1] René Descartes, The Philosophical Writings of Descartes, Vol. 1. Translated by John Cottingham and Robert Stoothoff. Cambridge Univ. Press: 1984, p. 17

A Characterization of Analytic Geometry

Uwe Hansen

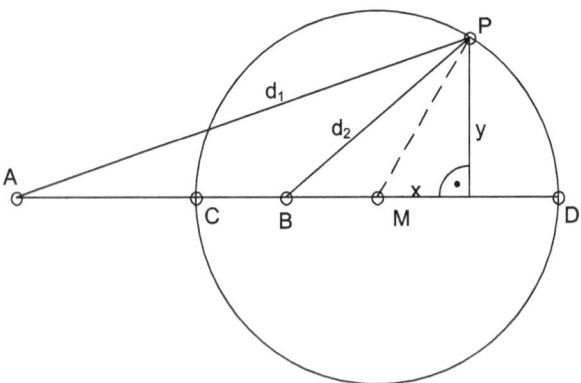

Figure 1

First point C is found, located between A and B, 4 cm. from A; and then point D, 6 cm. from B, mirroring A (see figure 1).

If further points P are drawn, the pupils guess that the points P lie on an ellipse – or could it even be a circle? An obviously possibility to investigate this is to consider the midpoint M of C and D and to determine P's distance from M. To do this, we drop a vertical line from P to AB and name the legs of the resulting right-angled triangle with hypotenuse PM x and y.

As AM = 8 cm and BM = 2 cm, using the Pythagorean Theorem we deduce (all lengths are in cm):

$$d_1^2 = AP^2 = (x+8)^2 + y^2$$
$$d_2^2 = BP^2 = (x+2)^2 + y^2$$

As $d_1 = 2 \cdot d_2$, therefore $d_1^2 = 4 \cdot d_2^2$ it follows that

$$(x+8)^2 + y^2 = 4 \cdot \left[(x+2)^2 + y^2\right]$$

this simplifies to

$$16 = x^2 + y^2$$

It follows that hypotenuse MP must always have length 4, i.e. P lies on a circle (circle of division, «Apollonius» circle). It makes sense to repeat this calculation with other proportions (e.g. 3 : 1, 4 : 1, 3 : 2).

From $d_1 : d_2 = 3 : 1$ and AB = 8   we find $x^2 + y^2 = 9$
From $d_1 : d_2 = 4 : 1$ and AB = 15   we find $x^2 + y^2 = 16$
From $d_1 : d_2 = 3 : 2$ and AB = 8   we find $x^2 + y^2 = 36$

These considerations lead to the following drawing:

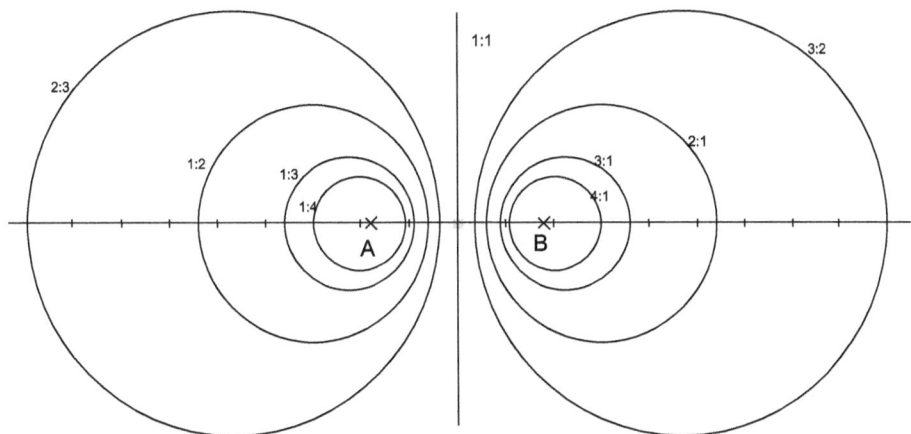

Figure 2:
Apollonian circle: all points of a circle have the same proportion of their distances to points A and B.

If in the previous example we assume that $d_1 = d_2$, so $d_1^2 = d_2^2$, then we find the equation of the perpendicular bisector of AB, e.g. $x = -5$.

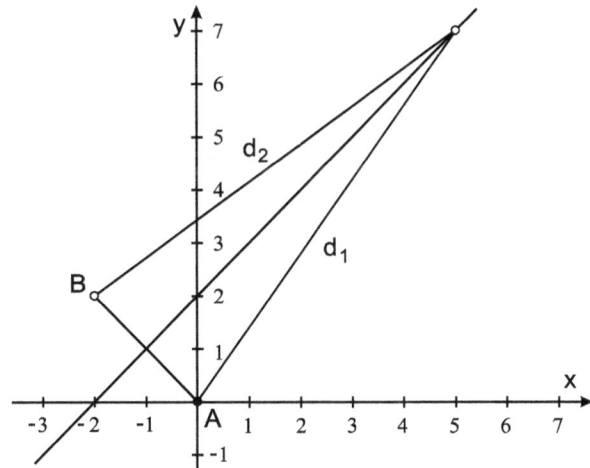

Figure 3

For more practice of the algorithm, the equation of a line may be introduced in this way. The pupils are now clear about how to describe points through the coordinates, so the following problem will be immediately comprehensible:

Determine the perpendicular bisector of AB given $A(0\,|\,0)$ and $B(-2\,|\,2)$.

In this case,
$$d_1 = x^2 + y^2$$
$$d_1^2 = (x+2)^2 + (y-2)^2$$

From $d_1^2 = d_2^2$ it follows that
$$y = x + 2$$

A Characterization of Analytic Geometry

Other equations of lines can be derived in further appropriate problems.

The following example can also be used as an introduction to the Cartesian coordinate system at the beginning of a block. It shows how the geometric content remains recognizable in an equation.

The hypotenuse AB of a right-angled triangle lies on a fixed line; endpoint A is also fixed. Let D be the foot of the altitude. The hypotenuse segment $k = DB$ has a constant length. Along what curve does C move as $l = AD$ changes?

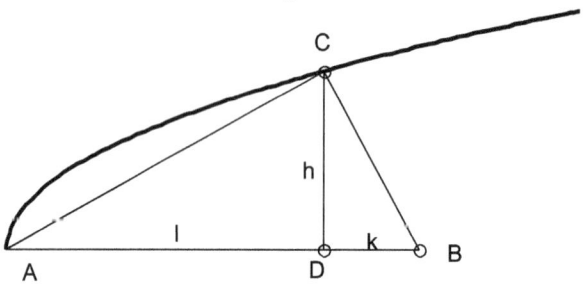

Figure 4

Based upon the right-triangle altitude theorem, we know

$$h^2 = l \cdot k$$

In order to make it clear that l and k are variable quantities, we set $l = x$ and $h = y$. Then it must be true that

$$y^2 = x \cdot k$$

whereby k is a constant.

In the same way as in the first example, the position of point C is determined by x and y. We write $C(x \mid y)$.

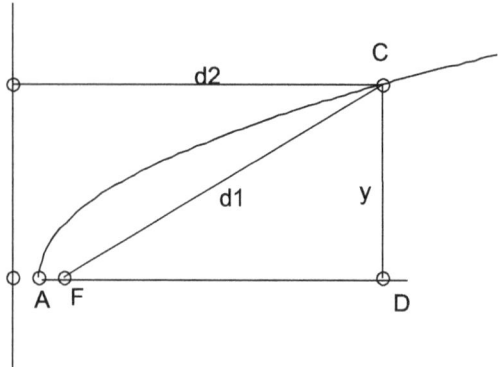

Figure 5

If we draw a few triangles, we begin to suspect that the point C lies on a parabola. This is proven by a calculation that shows that the parabola's definition is satisfied. We show that the point $F\left(\frac{k}{4} \mid 0\right)$ is the focus and the line $-\frac{k}{4}$ is the directrix.

For the segment $d_1 = FC$

$$d_1^2 = \left(x - \frac{k}{4}\right)^2 + y^2$$

As $y^2 = x \cdot k$, it follows that

$$d_1^2 = \left(x - \frac{k}{4}\right)^2 + x \cdot k$$
$$= x^2 + \frac{k}{2}x + \frac{k^2}{16}$$
$$= \left(x + \frac{k}{4}\right)^2 = d_2^2$$

Thus we have shown, that $d_1 = d_2$; C thus lies on a parabola. The equation $y^2 = kx$ thus signifies a parabola; it is a special expression of the right-triangle altitude theorem.

The equilateral hyperbola can also be used as an entry into a block, beginning with the following problem:

A rectangle has two sides lying on two mutually perpendicular lines that are given. Along what curve does the rectangle's fourth vertex move if the rectangle's area remains constant?

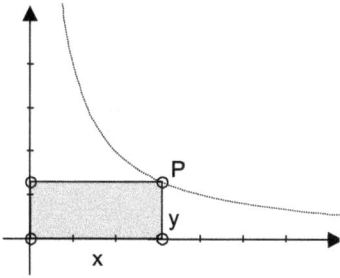

Figure 6

If we call the width of the rectangle x and the height y, it must be that: $y \cdot x = c$ (a constant), so $y = \frac{c}{x}$; this equation gives the condition for a point P's position. It is thus called the equation for the equilateral hyperbola. An obvious next step is to compare the equations $y \cdot y = c$ and $y + x = c$, and to graph corresponding points. The coordinate system can be developed with reference to one of these figures. The representation of points is thus introduced through a concrete curve.

A further possibility is to introduce a coordinate system as offered by the altitude theorem in conjunction with Thales' circle:

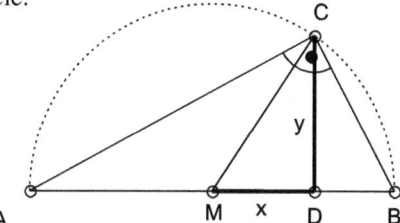

Figure 7

Let the Thales circle be constructed for the segment AB. For any point C on the circle, it must be true that $\angle ACB = 90°$. Find D, the foot of the altitude from C.

39

Let MD = x and DC = y. From the altitude theorem follows:

$$(r+x) \cdot (r-x) = y^2 \text{ (with } y = CD \text{ and } x = MD)$$

or

$$r^2 = x^2 + y^2$$

This equation is the condition for a point C to be a point of the circle; it is thus also called the «equation of the circle». It is, naturally, a direct result of the Pythagorean Theorem. It is entirely possible to start a block with this equation of the circle.

Through comparisons with the equations of the parabola and hyperbola, the goal of analytic geometry becomes clear to the student. Before its systematic development, a few typical equations can be treated.

The right-triangle altitude theorem can be extended in the following way. point P lies outside of segment AB. C is chosen so that

$$(r+x) \cdot (r-x) = y^2 \text{ (with } y = CD \text{ and } x = MD)$$

or

$$x^2 - y^2 = r^2$$

y is then exactly as long as tangent DC'! (Secant-Tangent theorem)

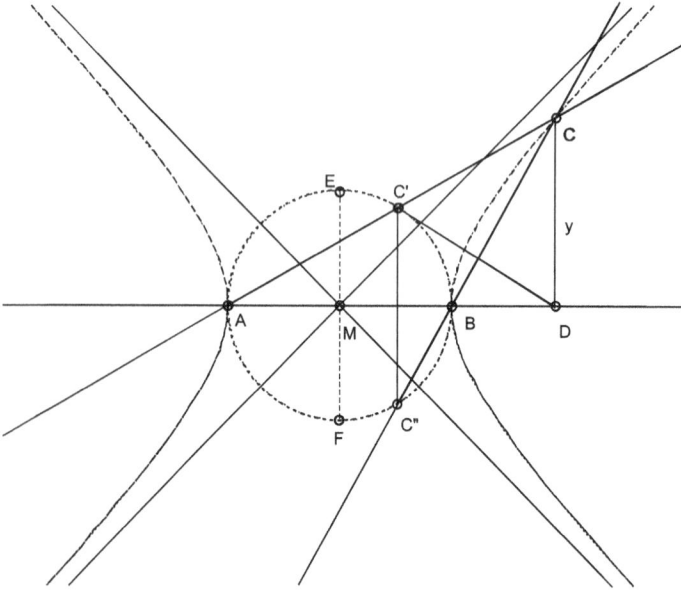

Figure 8

As, in addition, C is the intersection of AC' and BC" (C" is reflection of point C' across AB), the point C lies on an equilateral hyperbola, which appears here as an «inverted Thales' circle».

The hyperbola formula appears here in another form.

In this inversion, the two points of the circle E and F, which lie on the perpendicular bisector of AB, go to infinity. They become the intersections of the asymptotes with the boundary line of the line.

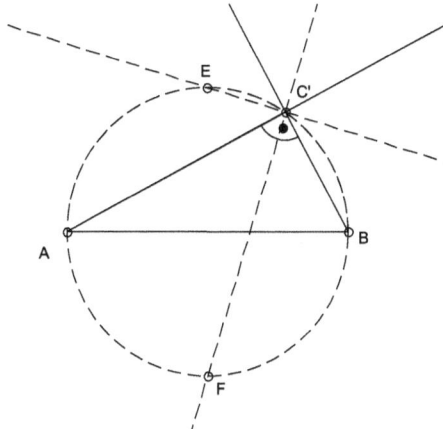

Figure 9

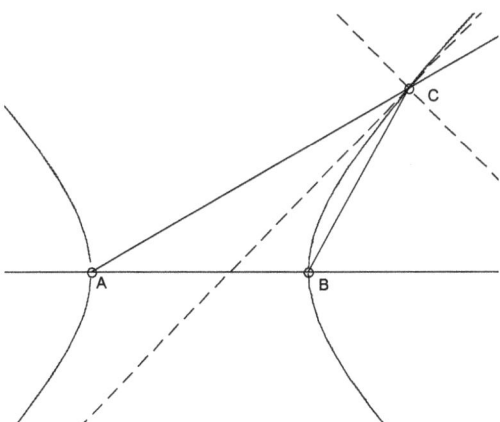

Figure 10

The following consideration demonstrates a corresponding connection:

In the circle of Thales, the two angle bisectors of AC' and C'B always go through the two points E and F. (See figure 9)

For the equilateral hyperbola the angle bisectors of AC and CB are correspondingly parallel to both asymptotes; that is, they pass through both points at infinity, which are the images of E and F (see figure 10).

In the previous examples, the middle term of the ratio (the geometric mean) played a decisive role in connection with the altitude theorem. This middle ratio leads to a quadratic relationship.

If between two quantities not one but two middle ratios are placed, then there is a cubic relationship.

I.e.: given two quantities a and b, we are looking for values x and y such that:

$$a : x = x : y = y : b$$

This problem is a generalization of the so-called Delian Problem: Apollo instructed the Delians to double the size of his cubic altar.

The mathematicians of ancient Greece understood this instruction as requiring them to increase the edge-length of the cube in such a way that the cube's volume would be doubled. Thus they sought two values x and y such that:

$$a : x = x : y = y : 2ab$$

In this case, thus $b = 2a$

From $\frac{a}{x} = \frac{x}{y}$ follows that $ay = x^2$

From $\frac{a}{x} = \frac{y}{2a}$ follows that $xy = 2a^2$

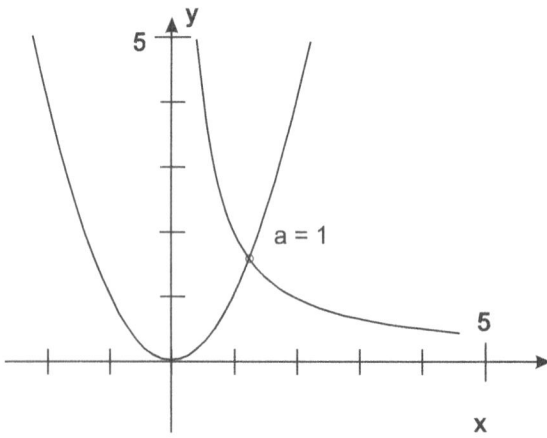

Figure 11

The first condition describes a parabola in coordinate space; the second an equilateral hyperbola. The intersection of the parabola and hyperbola determines the coordinates x and y (this is $x = a \cdot \sqrt[3]{2}$; see figure 11).

The connection between a, x, and y can be represented through the figure 12. Three similar right-angled triangles are used.

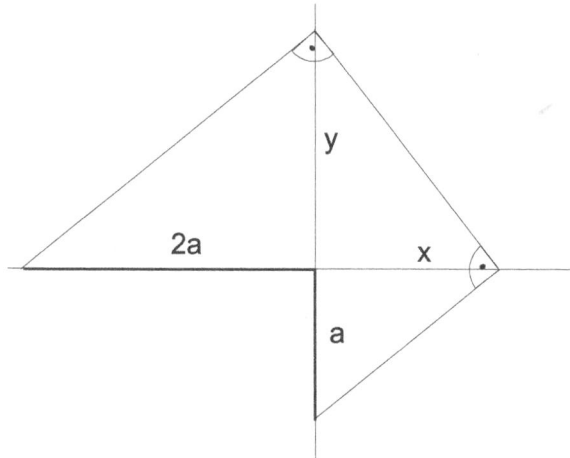

Figure 12

This task can serve as an entry-point into a main lesson block; it can also be sensible to treat it at the end of a main lesson block.

The considerations that led to the equations for a circle and a parabola can be transferred to the derivation of the equation of an ellipse or hyperbola.

Given a point F and line l that does not pass through F: on which curves lie the points P that are double so far from l as from F?

As in the first example, we determine the points C and D and the midpoint M of the segment CD. M is again the origin and the quantities x and y are introduced correspondingly.

Let F be located 3 cm from l.

As $d_2 = 2d_1$, so $d_2^2 = 4d_1^2$ and as $d_2 = y + 4$ and $d_1^2 = x^2 + (y+1)^2$

it follows that
$$4\left(x^2 + (y+1)^2\right) = (y+4)^2$$

or
$$\frac{x^2}{3} + \frac{y^2}{4} = 1$$

We recognize the relationship to the equation of a circle and the asymmetry of the variables x and y. If $d_1 = 2d_2$, we similarly arrive at the equation for a hyperbola.

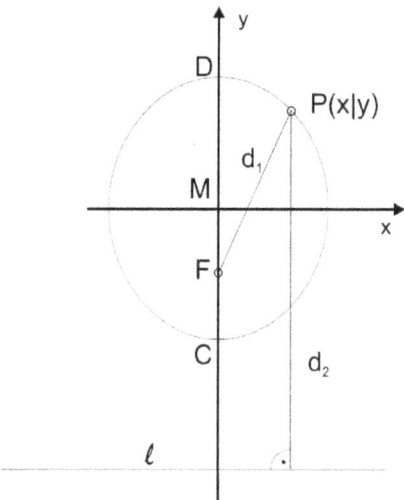

Figure 13

It is satisfying for pupils if the equations for a circle, parabola, ellipse, hyperbola and line can be compared at the beginning of the block.

In our mathematics teaching we must always try to keep the right proportion between inner activity, imagination and visual presentation. When calculating with equations it is easy to slip into a formal application of rules.

Inner activity is maintained and encouraged when the various images are modified and dissolved again. Equations are also «images» in so far as they view geometry from a particular angle, that is, through a particular framework, namely, the coordinate system. It is thus sensible to consider the same geometric form from various sides, that is, in various coordinate systems.

Reviewing the 9th grade geometry block on conic sections, we can use a coordinate system in which the position of a point is described through its distance from two fixed points A and B. We can describe these distances using x and y. In this system, x and y must be positive numbers and we must be careful that $x + y \geqslant AB$. Every number pair $(x \mid y)$ then defines two points that are symmetrically located with respect to AB.

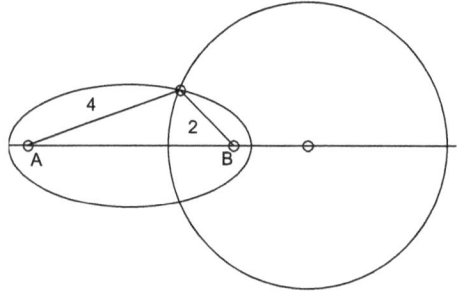

Figure 14

Intersection of the circle $x = 2y$ with the Ellipse $x + y = 6$. The solution is $x = 4$, $y = 2$.

The equation $ax + by = c$ gives Ellipses when $a = b = 1$; hyperbolas when $a = 1$ and $b = -1$ or $a = -1$ and $b = 1$. If $c = 0$, we get an Apollonian circle of division when a and b have opposing signs. In general we get ovals that can also contain concave dips, or Cartesian ovals.

The condition $x \cdot y = c$ leads to the curves of Cassini, which are lemniscates when $AB = 2$.

In another, particularly simple coordinate system pencils of lines are readily depicted; this coordinate system certainly may be used in 10th grade to clarify the connection between increases and decreases in the two variables.

The x and y axes are chosen as parallel lines. Every line that intersects both these axes can be specified by the coordinates of the intersection. Thus the equation $x + y = 6$, for example, defines a set of lines passing through the point A.

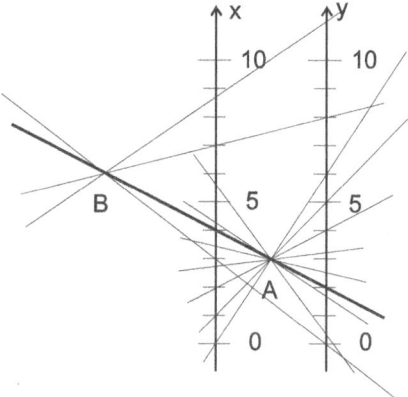

Figure 15

The eqation $2x - y = 6$ describes another pencil of lines that has B as its center.

If we connect points A and B with a straight line we have the solution of the set of equations

$$x + y = 6$$
$$2x - y = 6$$

that is $x = 4$ and $y = 2$.

In this system, all equations of the form $ax + by = c$ define pencils of lines, whereby the center can also be at infinity when $b = -a$. This coordinate system can be immediately understood by a 10th grader.

If we let the x and y axes intersect perpendicularly, we can in precisely the same way describe a line that intersects both axes, as long as this line doesn?t pass through the axes? intersection. Now the equation

$$x + y = 6$$

describes a locus of lines that envelop a parabola.

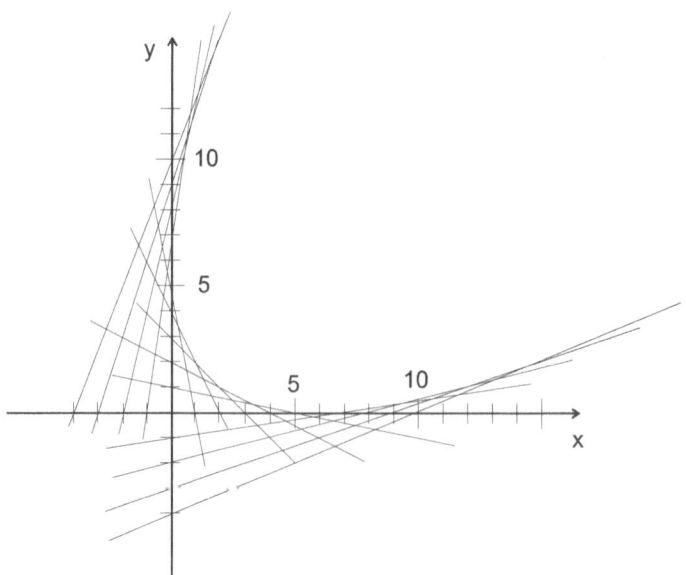

Figure 16

It is generally true that all equations of the form $ax + by = c$ are equations of parabolas in the form of loci of tangent lines.

The equation $x + y = 6$ can thus describe a straight line, an ellipse, a pencil of lines, or a parabola. It follows from this that these geometric images are equivalent from a particular point of view. This connection only becomes clear by considering them algebraically.

In the last-mentioned coordinate system, for example, an equation $x \cdot y = c$ describes a locus of lines that envelop an equilateral hyperbola.

To close, we should contrast an analytic proof with a purely geometric proof; we will demonstrate through a simple special case that an ellipse is an affine image of a circle.

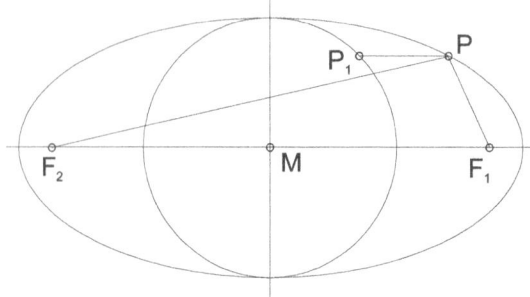

Figure 17

Let $P_1 (x \mid y)$ be a Point of the circle $x^2 + y^2 = 1$, then $P(2x \mid y) = P\left(2x \mid \sqrt{1-x^2}\right)$ is an affine image of P_1.

It is $r = 1$; let $F_1 \left(\sqrt{3} \mid 0\right)$ and $F_2 \left(-\sqrt{3} \mid 0\right)$.

Then

$$F_1P = \sqrt{\left(2x-\sqrt{3}\right)^2 + (1-x^2)}$$
$$= \sqrt{4x^2 - 4x\sqrt{3} + 3 + 1 - x^2}$$
$$= \sqrt{4 - 4x\sqrt{3} + 3x^2}$$
$$= \sqrt{\left(2-x\sqrt{3}\right)^2}$$
$$= 2 - x\sqrt{3}$$

We can similarly demonstrate that $F_2P = 2 + x\sqrt{3}$ thus $F_1P + F_2P = 4$.

We have thus shown that P is a point of an ellipse. F_1, and F_2 are the foci; the constant sum of the radial distances equals 4.

Geometric Proof:

For this proof an elliptical surface is produced by sectioning a cylinder (figure 18). Let the cylinder radius be $r = 1$; in addition, let the cylinder be cut so that AM has length 2. Let P_1 be an arbitrary point of the circle and the planes MAA_1 and NPP_1 be parallel to the cylinder's axis. By the similarity of triangles MAA_1 and NPP_1, NP is twice the length of NP_1, for MA is twice as long as MA_1.

This means that the plane E's intersection with the cylinder is a curve that is an affine image of the circle.

Now two spheres are place into the cylinder, touching the cylinder and the sectioning plane E. Let the two points of tangency be F_1 and F_2.

A generating line of the cylinder is drawn through P, intersecting the two circles where the spheres meet the cylinder at point U and V. As all tangents from a point to a sphere are of equal length, we know that:

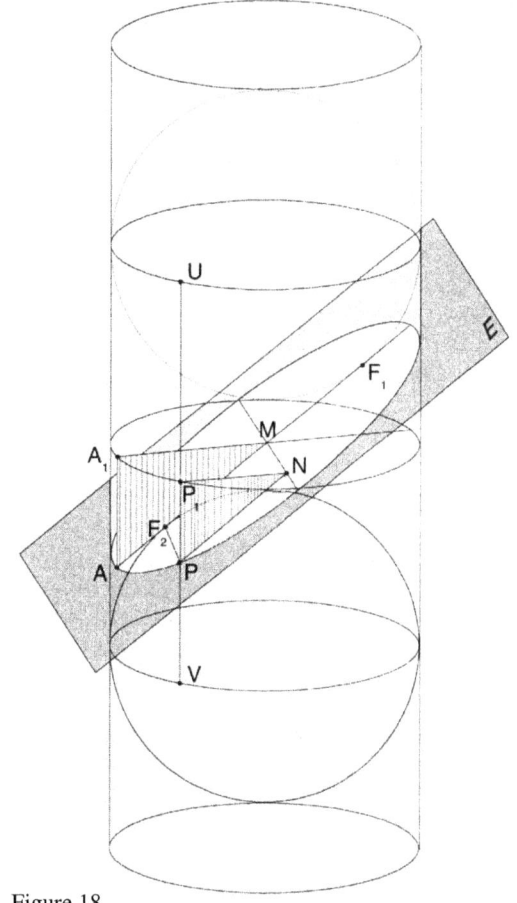

Figure 18

- $PF_1 = PU$ (tangents to the upper sphere)
- $PF_2 = PV$ (tangents to the lower sphere)
- thus $PF_1 + PF_2 = PU + PV = UV$, a constant.

Thus the curve of intersection is an ellipse with foci F_1 and F_2.
As $MA = 2$ and $r = 1$, $MF_1 = MF_2 = \sqrt{3}$ and we know that

$$PF_1 + PF_2 = 4$$

The contrast between these two styles of proof shows that the inner imagination is weakened for part of the first proof through the algebraic reformulation, as we are limited to logical conclusions. It is more easily possible to see the proof before us as a whole in the purely geometric proof.

Comment: There are many proofs that are simpler in a synthetic form than are the corresponding analytic proofs.

An example: Let P be an arbitrary point of the Thales? circle on AB. Let Q be a vertex of the square on the leg PB.

$$x + y = 6$$

describes a locus of lines that envelop a parabola.

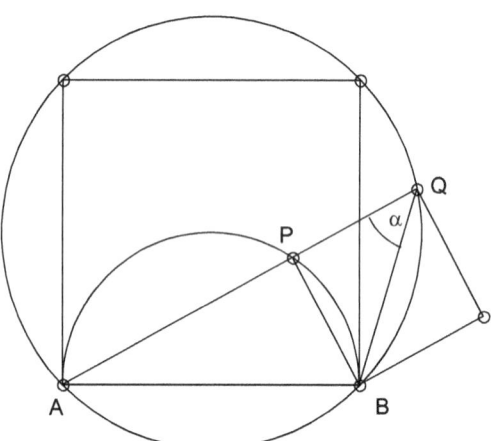

Figure 19

As P moves along the Thales' circle, Q also moves along a circle; this circle is the circumcircle of the square on AB.

It follows that α must be $45°$ (inscribed angle of a circle).

Stepping-Stones in a Projective Geometry Block

STEPHAN SIGLER

For me, to imagine space was fraught with great inner challenges. I found it impossible to find any reasonable way of considering it to be emptiness spreading infinitely in all directions, as the dominant scientific theories of the time presupposed. Through the new (synthetic) geometry, which I encountered through lectures and my personal reading, the imagination arose in my soul that a line which was extended infinitely far to the right would come back around from the left. Its point infinitely far to the right is the same as that infinitely far to the left. It seemed to me that by way of such imaginations drawn from this new geometry, space – otherwise fixedly staring into emptiness – could be taken hold of conceptually. [...] After the lecture during which this image first arose in my soul, I went out as if a huge weight had fallen away from my shoulders. A liberating feeling swept over me. As in my earliest boyhood, geometry brought me joy again.[1]

Curriculum indications for projective geometry

Steiner came to appreciate the clarity and orderliness of mathematical and geometric structures of thought, which he experienced as «salutary», when he was still a pupil.[2] They stimulated early questions about the relationship of his visions of a spiritual world – to him these seemed natural – to phenomena of nature. He spoke about these matters later in many lectures and held synthetic projective geometry in high esteem. He only made three brief comments, however, which can be understood as curricular indications; these were spoken during conferences with teachers at the Stuttgart school:

1. It seems to me that synthetic geometry holds great therapeutic promise.[3]

2. Follow up with elementary topology. Above all, bring to the children the concept of duality. You only need to teach them the very simplest aspects.

3. «These children are between 15 and 16. When they work through some first elementary ideas, up to the principle of duality in perspective, so that they are perplexed and amazed, and when they take an interest in Baravalle's dissertation, then you've achieved all that you should achieve. Have you started on descriptive geometry[4]

---

[1] Steiner, R.: Story of My Life, Chapter III.
[2] Ibid. Chapter II.
[3] Steiner, R.: Conferences with Teachers. March 1921. This was said in connection with planning for the Stuttgart Collegiate Courses.
[4] Steiner, R.: Conferences with Teachers. June 17, 1921. This quotation referred to the 10th grade.

The teacher addressed above explained what he had covered and added that he had covered relatively little of mechanics. Steiner recommended that he treat the parabola of flight to demonstrate how reality and a mathematical concept here coincide. Immediately afterwards, in connection with this, Steiner continued:

> «Philosophy begins with wonder» Well, that's partly false. When teaching we must stimulate a feeling of wonder at the end of a chapter, while in philosophy this feeling comes at the beginning. The children must be directed towards wonder. They must encounter something that takes hold of them completely. They must be brought to comprehend that they are encountering something before the magnificence of which Novalis himself would kneel.
>
> Something like Baravalle's dissertation – though he shouldn't grow arrogant – is of fundamental significance for a Waldorf teacher, above all because it demonstrates and greatly simplifies the transformation of mathematical concepts into pictures that can be visualized. [5]

A tradition arose in Waldorf schools, based on this comment, of offering at least one block on projective geometry. In contrast to Steiner's comment, however, this usually takes place in the 11th, not the 10th grade. I would like to explore the special character of projective geometry, as Steiner repeatedly described this. By considering this character in combination with the daily-experienced situation of 11th-graders, we can fully justify the sensible and well-grounded practice of waiting for the 11th grade to give this block. There are naturally colleagues who approach this differently.

The Character of Projective Geometry

In order to properly understand projective geometry's character, we should briefly picture how it first arose. The 19th-century discovery of possible geometries that contradict our visual space has proven to be quite significant for the evolution of consciousness; fundamental philosophical convictions that to this day shape our ordinary state of consciousness were thereby shaken. René Descartes (1596-1650) founded analytic geometry, with the help of which geometric problems could by solved by means of calculations utilizing a coordinate system. Geometry was thereby reduced to the knowledge of certain straight lines and calculations of their relationships. The equation of a sphere, e.g., is based solely upon x, y and z distances and a radius r; the Pythagorean Theorem joins these together in the equation $x^2 + y^2 + z^2 = r^2$.

A coordinate system prepares a mathematical scaffolding that enables us to manipulate special relationships completely abstractly. The three mutually-perpendicular coordinate axes provide us with a stable schema, ordering and orientating, as they are linked to our bodily organization. Originally they are generated from the latter through a process of abstraction by human beings. The

---
[5] Steiner, R.: Conferences with Teachers. Sept. 11, 1921.

thus-configured space gives us some security in existence as it corresponds to an unconsciously-experienced, inner, three-dimensional schema: above-below, right-left, and forward-backward.[6]

The popular understanding of space culminates in Newton's «absolute space», which must be thought of as a rigid, self-sufficient reality:

> It is the nature of absolute space to always remain uniform and motionless in the absence of any relationship to an outer object.[7]

Newton fails to explain what absolute space actually is, however:

> I will not explain time, space, location or movement, as these are well known to all. But I must observe that these quantities are commonly conceived solely in relation to the senses, giving rise to certain prejudices, to overcome which it is necessary to distinguish appropriately between their use in absolute and relative, true and apparent, and mathematical and conventional terms.[8]

This statement is amazing as it contradicts Newton's own empirical method, according to which the existence of absolute space would have to be proven by some method. If absolute space really existed, its existence would have to be absolutely independent of any object whatsoever. Absolute space is itself void of content, although packed with material objects, and serves as an empty container indefinitely extended in all directions. Every single object corresponds to a well-defined point in space. Each exists absolutely independently in space and has no real inner connection with any of its neighboring objects. Even if two objects begin interacting with one another, it is in a purely external manner that can be described in mathematical terms.

This view of space totally strips our image of the world of any human connection. The human being becomes an observer of an insubstantial, externalized world. Steiner described this as a constitution of soul typical of our times. [9]

For Immanuel Kant (1724-1804), on the contrary, space is an a priori category of our perception of the outer world. He differentiates the form and content of perception: The content is provided from outside while the form has its origin within the human being. Our knowledge of geometrical mathematics develops through our applying thinking to the pure category of space. Geometric forms and thoughts are not products of experience, but rather exist in our mind as a constructive process completely independent of experience. Mathematical laws are independent of the content of sense-experience and therefore cannot be evaluated with reference to the latter. These a priori laws underlie the world of human experience and thereby determine the characteristics of our mathematical and physical space.

---

[6] Steiner (1985) The Origins of Natural Science, Hudson: Anthroposophic Press. Lecture 3.
[7] Newton, Principia Mathematica, p. 25
[8] Ibid.
[9] Cf. footnote 1.

> Empirical perception is only possible by means of pure perception; thus what the geometer says of the latter is invariably true of the former. [10]

Thus geometry was irrevocably linked to the categorical structure of Euclidean space. Space is thereby not a quality that belongs to the «things in themselves» that, according to Kant, underlie the world's appearance. Space is only a quality of things as they appear to a perceiving agent. Through such categories of perception, the human being establishes the manner in which objects appear to him; through our reasoning we subsume sense perceptions under concepts and classifications which have their ultimate origin in the pure realm of reason.

If we could remove all subjective conditions of perception that are inherent in the human observer, then space would be missing. The particular conditions of sense-experience have nothing to do with the «things in themselves», but only make it possible that we experience anything whatsoever. We can therefore conclude that real objects can only appear to us spatially. If we give up the very conditions that make experience possible, space becomes nothingness. Thus Kant, as Newton before him, postulates space as something in a certain way stable and absolute, but with the limitation that this only applies to human perception, and there the world of appearances, not to the objects themselves. [11]

Long before Kant, Girard Desargues (1593-1662) had already taken up geometric problems whose solution and extension would place the above-described understanding of space in doubt. Desargues, an architect and engineer, became an important connecting link between empirical practice and mathematical theory. He unified all the drawing constructions of Renaissance artists, despite their diverse origins and appearance, from the standpoint of mathematical geometry. He thereby introduced for the first time the idea that the vanishing points of central perspective are representations of the intersections of parallel, infinite lines. With the aid of this principle he was able to describe the regular curves of the circle, ellipse, parabola and hyperbola as special cases within a unified concept of the conic section. The implications that this idea would have for mathematics as a whole went unnoticed by both him and his contemporaries for a long time.

Even 170 years later, Karl Friedrich Gauss (1777-1855), who studied the problem of the parallel postulate for many years, was for a long time uncertain whether to publish his ideas. They seemed too revolutionary for him, and he feared the «cries of the buffoons» and the «hornets-nest» he would stir up, as he once wrote in a letter. Nevertheless, the idea of a non-Euclidean geometry that was completely free of contradictions could not be held back, for Wolfgang Bolyai and his son Johann (1802-60) as well as Nikolai Ivanovich Lobachevsky (1792-1856) worked on the same problem contemporaneously to Gauss but probably relatively independently from one another; seeking to liberate the conceptual laws of geometry from the strictures of visual perception. In 1826, Lobachevsky published his first results, Bolyai following in 1831. It was much harder to achieve in geometry what had already been accomplished 100 years earlier in analytic

---

[10] Immanuel Kant (2003) Critique of Pure Reason. Dover. p. 116.

[11] For a more in-depth understanding of Kant's views I recommend studying Steiner's epistemological writings, in order to give one's teaching a philosophical orientation and basis. Cf. especially Steiner's Truth and Science.

mathematics, as the former had always been closely coupled to perception. Even today it continues to be difficult to consciously separate the purely conceptual and logical aspects from our visualizations, which always appear very convincing and immediately apparent.

From a modern point of view, Euclidean geometry appears as a special case of a much more general projective geometry. These ideas therefore met with resistance and only very slowly gained acceptance. It was only in 1860, when the correspondence between Gauss and the astronomer Hans Christian Schumacher was published, that the general public was forced to recognize and accept the discoveries in the light of Gauss' overwhelming authority in the field.[12]

The problematic nature of the parallel postulate and the discovery that this axiom is not necessary to establish a geometry without internal contradictions deeply disturbed a mathematician of the time for whom the question was far from being an intellectual, theoretical game. A shocked Wolfgang Bolyai wrote to his son Johann, having heard that he wanted to take up this question:

> You must not attempt to tackle parallels by any method; I know this path to its very end; I have also measured that bottomless night, which extinguished life's every light and pleasure. I call upon you in God's name; let the theory of parallels be. [...] I had resolved to sacrifice myself for truth, was prepared to become a martyr in order to present humanity with a geometry purified from this defect. I worked furiously at it, accomplishing far better work than was ever done before, but I have never been able to find a fully satisfactory solution. [...] I returned from this journey when I perceived that this night's ground could not be reached from the Earth; disconsolate, sad for myself and for the whole human race. [...] I have sailed past every peril of this hellish dead sea and returned from each with my mast in ruins and my sails in tatters. I date from that time the ruination of my humor and my fall.[13]

For the father, it was thus a deadly serious matter. When pupils hear such passages they smile disbelievingly. Despite this, they can sensitively sympathize with the dramatic struggle – but only after they have themselves begun to explore and experience the ideas of projective geometry.

Considering the character of projective geometry and its importance in the history of consciousness, this historical view is quite suggestive. Indeed, Steiner frequently treated this question, characterizing work with projective geometry as a training ground for the ability to achieve supersensible knowledge, on the one hand, and as a model for the scientific method generally, on the other. He fought vehemently against a one-sidedly formal treatment of mathematics, and thereby against using mathematics merely to quantify and master nature. For him, non-Euclidean geometry was a symptom of a longing for spiritual understanding.

---

[12] For a history of the critical reception of non-Euclidean geometry cf. Ziegler, R. (1987): «Die Entdeckung der nichteuklidischen Geometrien und ihre Folgen; Bemerkungen zur Bewusstseinsgeschichte des 19. Jahrhunderts». In: Elemente der Naturwissenschaft 2:87.

[13] Quoted in Meschkowski, H. (1954): Nichteuklidische Geometrie. Braunschweig. Translation by HG.

> I just want to point out how symptomatic it is that precisely in mathematics, a field that has maintained such extraordinary inner power, it has become quite clear how ready 19th century thought is to break through the boundary that separates the knowing human subject from the supersensory world. Even if these are frequently only bold hypotheses, just theoretical calculations, we still have to see what has happened in the field of mathematics as an expression of a longing for human understanding to extend beyond the sensory world.[14]

Steiner saw this happening precisely in the fact that non-Euclidean geometry invalidates the monopolistic claims of a Euclidean view of space: more worlds are conceivable than we initially experience. In order to not only conceive of, but also to experience these worlds, we must train our human powers of understanding:

> Now Plato looked upon mathematical science as a means of training for life in the World of Ideas emancipated from sense-perception. The mathematical images hover over the border-line between the material and the purely spiritual World. [...] When I think mathematically, I do indeed think about something my senses can perceive; but at the same time I do not think in terms of sense-perception. [...] From the mathematical figure I can learn to know supersensible facts by way of the sense-world. This was the all-important point for Plato. We must visualise the idea in a purely spiritual manner if we would really know it in its true aspect. We can train ourselves to this if we only avail ourselves of the first steps in mathematical knowledge for this purpose, and understand clearly what it is that we really gain from a mathematical figure.[15]

Steiner here presents an approach to purifying the activity of thinking and liberating it from sensory components through mathematical training. This relies partly on the modality in which mathematical concepts exist in our consciousness, related to but not directly within the sense world, and partly on the method through which mathematical ideas take shape, in which we relate and connect our thoughts in accordance with their content and in a totally conscious way sustained only by our own ego activity. In this way this kind of activity – especially in the field of synthetic projective geometry – forms a first step on the way to a higher imagination.[16] This prepares the ground for an acknowledgement of the significance of an imaginative element, since we are not treating geometric forms in an external manner and solely quantitatively, as in analytic geometry, but can penetrate into their inmost, characteristic and essential form. Naturally, projective geometry also has the formal nature of a tool that gives us appropriate concepts to control external nature. At the same time, this specific form of practicing mathematics doesn't have

---

[14] Steiner, Wege und Ziele des geistigen Menschen. GA 125, Dornach 1973, p. 79. Translation by H. Gilbert

[15] R. Steiner, «Mathematics and Occultism», from «Anthroposophical Movement», Vol.V No. 28 8th July 1928. German Volume: «Philosophie und Anthroposophie», GA 35

[16] Imagination is a term used to describe the first step of supersensible knowledge, as Steiner describes Occult Science. He describes imagination's connection with mathematical work in the lecture cycle Anthroposophy and Science (Mercury Press: 1991).

to remain merely formal and external, but can keep in touch with reality: When done properly, according to Steiner, projective geometry is the only area of mathematics that even in its content strives to reconnect with sensory reality. Otherwise, mathematics always has the quality of ignoring everything that is part of life and only considering the formal properties or spatial, geometric relationships. In this regard, Steiner even called upon mathematicians to apply synthetic projective geometry to the form of the human organism, for example:

> If the mathematician were so trained as to be interested also in what is real, – in the appearance of the heart, for example, so that he could form an idea of how through a mathematical process he could turn the heart inside out, and how thereby the whole human form would arise, – if he were taught to use his mathematics in actual life, then he could be working in the realm of the real.[17]

As is evident from the above quotation from his autobiography, in his youth Steiner had decisive experiences of projective geometry. He could thereby conceptualize differently the paralyzing emptiness and infinite widths of the thus-imagined space, which is supposedly only «available» for the events of the world, and felt that this was liberating him from a heavy burden. It's clear from this experience why Steiner hope that projective geometry would do «a tremendous amount for the healing» of humanity.

Pedagogical Consequences

The character of projective geometry and the three curricular indications described above indicate possible lessons and methods of teaching.

- The function Steiner attributes to projective geometry's imaginative quality doesn't allow for a purely formal instructional method systematically building up from axioms. It seems natural to work with visual experiences through drawing exercises followed by thoughtful observation. Therefore I almost exclusively discuss planar geometry. Steiner himself suggests starting from central perspective, thus beginning completely from visual experience. The following material can be structured so that students are led very gradually out of sensory experience; the elements at infinity should not be brought in as an abstract addition whose signification lies solely in their utility. Even though the elements at infinity retain no sensory qualities and could appear to be purely abstract assumptions, the teacher can strive above all to connect them to qualitative experiences that call upon more than just thinking. Indeed, what is needed is for pupils «to have something that calls upon their *whole* being.» Pupils will only be able to fully open themselves to new thought forms when they encounter

---

[17] R. Steiner, «Astronomy Course, Lecture I». Translation by www.awakenings.com/jcms/anthroposophy-and-goethean/45-rudolf-steiner-third-cycle.html. German Volume: Das Verhältnis der verschiedenen naturwissenschaftlichen Gebiete zur Astronomie, GA 323, Dornach 1983, p. 28

these in ways that take deep root in their bodily constitution. In my opinion, Steiner's explanations in the second and third lectures of the book Education for Adolescents mean that in projective geometry we must begin with particular, concrete phenomena, whose richness of form stimulates joy and can be observed with interest.[18] For this reason they should not be subsumed as special cases from a formal point of view.

- One important aspect of the lesson is the duality and polarity of configurations (see the second and third curricular indications). Normally we tend to think of space or the plane as filled out with points, which in accordance with an atomistic world-view serve as basic building blocks. In our customary way of speaking, we always say, «A line is composed of infinitely many points.» The line's essential quality is concealed thereby. A special formation which is dual to the usual point-space allows radically different conceptual horizons and forms of thought which are worth practicing.

- Another important aspect is the wonder to be evoked and the interest for what follows that this engenders.

- [cf. (3) of the curricular indications]. Such a sense of wonder can arise on a number of levels: First, the carefully developed constructions can generate a quality of openness for wonder. In the end, however, students are amazed at their own magnificent and striking life of thought. Not truth, but rather the beauty of truth is worthy to be admired, as Goethe expressed in his Proverbs in Prose.

The Developmental Situation in 11th grade

In what way does projective geometry address the particular developmental situation of eleventh-grade pupils?

In the eleventh grade we usually meet a clearly calmer situation: pupils give the impression of being more mature, confident and secure. In our direct, personal contacts with them they demand respect and individual acceptance as an adult equal, which they are often also instinctively given. The negative side is a lack of drive, weariness, and laziness. The feeling of being grown-up and the wish to lead one's own life, whereby the parents influence – and are able to influence – only slightly the configuration of their days and nights often has consequences for the bodily prerequisites of being able to take meaningful part in a class at 8 o'clock in the morning.

This demands of teachers in yet higher degree an approach to teaching for which it is really worth waking early! The teacher's own respect for and intimate connection with the material, which come about through working ever more deeply with it, are the fundamental prerequisites for pupils – especially at this age – to relate to lessons and find them fruitful. A finer inner life goes along with this withdrawal from the outer world, however; the remnants of puberty disappear

---
[18] Steiner, R. (1996) Education for Adolescents, Hudson: Anthroposophic Press

and developmental differences within a class even out. The feeling of class unity that developed over the previous years, by which many pupils feel themselves to be carried even into the tenth grade, often disappears almost completely. A community begins to form out of what the various individuals bring.

In the general attitude to learning, too, this individualization becomes apparent; the class divides itself at times into those pupils who work to the best of their ability and want out of themselves to take something up and learn it, and those who take longer to begin to direct their own thoughts and will-power. Their self-evaluation and their evaluations of others become significantly more realistic; this is often a painful process of recognizing one's own abilities and limitations.

The boys, too, turn away from being solely preoccupied with the outer world and attend more to their inner experiences. Deeper questions and contributions to lessons no longer come primarily as provocative comments through which the teacher must hear the underlying substance. Thoughts are experienced more as coming from within and want to be personally felt and judged. Thinking no longer serves the purpose of being a means to achieve the power to explain and control the world; instead, they want to expand their horizons and acquire direction of thought. They begin to clearly articulate philosophical and spiritual questions.

Projective geometry takes up this situation especially deeply, whereby, in my experience, it has proven to be better not to give this block too early in the year. The elements at infinity are only proven to be «real» when they are so proven by a person's own thinking. They pupils can't be supported by examples drawn from sensory perception, only by their own thinking activity, in accomplishing which they experience the surety and evidence of their own thoughts' validity. This means, however, that they must first free themselves from the familiar, secure viewpoint of traditional geometry and find support only in the experience of their own thinking.

If the elements at infinity are established axiomatically, then pupils will generally not experience anything more in projective geometry than that mathematics is once again an illogical, arbitrary and dry subject that one is made to learn for a test. This must manifest in how the lesson is taught, naturally. The pupils' thinking must take imaginative flight in order to demolish barriers, to independently wrestle through to truth. What is static, complete and objective can only be a means of inquiring further into phenomena and listening for their spiritual content.

If we look to see how the above considerations respond to the developmental situation of eleventh-grade youth, we can see that this block serves a key function. On the one hand, through the many constructions and the immediate experiences these engender, it can help pupils reconnect with their own willed activity. On the other hand, it addresses latently-present questions such as:

- Are there entities that live and act in the world yet are not perceptible to the senses?
- Do I, for example, have such a force in me?
- How do these stand in connection with the world?
- What can I experience of them and how do I establish a relationship to them?

A thoughtful penetration into and evaluation of such questions should not only bring further steps of understanding, but also unleash new capacities, activities and will-impulses in the pupils. In this way projective geometry can prepare the ground for large questions about the development of the human being and the world in twelfth grade.

Perhaps it is clear from the above that such goals cannot be achieved in tenth grade. There we work in virtually an opposing way. If we consider, e.g., surveying: what is achieved by way of mathematical knowledge of trigonometry, partially with a quite practical orientation, serves primarily to rationally solidify one's own soul. This is even made use of to the extent that each pupil «takes hold» of a landscape through measurement and calculation. Very briefly summarized, surveying is an experience of how purely rationally-acquired understanding makes possible a particular, more technically-oriented grasp of the world rather than a matter of delicately feeling one's way into a realm of uncertainty or of the unimaginable.

I am certain that it is possible to appropriately prepare for projective geometry in tenth grade, for example through exercises in perspective and central projections.[19] I've always experienced the introduction to and really conceptual penetration of the elements at infinity as being first viable in the eleventh grade. In the tenth grade, pupils took on the connections as more of an invention, disbelievingly, and then become to some extent dissatisfied and finally concluded: «ok, sure, two parallel lines intersect at infinity.» They could then successfully apply this formula. The tenth-grader's configuration of soul reveals itself again here! Conversations about this theme were sometimes very lively controversies, but didn't press through to the essence of the matter, remaining more at the level of an exchange of blows.

Representative moments of the block

Methodologically, I have always drawn upon Arnold Bernard's book Projective Geometry,[20] which provides convincing possibilities for applying Steiner's suggestions to teaching various topics.

Central Projection and Central Perspective

If we begin a block, as Steiner suggests, with central projections, we can lead the pupils very cautiously and initially visually toward projective geometry. The first tasks are always to project points, lines and figures from a vertical plane onto a horizontal plane, and vice versa.[21] Exact descriptions and justifications of the constructions are important here. The known characteristics of central projections should be established.

---

[19] Cf. the article by R. Rosbigalle in this volume.
[20] Bernhard, A. (1984). Projektive Geometrie. Stuttgart
[21] Ibid., p. 17

- Points are mapped to points, lines to lines.

- If a point is on a line, the point's image is on the line's image.

- The line of intersection of the two planes is a line of invariant points; thus it remains point-wise invariant.

I like to introduce the theme of vanishing points by asking if anybody has ever seen parallel lines. I don't touch on the question whether we always really see a line as a line, as this diverges from the main point. For many pupils, it isn't clear that a perceived image never shows truly parallel lines. A little time is needed before everybody is clear that we continually conceptualize the quality of being parallel into the phenomena of our visual space. Even short straight segments, such as two edges of a table in front of me, appear only approximately parallel, as objects that are more distant appear smaller – a basic property of our vision. Usually pupils can recall fairly quickly the perspective drawing they did in the middle school, in which two parallel lines met at a vanishing point which was situated on a horizontally-drawn horizon line. I have often had them draw a chess board or something similar in two-point perspective, as this can be connected to much of our further work (e.g. the harmonic division in the complete quadrilateral).

If we ask the next morning how high you must raise your vision in order to bring a vanishing point on the horizon, where sky and Earth touch, into view, a very lively conversation can ensue: you have to look straight out. What do you see when your vision runs parallel to the Earth, sky or Earth? You don't see the Earth any longer, since your line of sight doesn't meet the Earth's surface any more. Thus, the sky. Do you not see the Earth at all any more? No, for you look over and past the Earth. Then in order to see the boundary between sky and Earth do I have to lower my vision? If I try this, I see only Earth as long as my vision is directed downwards. I can raise my eyes a little and still see only Earth. If the direction of my vision is parallel to the Earth's surface, do I still only see sky? Is there even such a boundary? How must I look to see it? Is it vague or sharply bounded? Where are, actually, the original points of the horizon? Etc.

I stir up a lot of controversy here in order to make the difficulties inherent in this situation very clear to the pupils.

It's important here that it comes out in the end that there is only one ray of vision that is directed to the vanishing point on the horizon. This ray of vision, considered as a line, passes through our eye. We thus «see» this line only as a point (the vanishing point). This line must naturally lie horizontally above the horizontal plane of the Earth and be parallel to the parallels of this plane. What is actually surprising here is that we see a point, the vanishing point, as the intersection of two lines and a line (the horizon), that are totally unable to be found «out in the world» or in the ground plane.

If we want to construct the vanishing points in a spatial configuration as well, we can project e.g. the given triangles from the horizontal plane onto the visual image, the vertical plane, whereby Z is the eye's location. (See Figure 1).

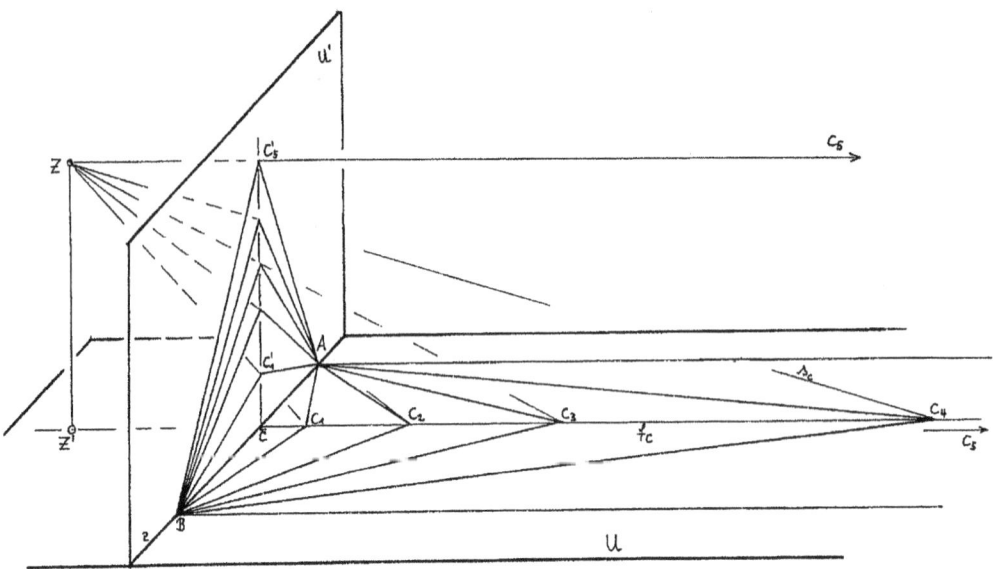

Figure 1

To draw points C'_1 through C'_4 and their corresponding image triangles is no longer difficult and is a review. How must we draw «image triangle» 5, however? At this point I conduct a very thorough, detailed and lively discussion with the pupils, touching on viewpoints such as the following:

- Let point C travel to the right along f_c with a certain, constant velocity. Thereby, C's image point travels upwards along a perpendicular (why?) to axis z, reducing its speed as it goes. This path should be imagined to be continuous.

- Over the course of this journey, what movement do e.g. the planes E_1 through B, C and C' and E_2 through A, C and C' make? Is it possible to prove through their positions that at C'_5 s_c must be parallel to f_c?

- The ray of vision s_c through Z describes a pencil of lines through Z. The ray of vision through C_5 must run parallel to the original image plane and thus parallel to f_c as well as to both of the triangle legs, so that it no longer intersects f_c.

- The construction method for the vanishing point is achieved as follows: draw the plan-ray f_c and ray of vision s_c parallel to the given parallels; is found where f_c intersects s_c. Erect a perpendicular to axis z at $\overline{C}$. The intersection of these perpendiculars with the ray of vision to C_5 is the sought-for vanishing point C'_5. Through this the horizon runs horizontally and parallel to z.

Pupils always answer the question, where then the original image point C_5 is when the triangle sides are parallel, by saying: «It is at infinity,» or «It doesn't exist.» I always encourage them then to precisely imagine the process of the disappearance: if we accompany in our consciousness the point C as the intersection of the lines AC and BC on its path to the right, how is it conceivable that it disappears into infinity? What does that moment look like when the two lines become parallel, yet I want to hold the point in consciousness? Pupils describe their experience at this boundary as a flickering; they reel and become dizzy. This furthest boundary, where the imagination touches on the unimaginable, is the grey area in which the still physically supported activity of the human being attempts to capture a corner of the purely conceptual, spiritual realm. The experience that pupils can have thereby proves to be effective in an on-going way, as they can then experience the further purely conceptual steps as a liberation.

What the pupils can be completely sure of and keep firm hold of is that when the lines become parallel there is no longer an intersection in the finite realm. I leave open in what sense it exists or not. If C_5 disappears into infinity, it leaves behind the two parallel lines in the finite realm. C_5 is thus only conceivable as the completed process of the lines' disappearance or becoming parallel. A clear direction is thus established.

There is now an opening to introduce the expression, «the point C_5 disappears into infinity in the direction f_c.» This disappearance has two aspects: on the one hand, we can understand thereby that the point no longer exists (in whatever sense) and on the other hand, it can be so interpreted that it is only hidden, thus no longer perceptible. At this stage, every pupil can choose for herself her preferred interpretation. Under no circumstances may the lesson be so presented that the elements at infinity are «assigned» to the students so that they are supposed to believe in their existence in so far as this is still imaginable.

At this point I completely relinquish a more precise conceptual definition of infinity. Through my approach and choice of further material, I try to proceed so that pupils experience this question as urgent and that they at least intuit that much depends upon the answer to it – on the one hand within mathematics and on the other hand related to the trust in their thinking that they want to acquire. The experience of the elements at infinity stands or falls with their insight and feeling that it is necessary to discover an answer to this question.

Considerations about the structure of the main lesson employing the example of central, linear collineations

Starting from a central projection, through continuously lowering the center of projection or viewpoint we arrive completely naturally at the central, linear collineation. After some preliminary exercises[22] I guide the pupils through a drawing in which a triangle is projected from a vertical

---

[22] Bernhard, pp. 45ff.

into a horizontal plane and the center Z passes along the whole vertical line through Z and Z' (see Figure 2).[23]

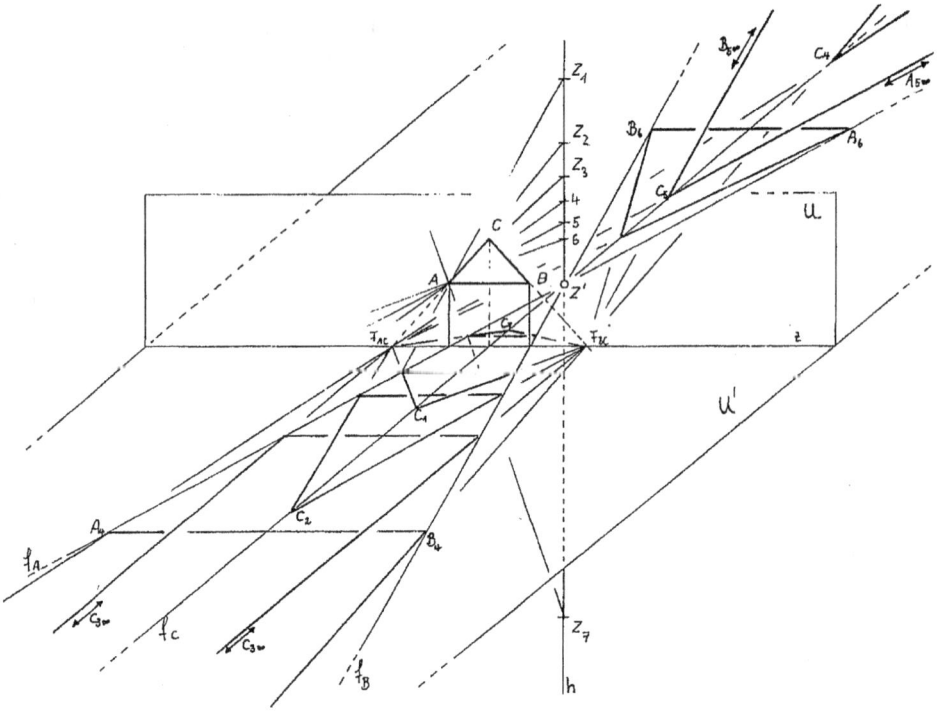

Figure 2

Using the example of this pedagogical situation, I want to describe how I organize a main lesson in line with Steiner's indications, taking the night into account.[24] Drawing upon examples from physics and history, Steiner divides a lesson into presentation, characterization, and, after the passage of a night, reflection. In physics, the experiment is performed in the presentation section, then that which has just been experienced is recapitulated by all, and after the night – thus only on the next day – one would work through the principles underlying the appearances.

I go through the drawing with the pupils (see Figure 2) in the «presentation section». The pupils have for this the example which I have drawn (the night before) with the help of an overhead projector on the board.

Pupils can work through the first three stations of the triangle by themselves (silently) if they are told to draw the visual rays through A and to be careful that the triangle sides A_iB_i always remain parallel. Sides A_iC_i and B_iC_i always go through the corresponding fixed points F_{AC} and F_{BC}. It becomes clear by the third triangle that the legs of the triangle become parallel and that point C_3 along f_c has disappeared into infinity.

---

[23] Ibid. p. 46, slightly modified.
[24] Steiner, Education for Adolescents, especially lectures 2 and 3.

If we construct the fourth triangle in the same way, the sides A_4C_4 and B_4C_4 diverge towards the front. Since they are no longer parallel, we now find the point of intersection C_4 behind the vertical plane. This can be determined quite naturally, since it arises out of the motion of the triangle's sides, which we consider to be continuous. At this moment, the drawing departs from what is visible and becomes abstract geometry, only following the principle that the legs of the image triangle must intersect at a point C_4 on f_c, as they are not parallel. This leap with the pupils has to be taken energetically. Experiencing the form's metamorphosis allows the next form to always be hinted at. The triangle legs have to open up at the front at some point, while the vertex C_i is defined by their point of intersection. Under no circumstances should this be discussed immediately, but rather on the following day. This is primarily successful when pupils live into the transformative process strongly. For this, it is essential to have a very clear, beautiful blackboard drawing which presents an overview of the process and concentrates in itself the complete visual process.

It's extremely important that none of the pupils draws along when something is developed on the board. Just as important are complete directions before the silent work, so that pupils can work uninterruptedly and thus enter into the process, really perceiving.

At the fifth station we can recognize that the ray of vision through A is parallel to f_A: A_5 thus disappears into infinity. The intersection of the parallels to f_A through F_{AC} with f_C is the point C_5. As the line connecting F_{BC} and C_5 is parallel to f_C, we can determine that B_5 also disappears into infinity.

If the triangle is projected from Z_6, the image triangle is again found in the finite realm, but behind the vertical plane. If center Z is now below the horizontal plane (Z_7), the image triangle appears between Z' and the vertical plane. Side A_7B_7 has overtaken C_7, however.

In this «presentation section», new phenomena, that is, the triangles that pass through infinity, appear for the pupils without being organized into a conceptual system: thus not theory-led perception and proofs of already presented hypotheses, but the direct encounter with novel, mysterious aspects in the full immediacy of experience. We must ensure that this is not just a matter of mere perceptual activity, or a half-conscious formation of judgments that group and assemble the perceived images. Pupils must come to a «conclusion» in which «the whole human being» is engaged.[25] They must have the feeling, «This is what happens as center Z descends.» A concentrated, peaceful mood is necessary for this, and sufficient time. The teacher should not explain too much; unnecessary speech is to be avoided. The matter speaks for itself, is self-expressive. All the elements and the way the figure arises are clearly penetrable for the students; they can be perceived «with understanding».

In this case, the phenomena are, on the one hand, the outwardly produced drawing with the various stages of the triangle metamorphosis, and, on the other hand, the experiences and thoughts that the pupil inwardly perceives through the activity of drawing. In the following characterization,

---

[25] Ibid.

the entire movement of the triangle must be examined once more, appealing to the imagination. With classes that can live strongly in their geometric imaginations, this can also be done with the blackboard drawing folded away, so that the recapitulation occurs wholly without external visual aids.

I have always tried to ensure that pupils experience the movement as proceeding continuously, grasping the individual stations as momentary snapshots of a unified process. It is important thereby that the relationships of motion are each reviewed previously, without, however, setting up precise rules in advance.

- If we consider the movement of the triangle in the horizontal plane, we see that for the first four stations the image point of C travels much faster on its invariant ray f_c than the image points of A and B on their invariant rays. From a certain point on, the relationships reverse and the image point of A and B begin to move faster than the image point of C. The image triangle disappears between stations 6 and 7 in point Z' and then reappears. C_7 now lies behind side A_7B_7. For a while, the image points of A and B are moving faster than that of C, a situation that reverses again, however, when the image triangle comes to lie on axis z.

- As the next step, Z's rapidity of movement on the vertical line h can be brought into relation to the movement of the image triangle: where are the regions in which Z travels very quickly but the image triangle hardly moves, and where is it exactly the opposite?

- How do the angles change in the course of the motion?[26]

During the characterization, we can also welcome emotional reactions and humorous aspects. Where have we gotten especially upset with ourselves? What is that for a mischievous triangle number 4, which goes through infinity? The mood can become inward and cordial. The pupils should inwardly «massage» the conclusions that they come to in the presentation section so that they achieve a personal connection to the facts, which they would otherwise relate to more distantly. The ego's rigid connection to the external facts loosens a little and is enlivened through the imaginative activity.

After a successful characterization, I can always perceive that the pupils experience an immediate sense of satisfaction and feel at ease. The presentation section is always more rigorous and demanding; in the characterization we can relax a little. For pupils, something comes about which is initially shut-off, not inviting being intellectually challenged. If the pupils immediately want to begin the conceptual work, either their dive into sensory experience and formation of conclusions have not been intensive enough, thus remaining intellectual and thus shallow, or the characterization has not been satisfactorily emotive, rounded-off or compendious.

---

[26] This theme can be gone into more deeply: if lines AC_i and BC_i are parallel, then angle $\gamma = 0$ and $\alpha = \beta = 90°$. The sum of the angles is 180° in this case, as well. If C_i goes back behind the vertical plane, angles α and β both become larger than 90°. If we think through the process by which a diminishes progressively, we see that the contribution of this angle to the sum of the angles must become negative. Even here, $\alpha + \beta + \gamma = 180°$. This makes sense in that γ's orientation has reversed itself in its passage through infinity.

I begin the next day's main lesson with a contemplative section. This is always a little shaped by antipathy: the pupils should be able to test out the acuity of their thinking, be «rebuffed», «take things too far», and «make fools of themselves.»[27]

We should examine the conceptual context and essence of the material. For this, the pupils' own concepts and judgments, which interconnections become clear to them and which not, are central, not what the teacher has to say or what has been chewed over for generations in textbooks. There is thus less focus on quickly and economically harvesting from the students the main mathematical material and more on considering phenomena in true dialogue, illuminating these from various points of view, and inwardly and outwardly weighing the consequences of the formal concepts: What is the significance of a triangle that passes through infinity for the geometry that has been learned hitherto?[28] What does it signify for me that I conceptualize this? Do I have to revise, modify and expand others of my images of the world? A jointly-experienced working atmosphere[29] should develop in which even those pupils who can't follow every detail can take part and grow thereby. Pupils who arrive late substantially disturb this process, so that I have gone over to only allowing such pupils in after the contemplative section has concluded, which can be as late as 8:45.

In this case, the diagram in figure 2 offers an inexhaustible supply of topics. Among others, I have worked on the following mathematical themes:

- The set of all visual rays through A form a plane perpendicular to the horizontal plane and passing through line h, on which the center lies. This plane intersects the horizontal plane in f_A. All image points thus lie on lines that pass through C'.

- Plane E_i, which is determined by triangle side AC and the corresponding center Z_i, intersects the horizontal plane in lines through the corresponding points A_i and C_i. As E_1 also contains point F_{AC}, which lies on axis z, all lines A_iC_i pass through F_{AC}.

- The precise mode of motion of the triangle's points and lines can thus by summarized as follows:

- Points travel along lines that pass through a point and lines rotate around points that lie on a line. Here a duality is hinted at that I usually, however, treat conceptually on the next day and depend via the theme «locus and envelope».

- This mode of motion also applies to the lines through A_i and B_i, as these all pass through point F_{AB}, which disappears into infinity in their direction, that is, in the direction of axis z. The rotation of the lines A_iB_i around this point is equivalent in this case to a parallel translation of these lines.

---

[27] R. Steiner, Conferences with the Teachers of the Waldorf School in Stuttgart, Michael Hall: 1967. v. 2, p. 69.
[28] Cf. footnote 28.
[29] The author uses the phrase «geistige Atmosphäre», which could signify a mental or a spiritual atmosphere; the border between these is less sharp in German than it is in English.

I don't treat the following questions, which may arise, in a conceptually precise manner, but simply establish them:

- Z passes through the vertical line exactly once, when the visual ray makes a 180° rotation through point A (no complete revolution!). The image triangle simultaneously goes through a complete cycle of transformation, however.

- If we consider station 4, imagining that we have depicted A, B, and C in a point-wise manner, then A_4 and B_4 are projected onto the upper side of the horizontal plane. Thinking this through consequentially, C_4 is projected on the underside of the horizontal plane (see figure 3).

- As points A and B disappear into infinity, what becomes of the line connecting A and B? Is it completely at infinity? Is it uniquely determined?

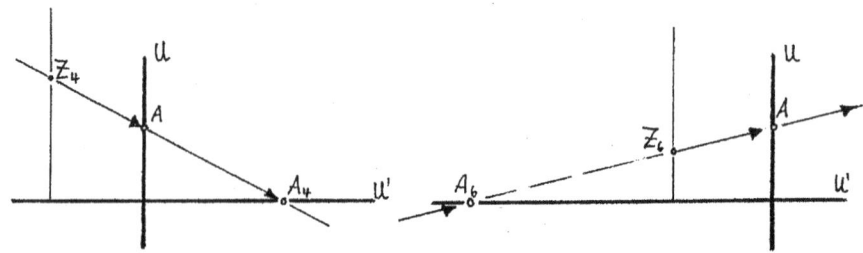

Figure 3

After this contemplative section, the following presentation section treats the central-linear collineation in the plane solely on the basis of its own mode of motion. I set up the exemplary figure for this so that the stations of the triangle precisely correspond to those of the previous figure. In addition, the starting points must be chosen correspondingly (see figure 4).

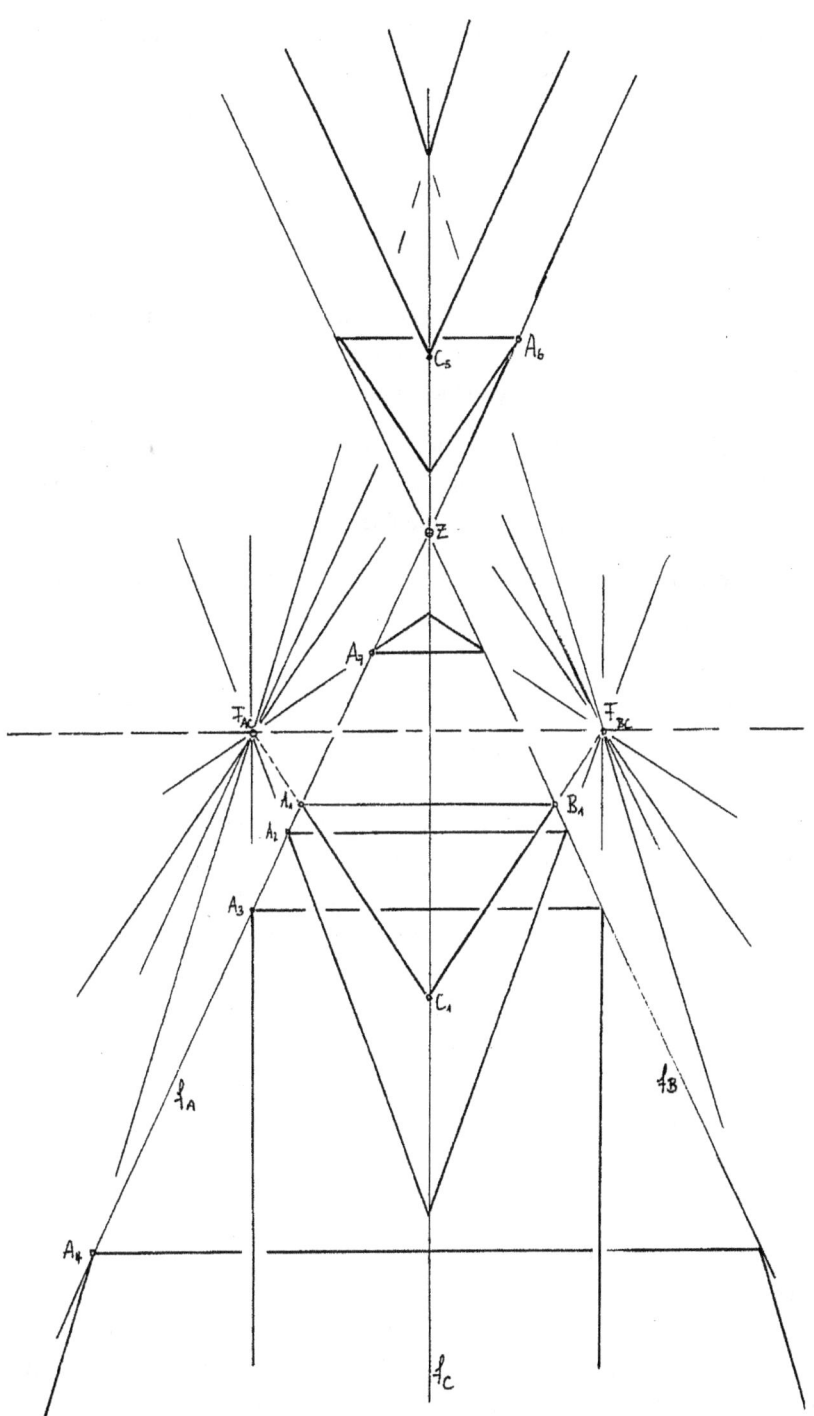

Figure 4[30] A_1, B_1, and C_1 are given; the starting points are A_2, A_3, A_4, C_5 and A_6.

[30] After Bernhard (1984), p. 48; slightly changed by author.

Further exercises follow, including the special cases that arise depending on the position of center Z and axis z in relation to the lines at infinity. In this way the various kinds of depictions that have been learned since the middle school can be grasped under the unified viewpoint of the central-linear collineation.[31]

Here, at the latest, the phrase «a point disappears into infinity in a given direction» will be abbreviated through speaking of points at infinity and the corresponding direction indicated. But here, too, one must be aware that there are always students who have not yet been able to truly experience the validity of their own thinking about the distant elements. For them we can emphasize the description of elements at infinity as being a shorthand, not so much as referring to concrete objects. The experience itself may come to them much later.

At this point, however, pupils usually press for a further conceptual penetration of the infinite. Here, above all, we have to establish that only one point at infinity lies on every line and that all the points at infinity (of a plane) lie on a line, the line at infinity.

The former is clear from all the previous work. For the latter, two aspects are ready at hand:

- In central projections, as points' images are points and lines' images are lines, the horizon as bearer of all the vanishing points in the visual image must be the image of a line whose points are all points at infinity: the line at infinity.

- With the introduction of the points at infinity, it is fundamentally clear that two lines always have one intersection and that every pair of points has exactly one connecting line. The line at infinity now also satisfies this condition precisely and thereby conceptually fits the laws of the geometry the pupils have already learned. Often pupils object that all points at infinity lie on a circle with infinite radius. The line connecting all points at infinity must thus be thought of as a circle. The various possible geometric relationships between a circle and a line would then have to be considered. As, however, every line has one infinite point in common with the line at infinity, and every point at infinity connects with every point of the finite plane by means of exactly one line, the connection of two points at infinity must also be a line.

If this three-stage build-up, with presentation, characterization and contemplation, including the night in-between, is successful, the lesson develops a special dynamic and a stronger impulse. Pupils connect with the unfolding content and can live into and with it. This is also revealed by the deep questions that pupils ask precisely in this block, sometimes quite overtly, and which are mostly directed to the relationship of one's ego to thinking and, as a next step, tentatively searching for the connection of the ego to the world and to reality.

---

[31] Ibid. Chapter 15.

Locus and Envelope: the Structure of the Projective Plane

I have always treated the theme of the division of a field of points by means of a number of lines as the next step, paralleled by the dual problem of the division of a field of lines by means of a number of points.[32] On the one hand, through this theme I develop the topological structure of the plane; on the other hand, it serves especially well to clarify the concept of duality. A plane filled with lines conceived as independent entities, in which fields of lines are separated from one another by points, that are indeed then discontinuous, but for our «point consciousness» overlap, calls forth the capacity to view the familiar from a new perspective.

I want to single out just one aspect of this linked to what we have treated already. If we consider the division of a field of points through three lines, four triangular regions arise: one lying completely in the finite plane and three that stretch out to and beyond the line at infinity. If we travel through region #2 in our imagination, we can begin at point A, go on to B, and then downwards toward C across the line at infinity. We point thereby toward the interior of the region with our right arms. If we have passed the line at infinity, we still point with the same arm toward the interior of the figure. It has apparently become the left arm, however! The rotational direction of the trilateral has likewise been reversed.

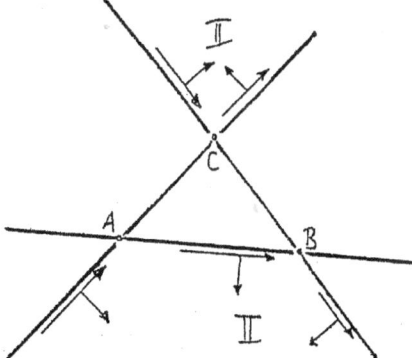

Figure 5, The division of a point field through three lines

To resolve this paradox we must imagine that we are now on the underside of the plane. This appears plausible as we have already encountered such phenomena in the central-linear collineation. The rotational sense of the triangle reverses itself when it crosses the line at infinity. Lines of sight through the original points A, B, and C must make a complete revolution if the triangle is supposed to return to the same points (see figure 2), for after a 180° rotation the triangle is actually located on the «underside» of the plane (see figure 3).

In order to make the phenomena in the finite plane accessible to the imagination, I demonstrate examples of planes on which «we can change sides» without crossing a boundary: the Möbius strip and the Klein bottle. The pupils experience these models ambivalently, and justifiably so; on

---

[32] The mathematical background for this is covered by Bernhard, pp. 53ff; L. Locher-Ernst (1957), Space and Counter-space; R. Burkhardt (1986), Elemente der euklidischen und polareuklidischen Geometrie, Stuttgart, pp. 14ff.

the one hand they recognize the ingenious simplicity of the correspondence and on the other hand they strongly sense the artificial character of these surfaces, which actually echo the relationships very imperfectly.

One has to be careful that no misleading imaginations slip in that could confuse pupils. After the magic of the earlier, astonishing discoveries, these surfaces invariably have a somewhat sobering effect, as they are fully accessible to the understanding.

Further possible themes

I have always taken pleasure in treating Desargues' Theorem as the foundation stone of many figures and demonstrating its connection to the central-linear collineation.

The projectively generated conic sections form a further, very substantial theme, as pupils can become familiar with the principle of duality from a completely different point of view. Aside from this it can be shown using examples how from a higher (projective) standpoint, diverse concrete phenomena (three curves that appear differently: ellipses, parabola and hyperbola) can be unified within an overarching concept. The theme connects directly to the ninth-grade geometric drawing block in Descriptive Geometry, in which ellipses, parabolas and hyperbolas are drawn and discussed as loci, symmetries, etc. In addition, the pupils will at one point become familiar with these curves from the point of view of analytic geometry.

The theorems of Pascal and Brianchon, including their special cases, are very rewarding topics to follow with.

I don't treat the subject pole and polar from a projective standpoint, but instead from a parallel analytic standpoint, in order to let the contrast be clearly felt.

In this list of mathematically exceptionally rich themes, which should be extended, I have always tried to choose those aspects that clarify how the infinite, as the archetype of the peripherally-working spiritual element, harmonizes with individual objects of the finite realm, or how universal conceptual elements take form and become differentiated as beings in the sensory realm of appearances.

Projective Geometry – the Main Lesson Block in the 11th Grade

KARL-FRIEDRICH GEORG

Preliminary Remarks

In addition to Rudolf Steiner's curriculum specifications for the eleventh grade, a projective geometry main lesson has found its place in Waldorf schools, generally as a replacement for the spherical geometry that was originally proposed. Through this augmenting of the Euclidean thought-world, relationships can be discovered that are not given merely through sense perception, and that only unfold through the intellect, through thinking. Through the synthetic approach and using the elements of geometry the relationships of position (incidence) are grasped and put into practice independent of any metric, the point being to bring the relationships into movement in the imagination. On this basis, central projections can be handled metrically in the 13th grade (when no *Zentralabitur* (central final examination) is prescribed). By means of challenging exercises (both computational and constructive) students can apply these projections in many different situations.

In the years since Rudolf Steiner gave new impulses to mathematicians to establish projective geometry as the basis for a new way of thinking in natural scientific research, this work has been carried out notably by George Adams (*Strahlende Weltgestaltung*, 1933), Louis Locher-Ernst (*Projektive Geometrie*, 1944; *Raum und Gegenraum*, 1957) and, especially as a basis for teaching, by Arnold Bernhard (*Projektive Geometrie*, 1984).

Experience over the span of three decades has shown, in a variety of ways, how important this main lesson is. Although the concepts of projective geometry are not difficult, they are in their very nature altogether new and require a way of thinking which is not given either by the Euclidean way or by the analytic method, namely a qualitative understanding of mathematical form. So students get to exercise forms of thinking that challenge them and develop them in a way that the ordinary mathematical curriculum can never do.

The following exposition corresponds to the content and sequence of a four-week main lesson. In some parts I have oriented myself to the book by Arnold Bernhard which has an immense wealth of material. I hope that this description of a main lesson block can be a useful aid, particularly for beginning teachers.

> God establishes himself without reason and measures himself without measurement.
> Should you be at one with him in spirit, O man, you will understand.
> *Angelus Silesius* (1624-1677)

> The actions of space and time are creation's powers,
> and their relationships are the hinges of the world.
> *Novalis* (1772-1801)

Projective Geometry   *Karl-Friedrich Georg*

> What is grasped in thought is also effective in the world.
> What lives in the world also comes to be revealed in thought.
> *Louis Locher-Ernst* (1906-1962)

1 Central projection

In the past the study of geometry was concerned with figures of finite magnitude. But since about the Renaissance, geometers and artists have increasingly occupied themselves with geometric inquiries that broke the bounds of the finite. Painters endeavored to portray buildings and other forms in space so that the spatial impression of the image agrees with the impression of sensory reality. They solved this problem with the help of perspective. We'll see that perspective is nothing other than a central projection. In a drawing, *Albrecht Dürer* vividly portrayed the technique of central projection:

From: Albrecht Dürer, *Underweysung der Messung mit dem Zirkel und dem Richtscheyt* [*Instruction in measurement with compasses and straight-edge*], Nürnberg, 1525.

A thread is stretched from a center (the ring on the wall) to each point of an object that is to be depicted. Between the center and the object is placed an image plane. Where the thread intersects the image plane, a point is marked: it is the image point of the point on the object. If we bring our eye to where the center is, we see each image point in the same direction as its object point. In geometric language: the set of object points (in general located in space) and the set of image points (always lying in a plane) are perspectively related; an image point and its object point lie in the same projection ray through the center. This way of forming an image is called *central projection*.

Examples of the use of central projection are photography and slide projection.

1. Problem: Project the given triangle *ABC* lying in the plane ε into the horizontal plane $\bar{\varepsilon}$ (Figure 1.1)

2. Problem: Project the triangle *ABC* from *Z* onto the horizontal plane $\bar{\varepsilon}$ (Figure 1.2)

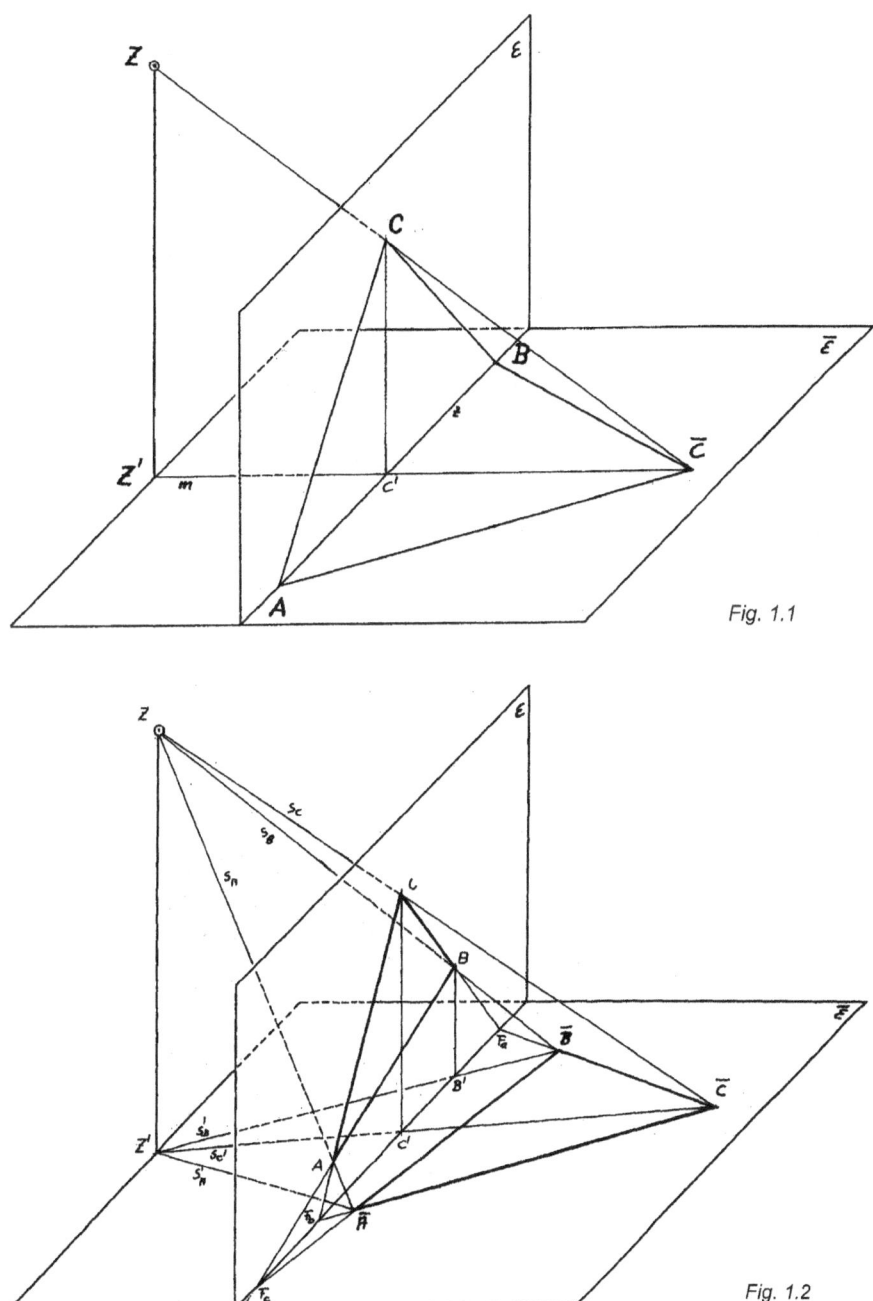

Fig. 1.1

Fig. 1.2

The extended sides a, b, c of the triangle in ε and their images $\bar{a}, \bar{b}, \bar{c}$ in $\bar{\varepsilon}$ intersect in the «axis» z. Whereas each point of the line a is projected onto a corresponding image point in $\bar{a}$, the common point of a and $\bar{a}$ in the axis z is the only point of a that is projected onto itself. It is called the «fixed point» of the line a.

3. Problem: The pyramid $ABCS$ (S vertically above B) stands on a table top. Project it from Z onto the «wall». (Figure 1.3)
4. Problem: Project the triangle ABC from Z onto the horizontal plane and then let the «candle» Z_1Z' burn down. (Figure 1.4)

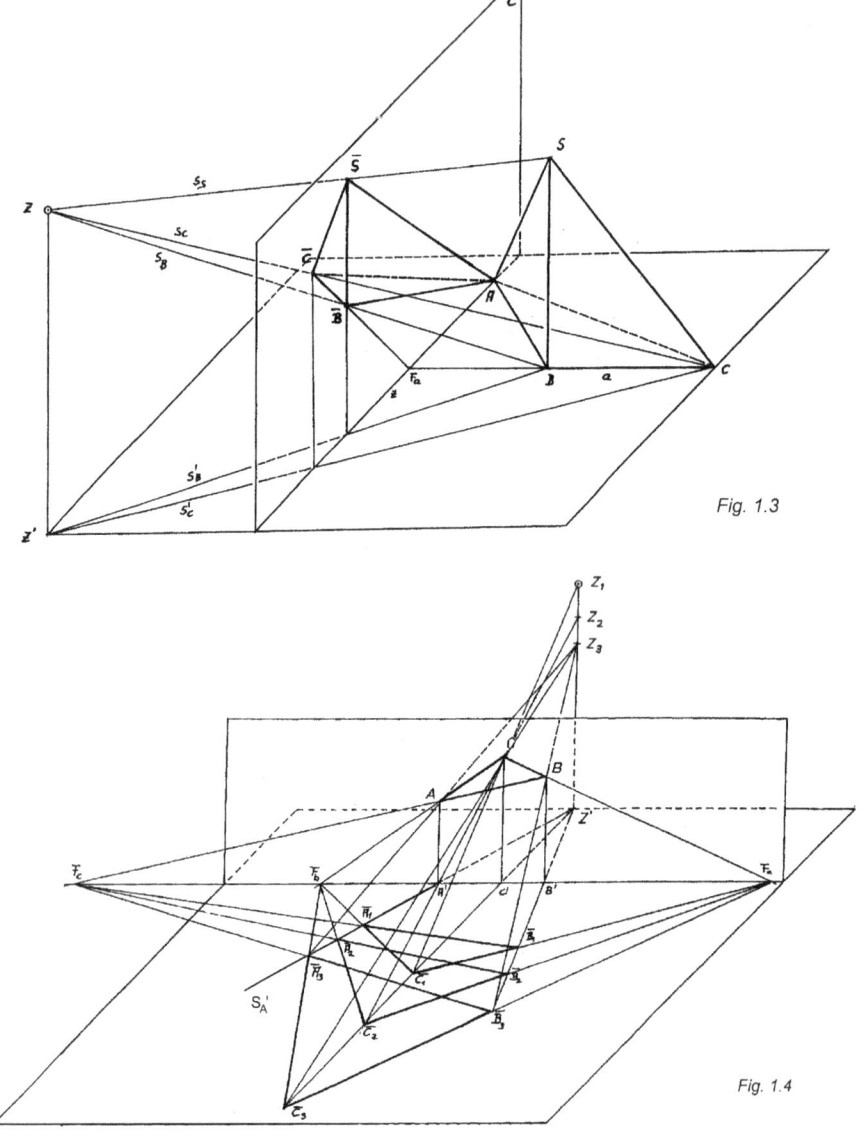

Fig. 1.3

Fig. 1.4

First we'll direct our attention to the point A: As Z_1 sinks down (positions Z_2 and Z_3), the image points $\overline{A_1}, \overline{A_2}, \overline{A_3}$ move along the fixed projection line s'_A of the projection rays rotating about point A. The same applies to the vertices B and C. The triangle's sides rotate around their fixed points F_a, F_b and F_c.

We can formulate two laws:

I. The vertices of the triangle move along (fixed) straight lines, which go through a *center* Z'.

II. The sides of the triangle rotate about fixed points, which lie in a *line* (axis) z.

We call such a controlled movement a **perspective collineation** or **homology**.

A second example of a homology is:

5. Problem: Project the square $ABCD$ from the center Z_1 onto the horizontal plane and then let the center sink down to points Z_2 and Z_3 (Z_3 has a special position!).

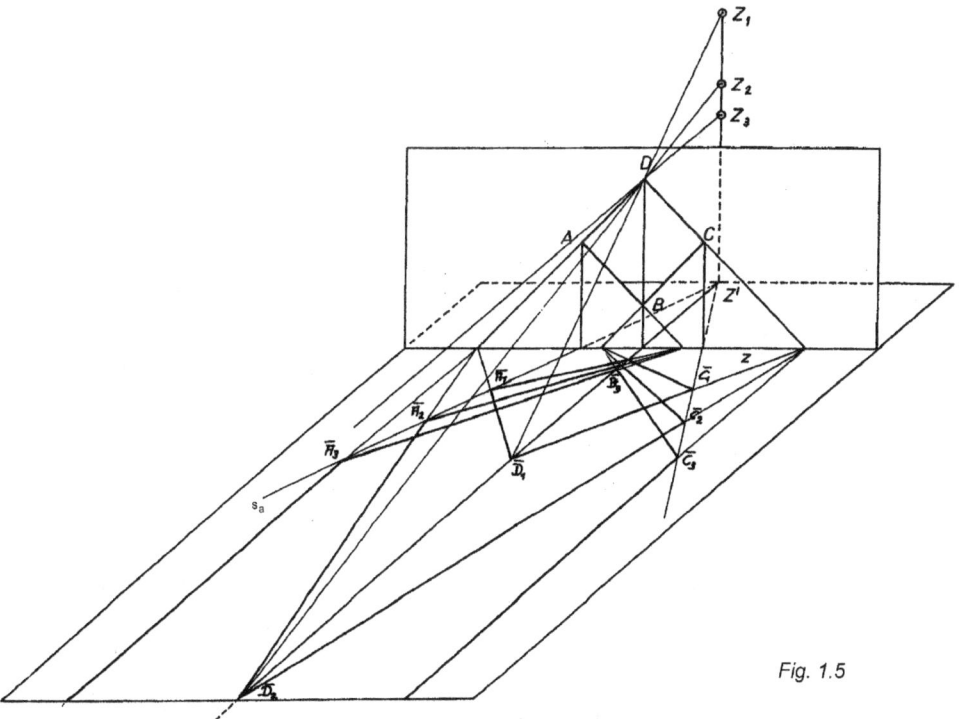

Fig. 1.5

2 The theorem of Desargues

When we project the whole configuration of Figure 1.2 onto a third plane, that is to say the original triangle ABC, the image triangle $\overline{A}\,\overline{B}\,\overline{C}$, the center Z, the axis z, the lines a,b,c and $\overline{a},\overline{b},\overline{c}$, the projection rays s_a, s_b, s_c, and the fixed points F_a, F_b, F_c, we get the following picture:

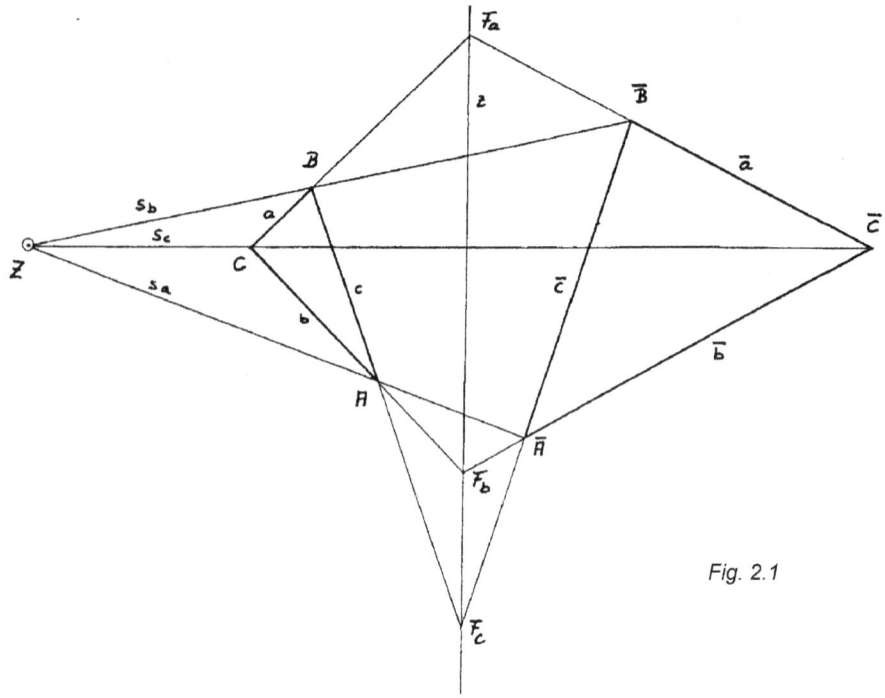

Fig. 2.1

We see that in this plane the following must be true:

> If the vertices of two triangles can be joined in such a way that the connecting lines meet in a center Z, then the points of intersection of the corresponding sides lie in a line z.

This law was discovered in 1639 by the French architect Girard Desargues (1591 - 1661) and is known in projective geometry as the «Theorem of Desargues»:

> If the three lines joining corresponding vertices of two triangles pass through a point, then the points of intersection of the corresponding sides lie in a line, and conversely.

In Figures 2.2 and 2.3 below, we have two different arrangements of the Desargues configuration. We shall partly change the notation used earlier in the central projection:

The lines joining the corresponding vertices of the triangles: p, q, r.

The points of intersection of the corresponding (extended) sides of the triangles: P, Q, R.

p, q, r go through Z; P, Q, R lie in z.

The law remains valid even if the positioning of the triangles is varied.

In studying the Desargues configuration, we recognize some peculiarities:

1. Symmetry in structure: 10 points $(A,B,C,\bar{A},\bar{B},\bar{C},P,Q,R,Z)$
   10 lines $(a,b,c,\bar{a},\bar{b},\bar{c},p,q,r,z)$.

2. Exactly 3 of these points lie in each of the 10 lines, and exactly 3 of these lines go through each of the 10 points.

3. Each of these configurations of 10 points and 10 lines can be understood as a relation of corresponding triangles in 10 different ways. This is because every point can take on the role of any other point and the same applies to the lines. So, for instance, each of the 10 points can play the role of Z as intersection point of the connecting lines of corresponding vertices; in the process, each line takes on the meaning of z as the line connecting the intersection points of corresponding sides (this is carried out as an exercise in Figures 2.4 to 2.13 which are not reproduced here).

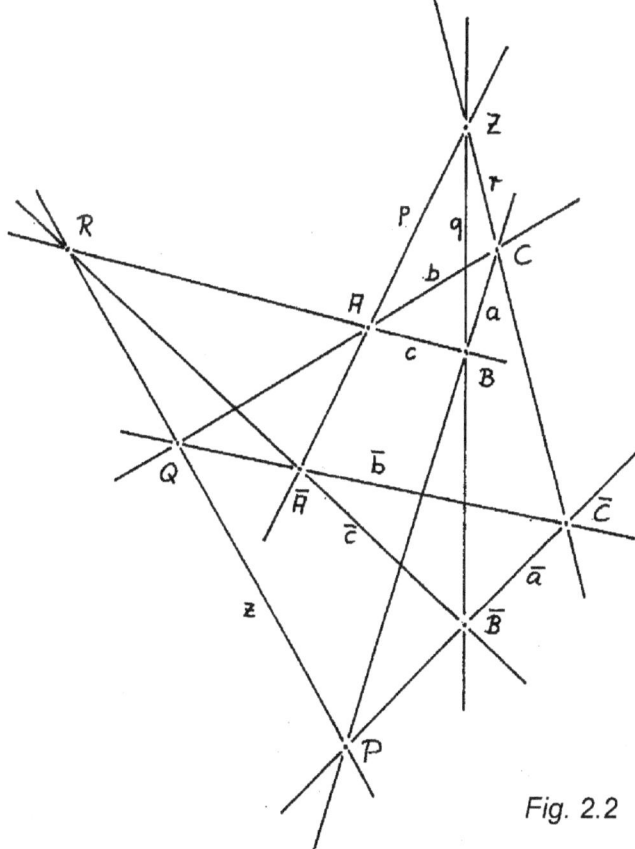

Fig. 2.2

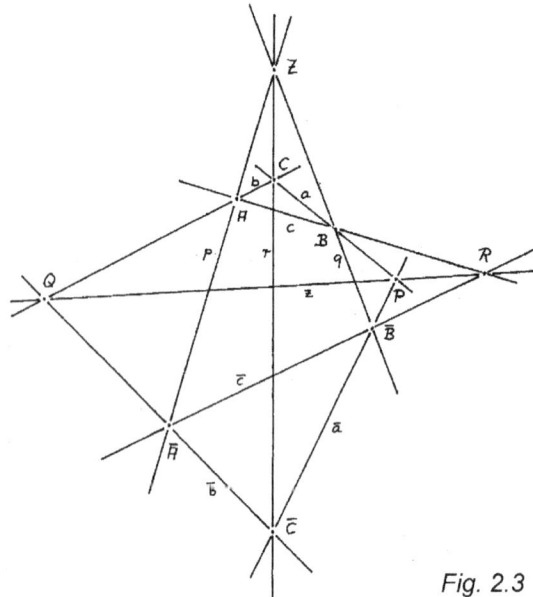

Fig. 2.3

3 A «growing» triangle

We now allow the triangle *ABC* of Figure 1.1 to increase in height in such a way that it remains isosceles (Figure 3.1). When the tip of the object triangle reaches position C_4 (the same height as the center *Z*), the projection ray is parallel to the line *m* and remains above the horizontal plane. The sides of the image triangle are also parallel to *m*. The projection ray to C_5 meets the horizontal plane $\bar{\varepsilon}$ in $\bar{C}_5$. The triangle's sides on the right are now «more than» parallel; the triangular area goes off into the distance on the right and reappears from afar on the left.

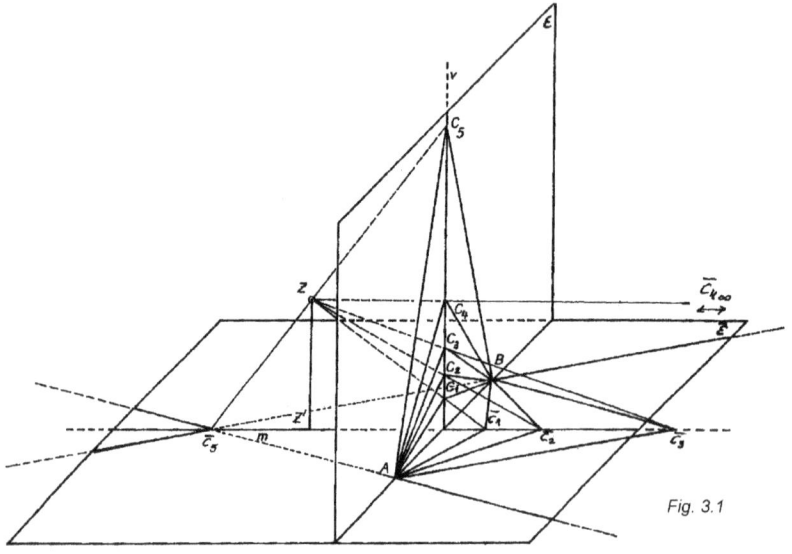

Fig. 3.1

4 From the finite to the infinite

4.1 The point at infinity (limit point) of a line

Now let's look at the correspondence of the points of lines v and m in Figure 3.1 in more detail (Figure 4.1):

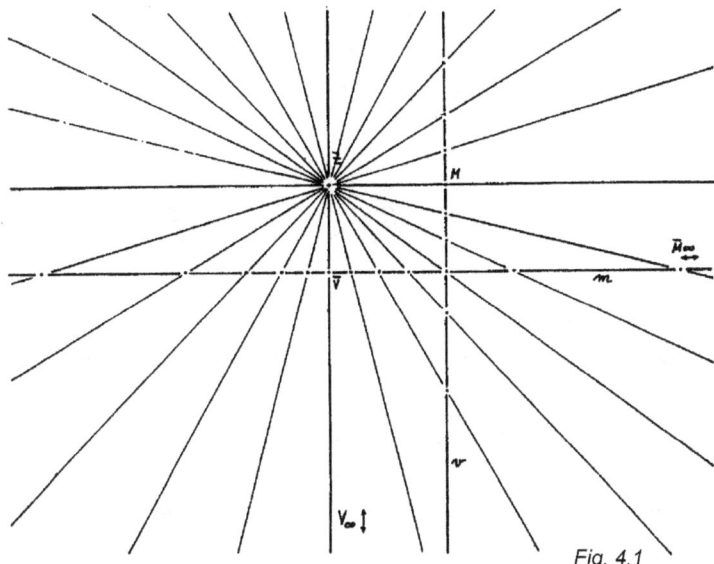

Fig. 4.1

A line is rotated around the center Z. It intersects the lines v and m, so that a point of v is paired with a point of m. When the straight line approaches the horizontal position, the one intersection point $\overline{M}$ in m moves faster and faster to the right, into the infinite. Shortly after the line is beyond the horizontal position, the one intersection point $\overline{M}$ in m comes back from infinity from the left. If the line reaches the horizontal position, the point paired with the one point M in v is the one infinitely distant point $\overline{M}_\infty$ in m. In the same way, when the rotating line is vertical, the point paired with the point $\overline{V}$ in m is the one infinitely distant point V_∞ in v.

As we observe the rotation of the line, it passes through the *totality* of the lines in Z, and the intersection points pass through the *totality* of the points of v and m. We call the *totality* of the lines in Z the **pencil of lines** in Z. The *totalities* of points in v and m we call **point ranges**. Both point range and line pencil are structures grasped purely in thought. We can conceive of these totalities but we cannot draw them. We can only draw individual elements – individual lines and individual points. The line in which we imagine the points to be we call the **bearer** or base of the point range; we call the point Z through which the lines are imagined to go the **bearer** or center of the line pencil.

We call the above-described pairing between points of the ranges v and m, mediated by the line pencil Z, a **perspective map** of the point ranges onto each other.

The point ranges m and v each have a single point at infinity (limit point) which, as a matter of principle, is no longer accessible as a mental picture – it can only be grasped by means of thought.

79

4.2 The line at infinity (limit line) of a plane

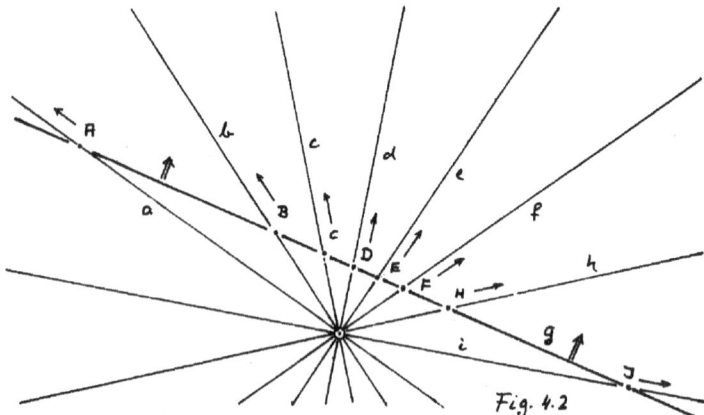

Fig. 4.2

An arbitrary line g of the plane intersects each line of a pencil in a unique point. If we let *g* move ever further outwards, then, in the limit, these points of intersection (which lie in *g* of course) become limit points of the plane. Since *g*'s property of being a line should not be lost, we can conclude from this observation that the set of all limit points of the plane has the limit line (line at infinity) as bearer. This limit line of the plane has exactly *one* point in common with every other line of the plane, that one point being the limit point of the other line. The limit line itself has no particular direction.

In the following construction (Figure 4.3) the tip of a triangle moves along a horizontal line *g*, at the height of the center Z. All points of the line *g* are mapped onto points at infinity (limit points). Conversely, the original image of each limit point lies in *g*.

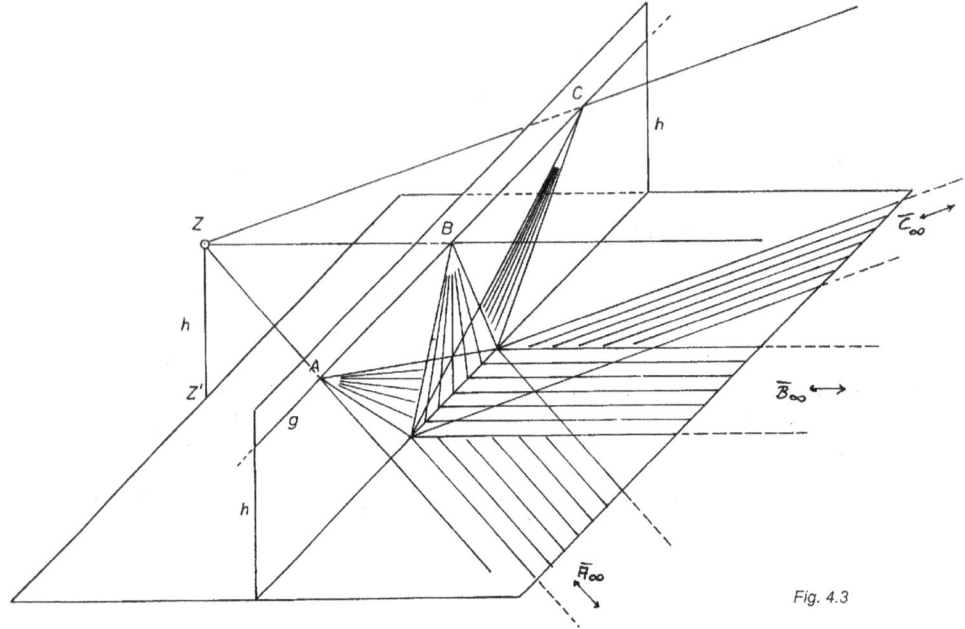

Fig. 4.3

The central projection of a line is itself a line and this suggests: The points at infinity of a plane all lie in a line, the line at infinity (limit line) of the plane (see above). The lines of a pencil of parallel lines have *one* common point at infinity. It is the bearer of the parallel pencil.

Let's observe what happens as concentric circles with a fixed center grow in the plane, including their tangent lines. In Figure 4.4, the tangents through some of the points of the circle are shown. The tangents move outward parallel to themselves. As the circles become increasingly larger, the curvature of the circles is reduced. In the limiting case when the circle's radius is infinitely large there is no longer any curvature, and the circle and all the tangents lie in the limit line g_∞ of the plane. Since all directions are represented among the tangents, g_∞ absorbs all these directions into itself.

As the circles grow, *all* the lines of the plane are covered by the tangents exactly once and the circles pass over *all* points of the plane.

We call the totality of all lines of the plane a **field of lines**. The totality of all points of a plane we call a **field of points**. If we think of the field of lines and field of points borne by the same plane together as a unity, we speak simply of a planar field. The planar field is the stage upon which plane geometry plays out.

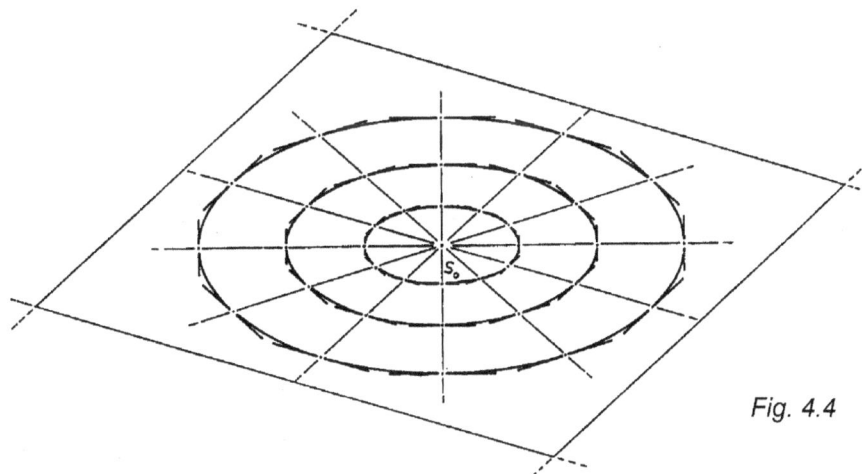

Fig. 4.4

4.3 The plane at infinity (limit plane) of space

An interesting question arises: What type of structure captures the totality of all the limit points as well as all the limit lines of space? First, we know that every ordinary line of space has exactly one limit point. Moreover, each plane of space has exactly one limit line. With a bit of thought we can see directly that any two limit lines always intersect in a limit point. So conceivably the two limit lines span a plane. To see this, we consider two «normal» planes which intersect in a line g. First, we know the following: The limit line of one plane intersects the line of intersection g in g's limit point. The same goes for the limit line of the other plane. Hence the limit lines of both planes pass through one and the same point, the limit point of the line g.

Thus it seems reasonable to *think* (not just imagine!) that all the limit elements of space lie in one and the same plane. We call this plane the limit plane (plane at infinity) of space. Like all other planes it appears to us in two aspects: both as a planar point-field of limit points and as a planar line-field of limit lines. As an *ideal structure* this plane delimits space and augments «Euclidean space», but with this ideal structure. We say that Euclidean space is extended to form «projective space» by means of this limit plane of space.

By means of the above observations we have expanded our consciousness over the whole of space. With the example of geometric imagination we have experienced something possible in cognition generally: expansion of consciousness.

4.4 The structure of the plane and the Moebius band

Let us take a long rectangular strip of paper that we glue together into a ring: a closed band, which has an inner and an outer surface.

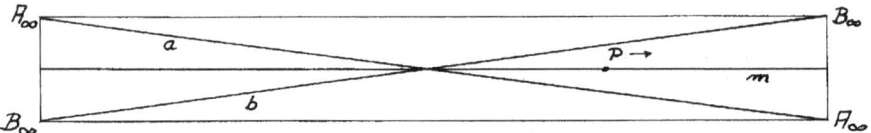

Suppose we see the paper strip as an infinite section of a plane containing the lines a, b and m, and now glue it together so that the two limit points A_∞ and the two limit points B_∞ coincide respectively. Then we must first turn the strip through 180°: we have now obtained the so-called Moebius band discovered in 1865 by August Ferdinand Moebius (1790-1868). This band has *only one side!* Each point can reach the «other» side without crossing the edge. Thus it has no «inner» or «outer» side, but one unified side. It also possesses *only one edge*. Starting out from a point of the «upper» edge, we reach a point of the «lower» edge which lies exactly opposite the starting point; continuing, we eventually arrive at the starting point again.

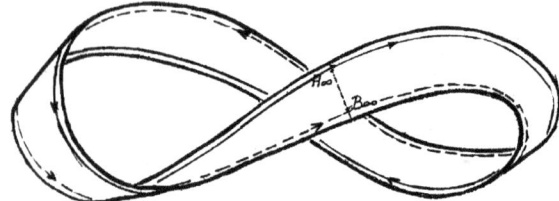

The Moebius band represents a one-sided surface and it possesses only one closed edge-curve.

If we imagine the band as wider, we obtain the model of a plane. As a whole, a plane is one-sided – which means that when we move in it through the infinite, we always emerge on the «other» side. A second passage is necessary to get back to the starting point. We are forced to the conclusion that the whole plane is a one-sided surface.

5 Exercises

5.1 If we include the limit elements ...

... we can see that the Desargues theorem retains its validity.

1. Exercise: Draw the Desargues configuration with $c \parallel \bar{c}$. Result: $R \to R_\infty$ (R becomes a limit point; Figure 5.1)

2. Exercise: As above, but $a \parallel \bar{a}$ as well. Result: $z \to z_\infty$; similar triangles in perspective (Figure 5.2).

3. Exercise: Let Z be a limit point. Result: affine triangles, axially related (Figure 5.3).

4. Exercise: Let Z and z be limit elements. Result: congruent triangles, translated (Figure 5.4)

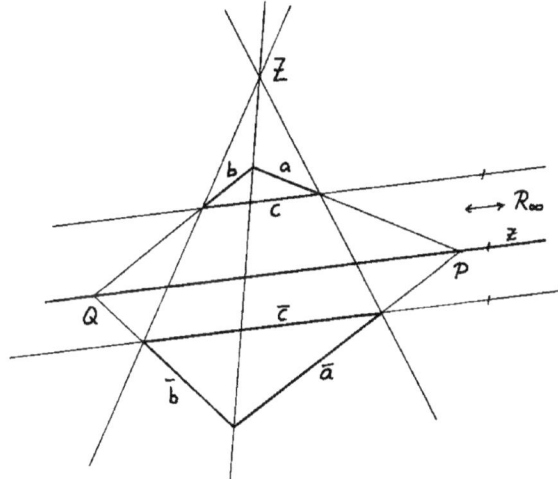

Fig. 5.1

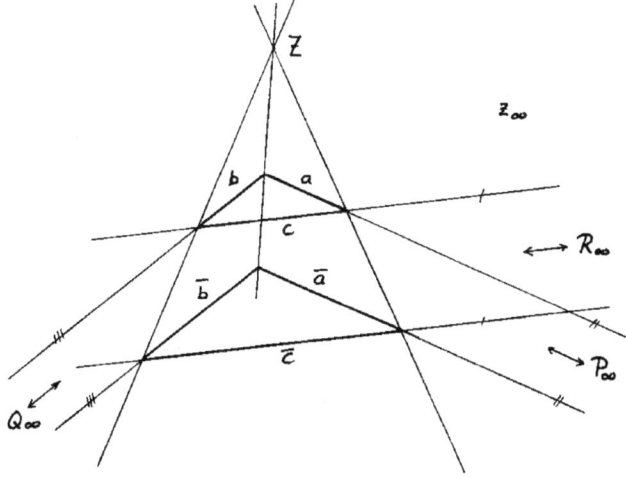

Fig. 5.2

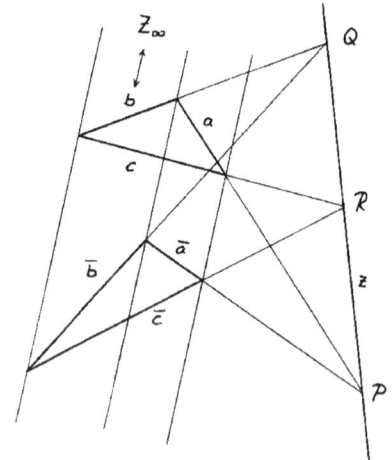

Fig. 5.3

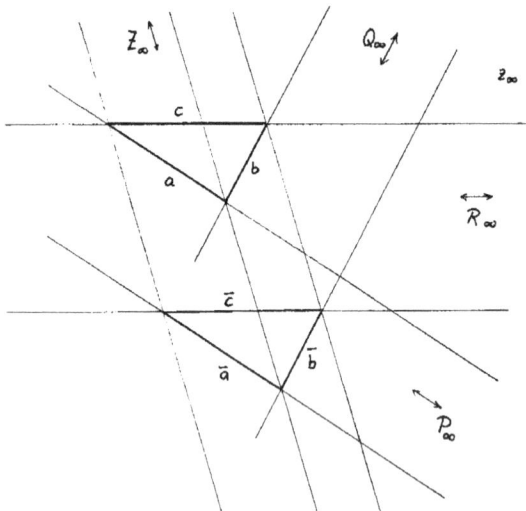

Fig. 5.4 a

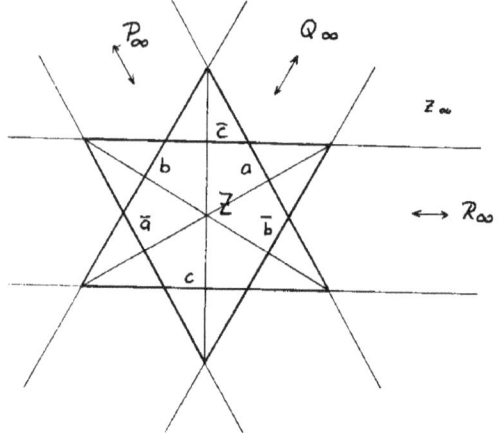

Fig. 5.4 b

These exercises can be done conversely: for instance, under which conditions are the triangles similar? Under which conditions are they congruent?

5.2 Transformation of a triangle

The points $\underline{A}$ and $\underline{B}$ remain stationary while C moves in a perpendicular line.

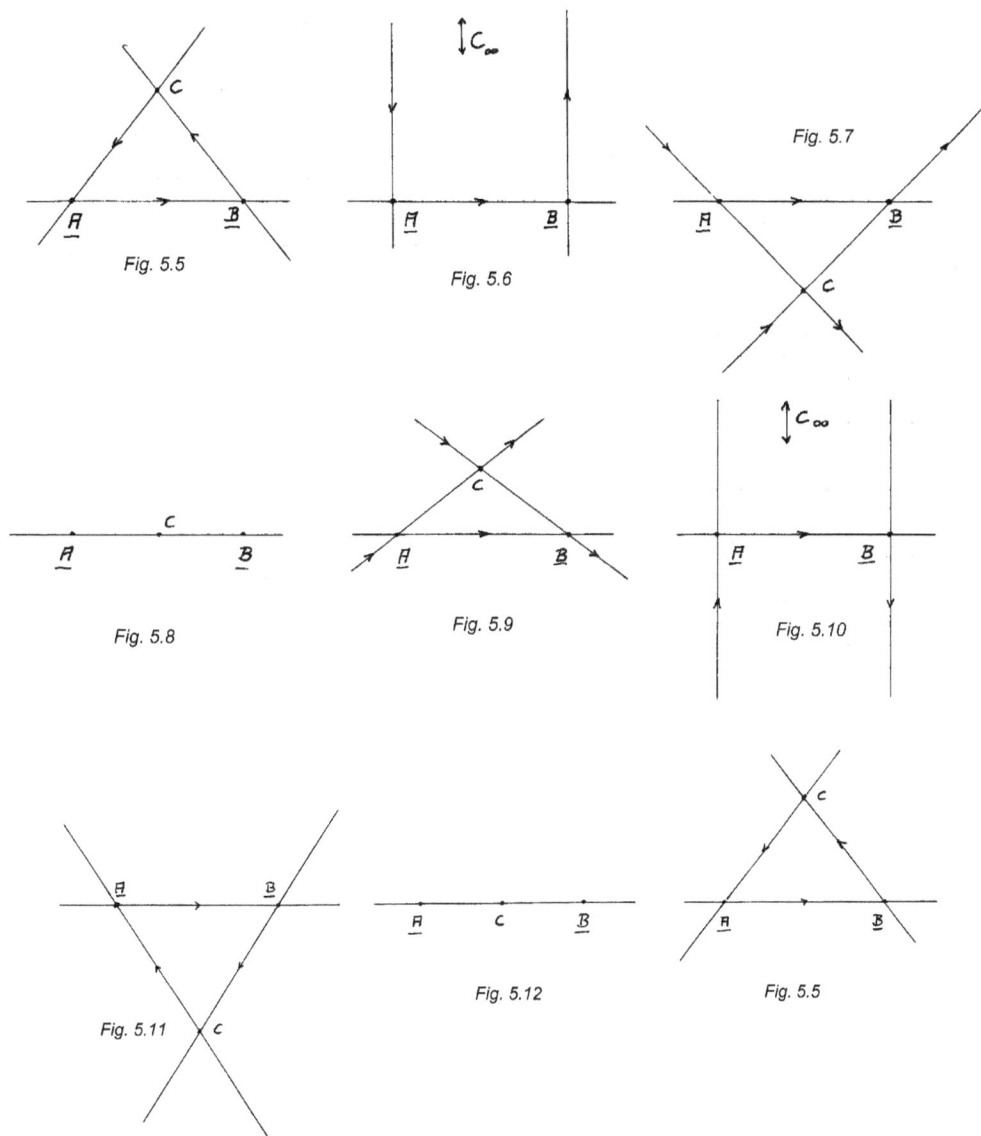

Fig. 5.5

Fig. 5.6

Fig. 5.7

Fig. 5.8

Fig. 5.9

Fig. 5.10

Fig. 5.11

Fig. 5.12

Fig. 5.5

After 5.7 we can continue in a different way, for example:

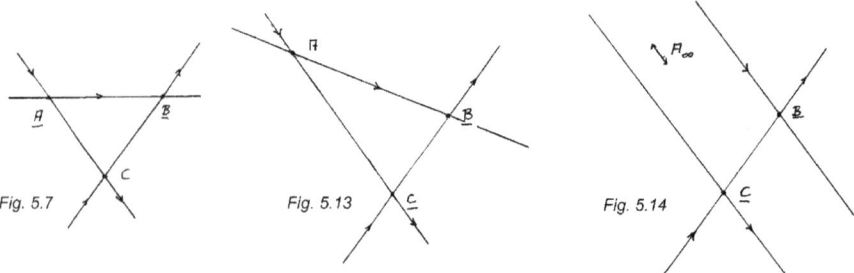

Fig. 5.7   Fig. 5.13   Fig. 5.14

5.3 Transformation of a quadrangle[1]

The transformation of quadrangles can also be practiced in diverse ways. For example, a problem of the following kind could be posed:

Forms are given at the beginning and end of a metamorphosis. The significant stages in between are required.

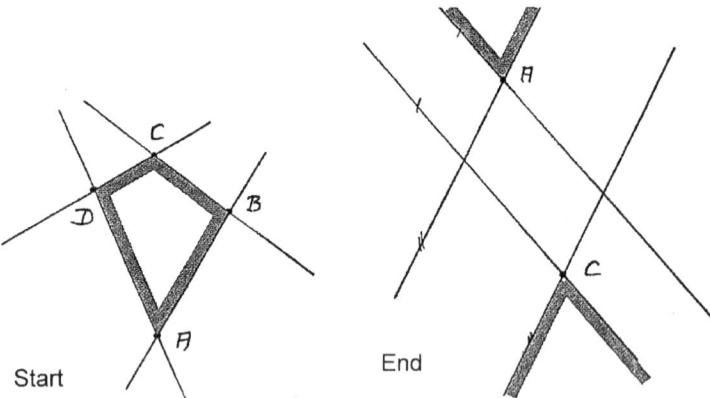

Start   End

5.4 About transformations of triangles

The triangles drawn differ in part from the usual idea we have of triangles. Usually, we imagine a triangle somewhat as follows:

- It is bounded by three finite segments,
- It has a definite area,
- The sum of the angles is 180°

In the sketch shown, the hatched area between the three straight lines would be a familiar triangle.

---

[1] the quadrangle is sometimes called «4-point», the corresponding figure is the «4-side».

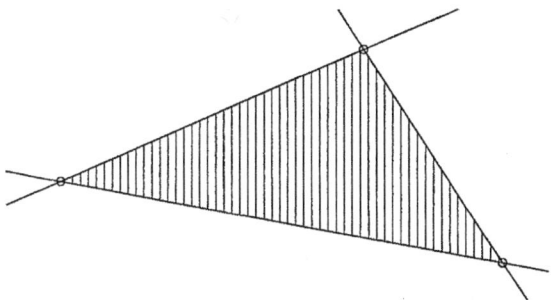

In our triangle transformation, the stages 5.7 and 5.8 take us to an essential change in form: we would not count them as triangles in the usual sense. Essential characteristics of the triangle 5.7 are: boundary segments going over the infinite, the infinitely large area, and the sum of the angles which can increase beyond 180° (up to 540°)

One possible continuation of Figure 5.7 is:

B and C remain fixed while A moves to infinity in the line AC (Figure 5.14). This triangle is so radically different from the form of the first triangle that we hardly recognize it as a triangle. We call such a transformation of shape a

metamorphosis.

Metamorphoses are changes where, within what changes, something constant can be observed. If, with our triangle transformation, we compare the initial form (5.5) with the final form (5.14), we see that a profound change in form has occurred.

Goethe's investigations of the metamorphoses in the plant kingdom are famous. Seedling – leafy plant – flowering plant – fruit bearing plant – all are one and the same plant, even though completely different (seasonally determined) forms arise. The changes can be quite extreme as long as the context in which the change occurs remains recognizable, as also the principle inherent in the changed object.

6 Harmonic division

6.1 Definition of harmonic division

If a segment $\overline{AB}$ is divided internally and externally in the same ratio, we speak of a harmonic division.

C divides the segment $\overline{AB}$ internally and D divides it externally.
Hence for the individual subsegments, the following holds:[2]

$$\frac{\overline{AC}}{\overline{CB}} = \frac{\overline{AD}}{\overline{BD}}. \tag{1}$$

Cross-multiplying (1) and dividing by $(\overline{AD} \cdot \overline{BD})$ gives respectively:

$$\overline{CB} \cdot \overline{AD} = \overline{AC} \cdot \overline{BD}$$

$$\text{and} \quad \frac{\overline{CB}}{\overline{BD}} = \frac{\overline{AC}}{\overline{AD}}. \tag{2}$$

(2) can now be interpreted as if $\overline{CD}$ is the segment to be divided, B the internal and A the external point of division.

Result: If $\overline{AB}$ is harmonically divided by C and D, then $\overline{CD}$ is harmonically divided by A and B as well.

A special case:
Letting the point D move to the right, we see that when $D \to D_\infty$, C is the mid-point of $\overline{AB}$. Analogously when $A \to A_\infty$, B is the mid-point of $\overline{CD}$.

6.2 The double ratio[3]

Equation (1) above implies

$$\frac{\frac{\overline{AC}}{\overline{BC}}}{\frac{\overline{AD}}{\overline{BD}}} = 1 \tag{3}$$

On the left side of (3) we have the ratio of two ratios. We call this the «double ratio» or «cross ratio» of the four points A, B, C, D of a line and write $(A, B, C, D) = 1$ for short. Only with the harmonic position does the double ratio have the value of 1.

---
[2] Ratios of absolute distances are formed without orientation by signs.
[3] The double ratio is sometimes called «anharmonic ratio» or «cross ratio»

6.3 Invariance of the harmonic division under projection

Theorem: If A, B, C, D are four harmonically related points in g, then, under a central projection, their four image points $\overline{A}, \overline{B}, \overline{C}, \overline{D}$ are harmonic in the line $\overline{g}$ as well.

Proof: We can see from the drawing on page 89 that by the Sine Rule the following holds:

$$\frac{\overline{AC}}{\sin \alpha} = \frac{\overline{AZ}}{\sin \varphi} \Rightarrow \overline{AC} = \frac{\overline{AZ} \cdot \sin \alpha}{\sin \varphi},$$

$$\frac{\overline{BC}}{\sin \beta} = \frac{\overline{BZ}}{\sin \varphi'} \Rightarrow \overline{BC} = \frac{\overline{BZ} \cdot \sin \beta}{\sin \varphi'}.$$

Since $\sin \varphi' = \sin \varphi$, it follows that:

$$\frac{\overline{AC}}{\overline{BC}} = \frac{\overline{AZ} \cdot \sin \alpha}{\overline{BZ} \cdot \sin \beta} \tag{4}$$

Furthermore:

$$\frac{\overline{AD}}{\sin \gamma} = \frac{\overline{AZ}}{\sin \sigma} \Rightarrow \overline{AD} = \frac{\overline{AZ} \cdot \sin \gamma}{\sin \sigma},$$

$$\frac{\overline{BD}}{\sin \delta} = \frac{\overline{BZ}}{\sin \sigma} \Rightarrow \overline{BD} = \frac{\overline{BZ} \cdot \sin \delta}{\sin \sigma},$$

hence:

$$\frac{\overline{AD}}{\overline{BD}} = \frac{\overline{AZ} \cdot \sin \gamma}{\overline{BZ} \cdot \sin \delta} \tag{5}$$

From (4) and (5) we obtain the double ratio for the points A, B, C, D:

$$(A, B, C, D) = \frac{\frac{\overline{AC}}{\overline{BC}}}{\frac{\overline{AD}}{\overline{BD}}} = \frac{\frac{\sin \alpha}{\sin \beta}}{\frac{\sin \gamma}{\sin \delta}} \tag{6}$$

We see that no reference is made in (6) to the line g, so that the double ratio depends only on the angles in Z.

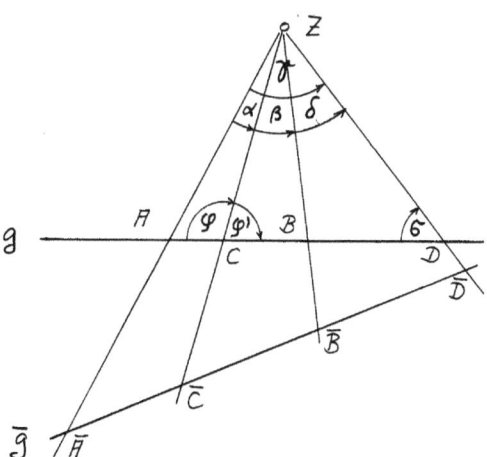

Were we to repeat the whole derivation using the points in the line $\bar{g}$, everything would work in exactly the same way and we would end up with:

$$\frac{\frac{\overline{\overline{AC}}}{\overline{\overline{BC}}}}{\frac{\overline{\overline{AD}}}{\overline{\overline{BD}}}} = \frac{\frac{\sin\alpha}{\sin\beta}}{\frac{\sin\gamma}{\sin\delta}}$$

which means that the double ratio is invariant under projection.

If the double ratio has the value 1, then we have harmonic division. The invariance holds in this case too of course.

We now make the following definition:

If, from a point G, we draw the four lines a, b, c, d through four harmonic points A, B, C, D of a line z, we call the lines *four harmonic lines*. We also say: the two lines a and b are divided harmonically by the lines c and d.

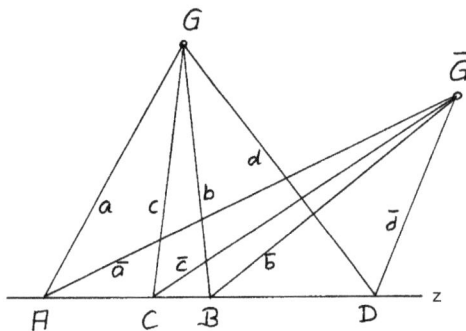

By a process exactly similar to the above, we conclude (the proof will only be possible after Chapter 7.5 on the principle of duality): Lines $\bar{a}, \bar{b}, \bar{c}, \bar{d}$ are *four harmonic lines* as well.

And the theorem formulated above leads to the «dual» theorem: If a, b, c, d are four harmonic lines going through G, then under a linear projection, the four image lines $\bar{a}, \bar{b}, \bar{c}, \bar{d}$ are harmonic in point $\bar{G}$ as well.

7 The complete 4-point and the complete 4-side – the fundamental harmonic configuration

7.1 The complete 4-point

A complete planar 4-point (Quadrangle) is formed from four initial points (basic vertices) A, B, C, D and their six connecting lines (sides). These six sides have three further points of intersection (extra vertices or diagonal points) P, Q, R whose connecting lines are the extra sides p, q, r. Extra vertices and extra sides together form what we call the **extra 3-point** or **diagonal triangle** (Figure 7.1)

Note: To see the relationships more easily, and as a help for the student, I color the drawings for the complete 4-point (Figure 7.1 and those following) and the complete 4-side (from Figure 7.4). For example, the first four points black, the 6 connecting lines blue, the three extra vertices green and the three extra sides red. In Figure 7.4, the four first lines are black, the six intersection points violet, the three extra sides red and the three extra vertices green. Thus when the fundamental harmonic configuration is drawn in Figure 7.6 and 7.7, all these colors appear in it. Coloring also helps the understanding of proofs (for example in Figure 7.8). In chapter 12 this coloring is taken up again, in the text and in the associated Figure 12.3.

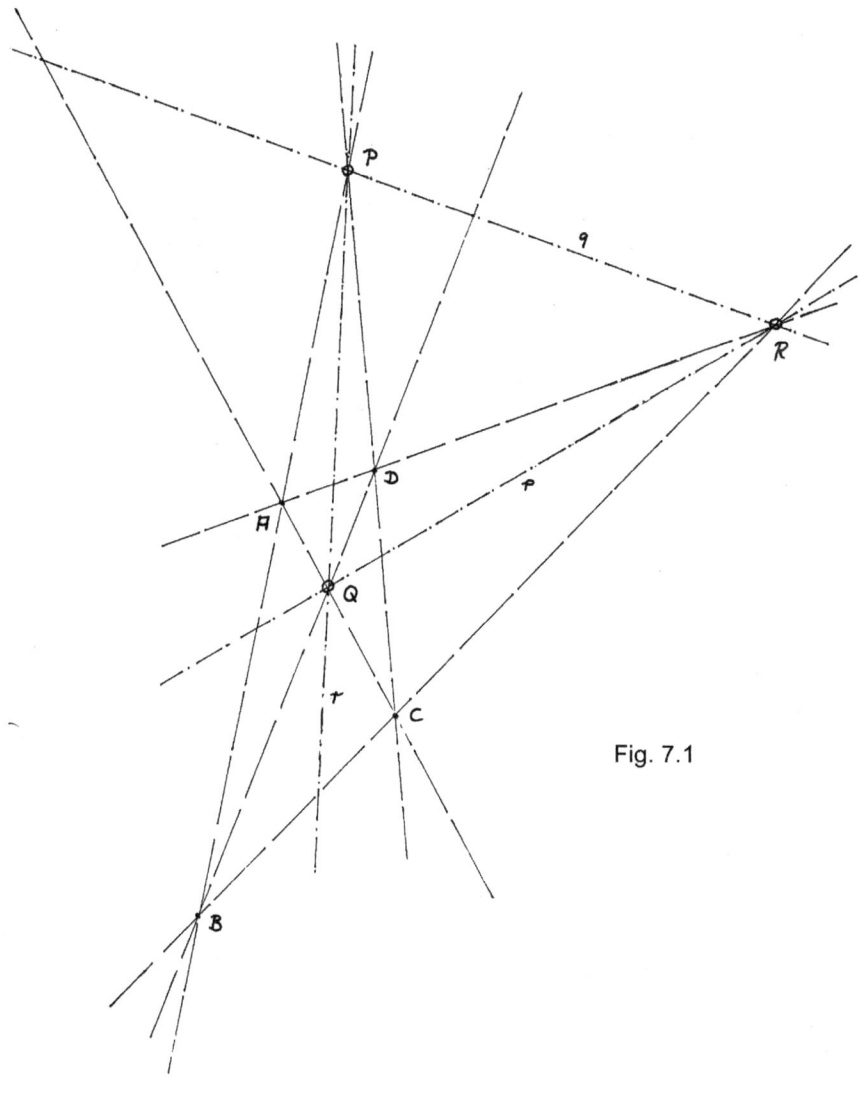

Fig. 7.1

7.2 The harmonic points in the complete 4-point

In the complete 4-point we see that in each extra side there are two extra vertices and two intersection points with the two sides of the 4-point that do not go through these two extra vertices.

The following law holds here: These four points are always harmonic, irrespective of the positions of the four vertices!

Thus, given three points, we can construct the fourth harmonic point with the help of a complete 4-point.

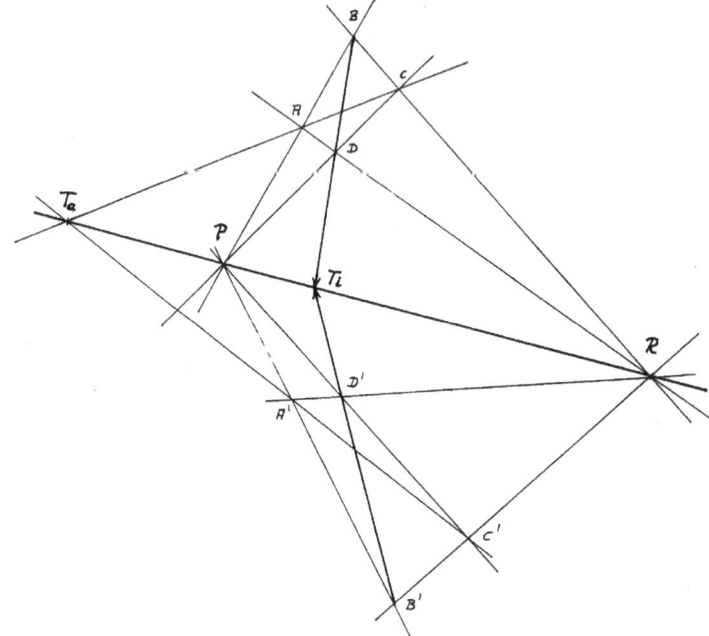

Fig. 7.2

We see that any other 4-point constructed in this way leads to the same point T_i.

We shall now show that T_i really is the fourth harmonic point to P, R and T_a (to simplify matters we take B to be B_∞).

Fig. 7.3

By the intercept theorems, we have:

$$\frac{\overline{PT_a}}{\overline{RT_a}} = \frac{m}{n},$$

and

$$\frac{\overline{PT_i}}{\overline{RT_i}} = \frac{\overline{PD}}{\overline{CD}} = \frac{m}{n}.$$

Hence

$$\frac{\overline{PT_a}}{\overline{RT_a}} = \frac{\overline{PT_i}}{\overline{RT_i}} \quad \text{(Q.E.D.)}.$$

The sets of four points in the six sides of the 4-point (in Figure 7.1) are also harmonic. They are the projections of the quartets of points in the extra sides (for example, q is projected onto the side $\overline{AD}$ by means of the center Q).

7.3 The complete 4-side

A complete planar 4-side (Quadrilateral) is formed from four initial lines (basic sides) a, b, c, d and their six points of intersection (vertices). These six vertices have three further connecting lines (extra sides or diagonal lines) p, q, r, whose points of intersection are the extra vertices P, Q, R. Extra sides and extra vertices together form what we call the **extra 3-side** or **diagonal trilateral** (Fig. 7.4).

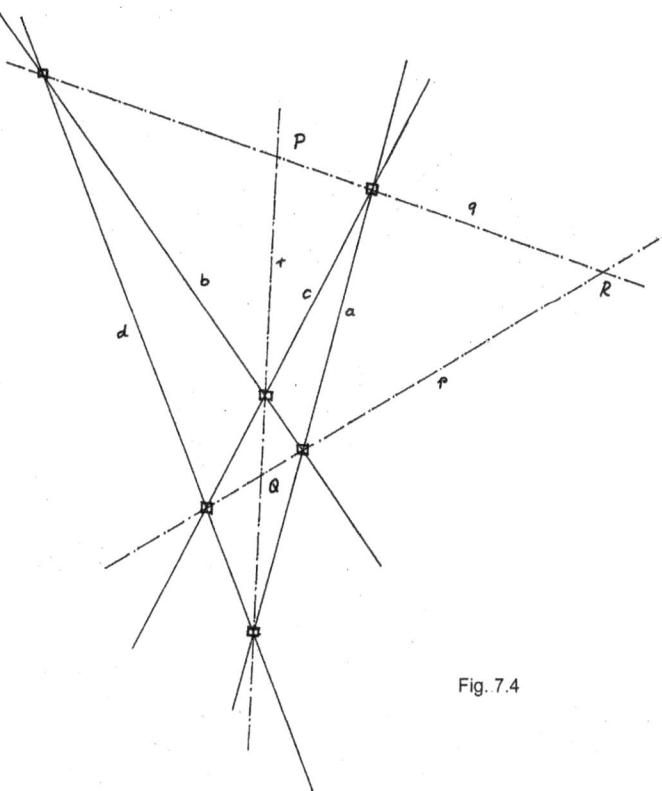

Fig. 7.4

7.4 Harmonic lines

The complete 4-side produces harmonic pairs of lines: If we join an extra vertex (such as Q) to the dividing points T_a and T_i in q, then these connecting lines (dashed) together with the two other extra sides (r and p) are four harmonic lines (Figure 7.5).

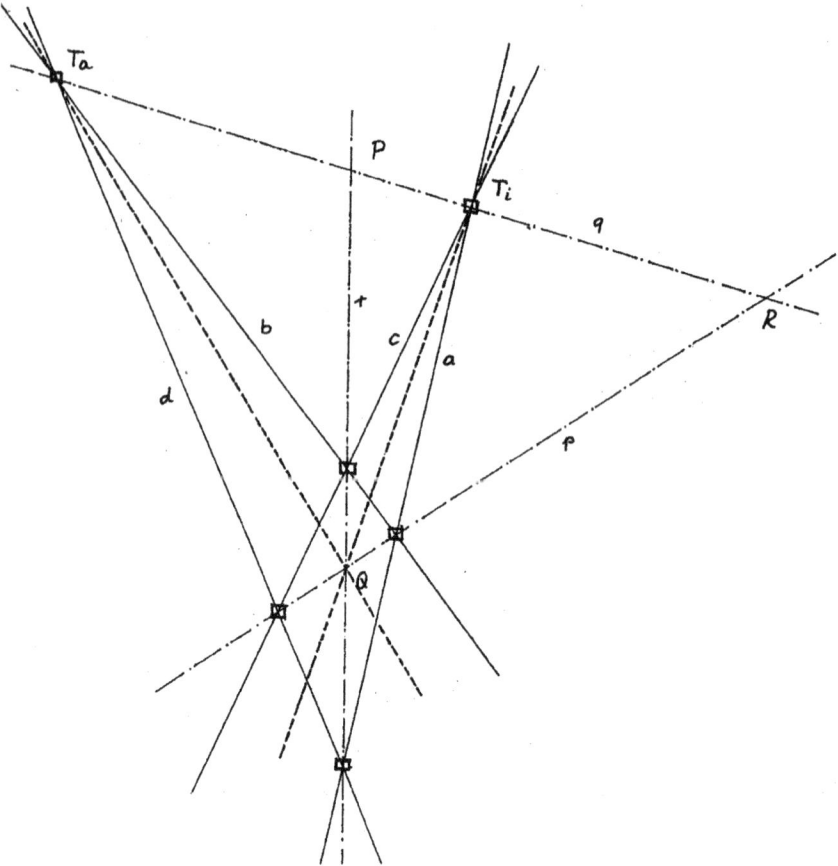

Fig. 7.5

If in all the extra vertices of the complete 4-side we draw the six harmonic dividing lines, these intersect in four points: A, B, C, D. We see that these «final» points are the initial points of a complete 4-point! And conversely: if we were to begin with these points as initial points and take the complete 4-point that arises further by connecting the harmonic division points of one extra side with the harmonic division points of the other extra sides, we would obtain four lines: a, b, c, d. These «final» lines are the initial lines of a complete 4-side.

The figure in which a complete 4-point and a complete 4-side with a common extra 3-point/3-side are woven into each other is called the **fundamental harmonic configuration** (Figure 7.6 and 7.7).

The fundamental harmonic configuration

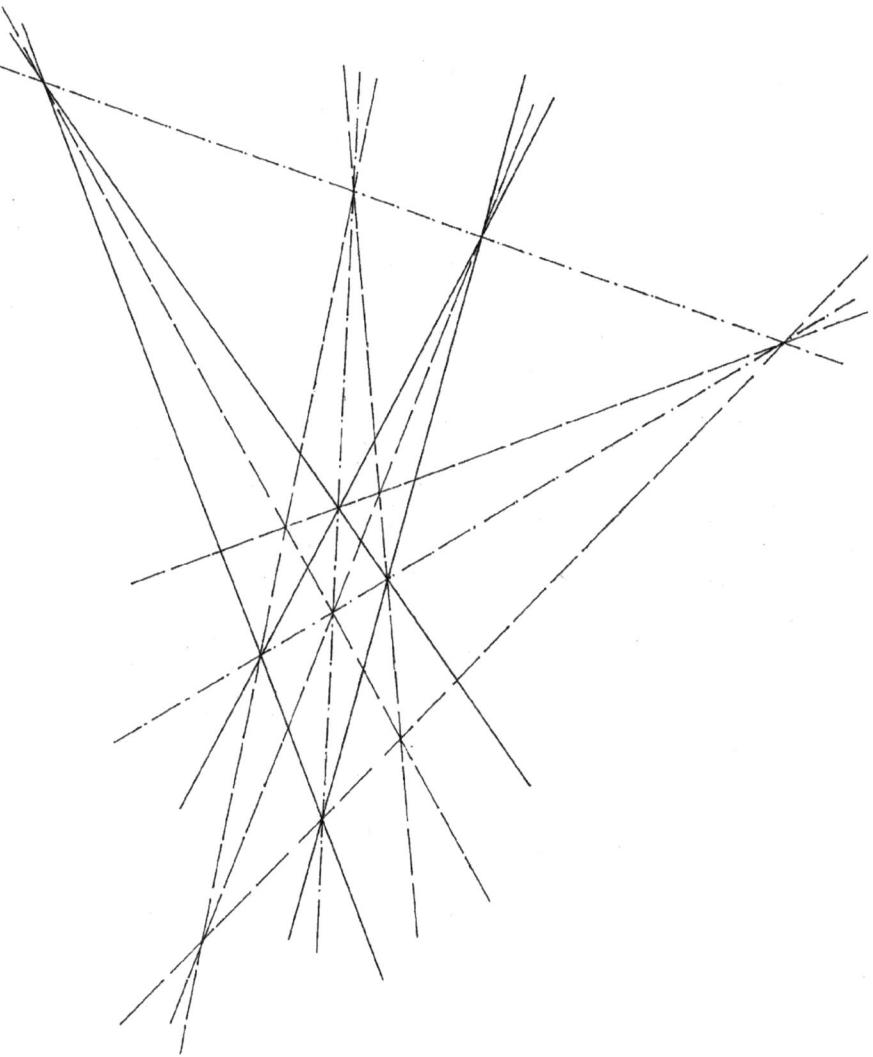

Fig. 7.6

Projective Geometry | *Karl-Friedrich Georg*

The fundamental harmonic configuration (with labeling)

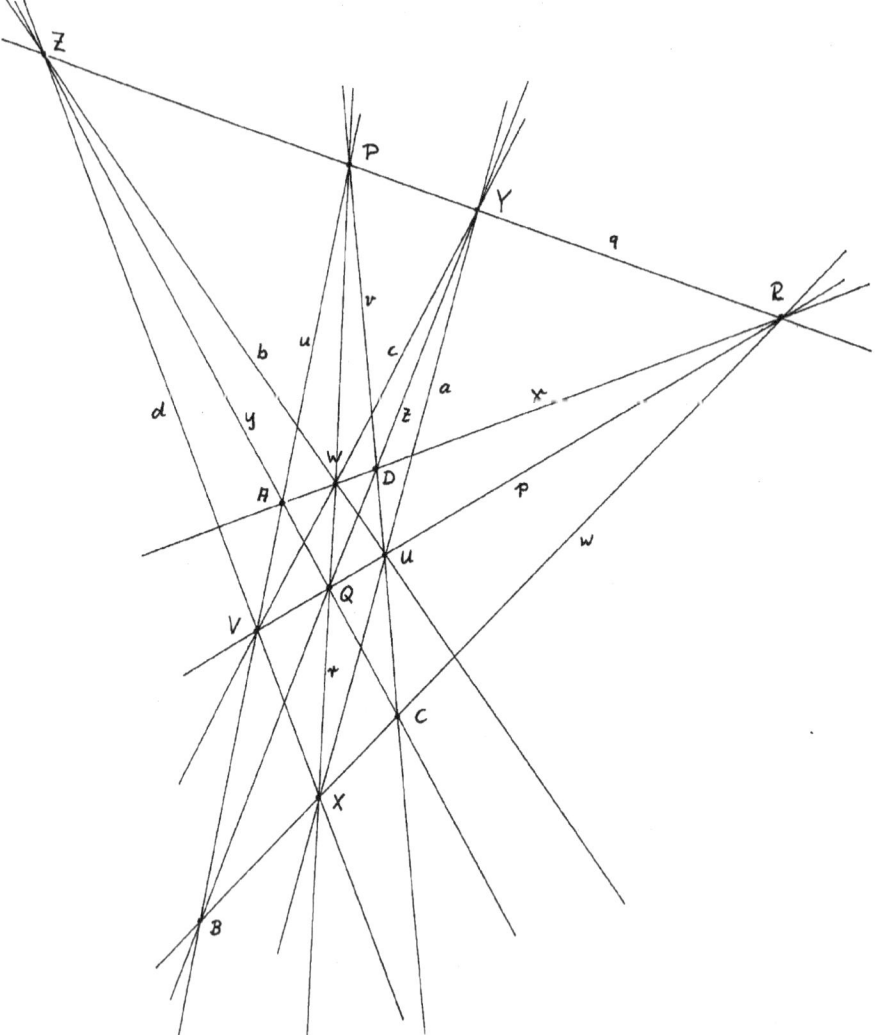

Fig. 7.7

Its genesis points to an important principle which is valid in all of projective geometry:

7.5 The principle of duality

In all the theorems of plane projective geometry which concern only incidence relationships between points and lines and the operations of intersecting and connecting, there are dual or «polar-opposite» propositions in the sense of the following table:

Basic form	Point	Line
Operation	connect	intersect
Incidence relations	lie in a line	go through a point

If a theorem of projective geometry has been proved then, by the duality principle, the dual counterpart is also a true theorem and needs no further proof.

We can clarify the dual symmetry in the structure of the fundamental harmonic configuration by the way we label the points and lines (Figure 7.7):

$$\text{complete 4-point} \begin{cases} 4 \text{ points } A, B, C, D \\ 6 \text{ connecting lines } u, v, w, x, y, z \\ 3 \text{ extra vertices } P, Q, R \\ 3 \text{ extra sides } p, q, r \\ 6 \text{ intersection points } U, V, W, X, Y, Z \\ 4 \text{ lines } a, b, c, d \end{cases} \text{complete 4-side}$$

Since in this configuration 13 points and 13 lines are woven together in this special way, it is also called the «13 configuration».

Note the following:

through A go y, u, x	in a lie Y, U, X
through B go u, w, z	in b lie U, W, Z
through C go v, w, y	in c lie V, W, Y
through D go v, x, z	in d lie V, X, Z
through U go a, b, v, p	in u lie A, B, V, P
through V go c, d, u, p	in v lie C, D, U, P
through W go b, c, x, r	in w lie B, C, X, R
through X go a, d, w, r	in x lie A, D, W, R
through Y go a, c, z, q	in y lie A, C, Z, Q
through Z go b, d, y, q	in z lie B, D, Y, Q

7.6 The fundamental harmonic configuration and Desargues' configuration

Let's disregard some of the points and lines of the fundamental harmonic configuration (Figure 7.6) and look at a subset of it:

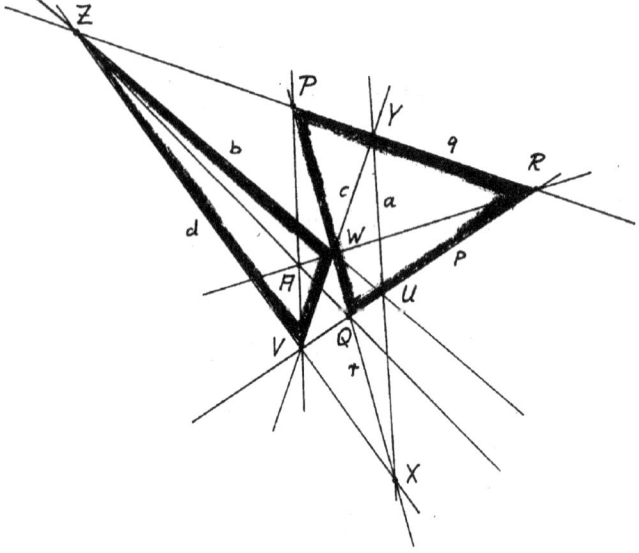

Fig. 7.8

We can see that a Desargues configuration is contained in this figure: point A is a center, the two related 3-points are marked, and the line a is the Desargues line associated with center A. Something similar can be found if we choose one of the other three points B, C and D as center.

7.7 Exercises on the fundamental harmonic configuration

1. In Figure 7.2 or 7.5, we imagine the extra side as a horizontal line h, in which we fix the (vanishing) points A, B, D. By means of the 4-point $1, 2, 3, 4$ we obtain the fourth horizontal point C.

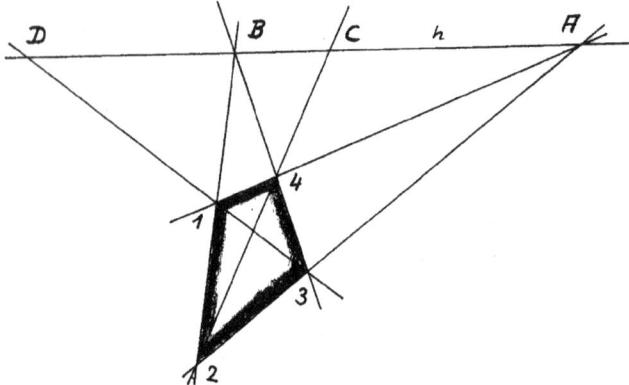

Fig. 7.9

2. As in the drawing above, but $D \rightarrow D_\infty$. C is now the mid-point of segment $\overline{AB}$.

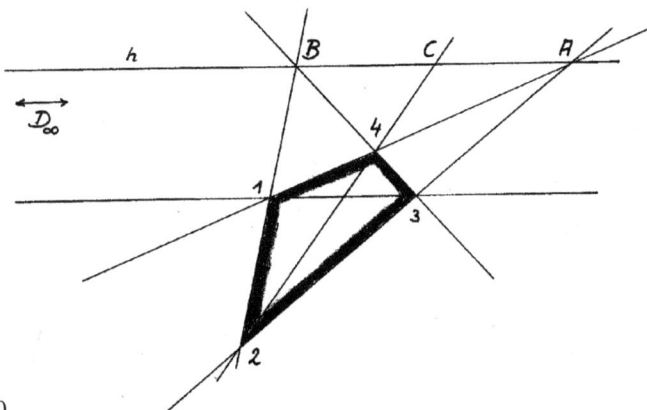

Fig. 7.10

3. As in Figure 7.9, but $A \rightarrow A_\infty$. B is now the mid-point of segment $\overline{DC}$.

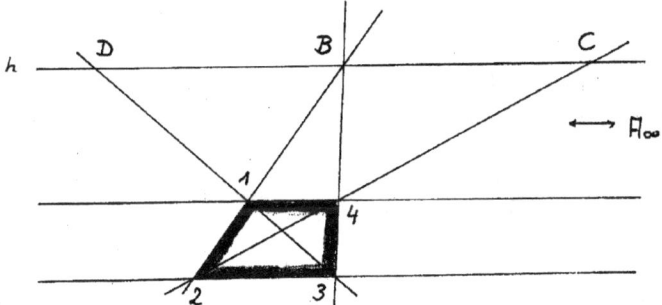

Fig. 7.11

4. $h \rightarrow h_\infty$, so we must give the three freely chosen points A_∞, B_∞, D_∞ as directions.

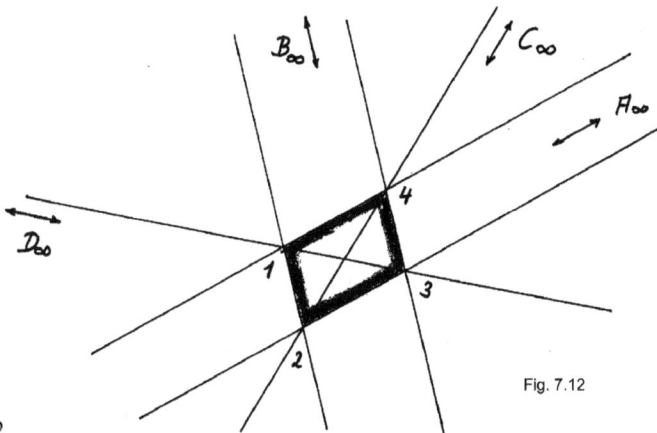

Fig. 7.12

5. The one 4-point can be expanded into a net of 4-points by adding further lines (the Moebius net – see Figure 7.13).

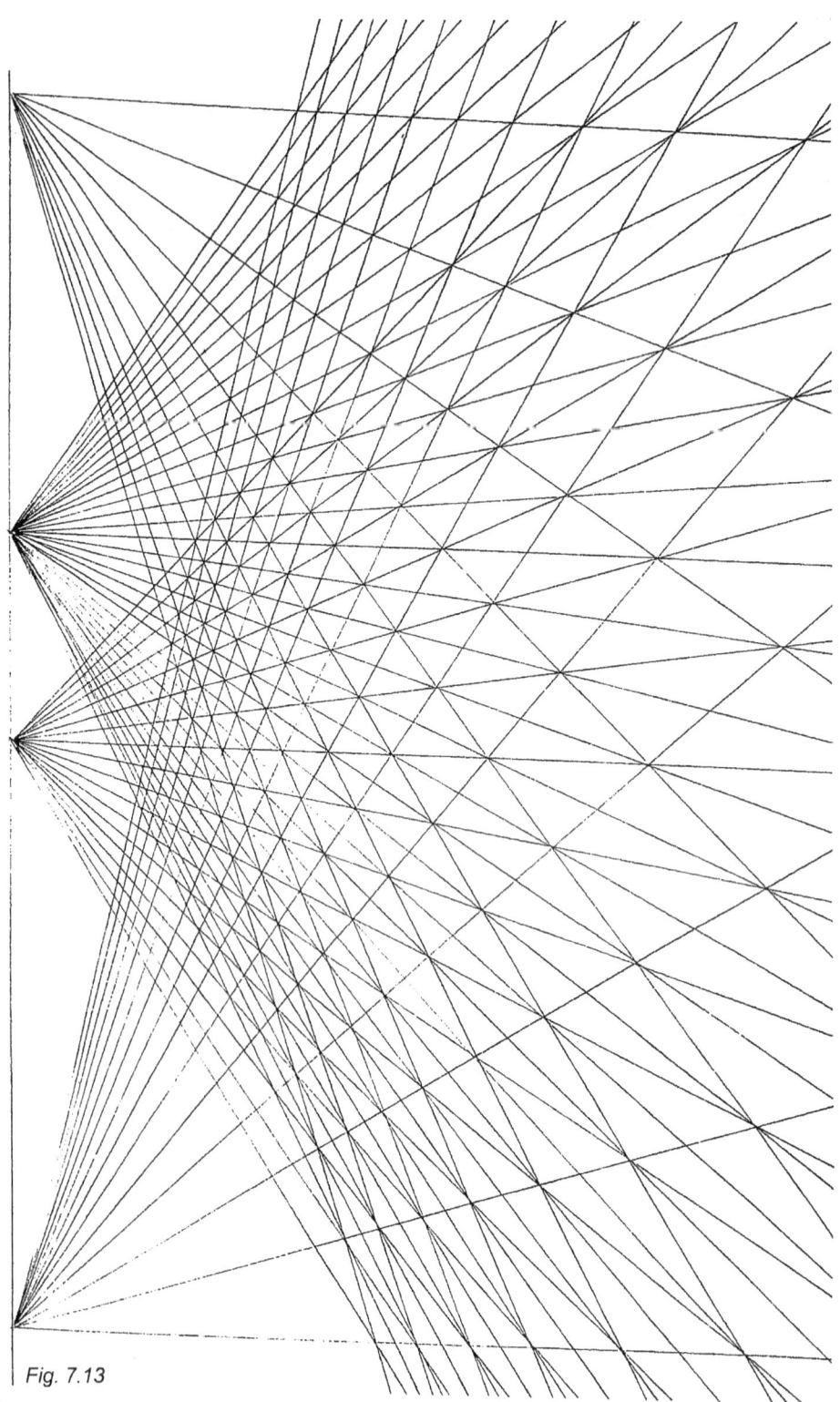

Fig. 7.13

As exercises:

6. Fundamental harmonic configuration constructed from a trapezoid: Fig. 7.14

7. Fundamental harmonic configuration constructed from a rectangle: Fig. 7.15

8. Fundamental harmonic configuration constructed from a square: Fig. 7.16

9. About the principle of duality.
   The theorem of Pappus has been known since antiquity. If three points A_1, A_2, A_3 lie in a line a and three points C_1, C_2, C_3 in a line c, then the three intersection points of corresponding connecting lines A_2C_3 and A_3C_2, A_3C_1 and A_1C_3, A_1C_2 and A_2C_1 lie in a line.

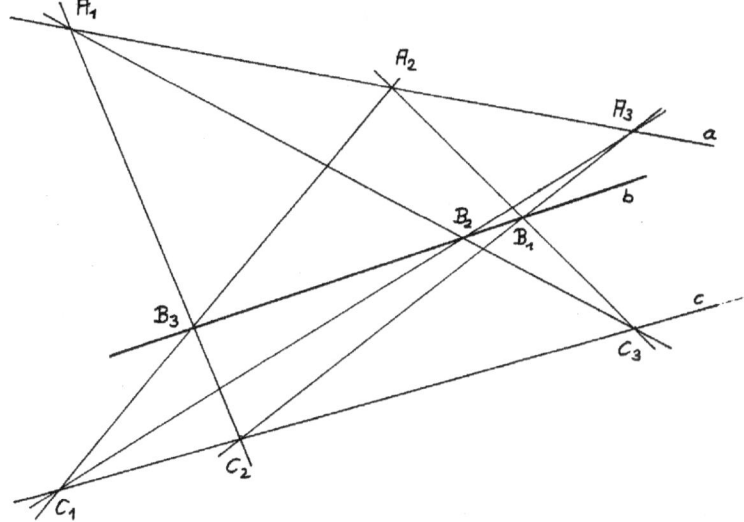

Fig. 7.17

We can see the correctness of this theorem by the following argument. If the theorem is true, instead of relating a and c with their sets of three points, we could just as well relate a and b, or b and c to each other. And in both cases we shall obtain the result that the intersection points lie in a line.

Problem: Form the dual theorem to the theorem of Pappus and draw it.
If three lines a_1, a_2, a_3 go through a point A and three lines c_1, c_2, c_3 go through a point C, then the three lines joining corresponding intersection points a_2c_3 and a_3c_2, a_3c_1 and a_1c_3, a_1c_2 and a_2c_1 meet in a point.

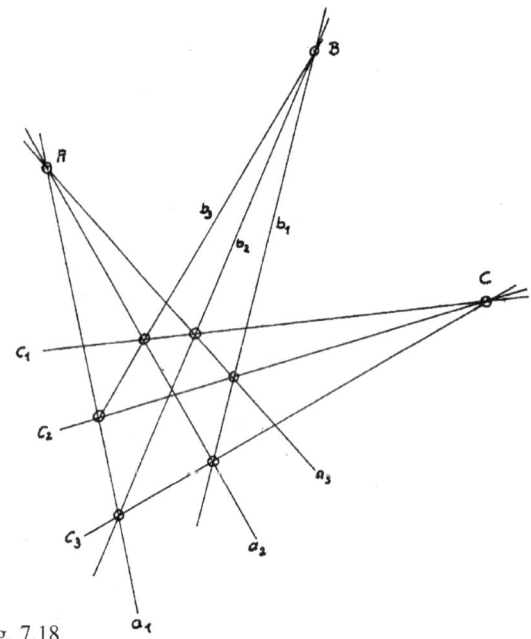

Fig. 7.18

10. Second example of the principle of duality:

    We dualize the following situation: If the lines of a pencil S are intersected by two lines a and b, we obtain intersection points $1, 2, 3, 4, 5, \ldots\ldots$ in a and $1', 2', 3', 4', 5', \ldots\ldots$ in b. We intersect the lines $12'$ and $1'2$, $23'$ and $2'3$, etc. to obtain the intersection points $I, II, III, \ldots$ These points lie on a line which goes through the point of intersection a and b.

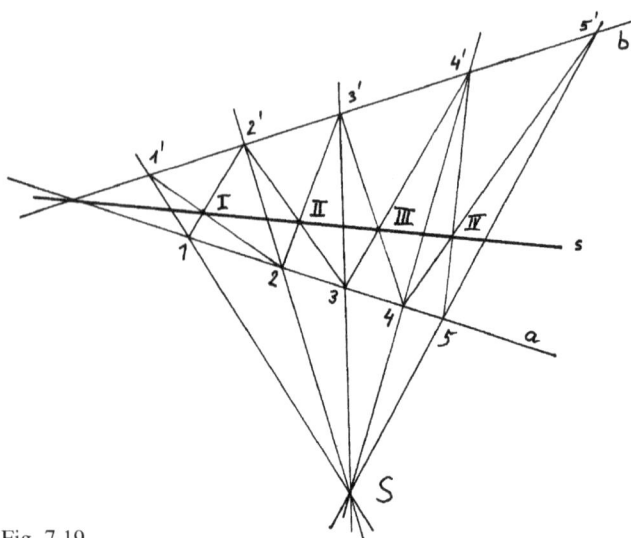

Fig. 7.19

First, the proof for Figure 7.19 (that s goes through the intersection point ab) using the theorem of Desargues. Consider any three lines of the pencil of lines.

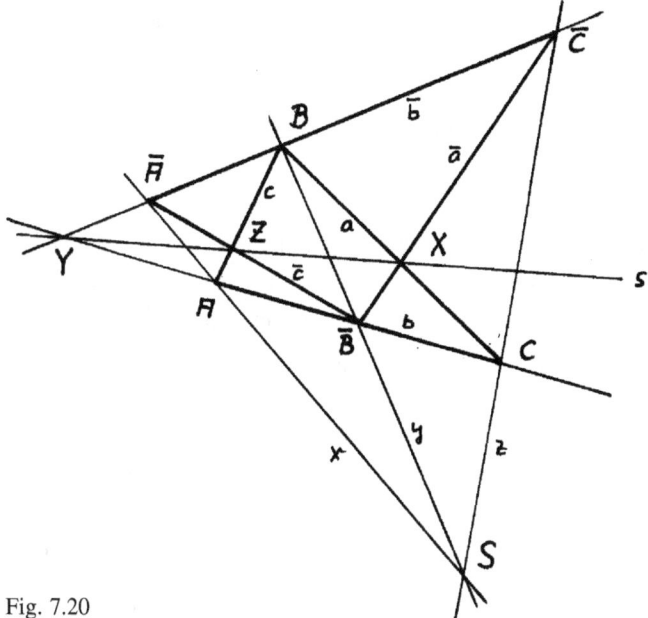

Fig. 7.20

Therefore this relationship is valid for all the lines of the pencil.

And the dualized situation is:

If the points of a range are joined to two points A and B, we get connecting lines 1, 2, 3, 4, 5, ... through A and $1'$, $2'$, $3'$, $4'$, $5'$,...... through B. We join the points $12'$ and $1'2$, $23'$ and $2'3$, etc. and obtain the connecting lines I, II, III,... These lines pass through the point S, which lies on the line joining A and B.

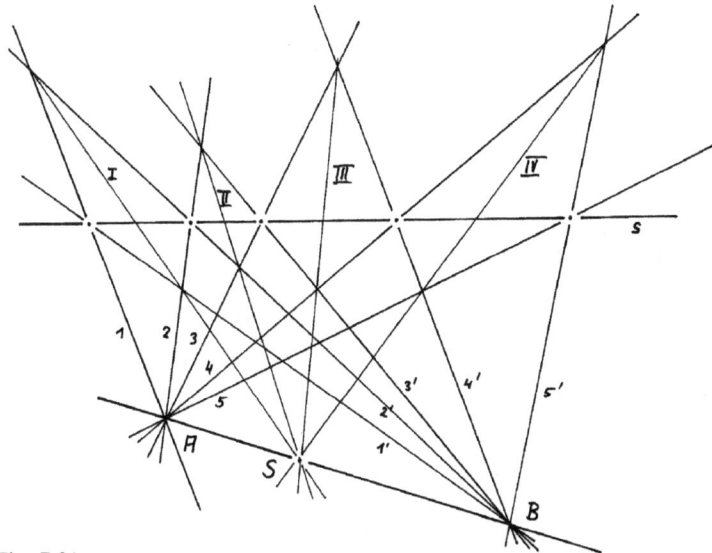

Fig. 7.21

8 The basic elements and basic forms of projective geometry

Point, line and plane are the elementary building blocks of geometry. We call them **basic elements**. They are ideal forms, even though to begin with they are apprehended in the world of experience. If, for instance, we think of the concept of a straight line, we have to admit that nowhere in the sense world do we see such a line appear precisely as such. If we try to imagine the fundamental elements individually we come upon the remarkable fact that none of the basic elements can be pictured as a whole. For example we only manage to picture a finite section of the plane. This fine distinction between mental picture and idea must be observed very precisely!

The three basic elements can also arise as structures, in fact each from the aspect of the other two:

1. We consider the plane as a structure of points:
   The plane is then the *bearer plane* for all the points that lie in it. The structure is called a *point field* and is denoted $\varepsilon(P)$.

2. We consider the point as a structure of planes:
   The point is then the *bearer point* for all the planes that go through the point. The structure is called a *bundle of planes* and denoted $P(\varepsilon)$.

3. We consider the line as a structure of points:
   The line is then the *bearer line* for all the points that lie in it. The structure is called a *point range* and denoted $g(P)$.

4. We consider the point as a structure of lines:
   The point is then the *bearer point* for all the lines that go through the point. The structure is called a *bundle of lines* and denoted $P(g)$

5. We consider the plane as a structure of lines:
   The plane is then the *bearer plane* for all the lines that lie in it. The structure is called a *field of lines* and denoted $\varepsilon(g)$.

6. We consider the line as a structure of planes:
   The line is then the *bearer line* for all the planes that go through the line. The structure is called *sheaf of planes* and denoted $g(\varepsilon)$.

7. We consider the plane as a structure of all the lines that lie in it and go through a point:
   The plane is then the *bearer plane* of point and lines. The structure is called a *pencil of lines* and denoted $\varepsilon(g; P)$.

8. We consider the point as a structure of all the lines that go through the point and lie in a plane:
   The point is then the *bearer point* of lines and plane. The structure is called a *pencil of lines* and denoted $P(g; \varepsilon)$.

Evidently the structures in 7 and 8 are identical.

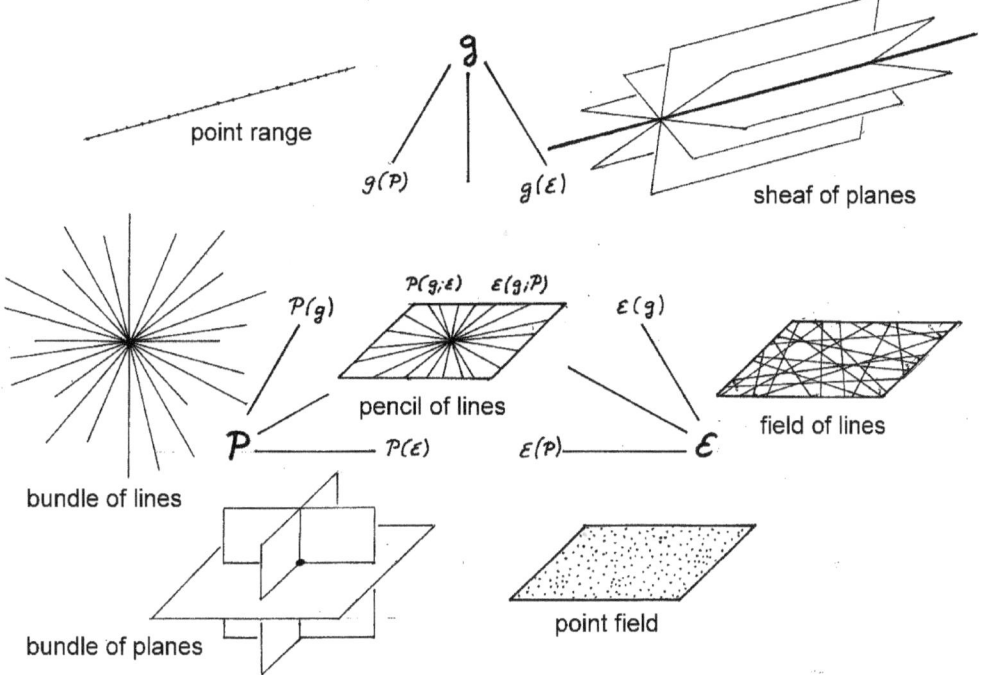

Fig. 8.1

Exercises: the common elements of two basic forms

Every basic form consists of an infinite number of elements of the same kind and a bearer (the one exception is the pencil of lines which has two bearers). In the line field, for example, the lines are the elements and a plane is the bearer.

If two basic forms of the same type are given, the question of common elements of the two forms naturally arises.

1. Two bundles of planes have in common all the planes of a sheaf (pencil of planes). The bearer of this sheaf is the line joining the bearer points of the two bundles:

$$P_1(\varepsilon) \cap P_2(\varepsilon) = g(\varepsilon)$$

2. Two line bundles have exactly one line in common, the line joining the two bearer points:

$$P_1(g) \cap P_2(g) = g$$

3. As point fields, two planes have in common all the points of a range, whose bearer is the

intersection line of the two planes:

$$\varepsilon_1(P) \cap \varepsilon_2(P) = g(P)$$

4. As line fields, two planes have in common exactly one line, the intersection line of the two bearer planes:

$$\varepsilon_1(g) \cap \varepsilon_2(g) = g$$

5. As point ranges, two lines have in common exactly one point provided they lie in a plane: their point of intersection:

$$g_1(P) \cap g_2(P) = P$$

6. As plane sheaves, two intersecting lines have in common one plane: their connecting plane.

$$g_1(\varepsilon) \cap g_2(\varepsilon) = \varepsilon$$

7. A point as bundle of planes and a line as sheaf of planes have in common exactly one plane if the line does not pass through the point:

$$P(\varepsilon) \cap g(\varepsilon) = \varepsilon, \text{ if } P \notin g$$

8. A point as bundle of planes and a line as sheaf of planes have in common the sheaf of planes if the line passes through the point:

$$P(\varepsilon) \cap g(\varepsilon) = g(\varepsilon), \text{ if } P \in g$$

9. A plane as point field and a line as point range have in common exactly one point if the line does not lie in the plane:

$$\varepsilon(P) \cap g(P) = P, \text{ if } g \notin \varepsilon$$

10. A plane as point field and a line as point range have in common the point range if the line lies in the plane:

$$\varepsilon(P) \cap g(P) = g(P), \text{ if } g \in \varepsilon$$

11. A point as line bundle and a plane as line field have in common a line pencil if the point lies in the plane. Point and plane are the common bearer of the pencil of lines:

$$P(g) \cap \varepsilon(g) = P(g)\varepsilon, \text{ if } P \in \varepsilon$$

12. A point as line bundle and a point/plane as line pencil have

a) the line pencil in common, if the two points coincide:

$$P_1(g) \cap P_2(g)\varepsilon = P_2(g)\varepsilon, \text{ if } P(g)\varepsilon \subset P(g)$$

b) one line in common, if the two points do not coincide but the bundle-point lies in the plane of the pencil:

$$P_1(g) \cap P_2(g)\varepsilon = g, \text{ if } P_1 \neq P_2, \text{ but } P_1 \in \varepsilon$$

c) no lines in common, if the two points do not coincide and the bundle-point does not lie in the plane of the pencil:

$$P_1(g) \cap P_2(g)\varepsilon = \emptyset, \text{ if } (P_1 \neq P_2), P_1 \notin \varepsilon$$

13. A plane as line field and a plane/point as line pencil have

    a) the line pencil in common, if the two planes coincide:

    $$\varepsilon_1(g) \cap \varepsilon_2(g)P = \varepsilon_2(g)P, \text{ if } \varepsilon_1 = \varepsilon_2$$

    b) one line in common, if the two planes do not coincide but the field-plane goes through the point of the pencil:

    $$\varepsilon_1(g) \cap \varepsilon_2(g)P = g, \text{ if } \varepsilon_1 \neq \varepsilon_2, P \in \varepsilon_1$$

    c) no lines in common, if the two planes do not coincide and the field-plane does not go through the point of the pencil:

    $$\varepsilon_1(g) \cap \varepsilon_2(g)P = \emptyset, \text{ if } \varepsilon_1 \neq \varepsilon_2, P \notin \varepsilon_1$$

14. Two point/planes as line pencils have

    a) one line in common, if the planes coincide and the points are separated: the line joining the points:

    $$P_1(g)\varepsilon_1 \cap P_2(g)\varepsilon_2 = g, \text{ if } \varepsilon_1 = \varepsilon_2, P_1 \neq P_2$$

    b) one line in common, if the points coincide and the planes are separated: the line of intersection of the planes:

    $$P_1(g)\varepsilon_1 \cap P_2(g)\varepsilon_2 = g, \text{ if } \varepsilon_1 \neq \varepsilon_2, P_1 = P_2$$

c) one line in common, if the line joining the two bearer points is also the line of intersection of the planes, the common line being this intersection and connecting line:

$$P_1(g)\varepsilon_1 \cap P_2(g)\varepsilon_2 = g, \text{ if } P_1 \in \varepsilon_2,\ P_2 \in \varepsilon_1$$

d) no lines in common, if neither the two planes nor the two bearer points coincide, and if the bearer points do not both lie in the line of intersection of the two planes, or the line joining the two bearer points does not lie in both planes:

$$P_1(g)\varepsilon_1 \cap P_2(g)\varepsilon_2 = \emptyset, \text{ if } \varepsilon_1 \neq \varepsilon_2,\ P_1 \neq P_2,\ (P_1 \notin \varepsilon_2 \text{ or } P_2 \notin \varepsilon_1)$$

9 The law of polarity

9.1 Preliminary exercise: comparison of Cube and Octahedron

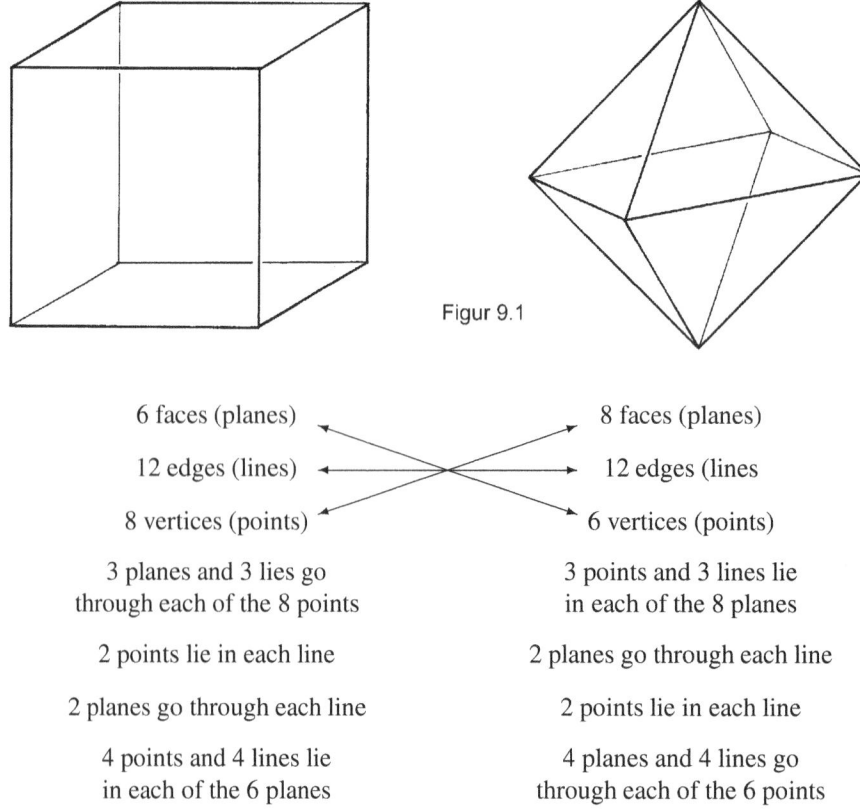

Figur 9.1

6 faces (planes)	8 faces (planes)
12 edges (lines)	12 edges (lines)
8 vertices (points)	6 vertices (points)
3 planes and 3 lies go through each of the 8 points	3 points and 3 lines lie in each of the 8 planes
2 points lie in each line	2 planes go through each line
2 planes go through each line	2 points lie in each line
4 points and 4 lines lie in each of the 6 planes	4 planes and 4 lines go through each of the 6 points

In comparing cube and octahedron we discern a regularity that suggests a fundamental law of space:

9.2 The law of polarity

Space conceals laws that are difficult to perceive directly. Yet after some practice we discern a fundamental contrast between point and plane. As mediating element between these, the line bears this contrast within itself, in that it can be characterized on the one hand as the intersection line of two planes and on the other as the connecting line of two points. In geometry, we call such opposites **polarities**.

Contemplating the triangular pattern of the seven basic forms (Figure 8.1) we notice something. If we replace each element with its polar element, we obtain essentially the same scheme. This means that for each basic form there is a polar opposite basic form. For example: the totality of all the lines through a point corresponds polarly to the totality of all the lines in a plane. That is, the line bundle and the line field are polar forms.

polar elements	$P \leftrightarrow \varepsilon$
	$g \leftrightarrow g$
polar forms	$P(g) \leftrightarrow \varepsilon(g)$
	$P(\varepsilon) \leftrightarrow \varepsilon(P)$
	$g(P) \leftrightarrow g(\varepsilon)$
	$P(g\varepsilon) \leftrightarrow \varepsilon(gP)$
polar operations	connecting $\leftrightarrow$ intersecting
polar position relationships	lie in $\leftrightarrow$ go through

9.3 Exercise

First draw a cuboctahedron and a rhombic dodecahedron. Then prove that these two solids are polar to each other.

Comparison:

Cuboctahedron	**Rhombic dodecahedron**
14 faces (6 four-cornered, 8 three-cornered)	14 vertices (6 four-faced, 8 three-faced)
24 lines	24 lines
12 vertices (all four-faced: 2 faces being three-cornered and 2 four-cornered)	12 faces (all four-cornered: 2 corners being three-faced and 2 four-faced)
Characterization with respect to points:	Characterization with respect to planes:
All vertices are equivalent in that 4 planes go through each: two planes in which there are four vertices and two in which there are three vertices.	All boundary planes are equivalent in that there are 4 vertices in each: two points containing four planes and two containing three planes.

Cuboctahedron	**Rhombic dodecahedron**
Also four lines pass through each point.	Also four lines lie in each plane.

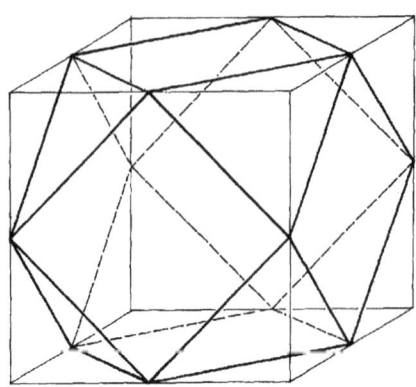 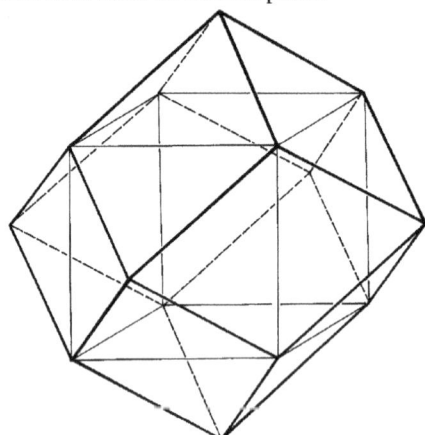

Fig. 9.2 Cuboctahedron   Fig. 9.3 Rhombic dodecahedron

Characterization with respect to edges:

2 vertices lie in each of the 24 edges and 2 planes pass through each edge, one four-cornered plane and one three-cornered plane.

Characterization with respect to planes:

The 14 faces are not equivalent. In 6 of the planes there are 4 points and 4 edges, in 8 planes 3 points and 3 edges.

Characterization with respect to edges:

2 faces go through each of the 24 edges and there are 2 points in each edge, one four-faced point and one three-faced point.

Characterization with respect to points:

The 14 vertices are not equivalent. 4 planes and 4 edges go through 6 of the points, 3 planes and 3 edges go through 8 of the points.

It is also worth noting that the cuboctahedron is inscribed in the cube while the rhombic dodecahedron circumscribes the cube.

9.4 Problem

«In a cube, starting at a vertex (point), join non-neighboring points that lie in the same plane.»

1. What sort of solid results?
2. What is the polar problem?

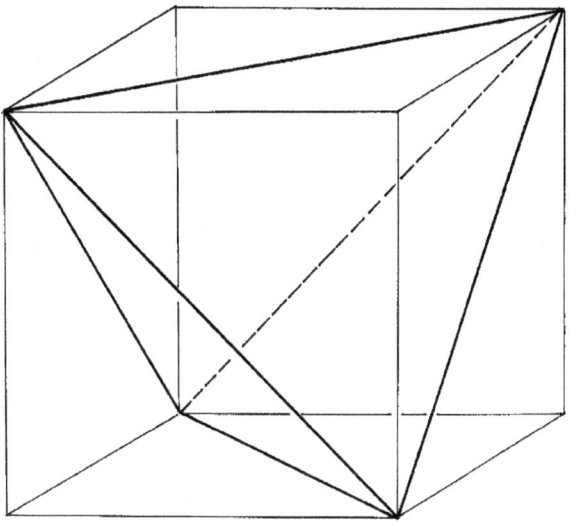

Figure 9.4

1. The result is a tetrahedron inscribed in the cube. The tetrahedron's vertices are also vertices of the cube.

2. The polar problem is:

«In an octahedron, starting from a face (plane), intersect non-neighboring planes that go through the same vertex (point).»

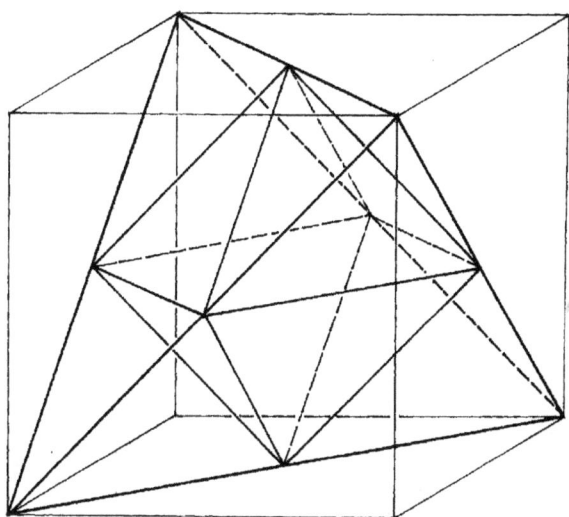

Figure 9.5

The result is a tetrahedron circumscribing the octahedron. The tetrahedron's faces are also faces of the octahedron.

9.5 A note about the Platonic solids

There are five solids that are entirely regular. These are described by Plato (427–347 BC) in his dialogue *Timaeus*. We can see that the hexahedron (cube) is polar to the octahedron. Likewise the pentagon dodecahedron is polar to the icosahedron. The tetrahedron is self-polar.

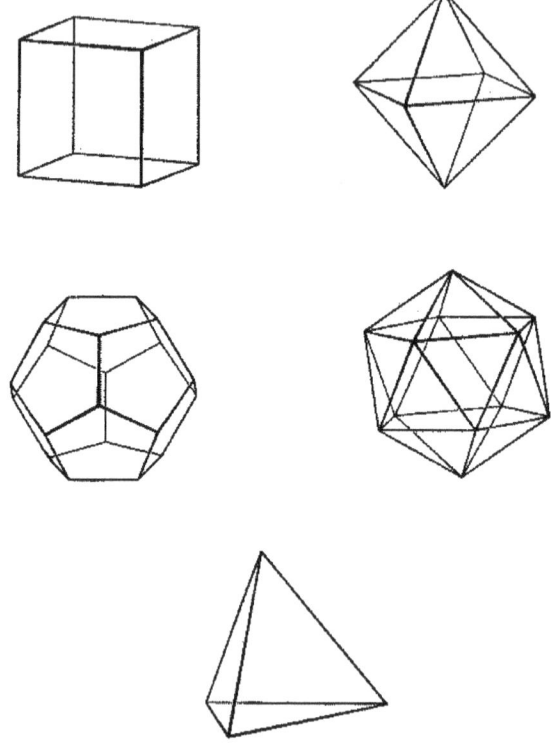

Fig. 9.6

9.6 Exercise

Polarize a double tetrahedron to find the polar solid.

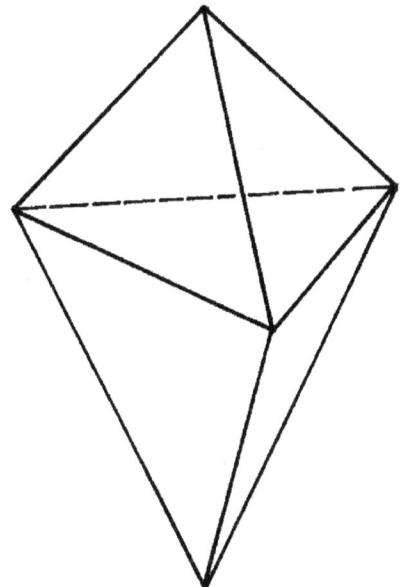

Figure 9.7
5 vertices (points)
2 vertices contain 3 faces (3-planes[4]) and 3 vertices contain 4 faces (4-planes[5]). Through 2 vertices go 3 lines (3-edges[6]) and through 3 vertices go 4 lines (4-edges[7])

6 faces (planes)
All faces contain 3 vertices (3-points) and 3 lines (3-sides). Each face contains 1 three-faced vertex and 2 four-faced vertices.

9 edges (lines)
Each edge (intersection line) contains 2 three-sided faces. 6 edges are lines joining a four-faced vertex and a three-faced vertex. 3 edges are lines joining 2 four-faced vertices.

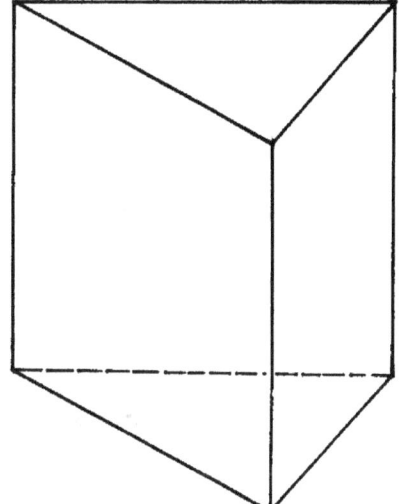

Figure 9.8
5 faces (planes)
2 faces contain 3 vertices (3-points) and 3 faces contain 4 vertices (4-points). In 2 faces are 3 lines (3-sides) and in 3 faces are 4 lines (4-sides).

6 vertices (points)
All vertices contain three faces (3-planes) and three lines (3-edges). Each vertex contains 1 three-cornered face and 2 four-cornered faces.

9 edges (lines)
Each edge (connecting line) contains 2 three-edged vertices. 6 edges are lines of intersection of a four-cornered face and a three-cornered face. 3 edges are lines of intersection of 2 four-cornered faces.

---

[4] trihedrons
[5] tetrahedral angles
[6] three-edged angles
[7] four-edged angles

9.7 Exercise: another example of polarization

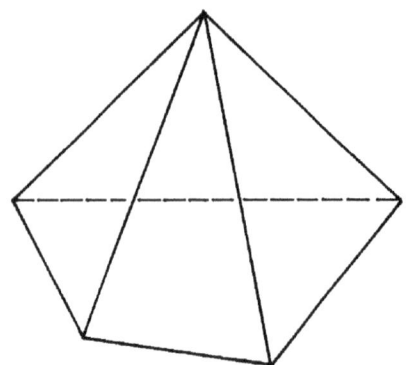

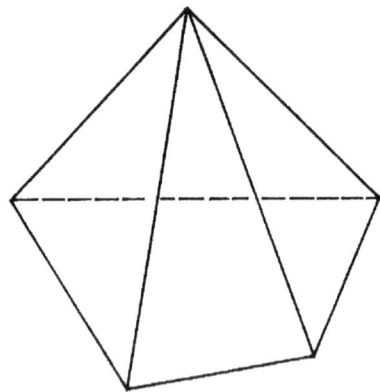

Figure 9.9a

5 vertices (points)
4 vertices contain 3 faces (3-planes) and 1 vertex contains 4 faces (a 4-plane).
4 vertices contain 3 lines (3-edges) and 1 vertex contains 4 lines (a 4-edge).
4 vertices contain 2 three-cornered faces and 1 four-cornered face.
1 vertex contains 4 three-cornered faces.

5 faces (planes)
4 faces contain 3 vertices (3-points) and 1 face contains 4 vertices (a 4-point).
4 faces contain 3 lines (3-sides) and 1 face contains 4 lines (a 4-side).
4 faces contain 2 three-faced vertices and 1 four-faced vertex.
1 face contains 4 three-faced vertices.

8 edges (lines)
4 edges are intersection lines of 2 three-sided/ three-cornered faces, and at the same time connecting lines of a four-faced/ four-edged vertex with a three-faced/ three-edged vertex.
4 edges are connecting lines of 2 three-edged/ three-faced vertices, and at the same time intersection lines of a four-cornered/ four-sided face with a three-cornered/ three-sided face.

Figure 9.9b

5 faces (planes)
4 faces contain 3 vertices (3-points) and 1 face contains 4 vertices (a 4-point).
4 faces contain 3 lines (3-sides) and 1 face contains 4 lines (a 4-side).
4 faces contain 2 three-faced vertices and 1 four-faced vertex.
1 face contains 4 three-faced vertices.

5 vertices (points)
4 vertices contain 3 faces (3-planes) and 1 vertex contains 4 faces (a 4-plane).
4 vertices contain 3 lines (3-edges) and 1 vertex contains 4 lines (a 4-edge).
4 vertices contain 2 three-cornered faces and 1 four-cornered face.
1 vertex contains 4 three-cornered faces.

8 edges (lines)
4 edges are connecting lines of 2 three-edged/ three-faced vertices, and at the same time intersection lines of a four-cornered/ four-sided face with a three-cornered/ three-sided face.
4 edges are intersection lines of 2 three-sided/ three-cornered faces, and at the same time connecting lines of a four-faced/ four-edged vertex with a three-faced/ three-edged vertex.

This pyramid is self-polar

If we analyze the individual elements in detail we find:

5 planes $\alpha, \beta, \gamma, \delta, \varepsilon$	$\leftrightarrow$	5 points A, B, C, D, E
e.g. α contains the 3-point PRM		e.g. A contains the 3-plane $\pi\rho\mu$
5 points P, R, S, T, M	$\leftrightarrow$	5 planes $\pi, \rho, \sigma, \tau, \mu$
e.g. P, R, S, T form the 4-point in ε		e.g. π, ρ, σ, τ form the 4-plane in E
8 lines a, b, c, d, p, r, s, t	$\leftrightarrow$	8 lines a, b, c, d, p, r, s, t
e.g. b is the connecting line RS		e.g. b is the line of intersection $\rho\sigma$
s is the line of intersection $\beta\gamma$		s is the connecting line BC

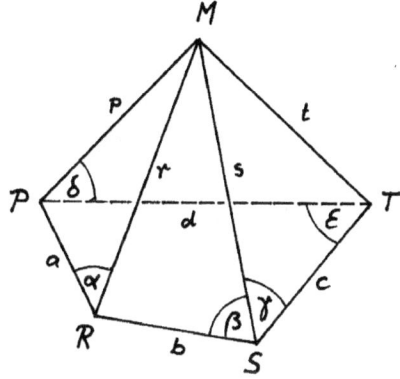

Figure 9.10a

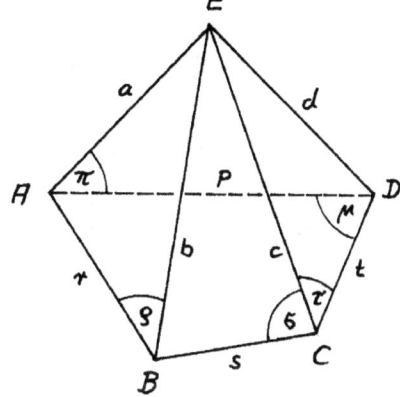

Figure 9.10b

9.8 The theorem of Desargues in space

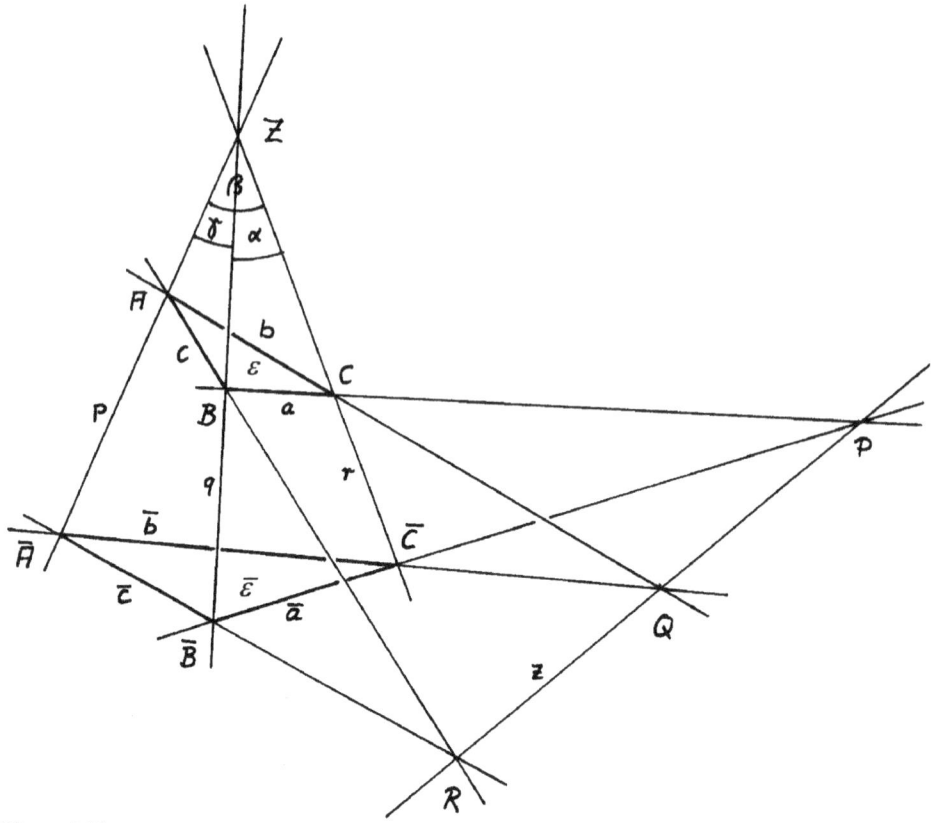

Figure 9.11

About Figure 9.11:

Two planes intersecting always produce a line (of intersection).

The three planes α, β, γ form the lines of intersection p, q, r and the point Z; the result is a 3-plane.

The four planes $\alpha, \beta, \gamma, \varepsilon$ form a tetrahedron with the six lines p, q, r, a, b, c and the four points A, B, C, Z.

The fourth plane ε and the fifth plane $\bar{\varepsilon}$ always intersect in a line, the «axis» z.

We shall now prove that the 10 lines and 10 points in the figure satisfy Desargues' theorem (compare Chapter 2).

a, b, c lie in the 4th plane ε and $\bar{a}, \bar{b}, \bar{c}$ in the 5th plane $\bar{\varepsilon}$. These two planes ε and $\bar{\varepsilon}$ intersect in z, hence all six lines of these planes form points of intersection with the line z.

a and $\bar{a}$ lie in plane α of the 3-plane through Z, hence meet in a point.

Result: $a \cap \bar{a} = P$; similarly $b \cap \bar{b} = Q$ and $c \cap \bar{c} = R$. P, Q, R lie in z.

The two 3-points ABC in ε and $\bar{A}\,\bar{B}\,\bar{C}$ in $\bar{\varepsilon}$ are «perspective» with respect to Z ($\alpha\beta\gamma$).

This (spatial) configuration contains:

10 lines $(a, b, c, \bar{a}, \bar{b}, \bar{c}, p, q, r, z)$ and **10** points $(A, B, C, \bar{A}, \bar{B}, \bar{C}, P, Q, R, Z)$ and **5** planes $(\alpha, \beta, \gamma, \varepsilon, \bar{\varepsilon})$.

In Figure 9.12 this configuration is polarized:

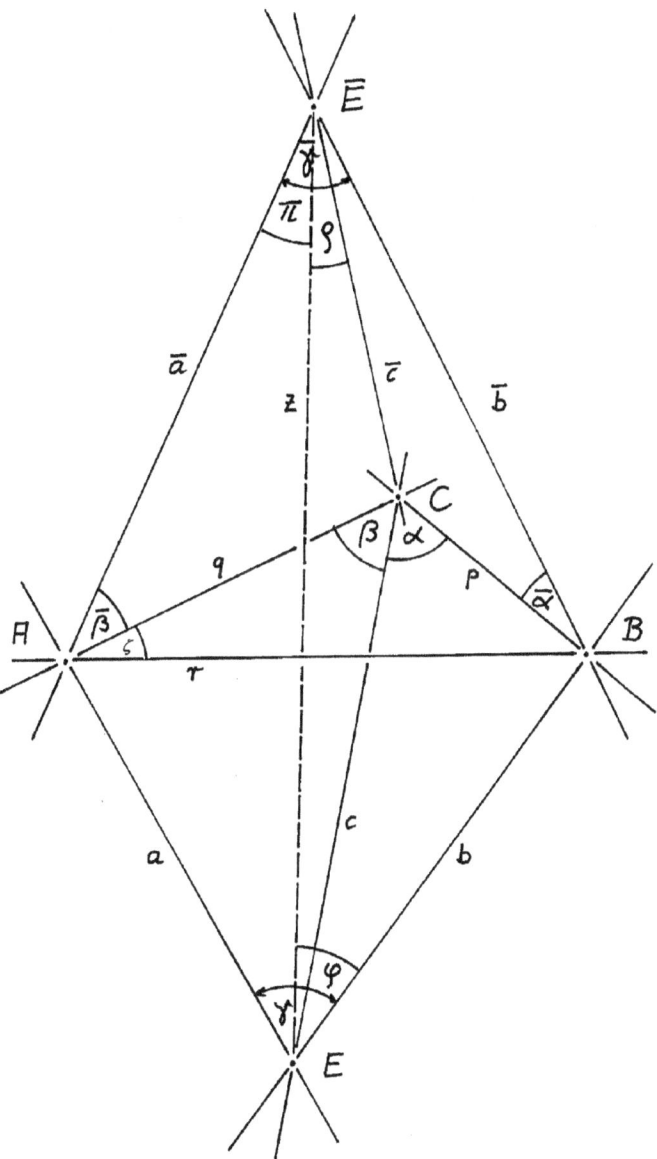

Fig. 9.12

Joining two points always produces a line (of connection).

The three points A, B, C form the lines of connection p, q, r and the plane ζ ("zeta"); the result is a 3-point.

The four points A, B, C, E form a tetrahedron with the six lines p, q, r, a, b, c and the four planes $\alpha, \beta, \gamma, \zeta$.

The fourth point E and the fifth point $\overline{E}$ are always joined by a line, the "axis" z.

a, b, c go through the 4th point E and $\overline{a}, \overline{b}, \overline{c}$ through the 5th point $\overline{E}$. These two points E and $\overline{E}$ are joined by z, hence all six lines of these points form connecting planes with the line z:

a and $\overline{a}$ go through the point A of the 3-point in ζ, hence they have a connecting plane.

Result: $a \cap \overline{a} = \pi$; similarly $b \cap \overline{b} = \varphi$ and $c \cap \overline{c} = \rho$. π, ρ, φ go through z.

The two 3-planes $\alpha \beta \gamma$ through E and $\overline{\alpha}\, \overline{\beta}\, \overline{\gamma}$ through $\overline{E}$ are "perspective" with respect to the plane ζ (ABC).

This (spatial) configuration contains

10 lines $(a, b, c, \overline{a}, \overline{b}, \overline{c}, p, q, r, z)$ and **10 planes** $(\alpha, \beta, \gamma, \overline{\alpha}, \overline{\beta}, \overline{\gamma}, \pi, \varphi, \rho, \zeta)$ and
5 points $(A, B, C, E, \overline{E})$.

9.9 Polar variations

Figures 9.13 and 9.14 show two polar sequences of variations of initial polar solids.

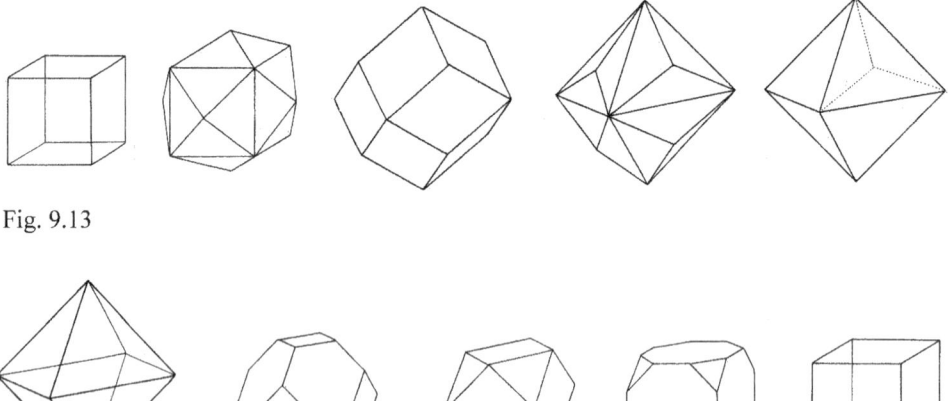

Fig. 9.13

Fig 9.14

In 9.13 four-edged pyramids grow out of the faces of the cube (hexahedron, A); at B a pyramidal cube is formed. When the height of the pyramids increases to half the cube's height a rhombic dodecahedron (C) is produced. Its three-edged vertices are made flatter and a pyramidal octahedron (D) is formed. The octahedron is the final transformation.

The polar transformations are shown in 9.14. Cutting off the octahedron's vertices produces a truncated octahedron (B). When the depth of the cut at each vertex reaches a quarter of the height of the octahedron, a cuboctahedron results (C). Its three-sided faces move outwards and a truncated cube is formed (D); the hexahedron (E) is the final metamorphosis.

10 The perspective cube

Two 4-points in different planes with a common horizon line (again the 2nd diagonals of both 4-points meet in the same point T – compare Figure 7.2).

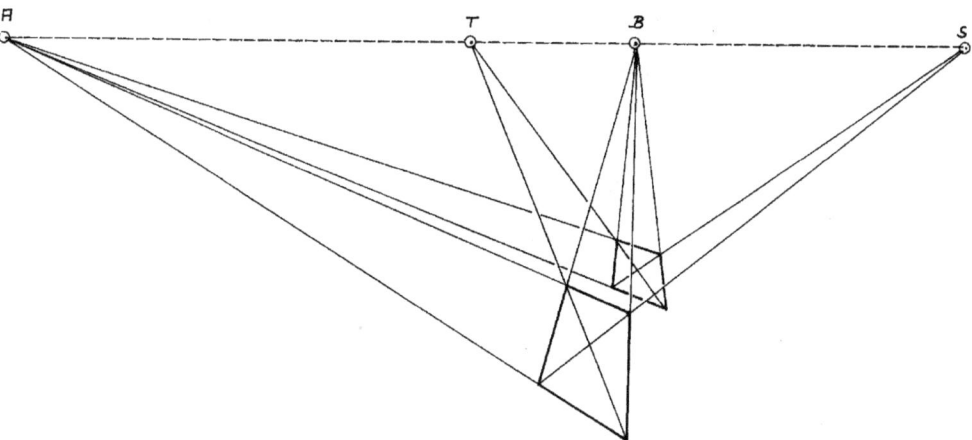

Figure 10.1

We connect corresponding vertices of the 4-points and obtain a three-dimensional form – a perspective cube. The new edges of the solid meet in one point C.

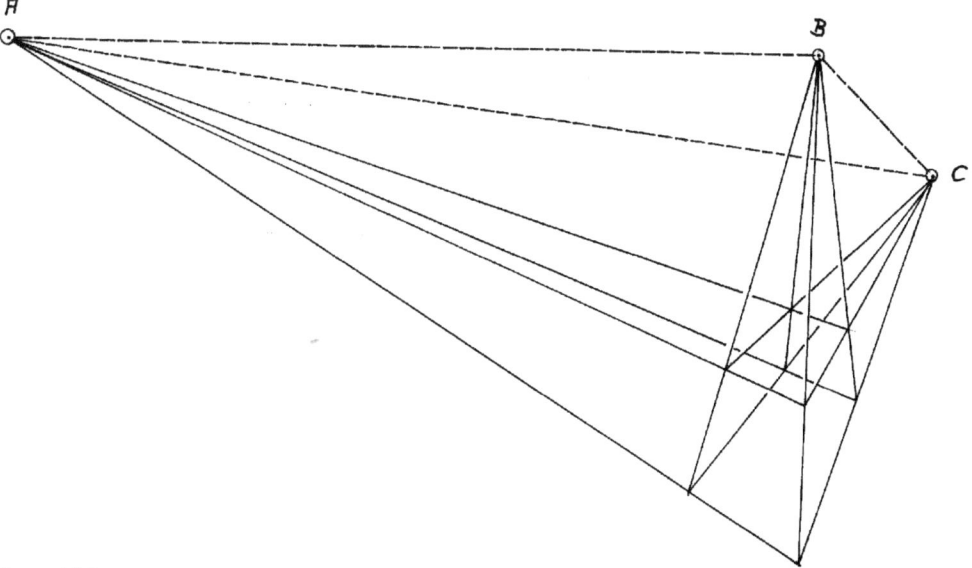

Figure 10.2

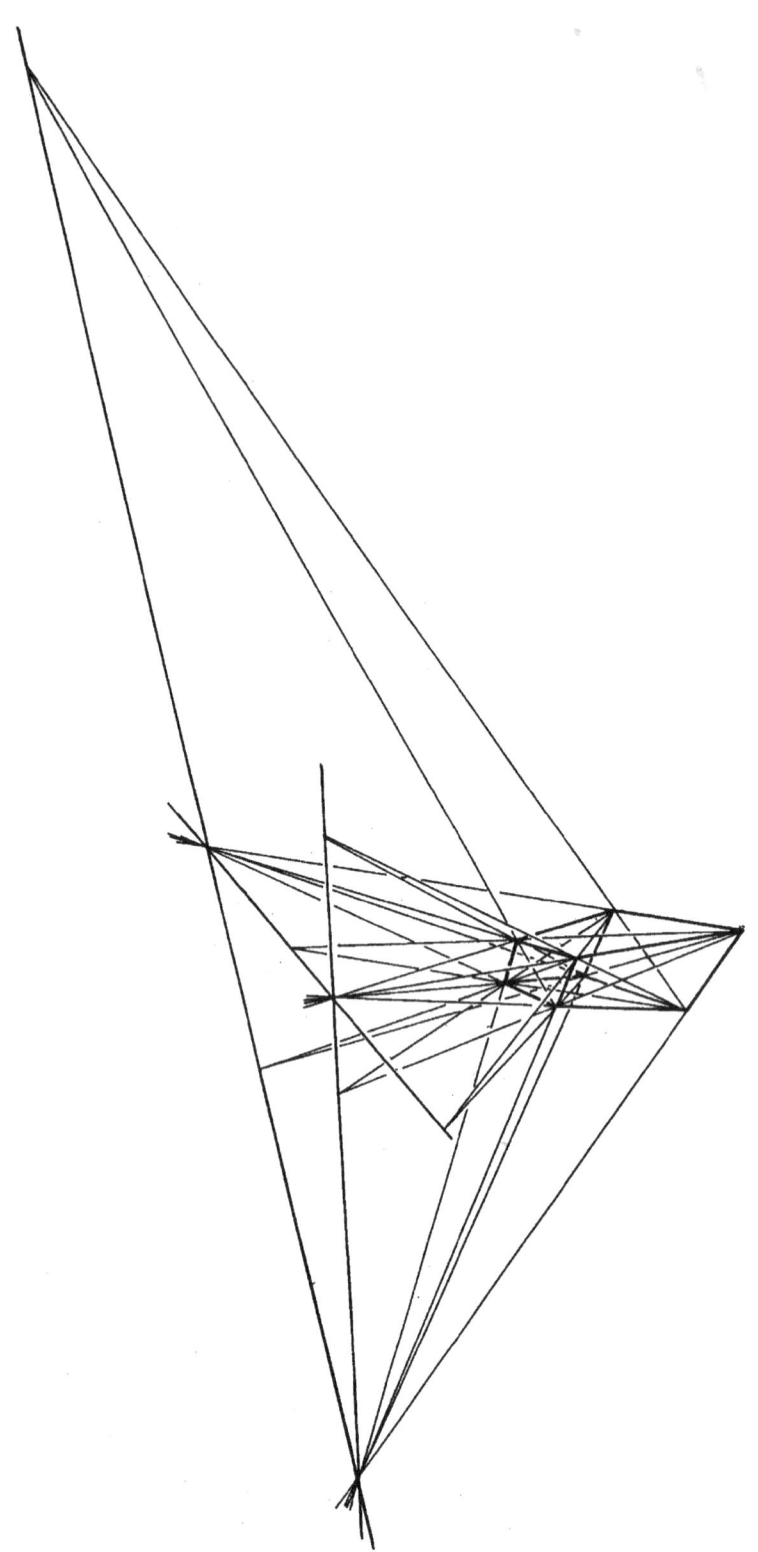

Figure 10.3

About Figures 10.2 and 10.3:

Lines in point *C* form sides of the cube, just as do lines in *A* and *B*. The three times four edge-lines originate in these three points. This form has (apart from the lengths of the edges and the right-angles between them) all the properties of a cube: 12 edges, 8 vertices and 6 faces. The three edge-forming points A, B, C form a 3rd plane which, like the two planes containing the 4-points, goes through the horizon line. Two planes also go from each of the other two sides of 3-point *ABC* to produce the hexahedron's faces. The eight vertices of the form in space result from the interweaving of the 12 lines and six planes originating in the 3-point. Four faces converge in the new point *C*, and even the diagonals of these four faces will meet in pairs in the appropriate sides of the 3-point if the figure is drawn accurately! In each side of the 3-point the diagonals form, together with two vertices of the 3-point, *four harmonic points* (Fig. 10.3 – compare with Fig. 10.1).

The form-creating elements (point, line, plane) are harmonically interwoven. We see that the entire form proceeds from the 3-point *ABC*. The 3-point is as it were the form's fundamental source (Fig. 10.2 and 10.4).

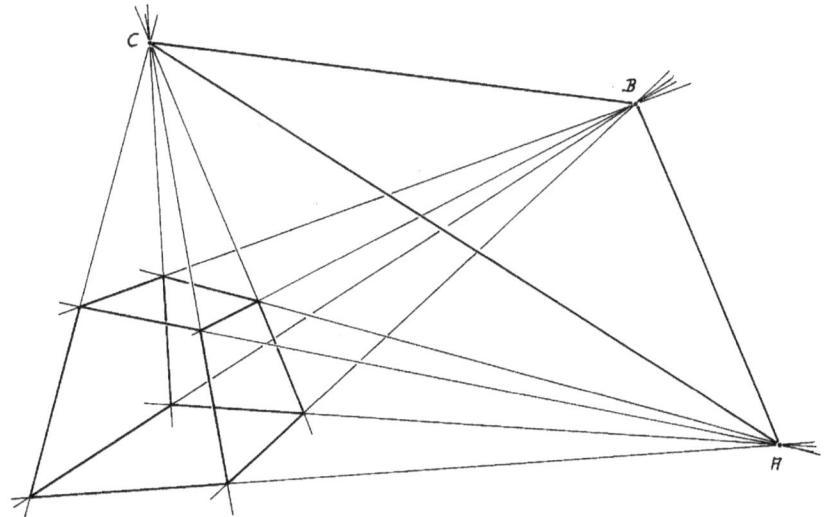

Figure 10.4: The perspective cube and the 3-point *ABC* which forms it.

Let's imagine that the plane of 3-point *ABC*, the «archetypal plane», moves and picture in our minds how the solid form changes as a result!

If we let the «archetypal plane» become the plane at infinity, then our general («perspective») cube takes on metrical properties: edges and faces become parallel (as for example in the parallelepiped of feldspar crystals) and in a special case of the right-angle, the cube is produced (Figures 10.5 to 10.7).

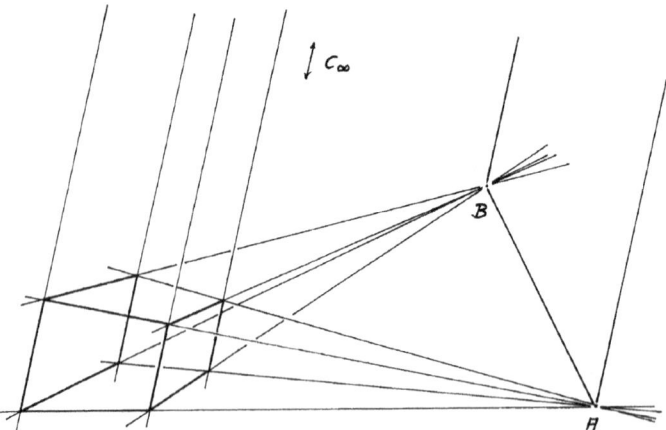

Figure 10.5: As 10.4 but $C \to C_\infty$

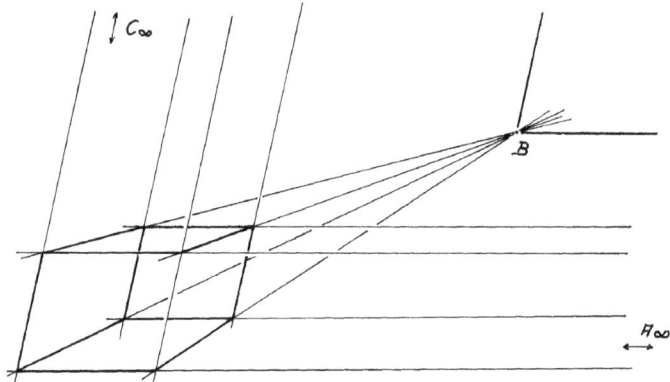

Figure 10.6: As 10.5 but $A \to A_\infty$ as well

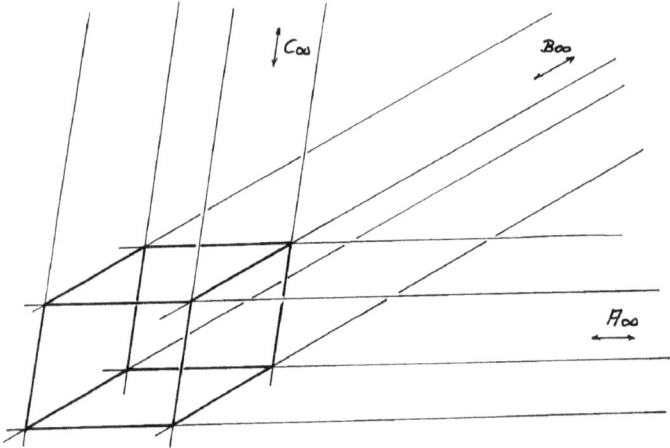

Figure 10.7: As 10.6 but $B \to B_\infty$ as well

11 The tetrahedron as 4-plane in space

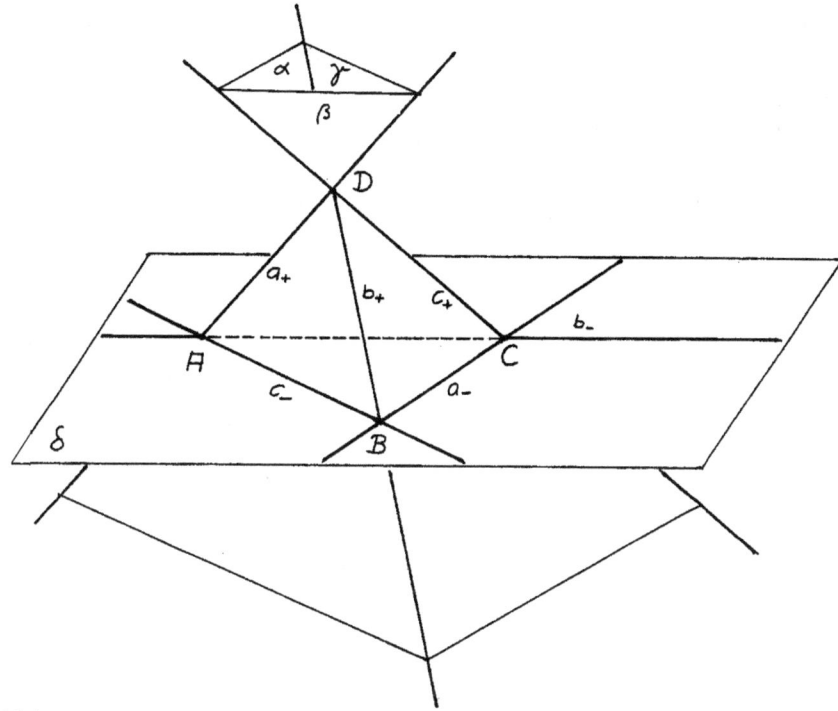

Figure 11.1

In general 4 points A, B, C, D in space form, with their 6 connecting lines (a_+, b_+, c_+, a_-, b_-, c_-), 4 connecting planes ($\alpha, \beta, \gamma, \delta$). The connecting lines form the edges of a (generally non-regular) tetrahedron.

Polarizing this gives:

Generally 4 planes $\alpha, \beta, \gamma, \delta$ form, with their 6 lines of intersection (a_+, b_+, c_+, a_-, b_-, c_-), 4 points of intersection (A, B, C, D); the lines of intersection form the edges of a tetrahedron.

Since the same object results in both cases, the tetrahedron can be regarded as a fundamental spatial form (in 9.5 we described the tetrahedron as self-polar). It is a harmoniously balanced object, complete in itself. It offers no opportunity for further construction.

12 The complete hexahedron

Suppose we choose a point E in the interior of the tetrahedron $ABCD$ with edges a_+, b_+, c_+ and a_-, b_-, c_- (see Fig. 12.1). Then the lines joining E with the tetrahedron's vertices intersect the respective opposite planes of the tetrahedron, and we obtain a hexahedron with the 6 planes $\alpha_1, \alpha_2, \beta_1, \beta_2, \gamma_1, \gamma_2$. The form consisting of three pairs of planes, 8 vertices and 12 edges we call a

simple hexahedron.

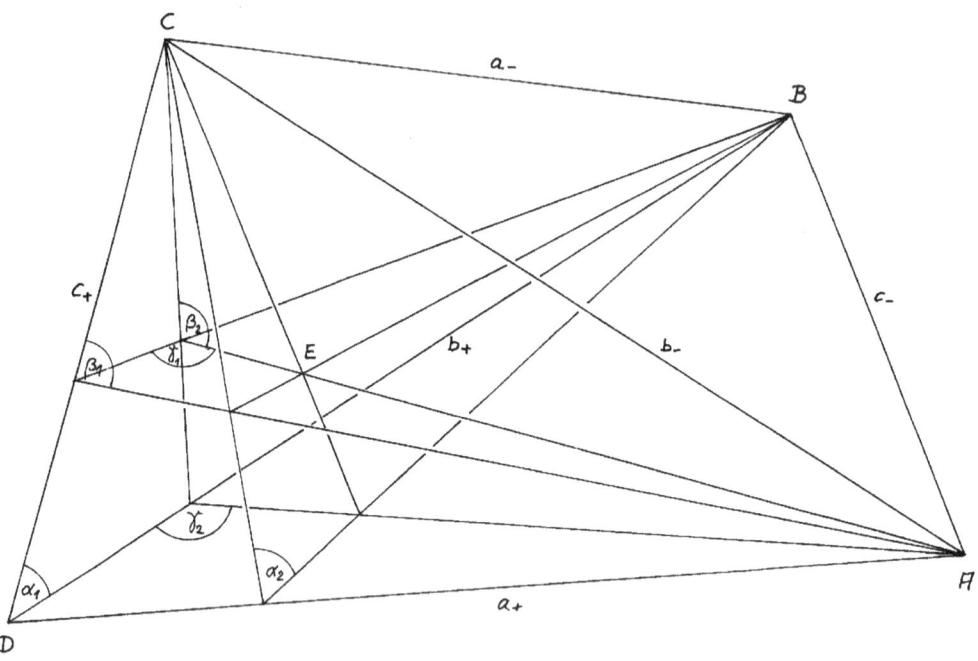

Figure 12.1 The simple hexahedron

If we now draw the four cross-lines (spatial diagonals) then any pair of these cross-lines forms a cross-plane. 2 such cross-planes go through each of the points A, B, C, D. They all belong to a bundle whose bearer is the "middle point" M (Figure 12.2). This

complete hexahedron

consists of:

12 points	12 + 1 faces	16 + 3 lines
8 vertices	6 faces	12 edges
A, B, C	6 cross-planes	4 cross-lines
middle point M	plane $\delta = ABC$	a_-, b_-, c_-

In Figure 12.3 a complete hexahedron is drawn. We recognize the 3 points (unfilled circles drawn green) through each of which go four edges. 2 opposite faces go through each of the sides (shown dashed) of the 3-point. Each of the four cross-lines intersects the plane δ of the 3-point in a point (drawn black). These 4 points are the basic vertices of a complete 4-point in the plane δ. The 6 sides of the complete 4-point are the lines of intersection of the cross-planes with δ; the vertices of the extra 3-point are green. Pairs of diagonals in opposite faces of the hexahedron meet in points (drawn violet) in the sides of the extra 3-point. These 6 points are the vertices of a complete 4-side that has its extra 3-side (red) in common with the 4-point (black points) mentioned (compare the fundamental harmonic configuration in Fig. 7.6).

The hexahedron is thus linked with a fundamental harmonic configuration in its plane δ.

Note: The colors of points and lines in Fig. 12.3 relate to the colors used in Chapter 7 (see the Note there). The structure of Fig. 12.2 too is revealed by the coloring: a_- orange, b_- violet, c_- green. The edges through A (TE, RS, PN, DL) yellow, the edges through B blue, the edges through C brown, the four cube diagonals (cross-lines through point M) red. The corresponding coloring of the polar Figs. 13.1 and 13.2 is as follows: Edges a_+ orange, b_+ violet, c_+ green. The edges in the plane α ($\tau\varepsilon = C_2B_2$; $\rho\sigma = B_1C_2$; $\pi\nu = B_2C_1$; $\delta\lambda = C_1B_1$) yellow, in β blue, in γ brown, the 4 cross-lines (in plane μ) red.

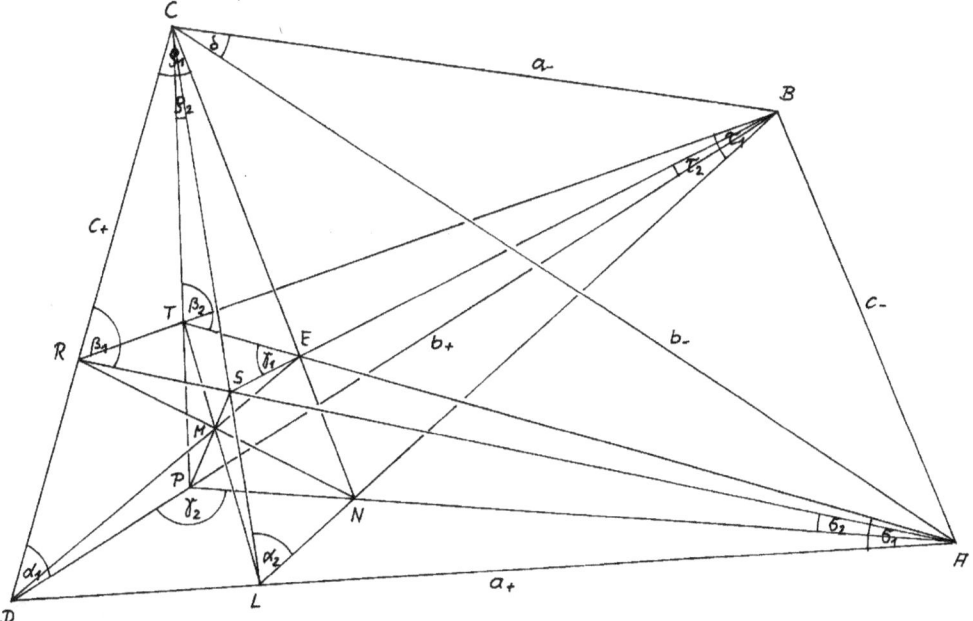

Figure 12.2 The complete hexahedron

If the plane δ is the limit plane δ_∞ and the directions A_∞, B_∞, C_∞ are mutually perpendicular, we obtain Figure 12.4.

Projective Geometry Karl-Friedrich Georg

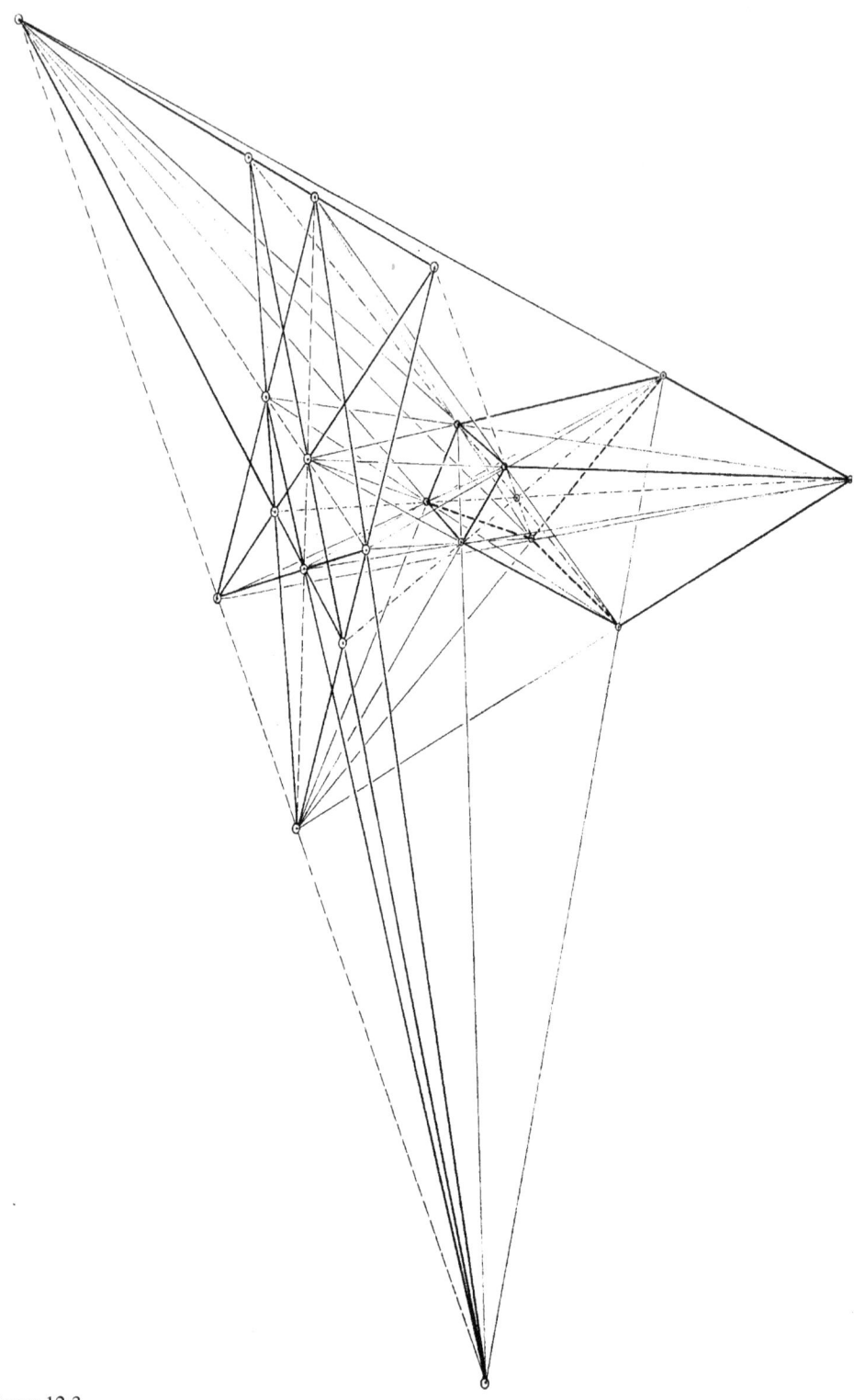

Figure 12.3

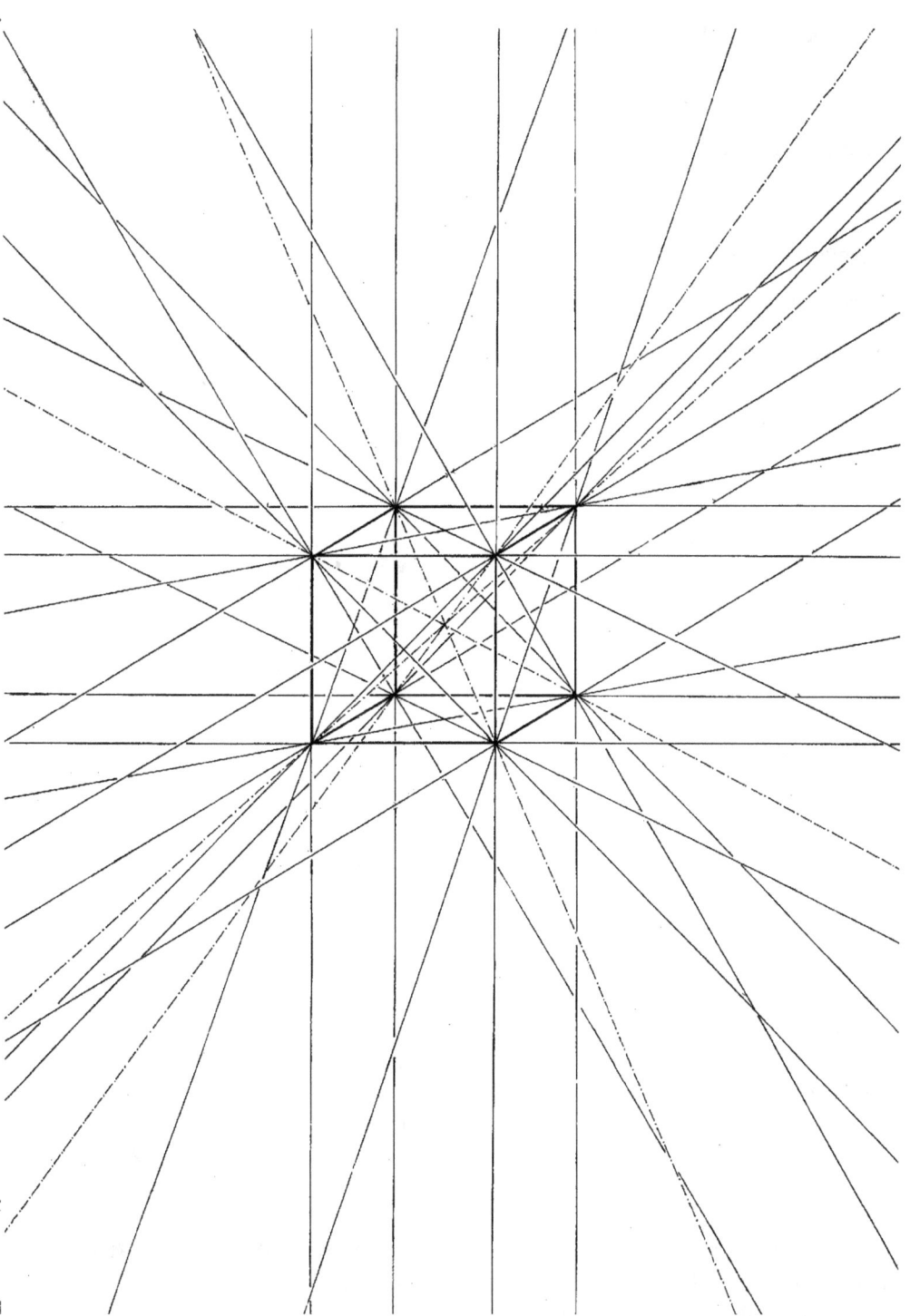

Figure 12.4

13 The complete octahedron

Before we polarize the complete hexahedron in order to obtain the complete octahedron, as a preliminary exercise we shall draw a simple octahedron as the form polar to the simple hexahedron.

The simple octahedron consists of

- 3 pairs of points
- 8 faces, and
- 12 edges.

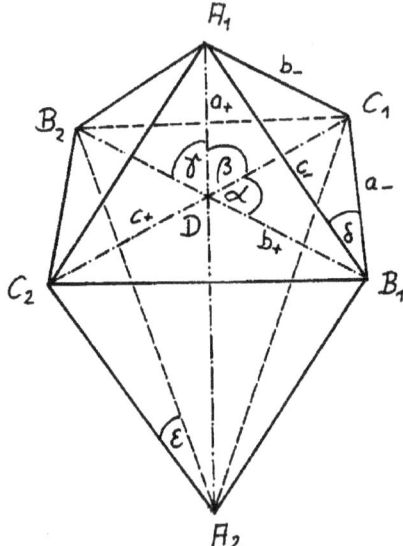

Figure 13.1

To obtain the form polar to the complete hexahedron we start from the tetrahedron $\alpha\beta\gamma\delta$ and carry out the polar «disruption» by adding an external 5th plane ε. In the edges a_+, b_+ and c_+ of the bundle D are the three pairs of points A_1, A_2 and B_1, B_2 and C_1, C_2. Any two of these pairs have a plane in common, namely α and β and γ. The 6 points also have 3 times four connecting lines which form the 12 edges of an octahedron. And the 6 points $(A_1, A_2, B_1, B_2, C_1, C_2)$ determine 8 connecting planes, the faces of the octahedron, as well.

We also consider the 4 cross-lines, the intersection lines of opposite faces of the octahedron (Figure 13.2). Pairs of these cross-lines form a cross-point (in the point of intersection of two opposite edges). There are 2 cross-points in each of the planes α, β, γ (S_1, S_2 in α; T_1, T_2 in β; R_1, R_2 in γ). Joining the 6 cross-points in threes produces the 4 cross-lines, which all belong to the same plane, the «middle plane» μ.

This **complete octahedron** consists of:

12 planes	12 + 1 points	16 + 3 lines
8 faces of the octahedron	6 vertices	12 edges
α, β, γ	6 cross-points	4 cross-lines
the middle plane μ	$D = \alpha\beta\gamma$	a_+, b_+, c_+

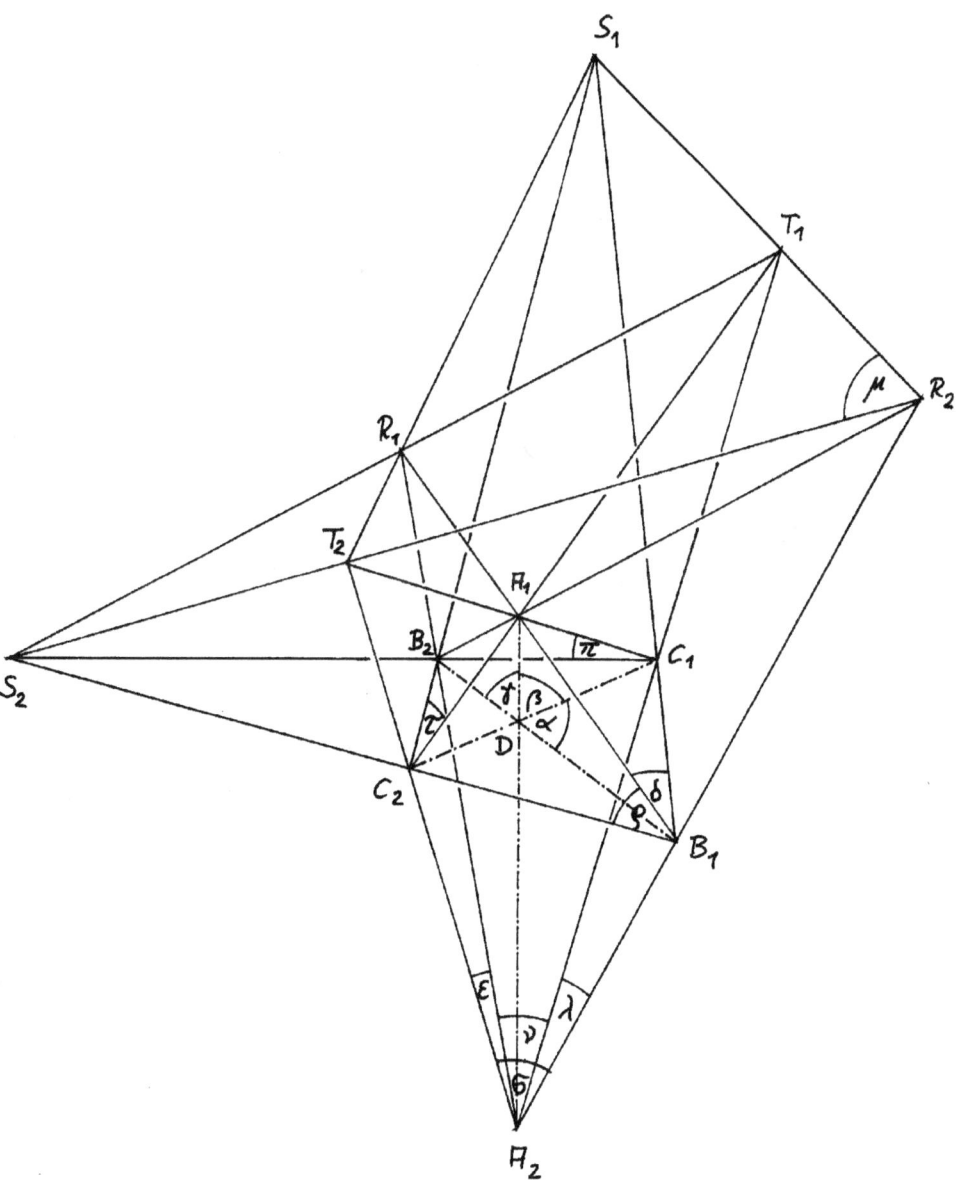

Figure 13.2 The complete octahedron

The polar correspondence is as follows:

Hexahedron	Octahedron
The constitutive 3-side in the plane δ with sides a_-, b_-, c_- and vertices A, B, C.	The constitutive 3-edge in the point D with sides a_+, b_+, c_+ and faces α, β, γ.
The 3 pairs of opposite faces (α_1, α_2), (β_1, β_2), (γ_1, γ_2).	The 3 pairs of opposite points (A_1, A_2), (B_1, B_2), (C_1, C_2).
The 4 pairs of opposite vertices (D, E), (L, T), (N, R), (P, S).	The 4 pairs of opposite faces (δ, ε), (λ, τ), (ν, ρ), (π, σ).
The 3 4-edges in A, B and C.	The 3 4-sides in α, β and γ.
The 6 diagonal planes (connecting planes of opposite edges in the above 4-edges): $\sigma_1, \sigma_2, \tau_1, \tau_2, \rho_1, \rho_2$.	The 6 "diagonal points" (intersection points of opposite sides of the above 4-sides): $S_1, S_2, T_1, T_2, R_1, R_2$.
The 4 hexahedron diagonals (cross-lines) through the middle point M produced by intersections of triples of the 6 diagonal planes.	The 4 «octahedron diagonals» (cross-lines) in the middle plane μ produced by joining the 6 «diagonal vertices» in threes.
We call this structure the complete hexahedron.	We call this structure the complete octahedron.

These two polar forms can also be brought together as follows. Suppose we choose the 6 middle points of the faces of the hexahedron as the 6 vertices of an octahedron. Then the «constitutive 3-side» of the hexahedron (a_-, b_-, c_-) and the «constitutive 3-edge» of the octahedron (a_+, b_+, c_+) augment each other to form a *tetrahedron*. M and D coincide, as do μ and δ (Fig. 13.3).

Fig. 13.3

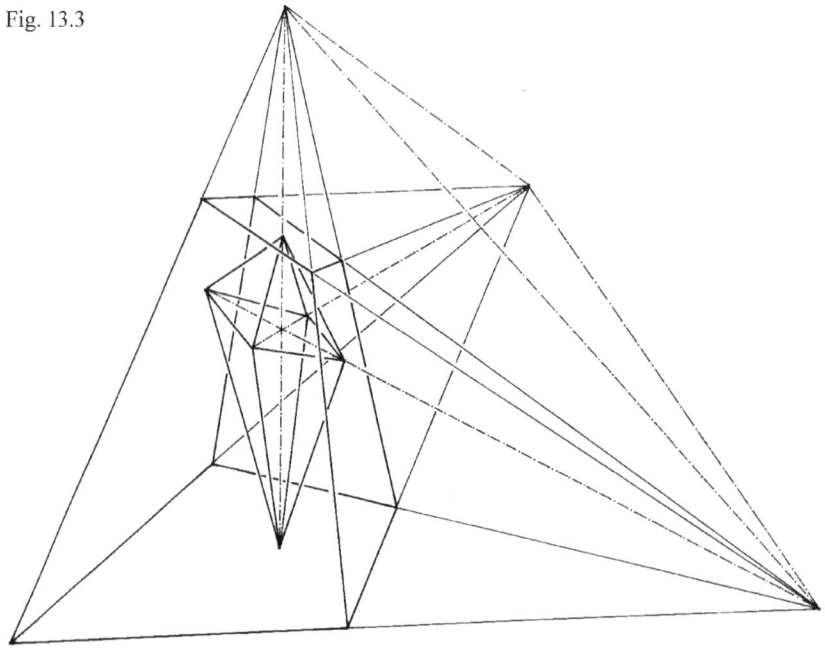

14 The fundamental structure

Suppose in the complete hexahedron we disregard the plane δ, likewise the lines a_-, b_-, c_- (the constitutive 3-side), but keep the points A, B, C. What remains is a form consisting of 12 points, 12 planes and 16 lines, of   the 8 vertices, the points A, B, C and the «middle point» M,

the 6 faces and the 6 cross-planes,

the 12 edges and the 4 cross-lines (Fig. 14.1).

Suppose in the complete octahedron we disregard the point D, likewise the lines a_+, b_+, c_+ (the constitutive 3-edge), but keep the planes α, β, γ. What remains is a form consisting of 12 planes, 12 points and 16 lines, of   the 8 faces, the planes α, β, γ and the «middle plane» μ,

the 6 vertices and the 6 cross-points,

the 12 edges and the 4 cross-lines (Fig. 14.2).

These two forms prove to be configured in exactly the same way.

4 lines and 6 planes of the form go through each of the 12 points, there are 4 lines and 6 points of the form in each of the 12 planes, each of the 16 lines contains 3 points and 3 planes of the form.

The form is self-polar!

That Figures 14.1 and 14.2 represent the same thing is shown by Figures 14.3 and 14.4. Figure 14.4 is the result of rotating Figure 14.2 clockwise through 90°. Conversely, in Figure 14.3 we can see an octahedron with opposite vertices M and C.

This form is called the REYE configuration after its discoverer; it's also called the *fundamental structure of space*.

> The fundamental structure is the self-polar form *common to the complete hexahedron and the complete octahedron*.

Like in the Desargues configuration where each of the points can be interpreted as Z, in the fundamental structure each of the 12 points can be regarded as the middle point M of a hexahedron, and each of the planes as the middle plane μ of an octahedron:

> The fundamental structure contains both 12 hexahedrons and 12 octahedrons.

Projective Geometry   *Karl-Friedrich Georg*

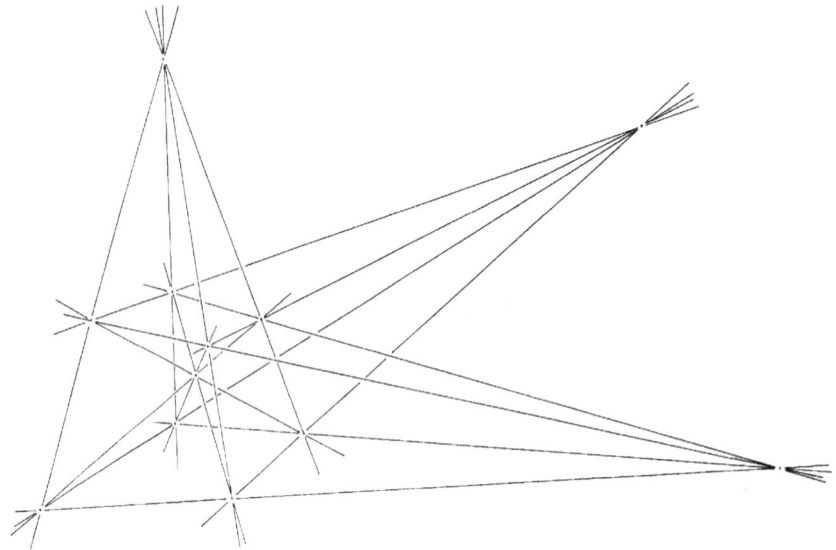

Figure 14.1

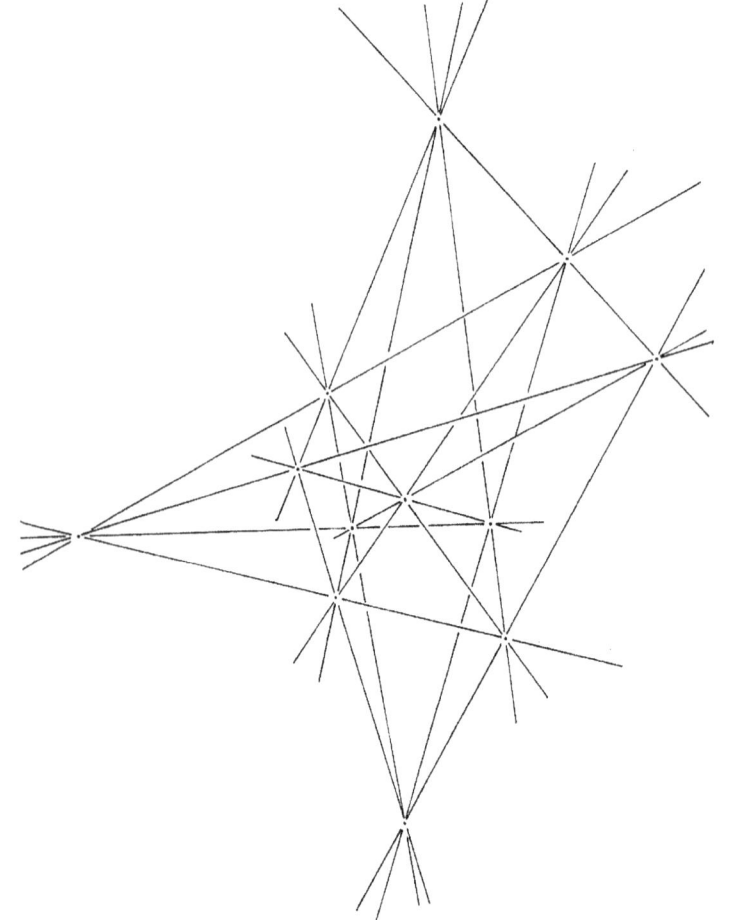

Figure 14.2

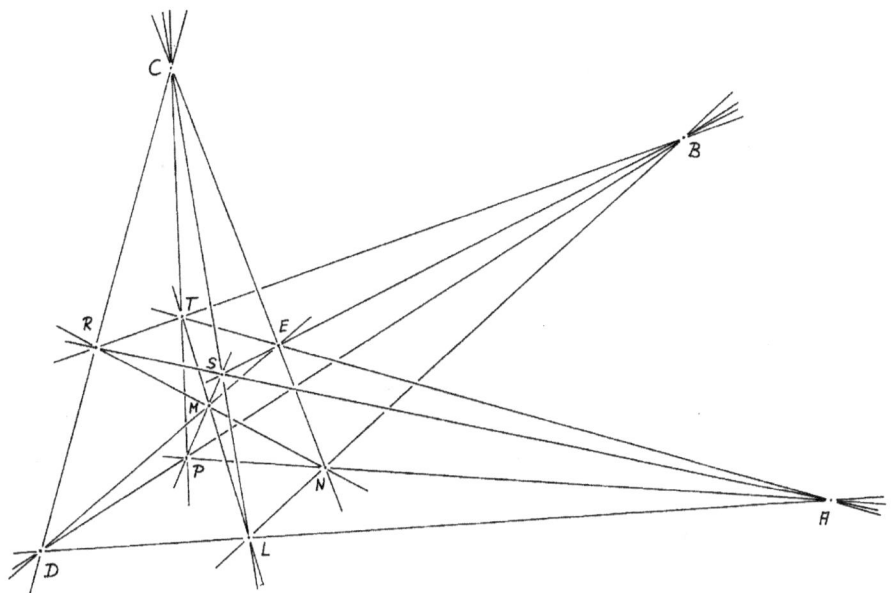

Figure 14.3

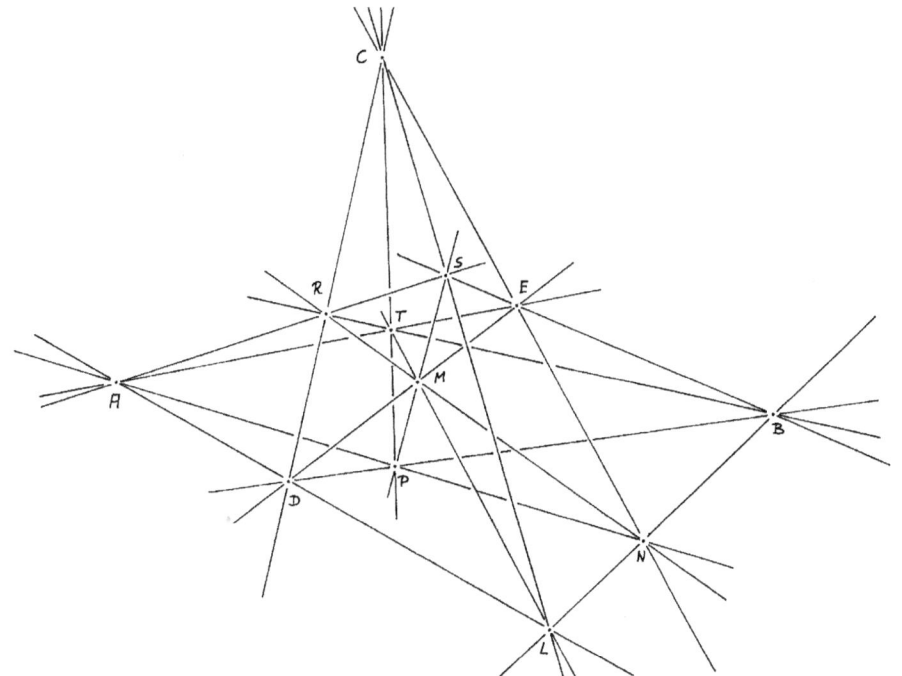

Figure 14.4

Exercises

1. Taking Figure 14.4 as basis, let the point *M* take up all 12 possible positions. Label the hexahedron vertices 1 to 8 in accordance with the adjoining sketch. Taking Fig. 14.4 as model, draw in each time the hexahedron's edges (blue) and cross-lines (red) (Figures 14.5 - 14.16).

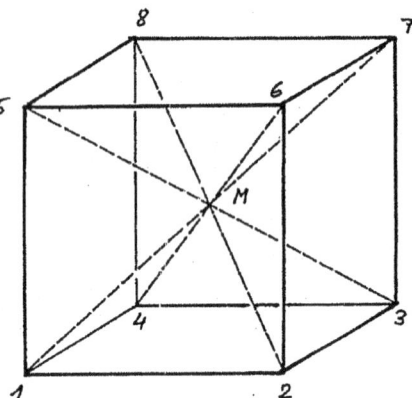

2. Taking Figure 14.4 as basis, an octahedron with vertices 1 to 6 can be drawn in accordance with the adjoining sketch, with the associated middle plane μ, in 12 different ways. In the model draw in the edges blue, the cross-lines red (Figures 14.17 - 14.28).

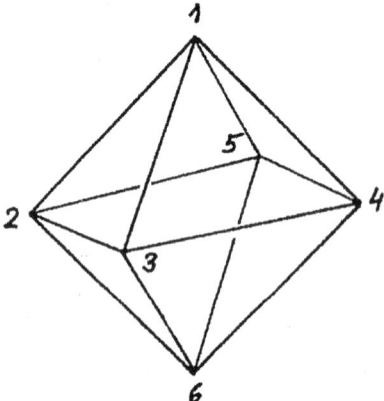

As illustrations of the exercises, two of the 12 possibilities are shown here (the blue lines are drawn as thick lines, the red as dashed lines). In Figures 14.6 and 14.10 (of the above series) the hexahedron's interior stretches over the limit plane of space and in Figure 14.20 the same goes for the interior (in the usual sense) of the octahedron.

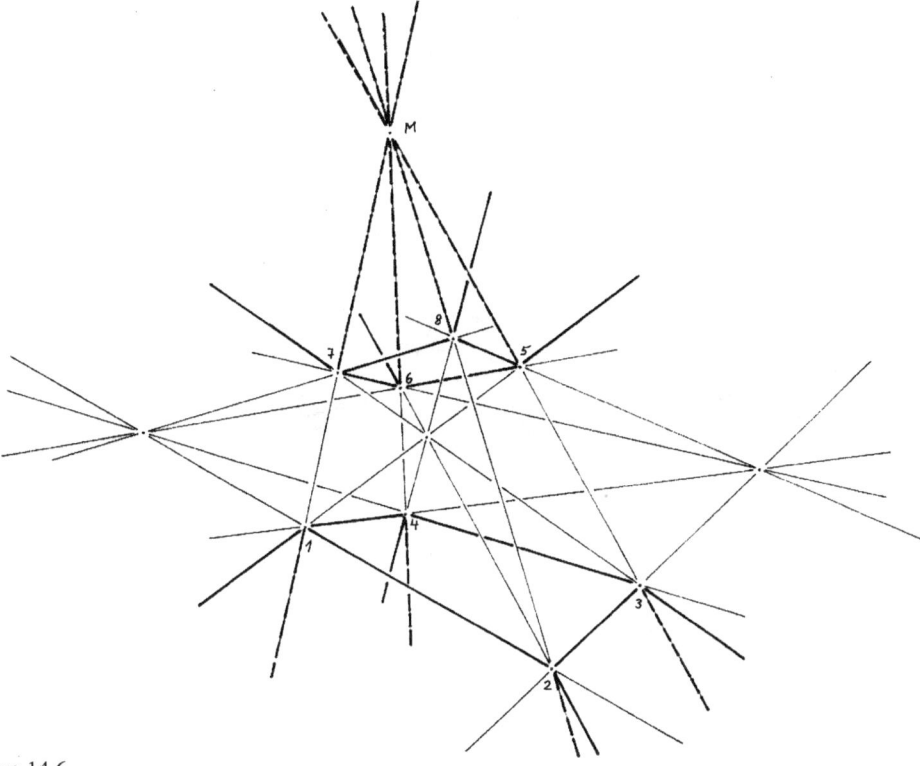

Figure 14.6

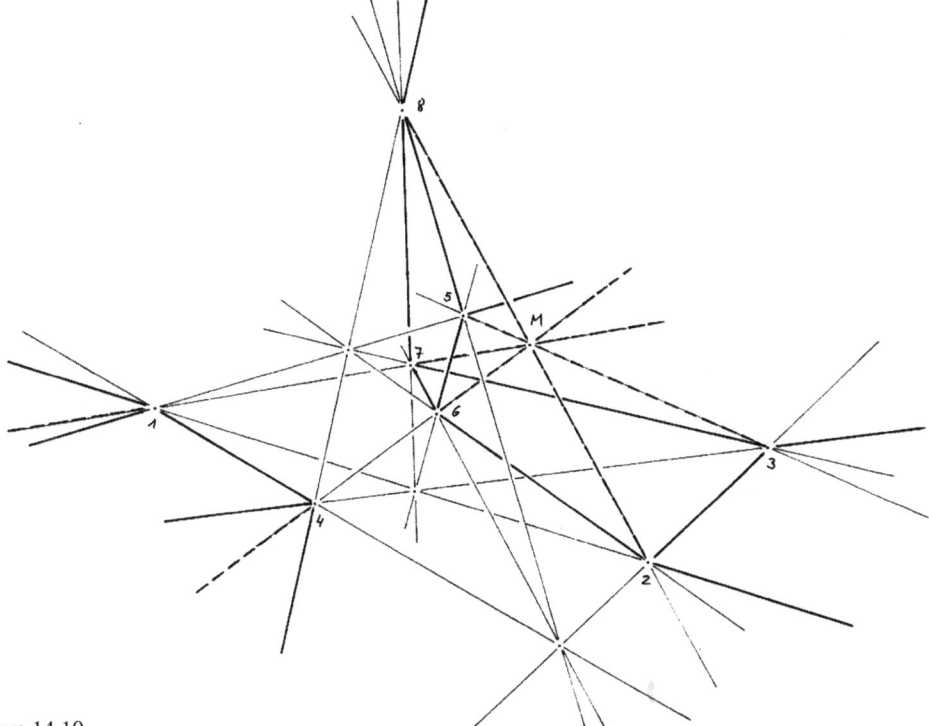

Figure 14.10

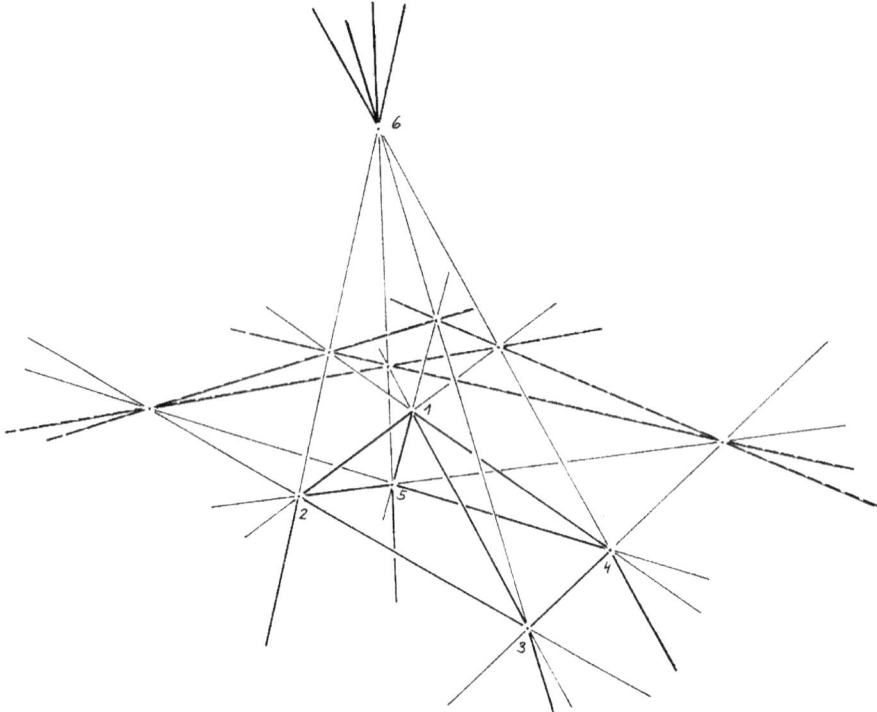

Figure 14.17

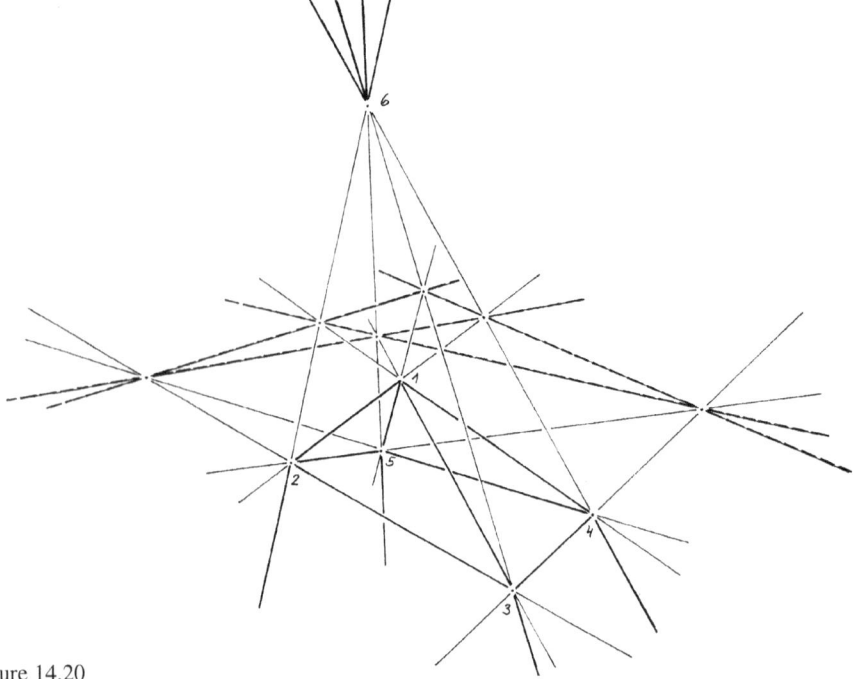

Figure 14.20

15 The conic section in the 5-point

In general, any five lines determine a five-pointed star. Depending on how these five lines are arranged, we can obtain the various conic sections.

First some important basic concepts:

1. If two point ranges a and b are projected centrally onto each other from a center Z, we say the point ranges are **perspectively** related. The relationship or mapping brought about between the ranges is called a *perspectivity*. The points $B_1, B_2, B_3, \ldots$ of b correspond perspectively to the points $A_1, A_2, A_3, \ldots$ of a (Fig. 15.1).

   If two line pencils A and B are projected linearly onto each other from an axis z, we say the line pencils are **perspectively** related. The relationship or mapping brought about between the pencils is called a *perspectivity*. The lines $b_1, b_2, b_3, \ldots$ of B correspond perspectively to the lines $a_1, a_2, a_3, \ldots$ of A (Fig. 15.2).

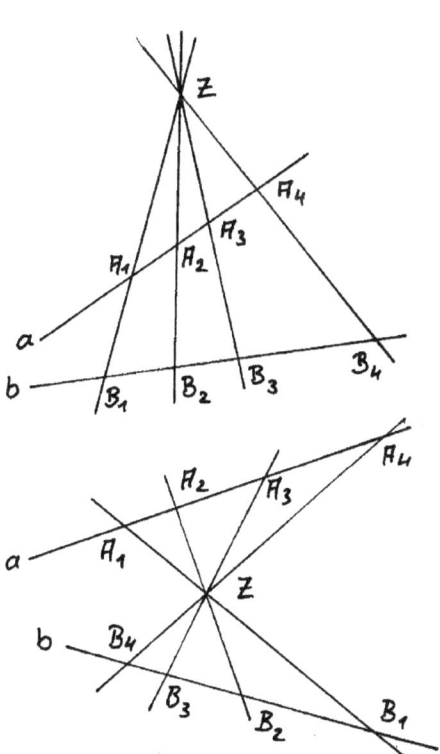

Figure 15.1

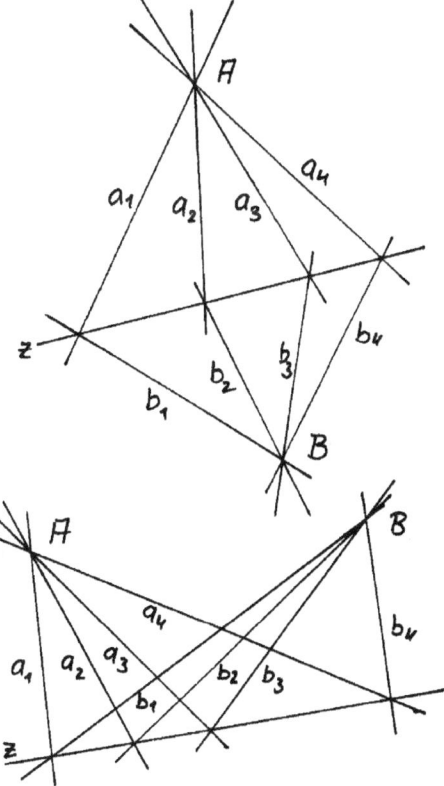

Figure 15.2

2. If a point range *a* is perspectively related to a point range *b* and the latter is perspectively related to a point range *c*, we say the point ranges *a* and *c* are **projectively** related. The relationship between *a* and *c* is called a *projectivity*. The points $A_1, A_2, A_3, \ldots$ of *a* and the points $C_1, C_2, C_3, \ldots$ of *c* correspond to each other projectively (Fig. 15.3).

If a line pencil *A* is perspectively related to a line pencil *B* and the latter is perspectively related to a line pencil *C*, we say the line pencils *A* and *C* are **projectively** related. The relationship between *A* and *C* is called a *projectivity*. The lines $a_1, a_2, a_3, \ldots$ of *A* and the lines $c_1, c_2, c_3, \ldots$ of *C* correspond to each other projectively (Fig. 15.4).

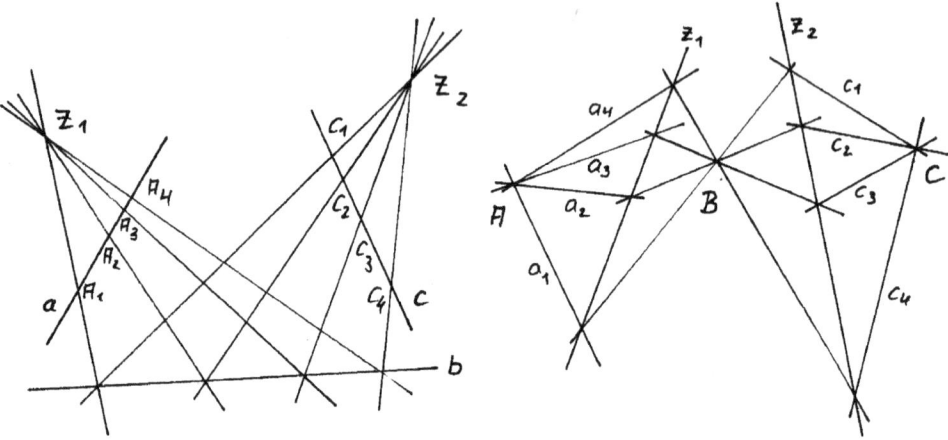

Figure 15.3　　　　　　　　　　　Figure 15.4

Construction of the ellipse:

Starting from the five-pointed star, connect the star's points round the outside so that the star is encompassed by the 5-side a', b', c', d', e'. In d' choose arbitrary points $P_1, P_2, P_3 \ldots$ and join these to E and C. Intersecting these connections with *e* and *c* respectively results in two projectively related point ranges in the latter lines. Projectively corresponding points $(E_1, E_2, E_3 \ldots$ and $C_1, C_2, C_3 \ldots)$ are connected. The connecting lines form the envelope of a curve. We repeat the same process starting from each of the other four sides a', b', c', e'. Between the 5 processes we obtain an ellipse inscribed in the five-pointed star (Figure 15.7).

We now dualize this construction by means of Figure 15.6:

Starting from the five-pointed star, intersect the star's lines round the inside so that the star surrounds the 5-point A', B', C', D', E'. In D' choose arbitrary lines $p_1, p_2, p_3 \ldots$ and intersect these with *e* and *c*. Connecting these intersections with *E* and *C* respectively results in two projectively related line pencils in the latter points. Projectively corresponding lines are intersected. The points of intersection form the arc of a curve. We repeat the same process starting from each of the other four points A', B', C', E'. And so we obtain an ellipse circumscribing the five-pointed star (Figure 15.8).

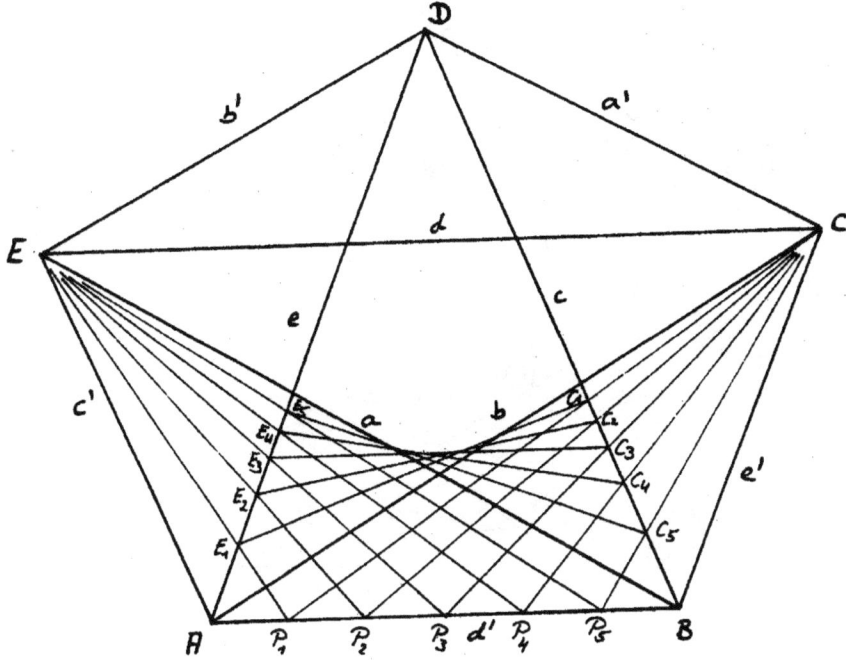

Figure 15.5

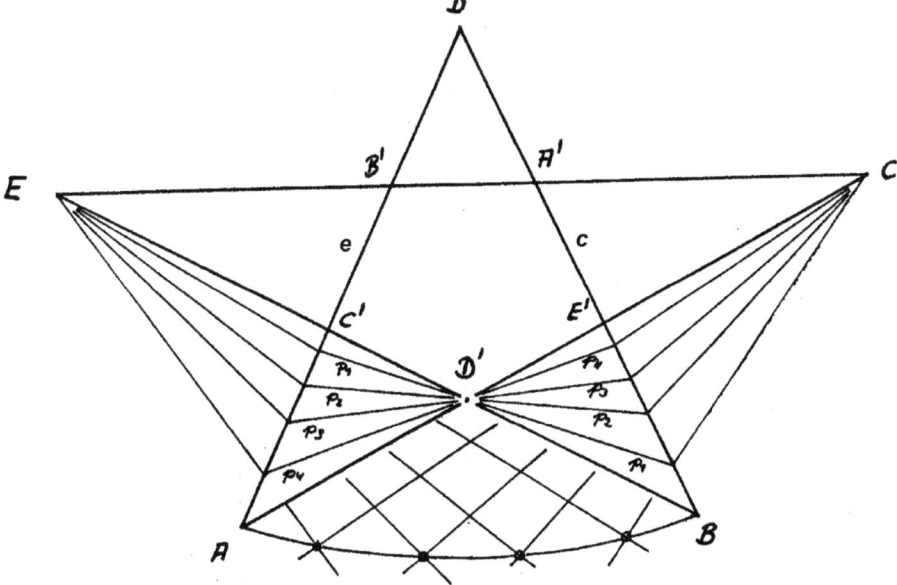

Figure 15.6

Thus two curves are associated with the five-pointed star, one constructed line-wise, the other point-wise.

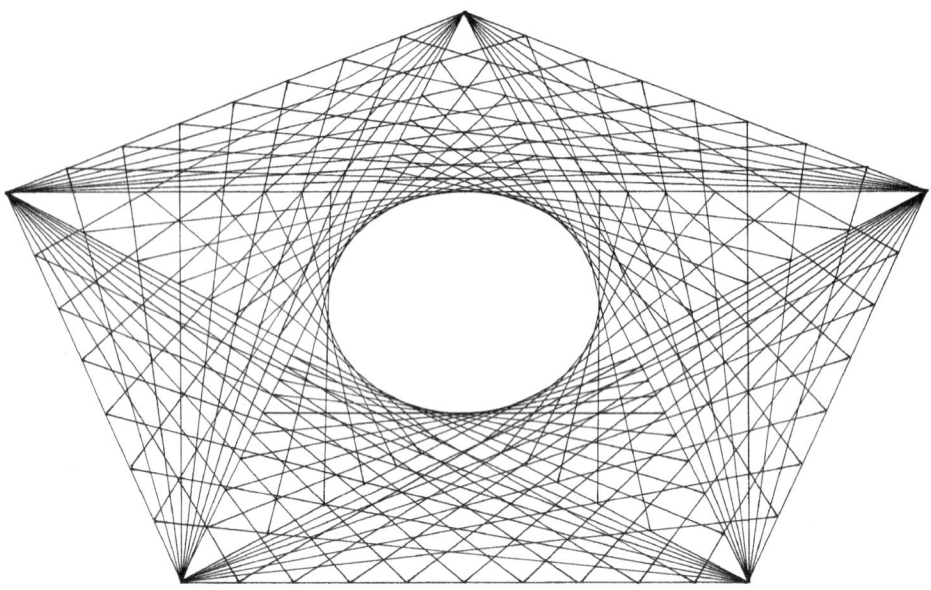

Figure 15.7

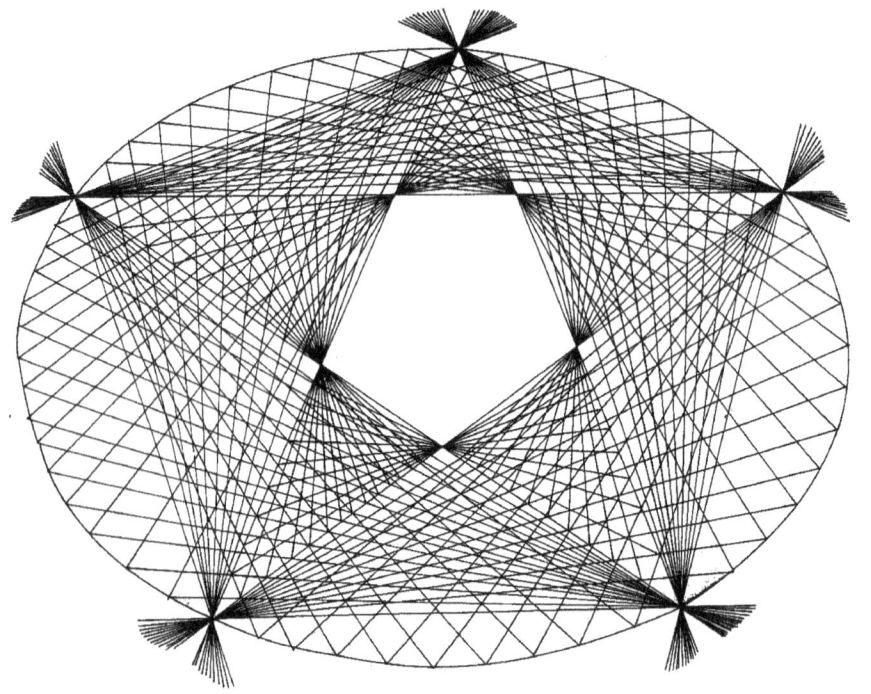

Figure 15.8

The positioning of the five lines (see Diagrams 1 to 3 below) determines which conic curve we obtain with the above-described construction, as follows:

	as inscribed curve	as circumscribing curve
in Diagram 1:	ellipse	hyperbola
in Diagram 2:	hyperbola	hyperbola
in Diagram 3:	parabola	hyperbola

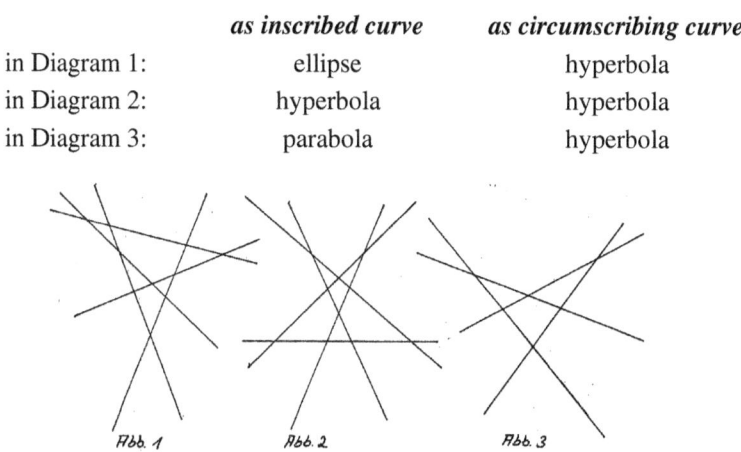

It is noteworthy that no circle is used anywhere in this construction: it is purely a matter of lines being intersected and points being connected. The curves are the outcome of a weaving between lines and points.

Aged 16 years, *Blaise Pascal* (1623–1662), the famous pupil of Desargues, lit upon the following theorem:

> If the points of a 6-point belong to a conic curve (so that the conic circumscribes the 6-point), then the points of intersection of opposite sides lie in a line (the Pascal line).

Not until 1806 was the dual theorem discovered by the 21-year-old *Charles Brianchon* (1785–1864):

> If the sides of a 6-side belong to a conic envelope (so that the 6-side surrounds the conic), then the lines joining the opposite vertices go through a point (the Brianchon point).

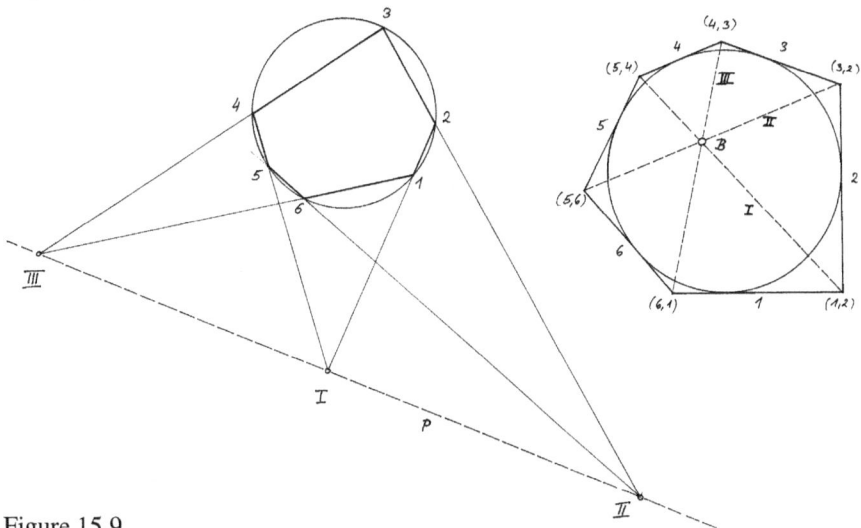

Figure 15.9

Using the theorems of Pascal and Brianchon we can look at our five-pointed star constructions of the conic sections afresh:

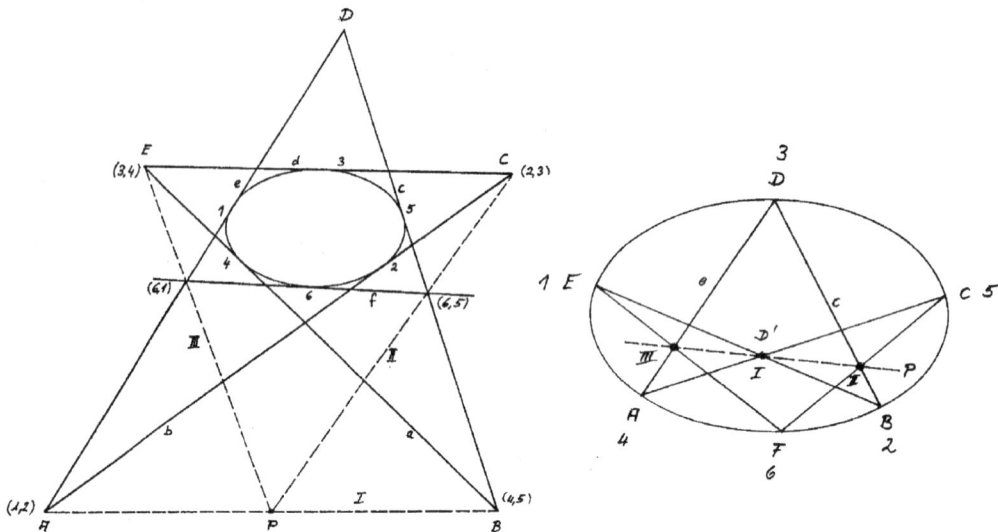

Figure 15.10

In the drawing on the left the point P at the bottom is the Brianchon point. If we let it move in line I, then line II sweeps through the pencil in C and line III though the pencil in E; the point ranges e and c are projectively related and f moves round on the ellipse.

In the drawing on the right p is the Pascal line. As p rotates about D', II moves along c and III along e. The line pencils C and E are projectively related and F moves round the ellipse.

These relationships explain the conic sections derived from the five-pointed star, and they can be the starting point for many interesting investigations into conics as well as curve forms in general.

Further related exercises:

Draw the Pascal line for the 6-point 1, 2, 3, 4, 5, 6 circumscribed by the conic (Figs. 15.11 and 15.12).

Karl-Friedrich Georg Projective Geometry

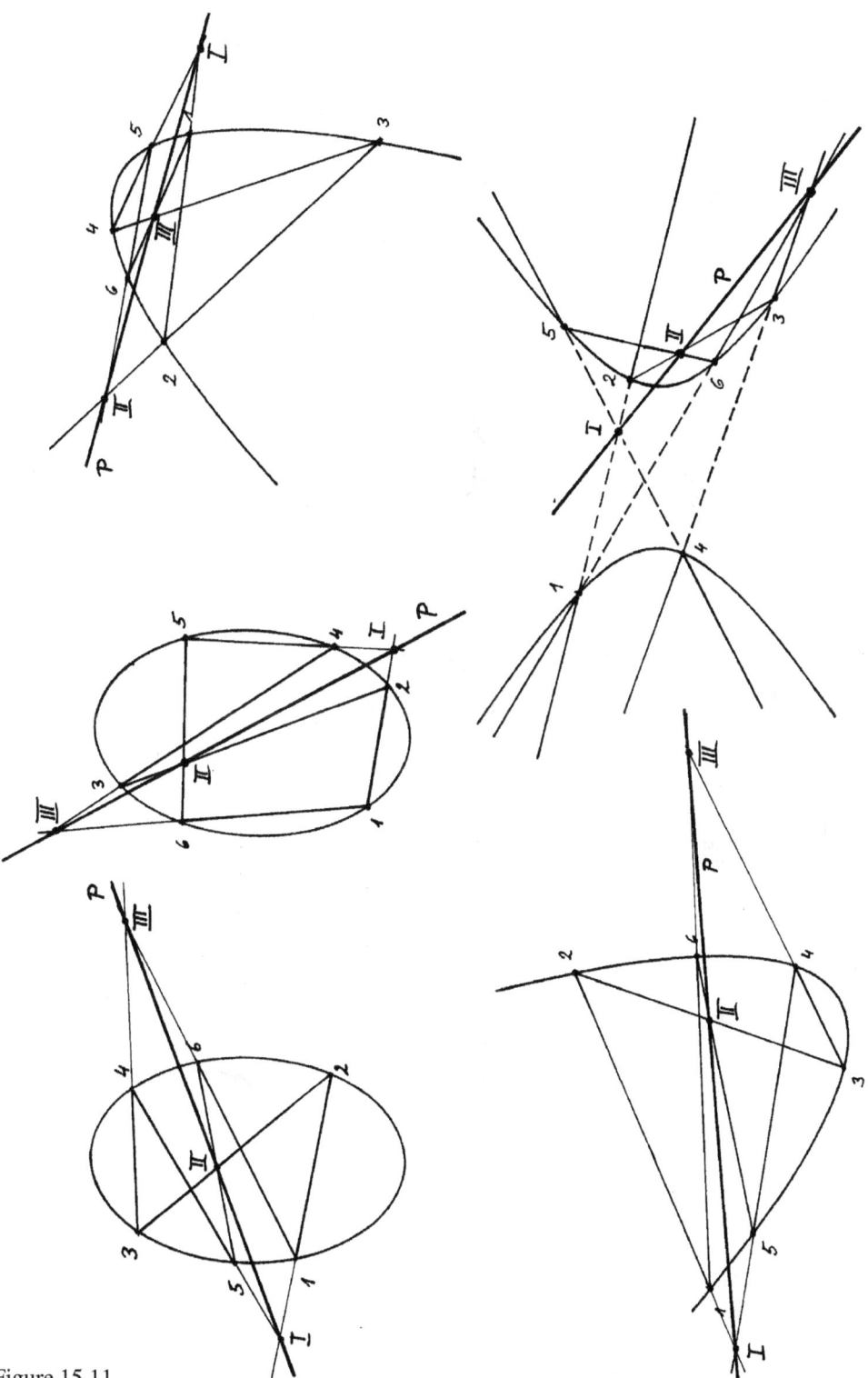

Figure 15.11

Projective Geometry

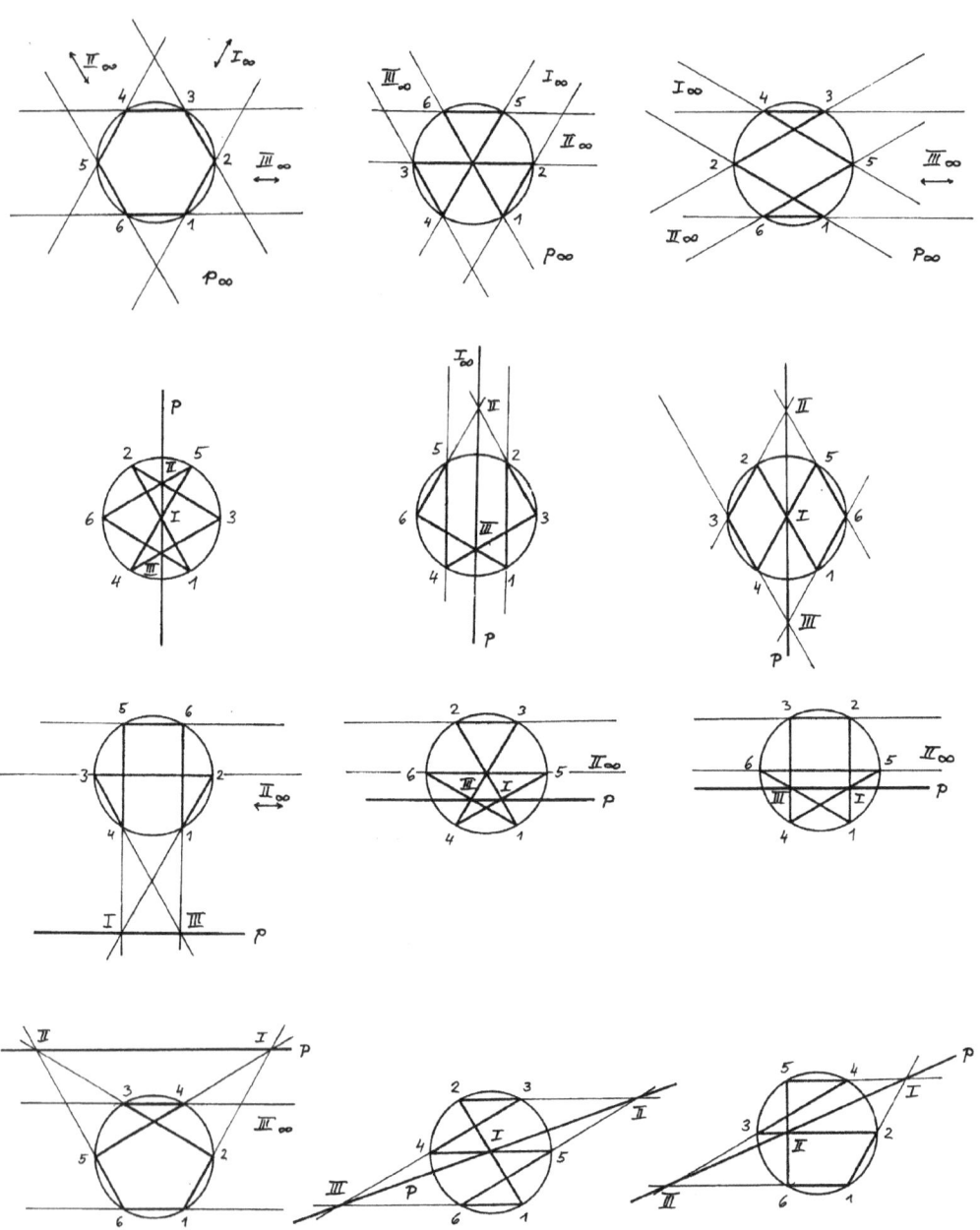

Figure 15.12

Draw in the Brianchon point in each case:

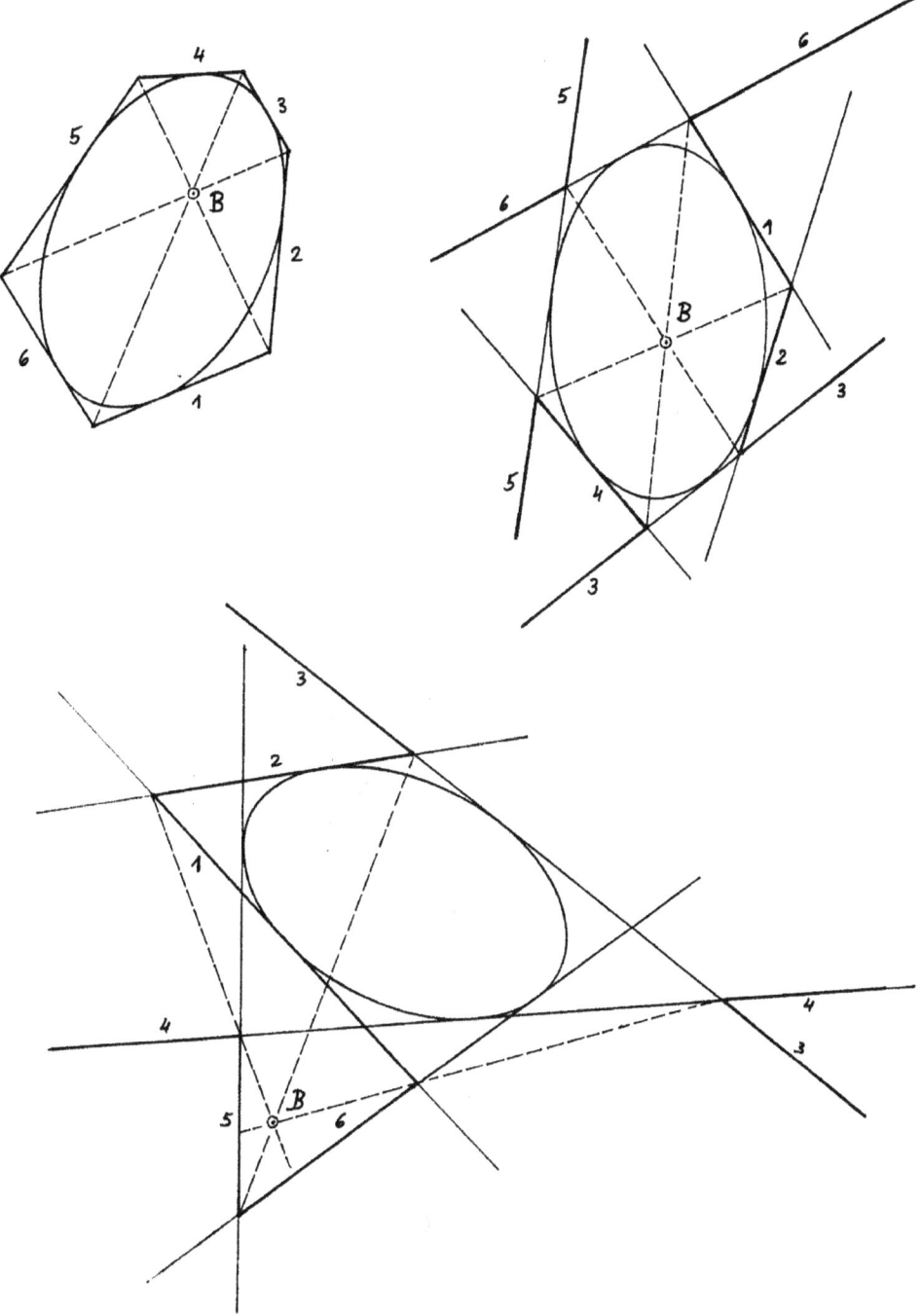

Figure 15.13

16 The conic section as central projection of the circle

(See Bernhard, Chapter 23)

If we centrally project a circle (radius r) we discover that:

$\quad$ with $\overline{ZZ'} > 2r$, the image curve is an ellipse (Figures 16.1 and 16.2)

$\quad$ with $\overline{ZZ'} = 2r$, the image curve is a parabola (Fig. 16.3)

$\quad$ with $\overline{ZZ'} < 2r$, the image curve is a hyperbola (Fig. 16.4)

The construction will be more accurate if tangents to the circle are projected along with the points. The image lines are then tangents to the image curve. In Figure 16.3 point 5 becomes a limit point and its tangent the limit line. In Figure 16.4, $\overline{ZZ'} = r$, which means the horizontal diameter 7–3 of the circle becomes the limit line of the image plane, and the tangents in 7 and 3 become asymptotes of the hyperbola, since their points of contact are projected onto limit points.

Taking these three cases together as a whole, we see that:

The parabola can be understood as an ellipse which touches the line at infinity, and the hyperbola as an ellipse which goes through infinity twice. The connection between the curves now becomes clear.

Project the circle from Z onto the horizontal plane.

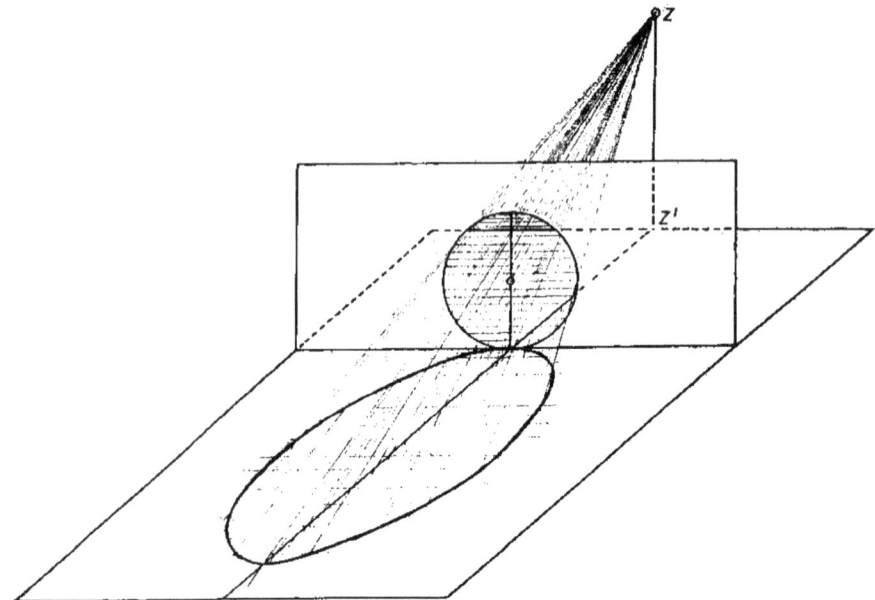

Figure 16.1

Project the circle from Z_1 onto the horizontal plane with the help of the two circumscribed squares.

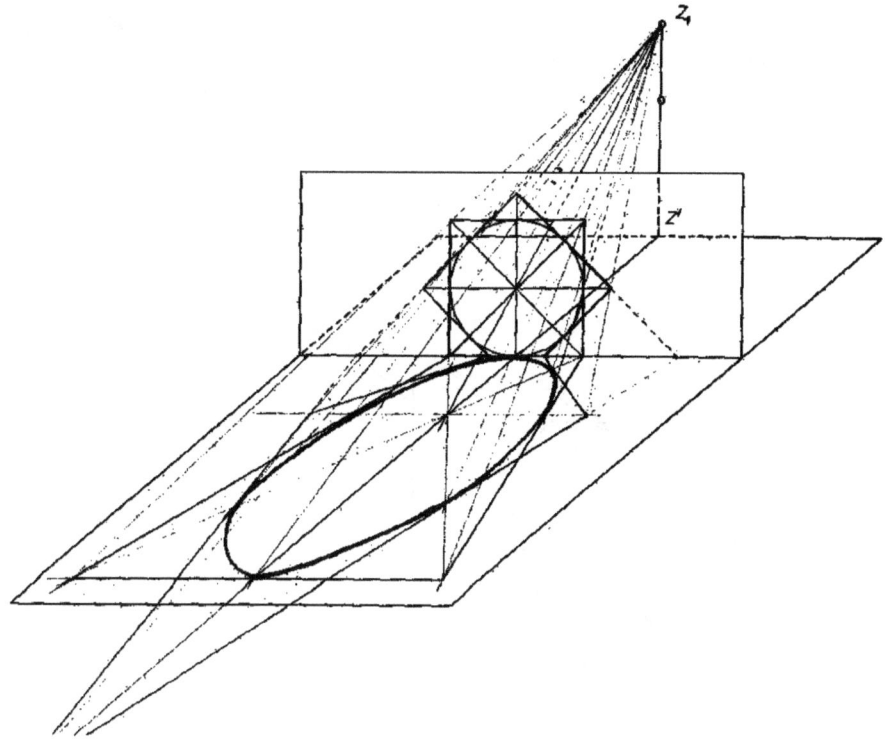

Figure 16.2

Project the circle from Z_2 onto the horizontal plane with the help of the two circumscribed squares. (The height of Z_2 is equal to the circle's diameter.)

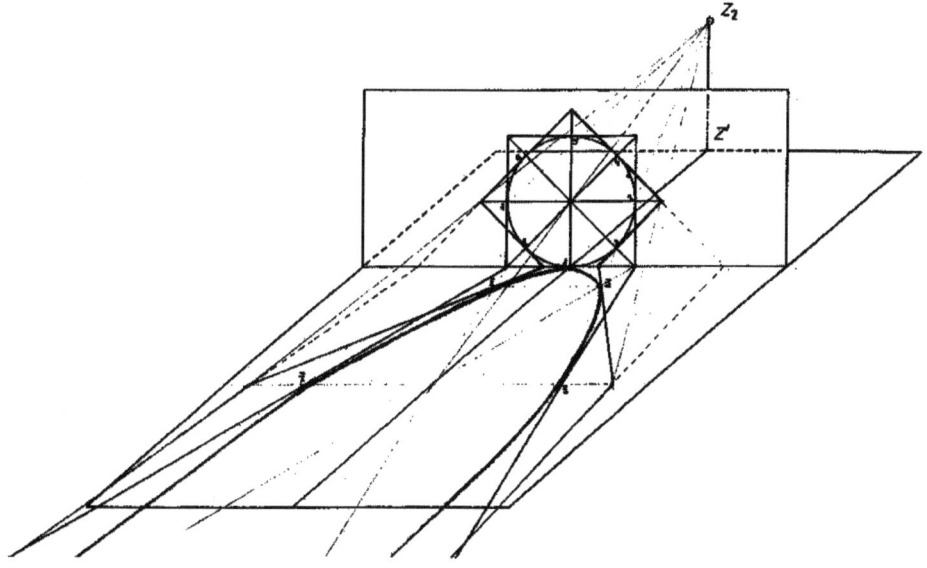

Figure 16.3

Project the circle from Z onto the horizontal plane with the help of the two circumscribed squares. (The height of Z is equal to the circle's radius.)

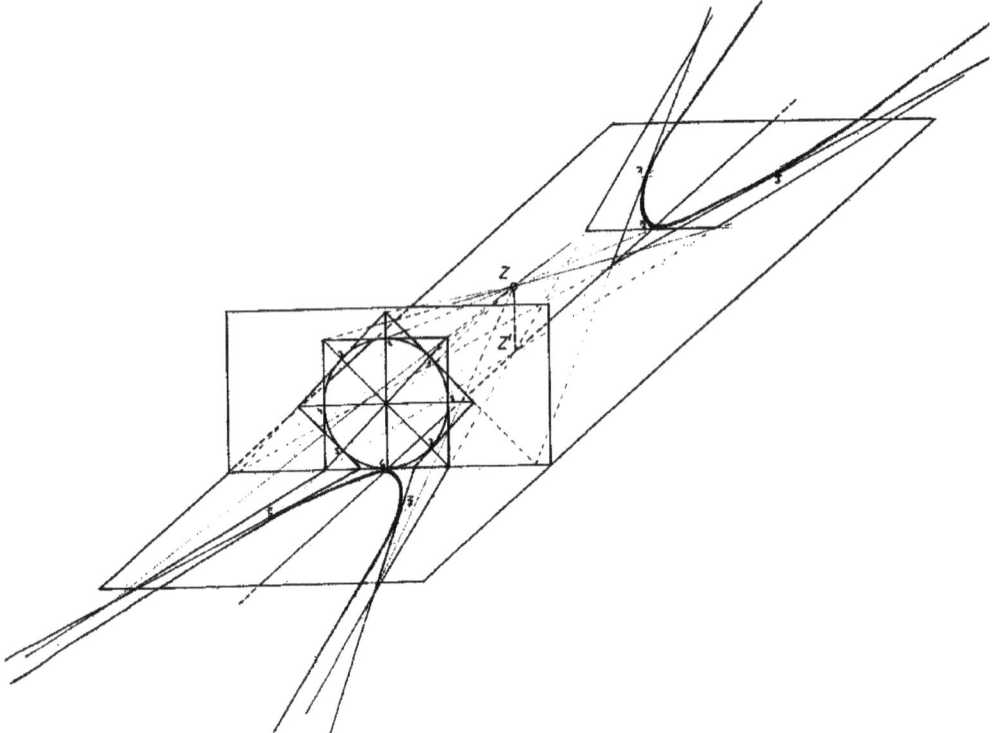

Figure 16.4

Projective Geometry

MARKUS HÜNIG

1 Foreword

Measurement and numbers are not in the foreground when it comes to projective geometry. Here we examine the position relationships of the geometric basic elements point, line and plane to each other. This geometry arose from the efforts of artists to exactly grasp space, in terms of perspective. It was further developed by the French mathematician Desargues ($\approx$1593-1662). Projective geometry reached its high point in the nineteenth century. At first, the twentieth century ignored it as being of little use. In more recent times, it has been rediscovered. For it offers a number of possibilities for application in communication technology: For instance, the often unavoidable coding of content in the Internet is performed with methods whose theoretical principles are provided by cryptography. These methods can be derived from those of projective geometry.[1]

The approach here represents a systematic construction from basic elements. Its content is continued in a block of the twelfth grade (polar theory, central projection, central collineation) and can be carried to the Abitur – where the standards of the states allow this. Years of practical experience for this exist.

With this, one possible path is offered; as can be seen from other contributions in this volume, it is in no way to be viewed as the only way.

For the material developed, relatively few exercises are carried out here. In the author's view, the few in the block notebook should suffice and the many further exercises carried out in a separate practice book.

2 Introduction of unreal elements

2.1 Vanishing points

From earlier years, we know that a *line* (in contrast to a distance) is unlimited in length. Given are a line g and a point A outside of g. Through A runs a line a, which intersects g at S. Now we turn a around A and observe the movement from S. Soon S will no longer be visible on the drawing – we can just imagine that this intersecting point exists. If a has been turned parallel to g, we can no longer imagine the intersecting point – one can only grasp it rationally. With further turning, S comes from the other side into the imaginable, and then into the visible realm. If a is parallel to g, apparently no intersecting point in the usual sense is present. Rather, the common element of the two lines is now their *direction*, which has taken over *the function of the point*. From the transition from S_4 to S_5 and further to S_6, it becomes clear that the «improper point» S_5 lies infinitely distant to both sides. Thus, we call this point a vanishing point. If we designate the

---
[1] See: A. Beutelspacher/ U. Rosenbaum: Projektive Geometrie, Vieweg, 1992

commonality of two different lines in the plane as «point», so we can call the common direction used point or distant point.

Apparently, two lines have a common *improper point* or *vanishing point* if they agree in their direction; so, the vanishing point always specifies a direction (direction in the plane or in space, without the sense of going through).

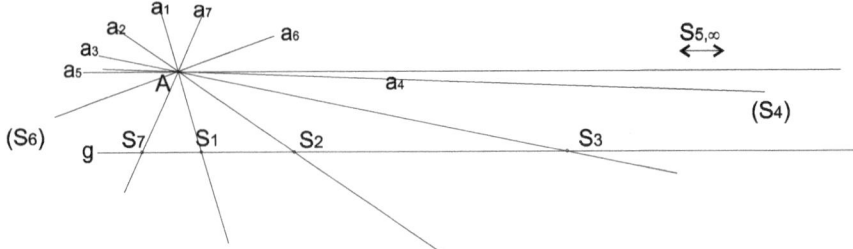

Every line has exactly one vanishing point. We must envision the line as a structure closed in itself, beyond this vanishing point. Here it is not necessary to distinguish between lines and rays (half lines).

We designate vanishing points with a double arrow of the corresponding direction; to the point name we add the index ∞. We will see that, in almost every regard, vanishing points can be treated as usual points. (Note: At this point, we do not make a distinction between a line and a row of points, whose bearer is the line. These explanations follow in a later chapter).

Examples:

1. Given are the point A and the vanishing point B_∞. We are seeking the connecting line g of A and B.
   Solution: The point B_∞ cannot be drawn directly. We can only make visible the direction cited by it. But a line through A goes exactly through the vanishing point B_∞, if it has the direction determined by it. So there is a line to be drawn through A, which has the direction of the given vanishing point.

2. Given are the points A, B and C_∞. The triangle (ABC) is to be drawn.

   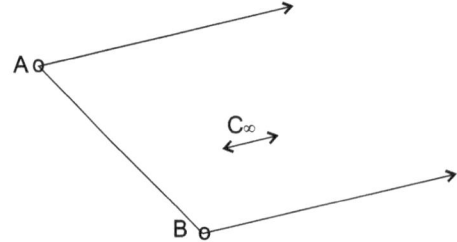

Note: Of course the triangle could also be drawn in the opposite direction. Then it would have the reverse orientation (in the sense of a revolution). As we will see in the next chapter, four triangles arise all together.

2.2 Vanishing lines

All vanishing points of a plane lie on the distant line. This is comparable to the horizon. As a help, we can think of the vanishing line as a circle with an infinitely large radius. Its turn is infinitely small – so it is a line. (*This idea must be overcome, because it does not correctly include all aspects of the vanishing lines. For instance, a point on the vanishing lines can never be localized in a certain direction – it always lies in the exactly opposite direction as well*).

Every normal line intersects the vanishing line at a vanishing point. The connecting line of two vanishing points (in a drawing plane) is the vanishing line.

The vanishing line of the drawing plane is not something that can be directly portrayed in drawings. To make clear that it is included in the drawing, we can write (g_∞) into the drawing.

Example: We produce the intersecting point A_∞ of the line h with the vanishing line of the drawing plane:

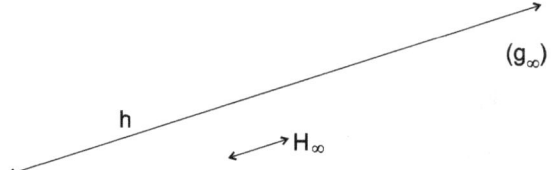

2.3 The vanishing plane of space

All parallel planes have a common vanishing line – that is, the intersecting line of two parallel planes is their common vanishing line. On the other hand, two planes with one usual intersecting line (not parallel planes) also have different vanishing lines. – All these distant lines lie in a common plane: the vanishing plane of space. As a help, this can be imagined as a sphere with an infinitely large radius. (Also this «crutch» must be overcome.)

Three-dimensional space only has one vanishing plane, as the drawing plane only contains one vanishing line. In drawings, one can only suggest the vanishing plane (for instance, (ε_∞)).

Note: In projective geometry, there are frequently illustrations in which the vanishing line is drawn in like a usual line. Here it is a matter of perspective representations in which the vanishing line is portrayed as the horizon. Strictly speaking, it would have to be designated with f', if the vanishing line itself is designated with f_∞ (the hatch mark designates an image)

3 Some basic concepts

3.1 Basic structures with their own elements as bearer

1. The point field – We call the set of all points of a plane a point field.

   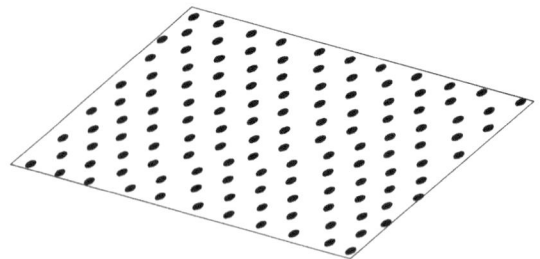

2. We call the set of all lines of a plane a line field (field of rays)

   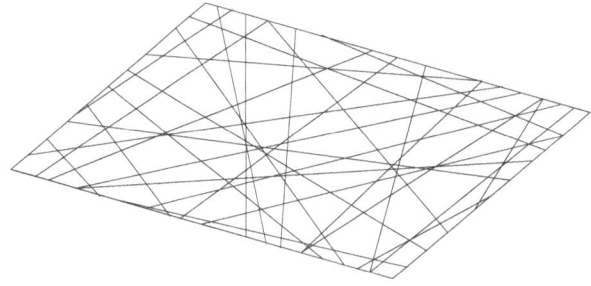

3. Together, all points which lie on a line form a point range

   The relevant line is bearer of the range. – A range is a plurality. And a line is a unit.

4. The set of all lines within the drawing plane, which go through a common point, we designate as pencil of lines. The point is the bearer of the pencil.

   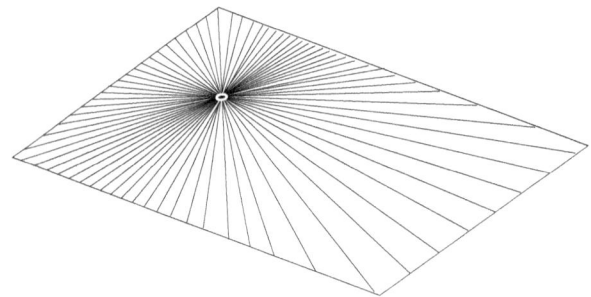

5. A bundle of lines consists of all lines of space, which go through a fixed point.

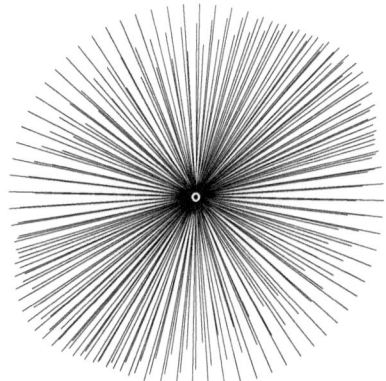

6. All planes, which have a common intersecting line, together form a plane pencil (sheaf of planes):

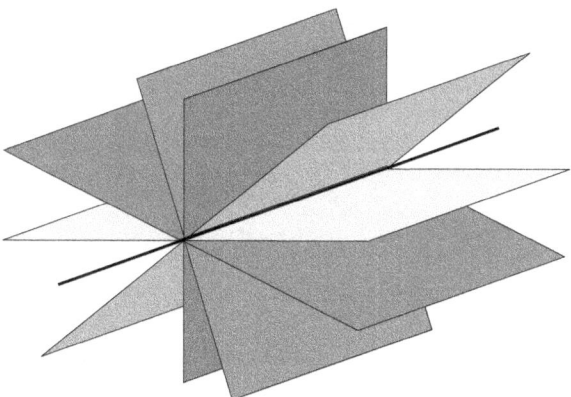

7. A bundle of planes, however, consists of all planes which go through a point

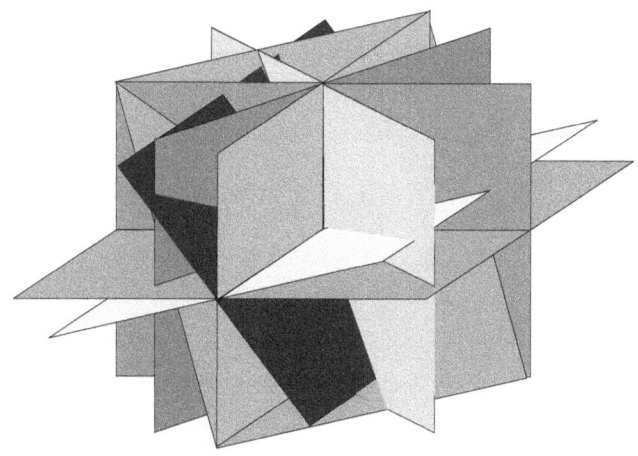

8. We call the set of all line bundles, whose bearing points lie on a line, a special linear complex.

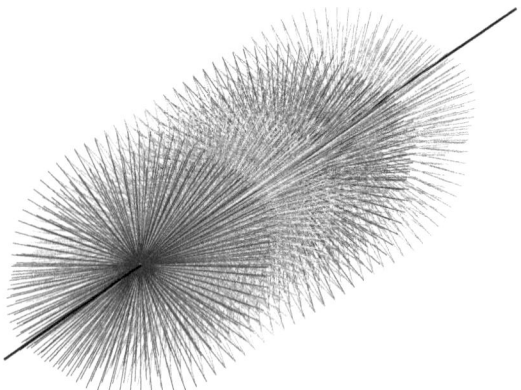

3.2 Basic structure with unreal bearers

The bearing elements of the basic structures can be vanishing points, vanishing lines, or the vanishing plane of space. Then the following structures result:

1. The point field, whose bearer is the vanishing plane of space:

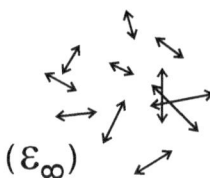

2. The line field on the vanishing plane contains nothing but vanishing lines (and in this sense cannot be represented).

3. A point row, whose bearer is a vanishing line, consists of all vanishing points of a plane:

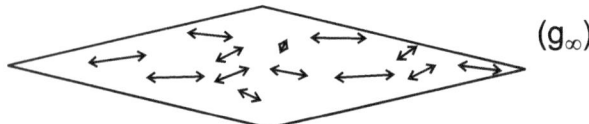

4. A Pencil of lines, whose bearer is a vanishing point, is a band of parallels in the drawing plane:

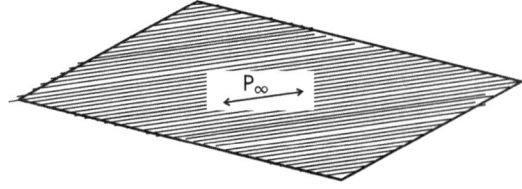

5. A line bundle, whose bearer is a distant point, is a spatial band of parallels (drawing is problematic)

6. A pencil of planes with a vanishing line as bearer is a band of parallel planes:

7. A plane bundle with a vanishing point as bearer:

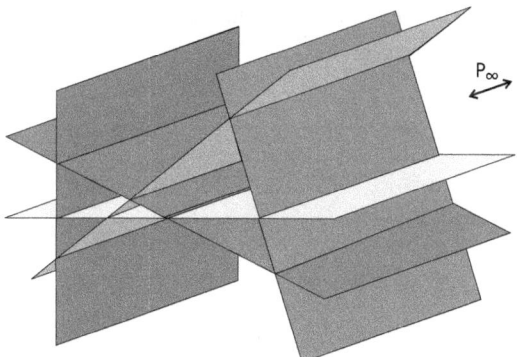

8. A special linear complex, whose bearer is a vanishing line, consists of all lines which run parallel to a plane:

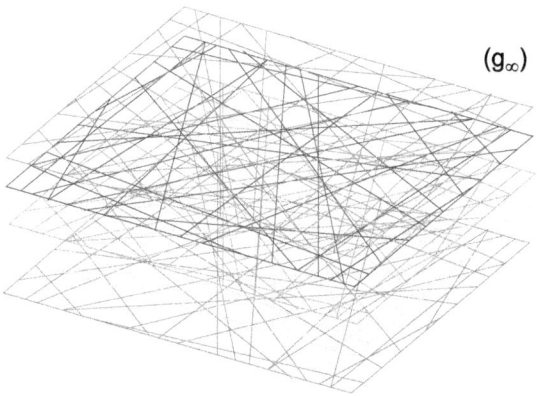

4 Arrangement of the plane

The plane can be the bearer of a point field as of a line field. It is easy to see that lines present can arrange the point field in different regions. Similarly, points lying in the plane can arrange the field of lines.

4.1 Arrangement of a point field by lines

1. by a line

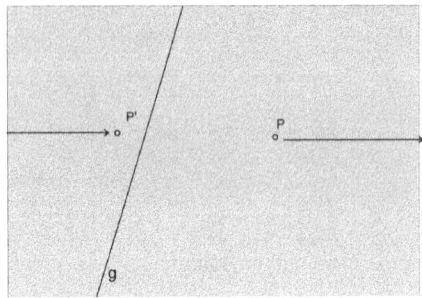

The point field is not split by *one* line: for P can move into the position P1 on the path over infinity, without crossing g in the process.

2. ...by two lines

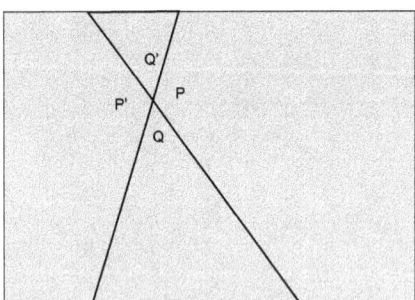

The point field is split into two areas by two lines. In each of these areas, there are two extreme positions for a «moving» point – namely, there where the two lines cross. Thus we name these areas «2-point areas».

3. by three lines:

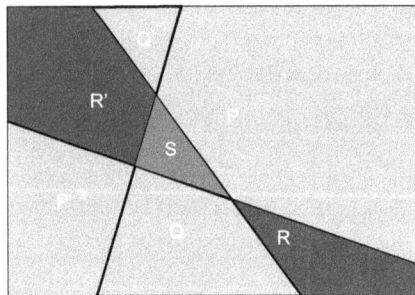

Here four 3-point areas arise: The points P, Q, R and S can move in areas with 3 extreme points. We can call each of these 3-point-areas a triangle- even though the first three do not correspond to the classical idea of a triangle.

4. by four lines:

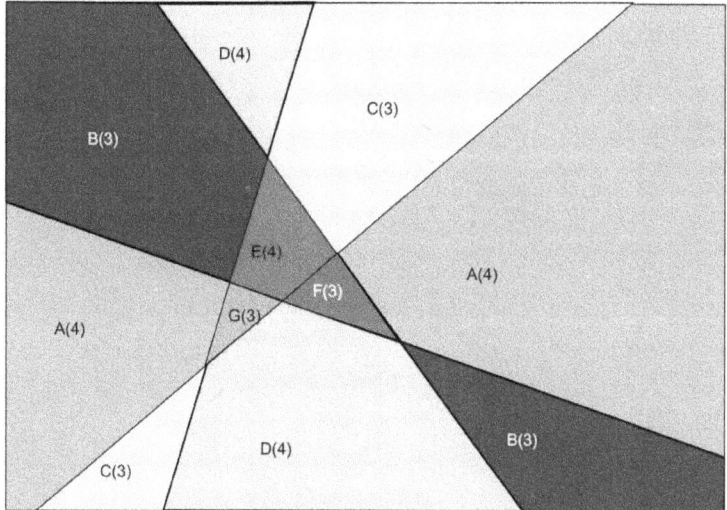

Here four 3-point-areas (trilaterals) and three 4-point-areas (4-lines) arise. The designation relates to a representative point in the area and the number in parentheses cites the possible extreme positions.

5. by 5 lines:

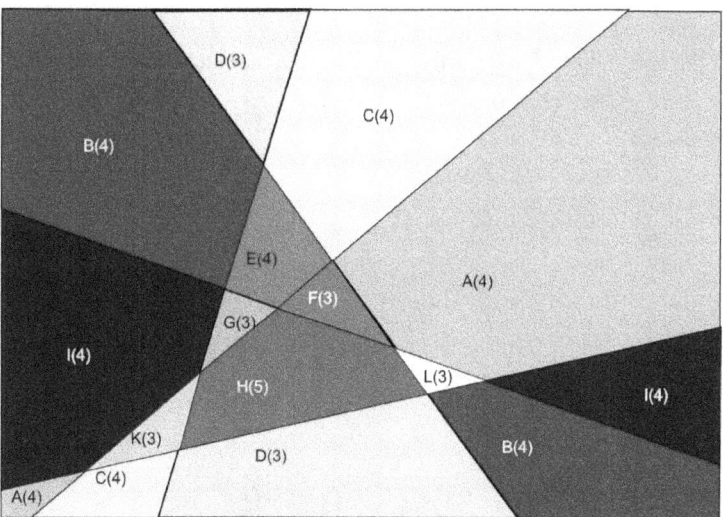

Now we have five 3-point areas, five 4-point areas, and one 5-point area. ? A good complementary exercise would be to draw such a situation with a 5-point area extending over infinity.

4.2 Arrangement of a line field by points

Analogously, points can now arrange the line field: Two lines belong to the same area, if the one can be transferred to the other without coloring over an arranging point. ?Since the areas of the line field can overlap, they cannot be portrayed by coloring the surface. Instead, a representative line is drawn in for each area.

1. ...by a point:

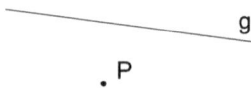

The line field is not yet arranged by a point; the line g can be shifted into any position, without covering over P.

2. by two points:

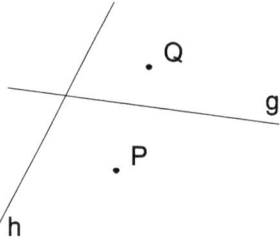

g cannot reach the position of h without covering over P or Q. g and h represent different areas of the line field.?With their freedom of movement, each of the two lines can take two extreme positions, since, in one way or the other, they lie on P and Q. Thus, we are dealing with two subsets.

3. by three points:

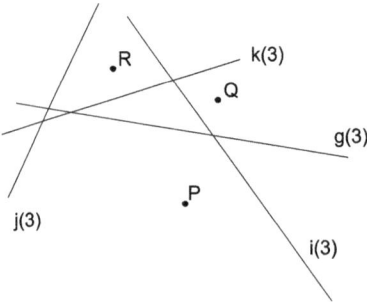

Here four 3-line-areas arise (or trilaterals – more later on this). Again, the representative lines are characterized by the number of extreme positions.

4. ...by four points:

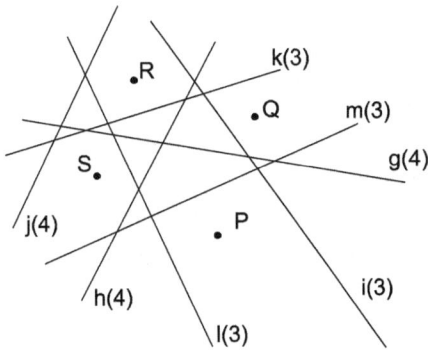

Four 3-line-areas arise and three 4-line areas.

5. by five points:

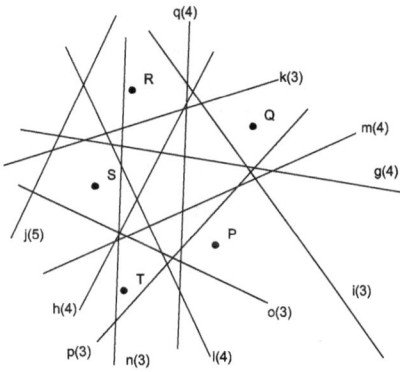

Now five 3-line-regions, five 4-line-regions and one 5-line region arise.

There is an apparent symmetry between the arrangement of the point field by lines and the arrangement of the line field by points: In regard to their position relations, they are completely of equal value. Here we speak of the duality of point and line in the plane.

If we go over into space, we perceive a corresponding duality of point and plane; the lines maintain a neutral mediation function. So the following bodies are structured dually to each other: icosahedron (20 surfaces, 12 corners, 30 edges), pentagon-dodecahedron (12 surfaces, 20 corners, 30 edges), hexahedron (cube) and octahedron.

Thanks to the role of vanishing points, the principle of duality of point and line can be pursued through the entire projective geometry of the plane. For each new discovery, we can show that it can also be found in a dual way.

5 The Desargues configuration

5.1 Introduction

Three points always lie in a plane; however, generally not on a line (they form a triangle). Within the drawing plane, it is a special case when three points lie on a line. Accordingly, as a rule, three lines will not intersect at a point, but rather form a «trilateral (3-side)».

So we view any two general triangles A_1, B_1, C_1 and A_2, B_2, C_2. Each triangle has three corner points which are connected by three sides-we wish to view these as whole lines.

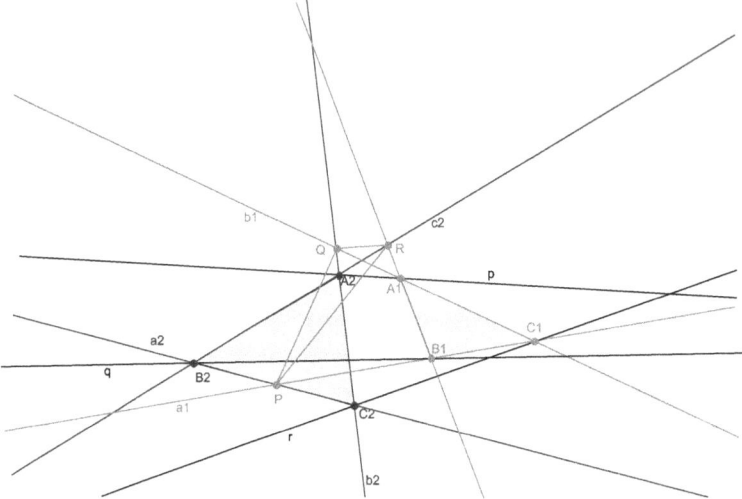

Now we can connect the corresponding corners A_1 and A_2, B_1 and B_2, as well as C_1 and C_2 with each other – in the process, three new lines arise – p, q, and r. Generally, these will form a trilateral with each other.

Accordingly, we can intersect the lines a_1 with a_2, b_1 with b_2 and c_1 with c_2; these three intersecting points (P, Q and R) will generally form a triangle. If we position the triangles such that the connecting lines of the corresponding corner points meet at a point Z, the following situation results:

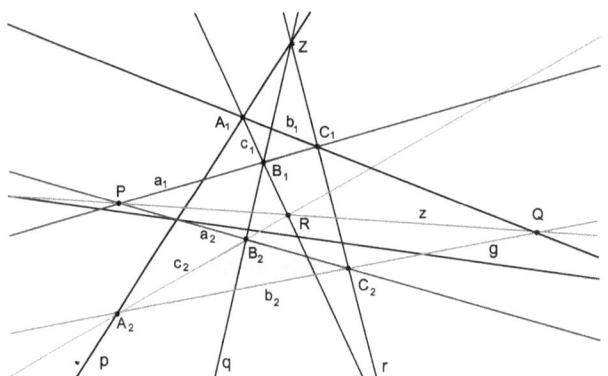

Observation lets us surmise the following (theorem of Desargues):

> If the connecting lines of corresponding corner points of two triangles intersect at a point, so the intersecting points of corresponding triangle sides lie on a line.

5.2 Proof of the theorem of Desargues

To understand the accuracy of the theorem of Desargues, it is helpful to imagine the whole configuration as a perspective image of a spatial structure: The triangle A_1, B_1, C_1 is the bottom of an «Indian tent». The tent poles are the lines p, q and r. This way, the triangle A_2, B_2, C_2 forms a type of in-between cover.

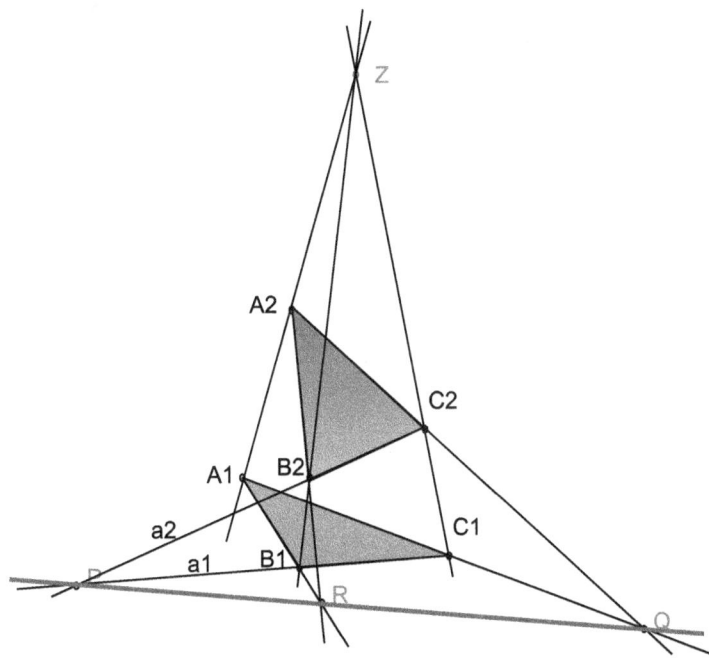

From the spatial arrangement, it is clear that the line z is the intersecting line of both triangle planes.

The lines b_1, b_2 and c_1, c_2 each lie in a common plane (they are no skew lines) that is, Q and R are indeed spatial intersecting points. They lie on the intersecting line z. The corresponding consideration for the lines a_1 and a_2 shows that P must also lie on this line. As seen spatially from z, the one triangle covers the other one; thus, we call them central-perspective to each other. At the same time, the corresponding lines meet as at a common horizon; we designate this property as axial-perspective. Thus, the theorem of Desargues can be formulated more generally:

If two geometric figures of the drawing plane are central-perspective to each other, so they are axially- perspective and the reverse is true.

5.3 Example problems

1. Given for one Desargues configuration are Z, A_1, B_2, C_2 and a_1; Q is supposed to be a vanishing point.

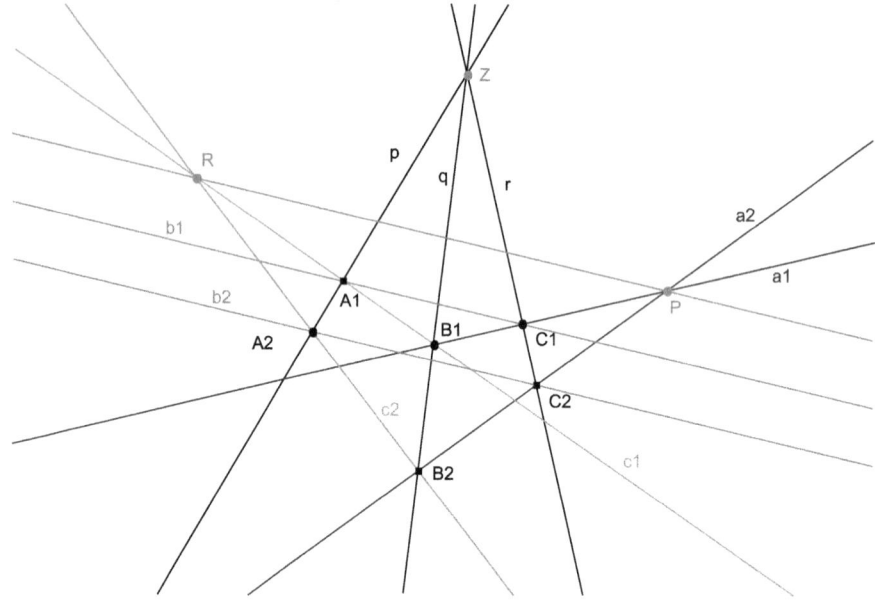

2. Given are two lines g and h, whose intersecting point lies outside of the drawn area, as well as a point P. – On the page, construct the connecting lines of P to the intersecting point of g and h. We grasp g and h as the lines b_1 and b_2 of a Desargues configuration; we add the missing parts and, at the end, construct z.

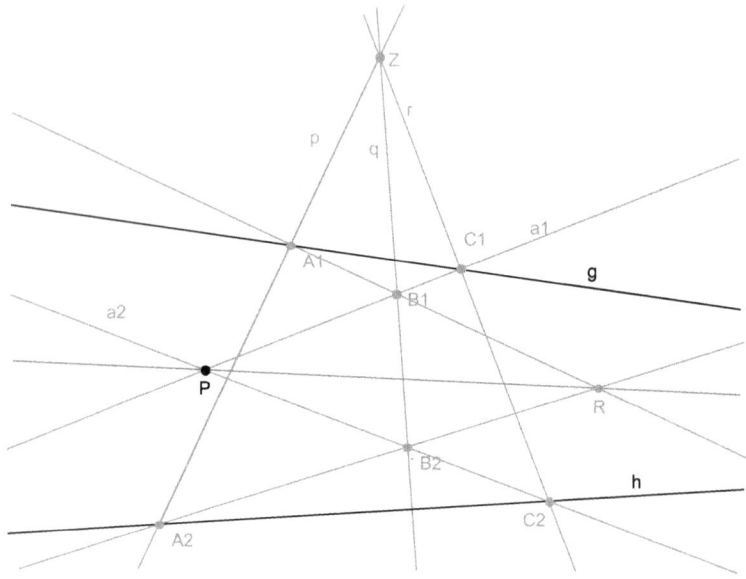

5.4 Ten viewing angles and dual relationships

The Desargues configuration consists of two triangles with three lines and three points, and the points Z, P, Q, R as well as the lines p, q, r and z – all together, it consists of 10 lines and 10 points.

In the process, three lines go through each point and three points lie on each line.

If we leave out all the designations, it is no longer possible to determine which of the ten points is Z. In fact, each of the ten points can take over the role of Z and every line can be z.

For this, we can distribute ten copies of the same Desargues configuration to the students and, according to the point of Z, let them search for the two triangles. – The first (larger) drawing can serve as model, with the cases $Z = A$ and $Z = B$ carried out.

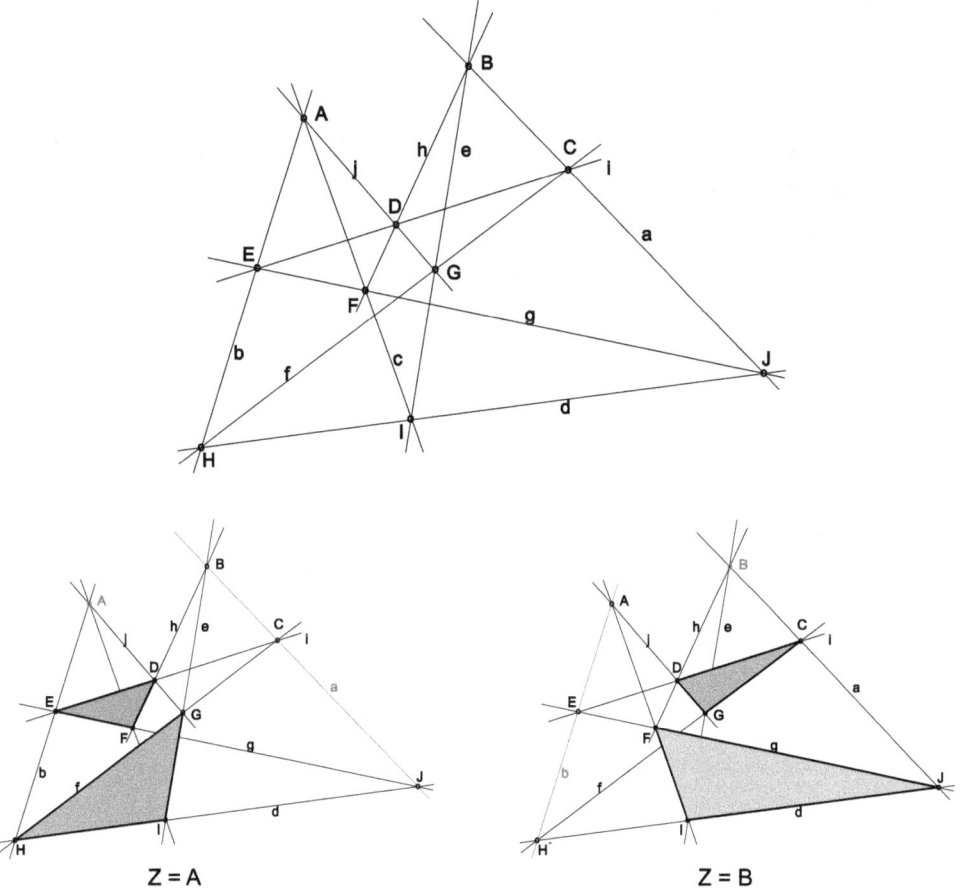

It is clear in the previous drawings that a line in the role of z corresponds to each point, viewed as the center. In this configuration, these two elements face each other in a dual manner: In fact, the statement «The connecting lines of corresponding corner points intersect at a point» is the exact dual statement to «The intersecting points of corresponding triangle sides lie on a line». – It is not surprising that the exact dual structure leads to a like configuration.

1.	We begin with a point, through which three lines run.	We begin with a line, on which three points lie.
2.	On each of the three lines, a further point is selected.	An additional line is drawn through each of the three points.
3.	The three points are connected by three lines.	The intersecting points of the three lines are marked.
4.	Steps 2 and 3 are repeated with new points.	Steps 2 and 3 are repeated with new lines.
5.	The intersecting points of two corresponding lines from steps 2 to 4 are marked.	Two corresponding points from steps 2 to 4 are connected by lines.
6.	The three intersecting points arising lie on a straight line.	The three lines drawn meet at a point.

At this point, further exercises on the dualization of relationships can be added. The following is cited as an example of such a dualization exercise:

Given are two lines *g* and *h* intersecting in the diagram; their intersecting point is S. On *g* are the points A, B, C and on *h* the points P and Q.

Draw in all connecting lines of the points provided and label these. Finally, produce a dual figure.

Model:

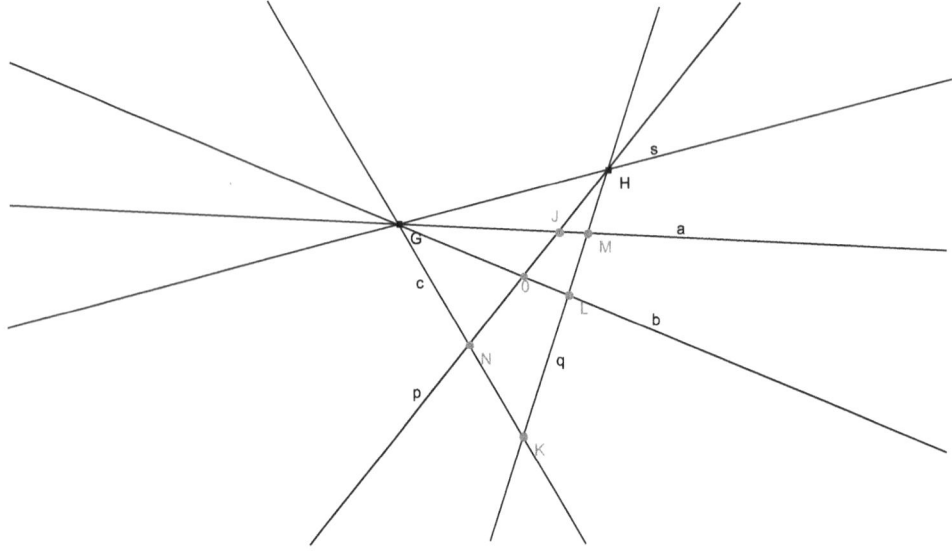

Dual figure:

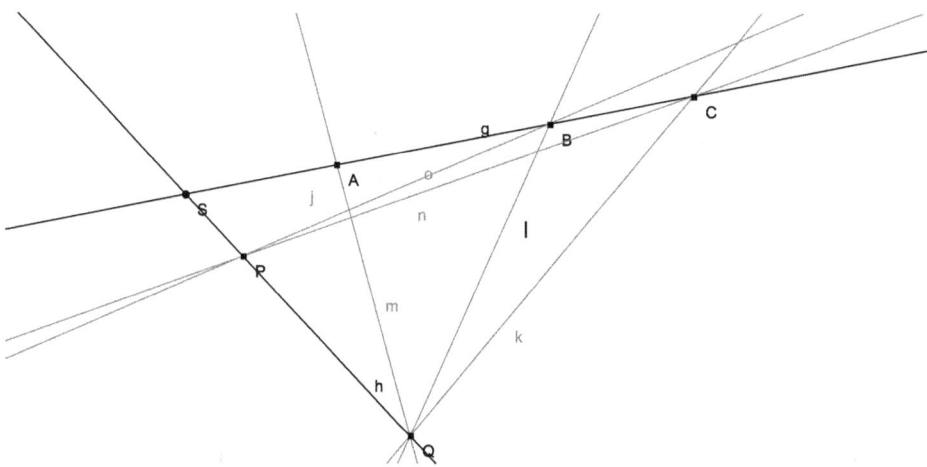

There are geometric figures which are dual to themselves (for instance, the Desargue configuration). This applies especially for a triangle: It consists of three points which are connected by three lines or three lines, which intersect at three points. Thus, triangle and trilateral differ through their origin but not in their appearance. This is different with a 4-line.

6 Complete 4-line, complete 4-point and harmonic position

6.1 Complete 4-line and complete 4-point

Four points can be connected by six lines; four lines have six points of intersection with each other. With this dualism, we want to construct a 4-line and a 4-point and next to each other.

4-line:

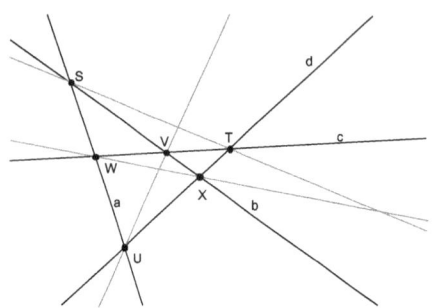

4-point:

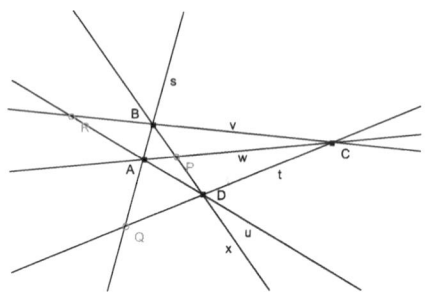

We begin with four lines a, b, c, d, which meet at six points $S = a \cap b$, $T = c \cap d$, $U = a \cap d$, $V = b \cap c$, $W = a \cap c$, $X = b \cap d$.

Of the six points, three lie on each line; so, for each of these points, one further point remains, with which it is not connected by a line. A further line can be drawn through these two corner points – altogether, 3 lines: $p = XW$, $q = ST$, $r = UV$.

We begin with the four points ABCD. Six connecting lines can be drawn in: $s = AB$, $t = CD$, $u = AD$, $v = BC$, $w = AC$, $x = BD$.

Besides at the previous points, these meet at three further points:
$P = x \cap w$, $Q = s \cap t$, $R = u \cap v$.

What meaning do the three points or three lines have in the sense of a «classical» 4-point?

According to the way we look at the 4-line, each of the three lines can be a diagonal. If we add the intersecting points of the three diagonals, we have four points on every diagonal. We call the 4-line, completed by its diagonal trilateral, a complete 4-line.

According to how we view the 4-point, each of the three points can be a cross point of the diagonals. If we draw in the connecting lines of these three points to each other, four lines go through each of the points. We call the 4-point, completed by its diagonal point triangle, a complete 4-point.

Now we will turn to the four points which arose with the 4-line on the diagonals and investigate their special place relationships.

6.2 Harmonic points

We construct a complete 4-line such that the line through A and B lies horizontal and the points P and Q of the diagonal trilateral lie on this line. (The points A and B thus correspond to the points U and V in the drawing on the previous page left. The bearing line of our 4 points corresponds to the line *r*.) While we leave A and B fixed, we let P move from right to left and observe the movement of the point Q.

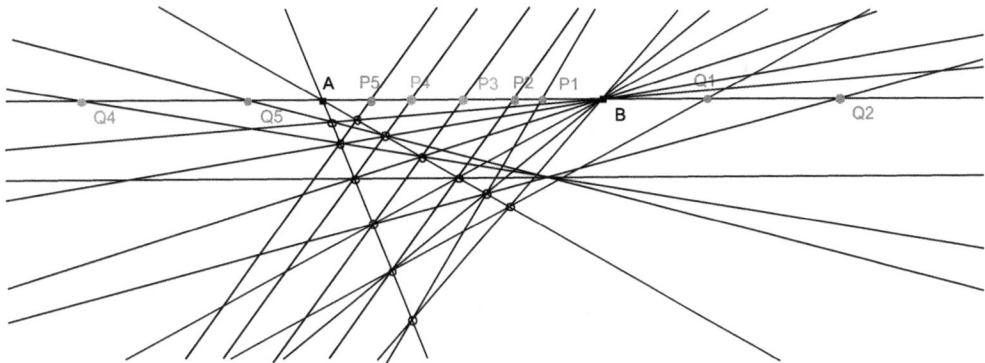

The position of Q seems to be determined by the position of A,B and P. If P approaches B, Q comes toward it from the other side. If P lies in the middle, between A and B, then Q is a vanishing point. If P approaches A, then Q comes toward it from the other side.

From the observation, it can be supposed that: $\frac{\overline{AP}}{\overline{PQ}} = \frac{\overline{AQ}}{\overline{BQ}}$ that is, P divides the distance AB in the same ratio internally as Q divides the distance externally. – We speak of an harmonic partial ratio: the four points A,B,Q,P are four harmonic points (four points of position in harmony, one harmonic point range).

The accuracy of this supposition is to be proven in the following chapters.

6.3 Proof of uniqueness

At first, we must be certain that the position of Q is really determined by A, B, and P and does not depend on the choice of the 4-line. From A,B and P, we construct a further 4-line. We can easily see that both 4-lines are in perspective to each other. Thus, the diagonals producing Q also intersect on the line AB. So the position of Q is independent of the choice of the 4-line.

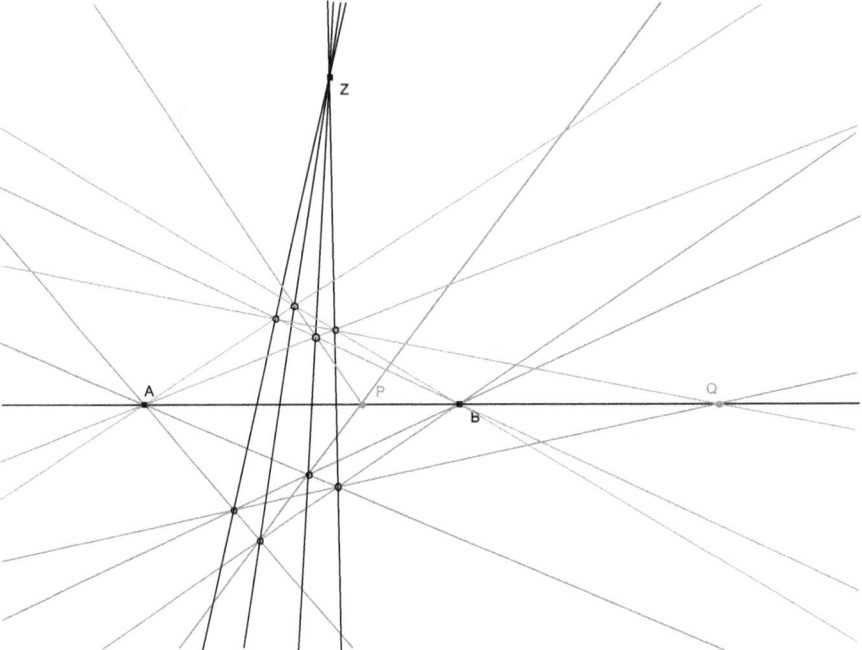

We can let the pairs of points A,B and P,Q exchange their roles, without having the relationships change.

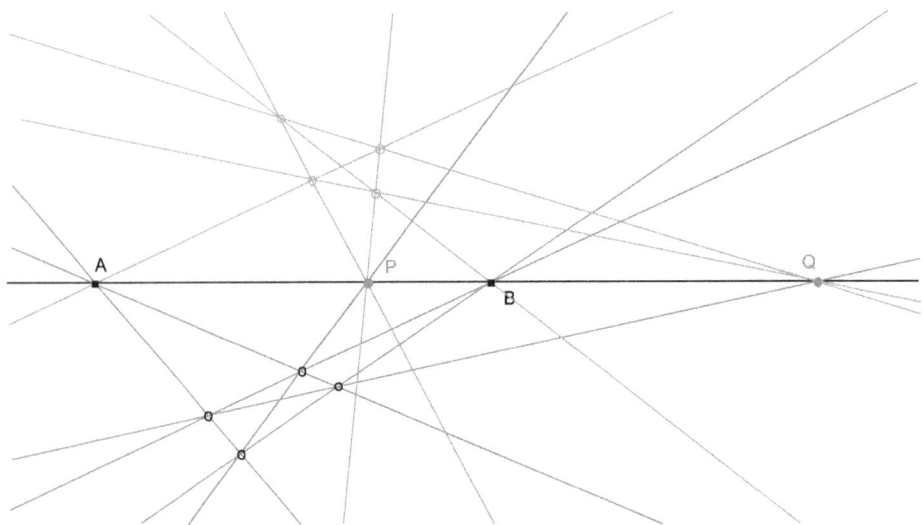

6.4 Harmonic lines

The four lines in each of the diagonal crosspoints of the 4-line correspond to the four harmonic points on the diagonals of the 4-point.

Also here we can make similar observations on movement as with the harmonic points. In association with the points, we call these four lines harmonic lines.

4-point: A, B, C, D; diagonal points: P, Q, R; harmonic line set in Q: t, r, s, p.

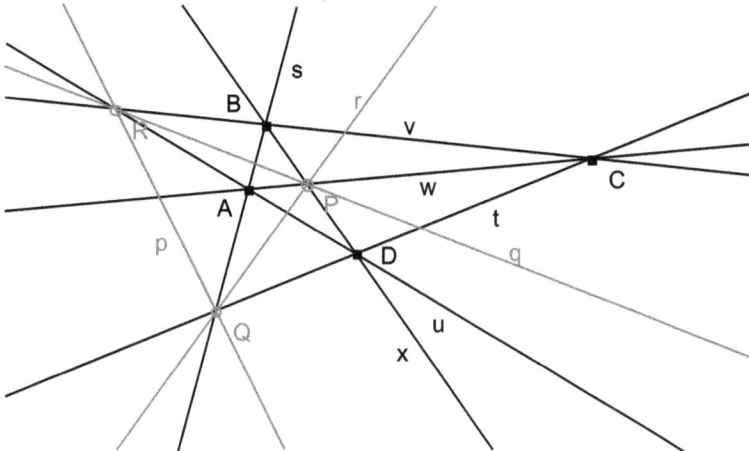

If we think of this as a 4-point, the four harmonic lines each comprise an angle of 45° at the midpoint of the 4-point. This represents a special case of harmonic lines.

6.5 The invariance of the harmonic position

Now we take a look at a complete 4-point, adding some resulting points of intersection: the points characterized as circles: $\mathfrak{T}, \mathfrak{U}, \mathfrak{V}, \mathfrak{W}, \mathfrak{X}, \mathfrak{Y}$.

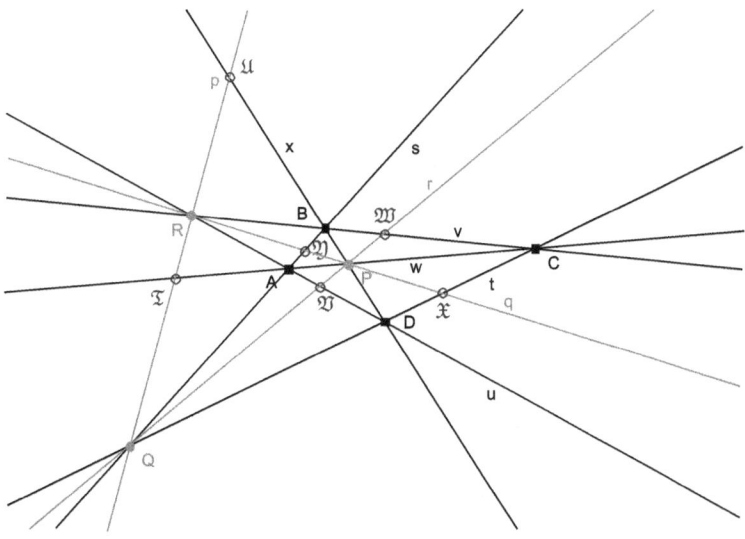

Now we look at the lines *s, t, v, u*: With each other, they open a *4-line*. Its diagonals are the lines *x, w* and *p*.

Thus, the points Q, 𝔗, R and 𝔘 are in a harmonic position.

Analogously, we can find the 4-lines which are responsible for the harmonic point range Q, 𝔙, P, 𝔛 or R, Y, P, X.

The four harmonic lines which proceed from P intersect *p* at a harmonic point range.

On account of the non-ambiguity shown in V.3, this relationship results for every line which is intersected by this harmonic line set.

Thus the following applies:

1. If we connect four points of a harmonic range to a point outside the bearing lines, then a harmonic line set results there.

2. If we cut the four lines of a harmonic set with a line which does not go through the bearing point, a harmonic point range appears on this.

Or:

> The harmonic position is invariant to the (projective) operations of connecting (to a point) and intersecting (with a line).

6.6 The harmonic partial ratio

With the help of our previous knowledge, we can show that harmonic division can be represented as a ratio or anharmonic ratio. This involves two steps.

1. We show: For every harmonic point range, there is a point O outside the bearing lines so that the connecting lines are perpendicular to the four points by pairs. That is, they intersect at an angle of 45°. For this, we draw the Thales circles over AB and PQ.

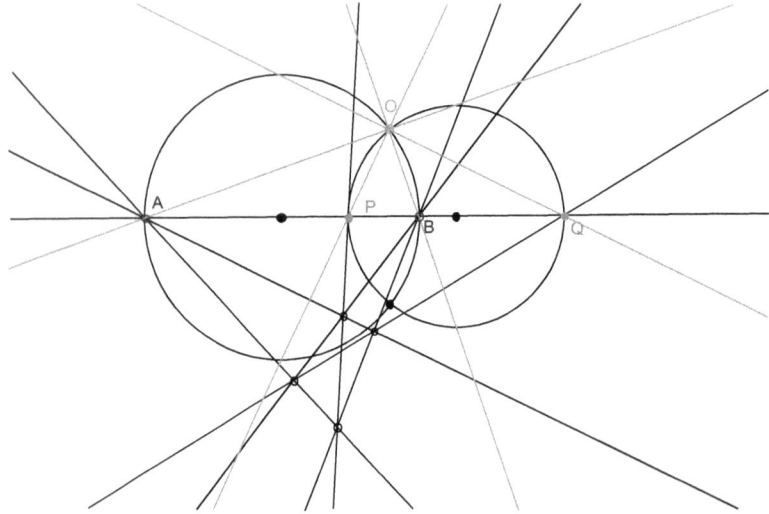

As we see, a harmonic line set must appear at o; on the other side, the four lines stand perpendicular to each other. Because of unicity, all four (or eight) must have an angle of 45 degrees.

2. We draw this special case (which can always be produced) and prove the supposition from V.2 with the help of similar triangles. Assertion:

$$\frac{\overline{AP}}{\overline{PB}} = \frac{\overline{AQ}}{\overline{BQ}}$$

Proof: From Q and P, the vertical lines are drawn in on the line AO. The triangles (ALP), (AOB), and (AMQ) are similar; thus, the length ratios on the line AM equal those on the line AQ.

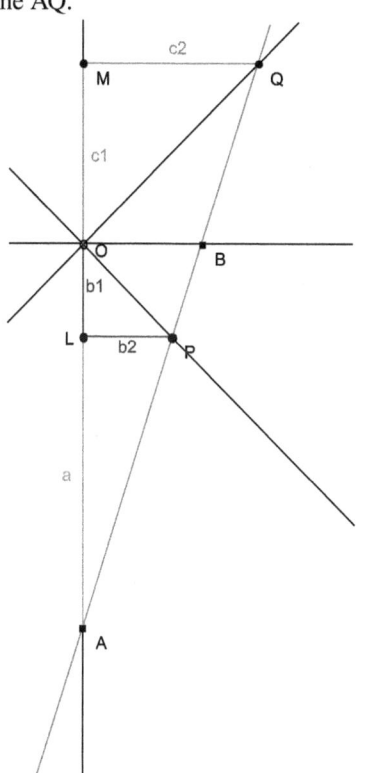

Thus, it is sufficient to show:

$$\frac{\overline{AL}}{\overline{LO}} = \frac{\overline{AM}}{\overline{OM}}$$

Now the angle (POL)=45°. That is, the triangle (OLP) is isosceles. Thus $b_1 = b_2$. Similarly $c_1 = c_2$. With this, the following applies:

$$\frac{a}{b_2} = \frac{a+b_1+c_1}{c_2}$$

thus

$$\frac{\overline{AL}}{\overline{LO}} = \frac{\overline{AM}}{\overline{OM}} \quad \text{q.e.d.}$$

Thus, for the harmonic ratio of the four points A, B, P, Q this applies:

$$\frac{\overline{AP}}{\overline{PB}} = \frac{\overline{AQ}}{\overline{BQ}} \quad \text{or} \quad \frac{\frac{\overline{AP}}{\overline{PB}}}{\frac{\overline{AQ}}{\overline{BQ}}} = 1$$

For the harmonic ratio, the anharmonic ratio has the value of 1.

Note: Since only distance lengths are being observed here, these always have a positive value. Thus, the anharmonic ratio is +1. In some areas of geometry, the sense of traversing must also be taken into account. This is put down in the sign (in the vector computation, $\overrightarrow{AB} = -\overrightarrow{BA}$). Then the anharmonic ratio has the value of -1.

7 Attachment: Suggestions for Exercises

Work on this material is always accompanied by fitting practice problems – in the author's opinion, these should be carried out in a separate workbook. In the following, some suggestions are given which show how problems can be varied with minor changes.

1. Given are three lines a,b,c in a general position.

    a) In how many and which areas do the intersecting points of a, b and c divide the plane (as line field)?

    b) Now comes the vanishing line g_∞ as the fourth line. Produce the complete 4-line with a diagonal trilateral and designate one harmonic point range that has appeared.

2. Given are three points A, B, and C

    a) In how many and which point areas do the connecting lines of A, B, and C divide the plane (as point field)?

    b) Now a further point Doo is given. Construct the complete 4-point with diagonal point triangle and designate one harmonic line set which appears.

3. Given are three lines a_1, b_1, c_1 in a general position, as well as the point Z and the line z. By coloring in your drawing, show

    a) which elements of the Desargue configuration are determined by it

    b) that there are several more possibilities to complete the Desargue configuration (carry out two different possibilities in different colors and cite which element you have determined with which limitation of choice).

4. Given are two lines g and h in a general position; on g lie the points S, T, U and S, V, R lie on h. Further, there is a point P which does not lie on g or h and lies on a line with no two of the other given points. – Draw in all possible connecting lines of the points and designate these. Finally, produce the complete dual figure.

5. Given are the vanishing points P_∞ and $A_{1\infty}$ (angle between is 38°); further, the points R, C_2, and Z in general position. Through coloring your drawing, show

    a) which elements of a Desargue configuration are determined by it;

b) that there are still several possibilities for completing the Desargues configuration (see 3b).

6. Given are a line h and the points A, B, and Q on it (in this sequence), with the measurements $AB = 10\ cm$ and $BQ = 7\ cm$. Construct the fourth harmonic point P and check whether the harmonic ratio equals 1 you should do this though measurement and calculation.

7. Construct the four harmonic points A, B, P, Q so that $AQ = 18\ cm$ and $PQ = 13\ cm$.

8. Construct a regular hexagram (edge length of triangles $AB = 5\ cm$). Show that the two triangles are perspective to each other – that is, indicate the center, the line joining centers and the points P, Q and R or draw these in.

A Path to Projective Geometry

ROLF ROSBIGALLE

1 Foreword

In the tenth grade, the teenager can gain a clarity of thought which has progressed beyond the more chaotic consciousness of the ninth grader. This clarity, which stabilizes the feeling for life, is acquired through the discovery that the student's own thinking «fits the things of experience» (Martin Wagenschein) – just look at trigonometry and surveying.

This can be taken further to a first inquiry in the realm of what can no longer be imagined, but can only be grasped with pure thinking. As will become apparent, projective geometry is a suitable means for this. The theme of geometry, which dominates the 11th grade, brings along with it the question of the proper sequence in time. At this age, the acquired inner security and the inwardly-sensed need for liberation from the conventional experience of surrounding space allow for a «free-floating» treatment of geometry. This would be unthinkable in the ninth grade and something to be handled carefully in the tenth.

On the other hand, I have occasionally experienced that geometry in the newly-found coordinate system – the coordinatization yielding the x- and y- coordinates from the angle and length measurements obtained from surveying – can so solidify idea and thought that a grasp of the basic ideas in synthetic projective geometry becomes more difficult. Thus I prefer treating the latter in the first part of the school year.

«Vector geometry in visual space» and «algebraic curves in construction and analysis», treated in connection with classical analytical geometry, give rise different impulses. I like to focus on these in the second half of the 11th grade.

The subject under consideration deals with freedom and necessity, requires the free acquisition of ideas and verification of their meaningfulness, and all that virtually without prerequisite knowledge.

The path leads over experimental action and self-discovery; until finally, out of the inner consistency which thereby emerges, necessary concept-formation takes place, which leads to harmonic wholes distiguished by their lack of exceptions. And then the real astonishment sets in, that has, so to speak, cognitive charakter. (R. Steiner, Konferenzen). One of these wholes is the geometric metamorphosis, which can be experienced cognitively through the vehicle of drawing. It is an excellent possibility for developing moveable perception and thought. In this way, one develops the possibility of fully grasping transformational processes.

Here I present a path into plane projective geometry which doesn't assume any previous acquaintance with space. In this case, I think it is worth trying to dedicate at least one instructional unit to the transition into space (perhaps in grade 12) – and to at least prepare for an experience and grasping of «Space and Counterspace».[1]

The articles in this work and several chapters in A. Bernhard, Projective Geometry, offer stimulation for this, aside from the extensive portrayals of L. Locher-Ernst, Olive Whicher and George Adams.

These concepts point to future new ways of observation in the natural sciences and they are contemporary forms of thought. Here the Waldorf School has a special educational role to play, for hardly any other type of school handles this domain.

Since the most important topics of projective geometry exceed the limits of a school course, there is a need for an artful selection, oriented on examples, for the 3- to 4-week main lesson offered in the 11th grade.

So there is a need for an adept selection for the main lesson of three to four weeks in the eleventh grade.[2]

Any block should portray a rounded totality in which the one thing fits into the other- at the end, a convincing totality of connections should «light up», not merely a concatenation of attractive material that moves the mathematician's heart – which doesn't make the choice of material any easier, but may convince the student!

I remember the recommendations of R. Steiner in the third lecture GA302 («Knowledge of man and the organization of instruction») on the division of different phases of learning into two main lessons on consecutive days. This way, the night is taken into consideration which is prescribed there for the subjects of history and physics. This implementation is effective and can be viewed as the pedagogical strength of the main lesson blocks (together with the rhythmic part and other pedagogical measures).[3]

It is important to me to «take along» students who have difficulties understanding the contents, so that they at least understand the fundamentals – and so the inner logical consistency of the subject becomes a need. This way, one can help prevent a schematic conditional learning which is so prevalent today. If we create a fullness and push on into higher realms, no talented student will be «underchallenged».

2 The course in the tenth grade

Experience has taught me that in order to achieve a deepened concept formation in the 11th grade, it makes sense in the 10th grade «to teach the first elements of position geometry... concepts of duality.. only that of first things.»[4]

---

[1] See other contributions of this collection and the book of this name by L. Locher-Ernst. Further statements on the literature are found below.

[2] According to the lesson plan, eight weeks of a block are assigned to math, and this is necessary-even if this cannot be realized for technical reasons.

[3] See my article in «Mathematikthemen fuer die neunte Klasse», Kassel, 1999.

[4] R. Steiner, Conference on June 17, 1921. Also see the conference on September 11, 1921.

I do avoid talking about «infinity» (see below) and let exceptions remain exeptions. I have always experienced a conceptually clear treatment at this class level as limited and premature – as when, ten years ago, on the basis of advice from collegues, I taught the «projective geometry» block in the 10th grade.

At this point, I will briefy describe a possible course of instruction. A similar procedure with another choice of theme is described below.

Mostly during practice time in the last part of the 10th grade, I have taught the Theoremof Pascal[5] (limited to the circle) through a construction problem. The theorem is conveyed as follows:

- Choose six points on any circle

- Number the points arbitrarily

- Connect these in the numbered sequence and thus obtain a hexagon with the sides 12, 23, 34, 45, 56, 61

- Intersect the extended sides (opposite) 12 and 45, 23 and 56, 34 and 61 with each other.

- What stands out?

Now diverse independent constructions can be produced (see appendix) and for easier beginning, work sheets are prepared. These are minimally provided with a circle, to prevent the project failing for lack of a compass. Then, when one hadgathered the discoveries from the construction pages, we get to this formula (not insignificant are the unusual «non-Euclidean» hexagons which just appear):

> When the corners of a hexagon belong to a circle, then the intersecting points of the opposite sides lie on a straight line.
> Exception: at least one pair of opposite sides is parallel.

In a corresponding way, the theorem of Brianchon is assessed, which we try to formulate analogously:

> When the sides of a hexagon belong to a circle[6] then the joining lines of the opposite corners intersect at a point.
> Exception: At least two connecting lines are parallel.

---

[5] For this chapter, see the literature cited and the other contributions of this collection.
[6] Tangents belong to a circle, and secants do not-this seems plausible. This formulation can be prepared through suitable construction.

Through comparison of the two theorems (in the third practice hour, with repetition of the previous), that which we call duality attracts our attention (see below.) and we have what we can formulate as a central «plausible conjecture»

The Pascal theorem can be expanded and deepened through transfer to an ellipse, parabola and hyperbola. With the help of the constructions of the Pascal configuration, this can be explored on the worksheet supplied. The students experience this as very exiting. Does this expansion beyond the circle apply for the theorem of Brianchon? And, indeed, this supports our assumption that the dualization of a correct theorem must be correct – if we think away the exceptions!

Moreover, through drawing, it becomes plausible that the theorem does not apply, if the corner points do not lie on one of the four curves. I avoid the term conic section in so far as students have not become familiar with these curves through intersection of a cone with a plane.

If we get this far, a seed is laid for what follows. At this point, we should prevent rather than encourage talk of vanishing points and infinity. For the most part, thinking is not advanced enough to grasp the infinite. It can only be a (therefore misleading) mental picture here.

3 The first block portion in the eleventh grade

Many times, I have taken the path over central projection:

1. Observations of historical illustrations, comments on the discovery of the laws of perspective- Leonardo, Duerer

2. Through developments by drawing, central projecting, burning candle- centered and linear collineation, geometric metamorphosis, theorem of Desargues, etc. in the sense of the chapters 11, 3, 4, 5, 12 according to A. Bernhard.[7]

3. Here many possibilities exist for further treatments.

One disadvantage is that the step from the practiced central projection to the exclusive activity in the plane (centered, linear collineation) bears the danger, at least with weaker student, that they fall back into the spatial view.

This approach has proven effective and has little risk in the sense of guiding of instruction and of discussion. And it can well be tied to everyday experience and, for instance, knowledge of painting and drawing.

In what follows, I describe another effiecient path which creates a certain abundance of plane geometric experiences and develops as it were from a free geometric activity. It draws students of the most diverse types into an experimental creative process and makes them capable of judgement. From this, concept formation arises in some measure by inner necessity. To do justice

---

[7] A. Bernhard, Projective Geometry, Stuttgart 1984.

to beginning teachers, I aim to prvide a representation which is closely tied to how a class (led according to my practice) might actually turn out, including detailed hints. The idea is to sketch the later course in big strokes and with reference to already existing guides.

4 The relation of two triangles

If this is the first main lesson block hour, we need – after rhythmic practice – empty table tops and quiet attention. Then, the teacher can draw two triangles on the board, with the sides as distances.[8]

He designates the corners as A, B, C resp. A_1, B_1, C_1. Then he connects corresponding corners of different colors with lines stretching over the whole board. Since it is formed from sides, a 3-side (trilateral) arises from the lines $AA_1 BB_1$, ACC_1. Then he extends the sides of the triangles to the edges of the board. The intersecting points of corresponding sides form a triangle. He quietly repeats the same construction on the side board with identical triangles whose initial positions have been slightly varied.

For the experimental drawing phase of quiet, independent work that follows, the teacher distributes a worksheet with two suitable triangles and designated corners. This is helpful as a «push» for some students. The students are directet to produce other pairs of trilateral-triangle through the transformation of the triangles in position or form on new pages. Agreement is reached on uniform coloring of triangle and trilateral. Frequently, one cannot get the configuration down on paper. DIN A3-format copy paper makes it easier and helps avoid unnecessary problems. The question quickly arises whether, if not on the paper, there are intersection points somewhere farther away. These can usually be quickly determined; there also occur cases of parallel lines, and sometimes many. But these are less frequent than intersections. And we will endeavor to shape the configuration so that it fits on the paper. Finished drawings can be immediately hung on the wall next to each other.

After some time, an array of configurations has appeared. Some students allow themselves to become confused by their own drawings and «see nothing more» (not the trilateral and not the triangle). And the hanging helps them to «see» again. It speaks for itself. Some students will quickly discover characteristics of the transformation. One can approach these students, in case they themselves don't ask, and engage them, ask them supportive questions lead them to further investigations, such as: does this work with quadrilaterals a well? Try it but don't tell. The young people must feel understood otherwise the teacher has not prepared well.

We should not try to prevent creative chatter and relevant communication with neighbors.

Once the intensity level is adequate, one can hang the rest of the drawings, the class gathers to observe them, and takes the time to take a look at each one. What stands out? One gathers all

---

[8]To attain the configuration, he considers how these triangles must lie; as needed, he makes inconspicuous drawings on the board. Continuation next page. Even if he is structurally familiar with projective geometry, the beginner will have to practice a good bit- until he can move in it, in terms of construction, and view the configurations as if «living in them».

the observations; all are useful, even those that seem worthless or incorrect. Much is corrected and students correct themselves. And the teacher attempts to understand all that is said as it was intended. Technical language is not yet required. After summarizing, we note on the board: what is essential and what is rather accidental? Do we have to hang the drawings differently? Which belong together, which do not? It may be, one has to hang the drawings in a new order, possibly as a developmental sequence – one incites a kind of exact feeling. One simply follows the ideas which are expressed and the teacher moderates. One is led to a remarkable discovery, for despite how the original triangles were selected:

The smaller (more point-formed) the trilateral becomes, the flatter (more line shaped[9] the triangle becomes. And the reverse is true.

(The formulations of the students result in this or something similar. The teacher accepts them, lets them undergo improvement and inserts nothing of his own).

This theorem can be put on the board in the lower third. In the upper part of the board, onewould describe how we proceeded – with the heading «Two Triangles – Their Relation». Often, there is not trilateral or triangle on the paper, no matter how large it is. Parallel lines prevent it. But the discovery appears so convincing, that even such exceptions don't threaten its perceived validity.

The assignment for the next main lesson day can be that everyone constructs his own stringent sequence of development from about eight to ten drawings, constructed and assembled with the above central assertion in mind. One can begin to work on this in the remaining instruction time.

A description of the construction rules by students removes any unclarities and draws the other students into the process. A comparison of both configurations brings up the question: What has changed? How could one carry out further changes of the initial triangles? Can one in each case foresee what the consequences of a change will be for the configuration as a whole? Well, we have to try it out.

At the end of the rhythmic part of the second main lesson, one can carry out the following fairly common exercise, that a student once so described (in a homework assignment):

«We imagine a horizontal line that is intersected by a line in the same plane vertically – the line is placed so as to turn. If we turn the latter line, its point of intersection moves. If the lines are parallel, then its point of intersection lies very far away - but it could still be grasped by calculation. If, in this position, the line to be turned is turned by a very small angle, the point of intersection moves a good bit. If we turn the line further, until both lines are parallel, there is no more intersecting point. But, with further turning, a point of intersection arises immediately. But it lies on the opposite side...»

This way, we keep the students alert and have a transition to the observation part (also see article by S. Sigler). Of which situatin from yesterday does this remind us? The conversation deepens

---

[9] I let line and straight line appear as synonyms.

what was done and discovered yesterday. What was actually present at the end of the developmental sequence?

At the end, we had two triangles, whose joining lines of pairs of corresponding corner points run through a point. And then the points of intersection of the (extended) sides lie on a line.

We can also express this conversely; for, in the drawing, both things occurred simultaneously. And we must take the exceptions into account.

Now we can use a board on rollers with the previous day's formulation written on it. We add the formulation cited above. This can be refined based on a student's suggestions – alternatives are sought and noted. Finally, the teacher makes a suggestion-one which Arnold Bernhard often uses and is pleasing to the students.

If two triangles are centered, then they are also aligned and vice-versa. [10]

This formulation is wonderful. All the same, we continue to polish what's already been collected on the board, until the teacher – via dictation – finally writes a very harmonic formulation, in exactly the sequence he desires, on the left side of the board. Calling out is acceptable here. And the supposition below appears:

«Theorem of Desargues»

| If the joining lines of corresponding vertices of two triangles pass through a point, then the intersection points of corresponding sides lie on a line. | But also the converse | If the intersecting points of corresponding sides of two triangles lie on a line, the connecting lines of corresponding corners pass through a point. |

Unless there are parallel lines in the configuration.

In a profound way, the students are struck by the «thing itself»; here the core of the matter is expressed

Pass through...	As a contrast	Lie on...
lie on		pass through...
joining lines		intersecting points...
intersection points		connecting lines
vertices		sides
sides		corners
point		line
line		point

So there is a remarkable symmetry of paired concepts, which – with an exchange – allow the two halves of the board to go over into each other. This can be developed in conversation and put on the board.

---

[10] The german term is: «Sind zwei Dreiecke zentriert, so sind sie auch liniert, und umgekehrt.» The term «zentriert-liniert» was introduced by A. Bernhard»

Now one has now conveniently recorded on a movable blackboard a set of observations and can bring them into play at just the right moment (see below). On the central blackboard, we have a attractive and clearly drawn Desargues figure, but only the points and lines. The teacher can also have this prepared on an overhead. What is taking place here? What properties does it have? The following observations are then to be discussed:[11]

- It consists of ten lines and ten points.

- On each line lie three points, and three lines pass through each point.

- Each line can take over the role of the axis and each point take over the role of the center.

- Once the center or the axis is selected, the rest of the configuration is completely determined.

Now we can practice the «seeing of the triangle» as follows:

One student goes to the board and determines one of the ten points as center. Now he tries to form the appropriate configuration from the figure. He looks for the two triangles and axis and marks them It's a matter of finding the correct combinations; the other students are just as intensely engaged in the task, and can give him hints and suggestions. The teacher is there only as moderator. As an example, we can offer the following approach: The projector is turned on and the projected Desargue figure (black on transperent sheet) appears so clearly on the board that we can complete the process above with another center. This exciting process for the students can, according to need and time available, be continued to the end. Teacher and student can alternate activity.

In any case, about a half hour should be available for quiet work until the end of the main lesson. It's not necessary that the board work be copied. It could be that a student produces a perfect copy which can be distributed. At this point, four different Desargues figures can be distributed as model worksheets (see attachment) – the assignment is to develop all ten possible configurations for the first figure. For the other three sheets (with increasing difficulty) he can produce ten identical copies by pricking holes through the paper. A possible homework assignment is to complete at least three of the four configurations.

Through this training of seeing, this gemetricalla fundamental theorems can «take root»[12]

Moreover, there are enormous differences in the capacity for «seeing». And it is not necessarily connected to the mathematical abilities of the individual. Often students who have difficulty with math find access here. And adults who deal with this the first time often have the greatest difficulty in «seeing configurations».

---

[11] See, for instance, A. Bernhard, L. Locher-Ernst, and others –or the other compositions of this notebook.
[12] Peter Buck, Einwurzelung und Verdichtung-Tema con variazione on the two metaphors of Wagnerschein-Didactics, Duernau 1997.

It is crucial for the completeness of our thinking activity that the following is taken into account.. And I do this in the skill classes running parallel to the block.[13]

This is to avoid overtaxing the thought process of the main lesson time. The theorem of Desargues treats the simultaneous central point of similarity and linear aspect of triangles. If no student has asked this, the question should be posed: Who says this doesn't apply for quadrilaterals or polygons? Otherwise, what is the theorem worth? We should pursue this through construction exercises, as is portrayed by A. Bernhard in chapter 17 (See practice sheet in the attachment). Here a deeper understanding sets in. And, as with other things represented here, the path to knowledge goes through «doing it oneself». Only then is real knowledge developed.

How far are we now? We consciously elect not to introduce any ideal elements (elements at infinity) – so that the many exceptions and special cases do not undermine the ideas and relationships found.

Since we have had the preview in the tenth grade, it is advisable to bring up the theorems of Pascal and Brianchon in the next main lesson. (If there was not this preparation, the instructional segment described should carried out in more detail - for instance, according to the model of the Desargue theorem).

After taking up the previous day's material in connection with the theorem of Desargues, we could proceed as follows: The teacher opens the two wings of the blackboard and, to the outside left, we see a Pascal figure - and, to the right, a Brianchon configuration. Then comes the development of further configurations for both theorems in the middle of the board. We involve the students with questions, so that the subject is again present for them. Together, we develop the verbal formulations of both theorems – and note them next to each other in the middle of the board:

If the vertices of a hexagon belong to a circle, then the intersection points of the opposite sides lie on a line.	If the sides of a hexagon belong to a circle, then the connecting lines of the opposite corners intersect at a point.
Exception: At least one pair of opposite sides is parallel.	Exception: At least two connecting lines are parallel.

Here we can refer to the «remarkable symmetry» of the theorem of Desargues and find this here again – in any case, when we none of the indicated exeptions are present. So we can exchange all the concepts of a geometric theorem, according to the given pairing, and gain thereby another true geometric theorem. This we call the principle of dualism in the plane. Olive Whicher calls this the archetypal connection of the elements of the plane:

The line relates to the point the point, to the line.

---

[13] Usually in Germany there exit one or two «skill classes» during a week additional to the main-lesson block.

Now let's go back to the simplest geometric situation:

The teacher marks two points on the board and connects them with a line. How may lines are there? Exactly one! How can we express this set of circumstances?

1. Two lines have exactly one joining line
   - and the dual statement for this?

2. Two lines have exactly one point of intersection, unless they are parallel.
   - Does this mean the beautiful dualism applies only with exceptions?
   - What would we have to do to have both of these fundamental facts really dual?
   - What conditions would have to be fulfiled?

(The above does not necessarily simulate the desired questions and answers between student and teacher. It just shows the thought process which can result in an exchange. We notice that the awakening of mental forces is completed through conversation. This can be carried out on all configurations, which hang on the pin board or are on the blackboard from the first main lessons.) also those arising from the mental exercises described above

Together, one hammers out the new concepts: the common point belonging to each family of parallel lines, and the fact that this common point is different for each family of parallel lines, and also unique; and the consistency of this with 2), but also, in light of 1), the necessity of recognizing a unique («new») line which joins together all the newly created points. – see overview from notebook on page 197

The result is that, by a free act, we have achieved a resolution, which was initially suggested by the unsatisfactory situation arising out of the incomplete symmetry of the theorem of Desargues, and other pairs of harmonically-related theorems (e.g., Pascal and Brianchon). And this is subject to the necessity of proving their compatibility with the phenomena of intersection and joining. This is indeed the case, and the perspective is opened for finding a new, valid theorem from one recognized as valid- through dualization. We can do this well with the theorem of Pappos. We become familiar with it in its diverse forms through construction. Then the dual theorem can be developed verbally. Through construction, we see that a new correct theorem results – and what a beautyful one it is (See the following pages – they come from main lesson books).

Now students will not just want to enjoy it. They will naturally ask the question, what can one do with it? An answer in the strict sense is provided by the generation of enveloping curves of second order out of the Theorem of Pappus, and of point curves of second order out of its dual form. This theorem is closely connected to the fundamental theorem[14]

If we continue the Pappos construction by assigning to a further freely-chosen element its corresponding one and and then join (resp. intersect) this pair of elements, a line-wise (resp. pointwise) conic arises. (See page 2 and 3 of student notebook).

---

[14] See L. Locher-Ernst, Projective Geometry, Dornach, 1980 , p.95f and p.122f, as well as Olive Whicher, Projective Geometry, Stuttgart 1970, p.80ff

The students find this fascinating , also in connection with the various methods for producing these conic curves which were learned earlier. Here there is an extensive field for practice. This is the adventure of discovering different conic curves, according to the arrangement of basic elements of the Pappos figure. It is suggested that the teacher produce multiple work sheets which enable the curve to appear harmonic on the page.[15]

It is frustrating to the students to repeatedly experience that, with a freely-chosen arrangement, he fails to get the desired figure on the sheet of paper, even when one worksworking with DINA3 format. But all this can be treated at this or a later point of the block progression.

4.1 Further course and overview

However we treat it , there is another connection in which the inclusion of elements at infinity is certain and that is the uninterrupted transformation of figures of the plane in itself. The goal is geometric metamorphosis.[16]

The path follows, for example, the complete transformation of a triangle in the plane.[17] It is not necessary but is stimulating to introduce the «centered-aligned-collineation» as a «moving medium» and to carefully discuss its properties (See A. Bernhard, Chapter 15). From here, multiple connections can be found to what has been treated before. This can be seen here in the theorem of Desargues.

---

[15] A stimulating partially demanding collection of diverse constructions is portrayed in the book by Angelo Andes Rovida, Exercises on Synthetic Projective Geometry, Dornach 1988

[16] A proven didactic composition is present in A. Bernhard , Projective Geometry, Stuttgart 1984

[17] See A. Bernhard, Chapter 12, p. 47, only viewed in the horizontal plane.

Pascal-Theorem

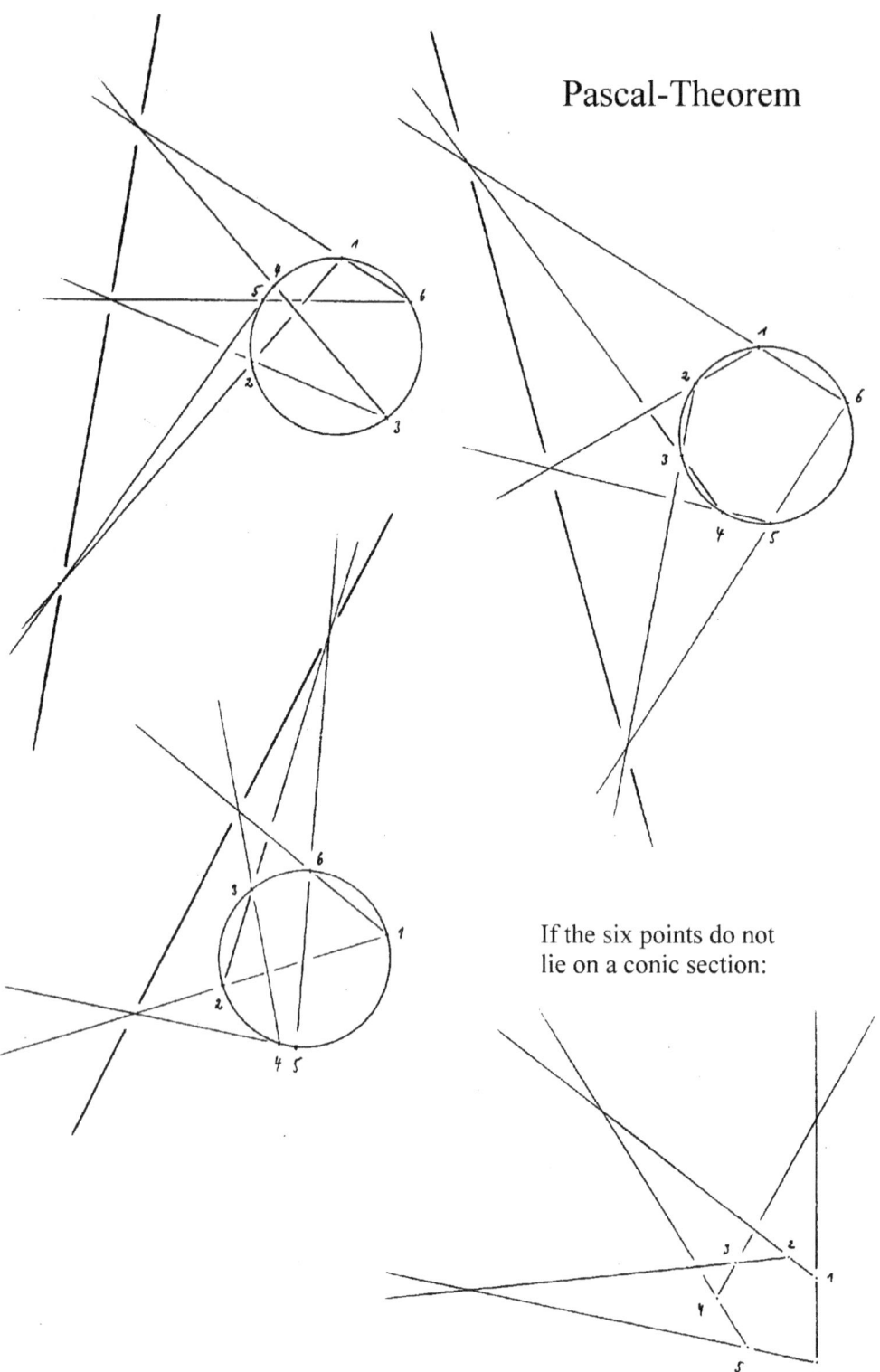

If the six points do not lie on a conic section:

Brianchon Theorem

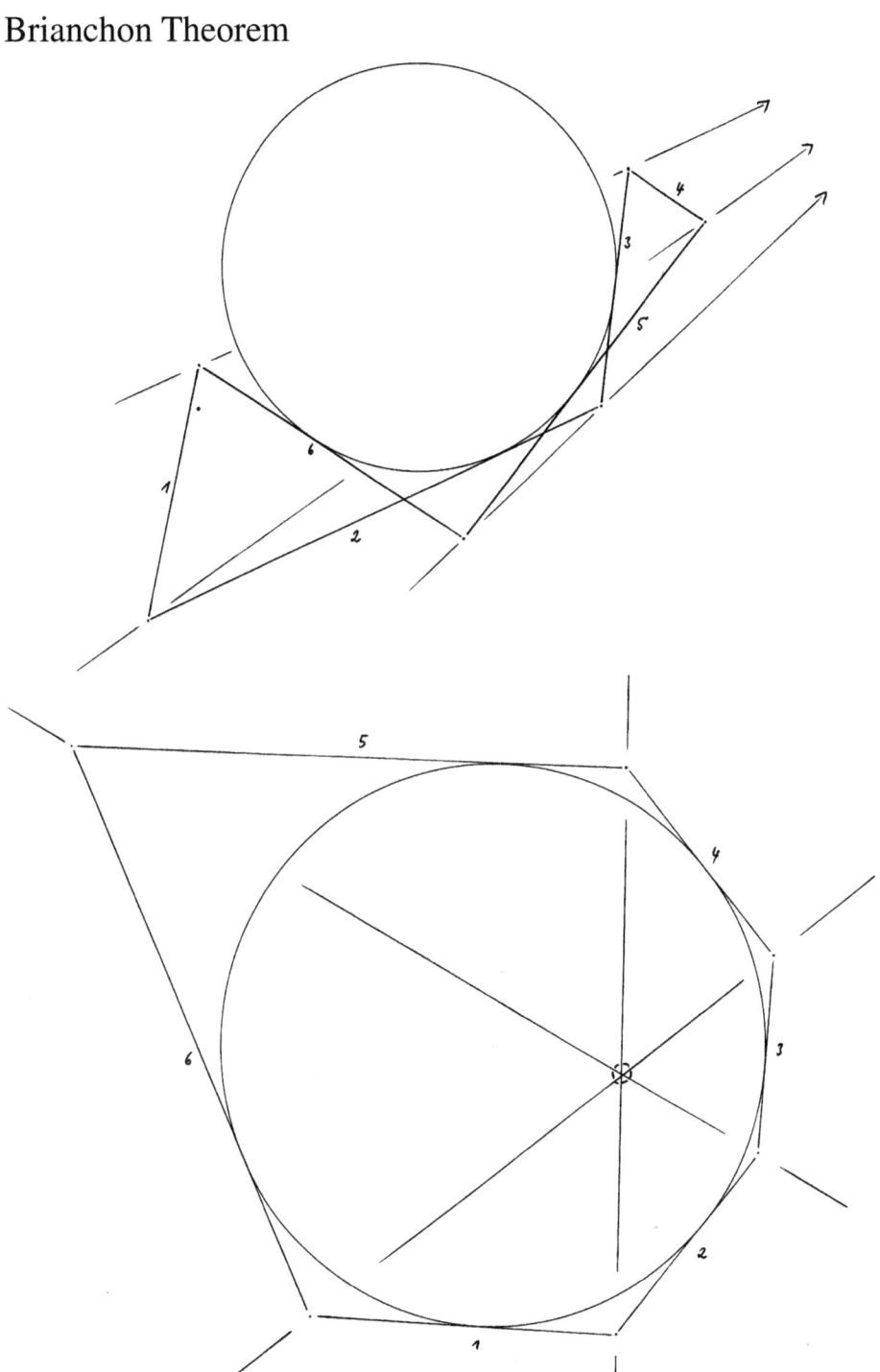

Worksheet 1

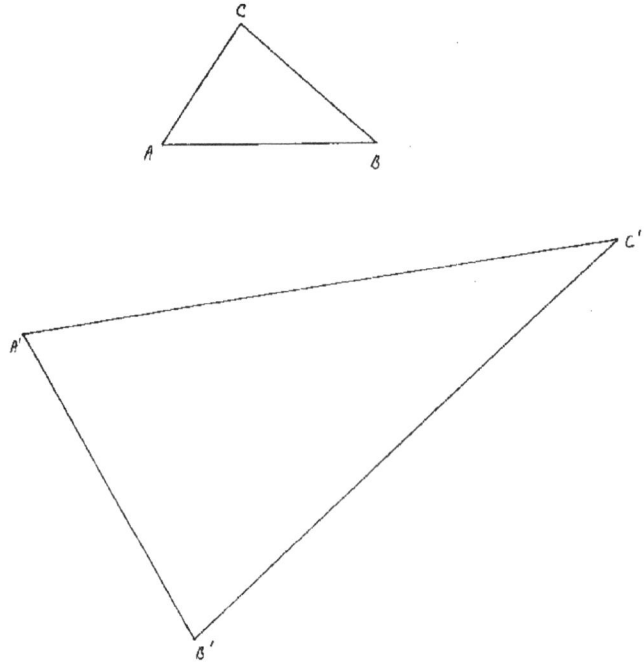

A relatively simplified worksheet 2 for students who have experimented in vain

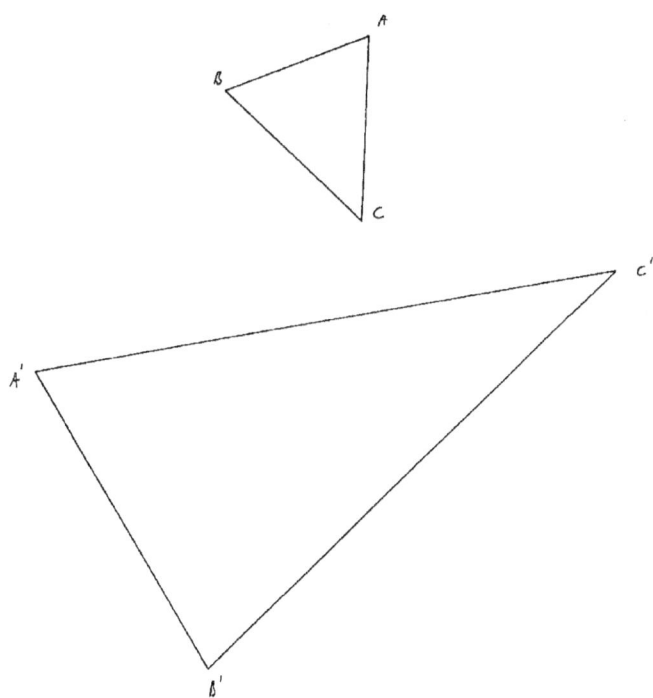

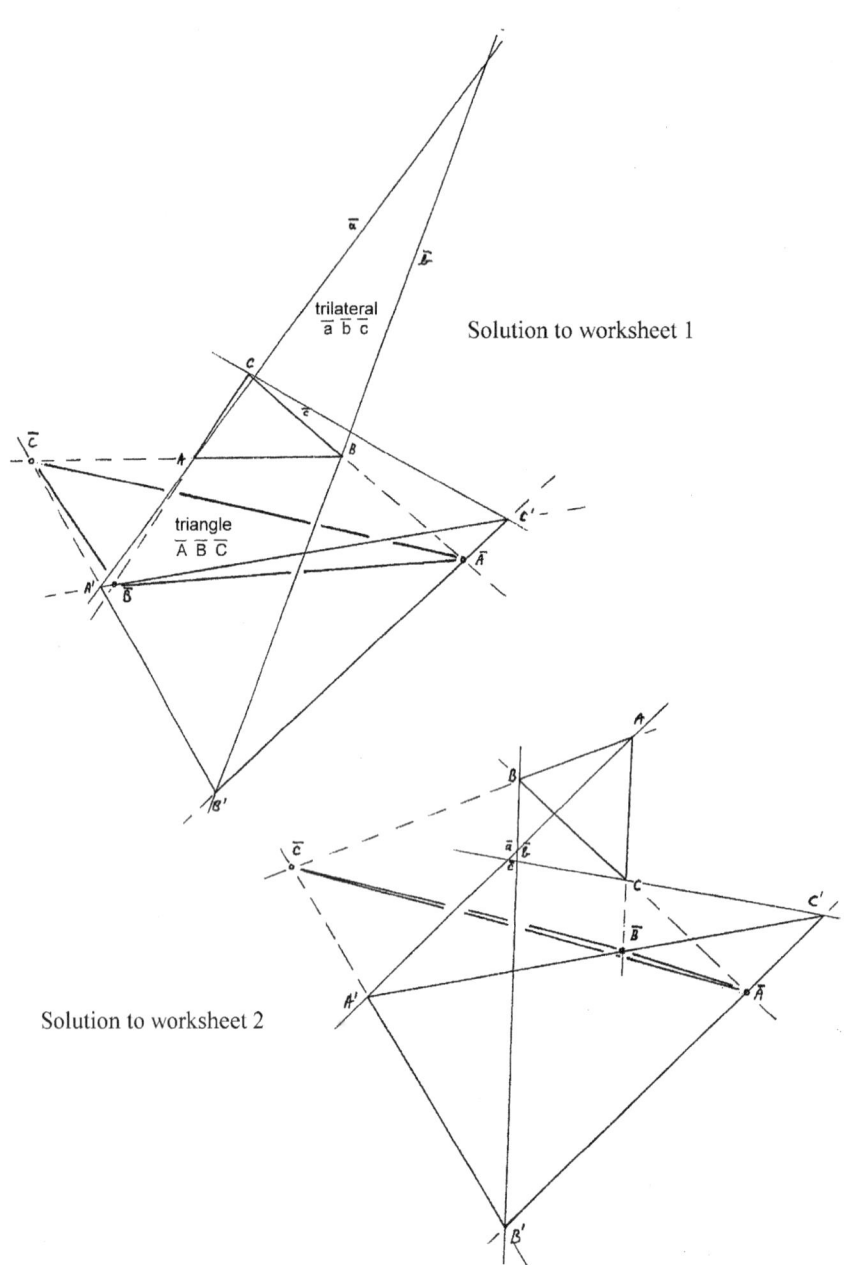

Worksheet for Desargues 1

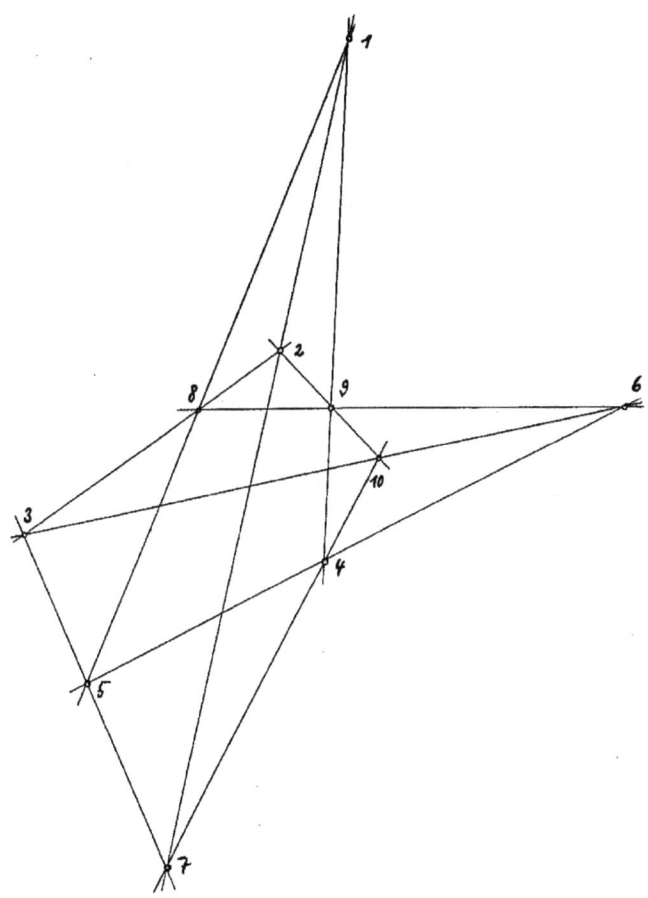

Worksheet for Desargues 2

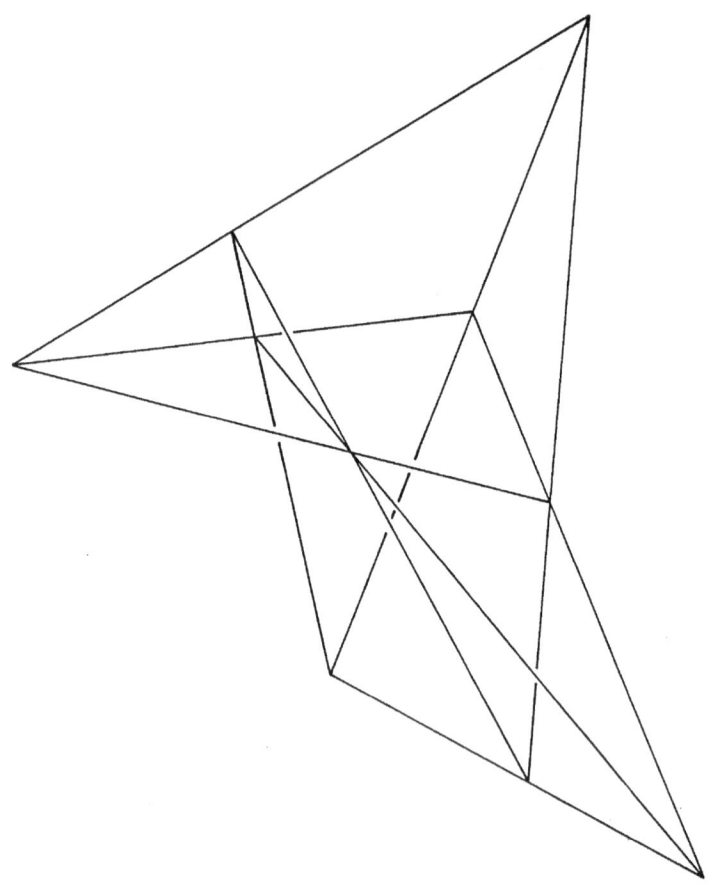

Worksheet for Desargues 3

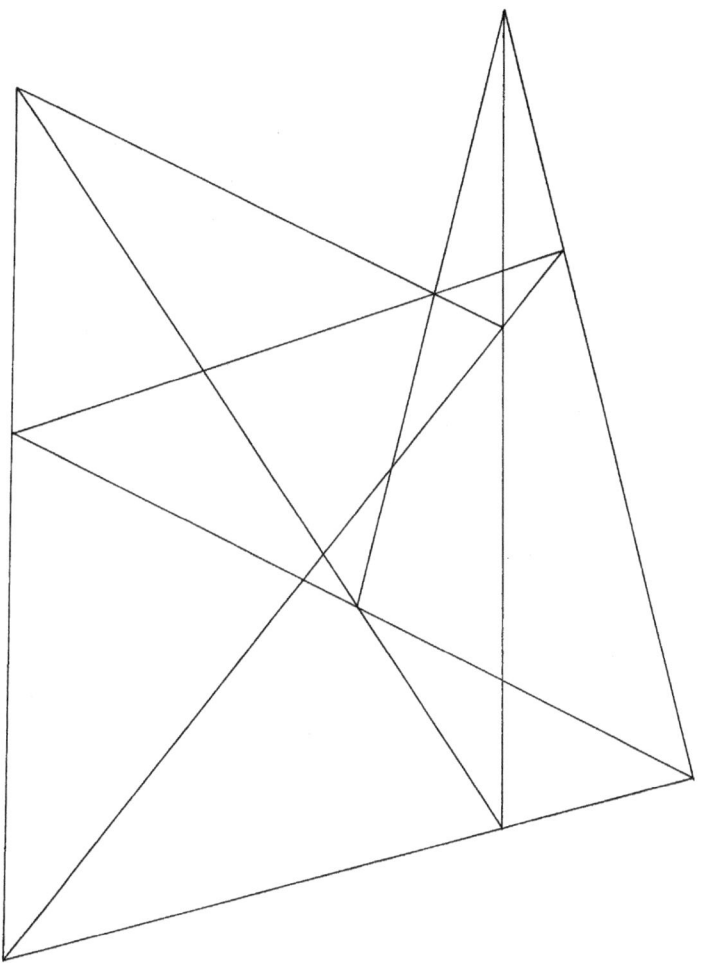

A Path to Projective Geometry *Rolf Rosbigalle*

Worksheet for Desargues 4

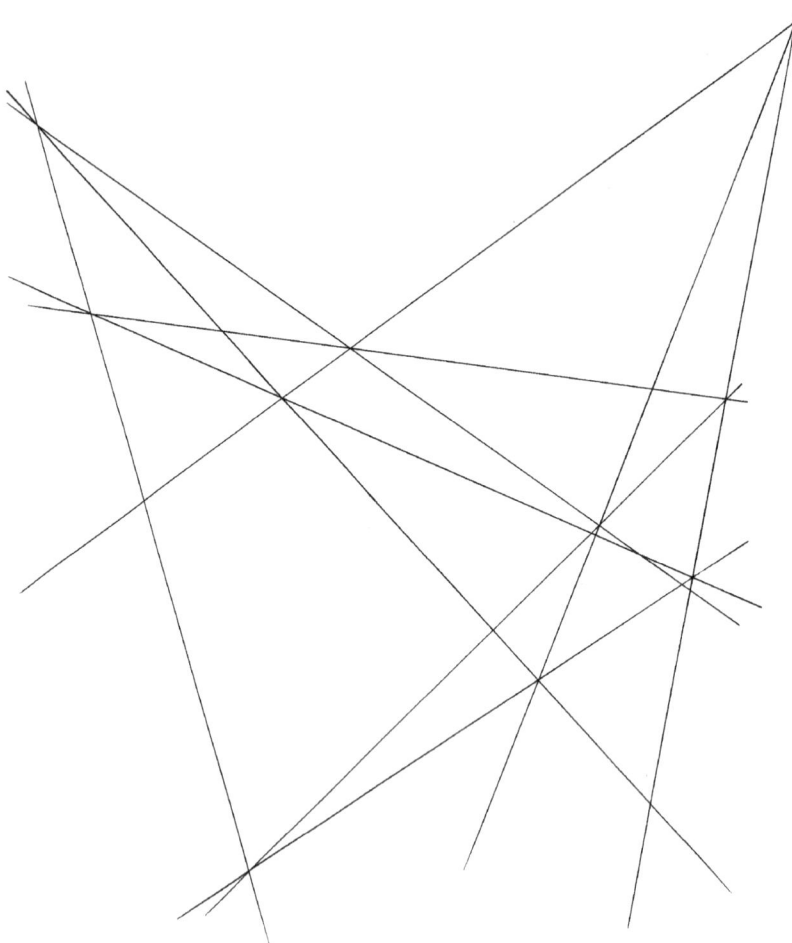

Worksheet a)

Which pairs ar centered, which are not?

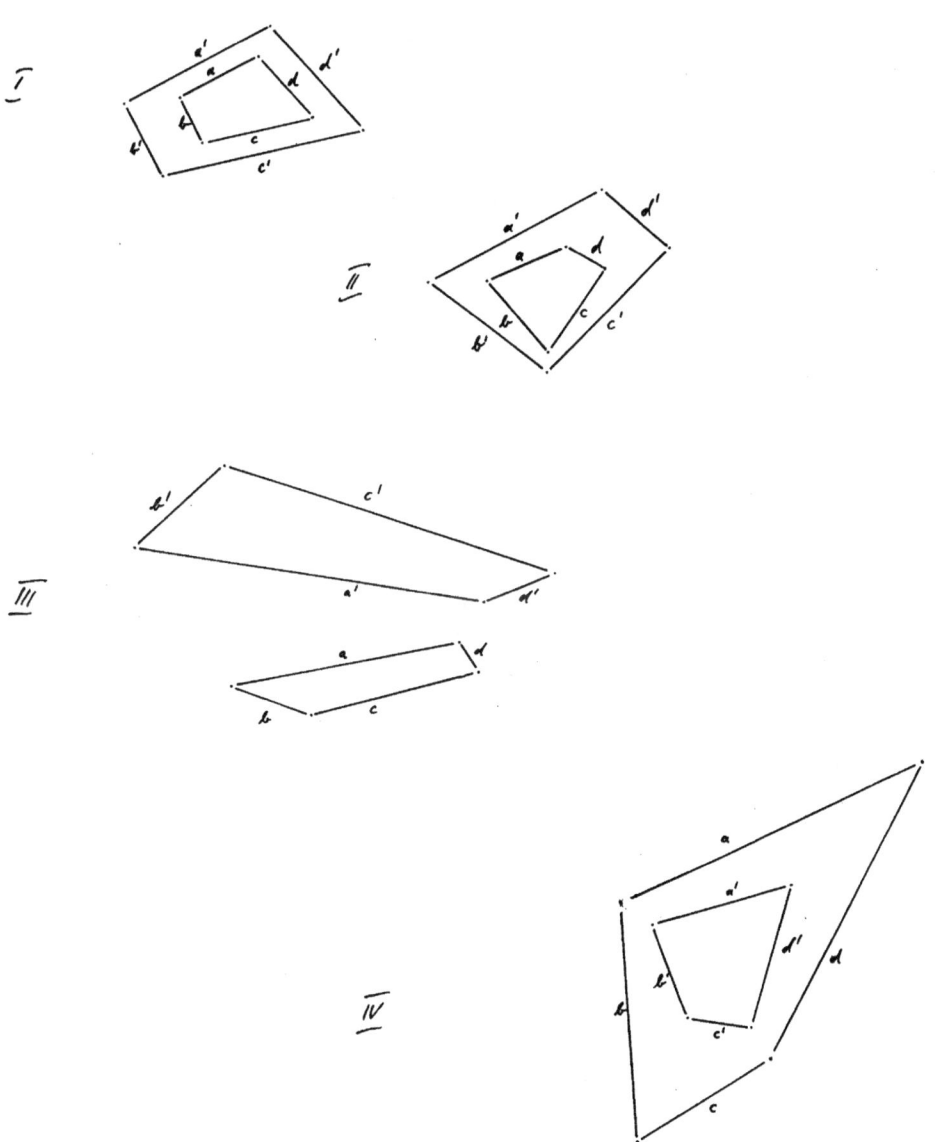

Worksheet b)

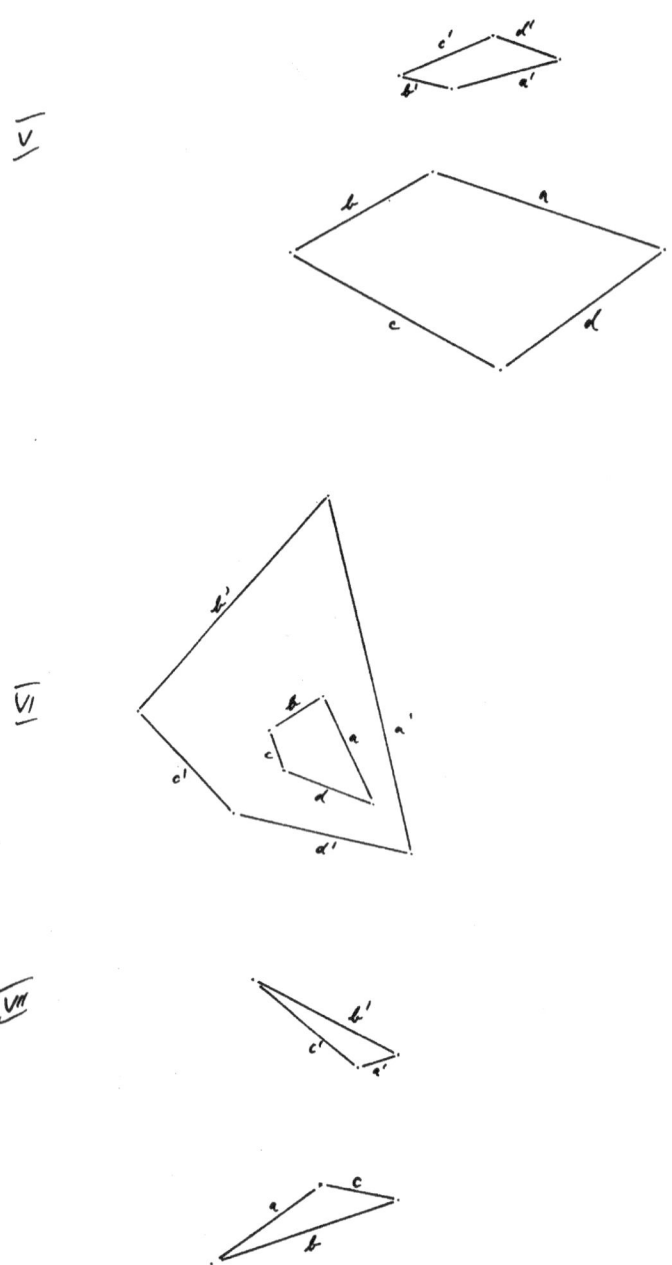

Some examples from student's notebooks:

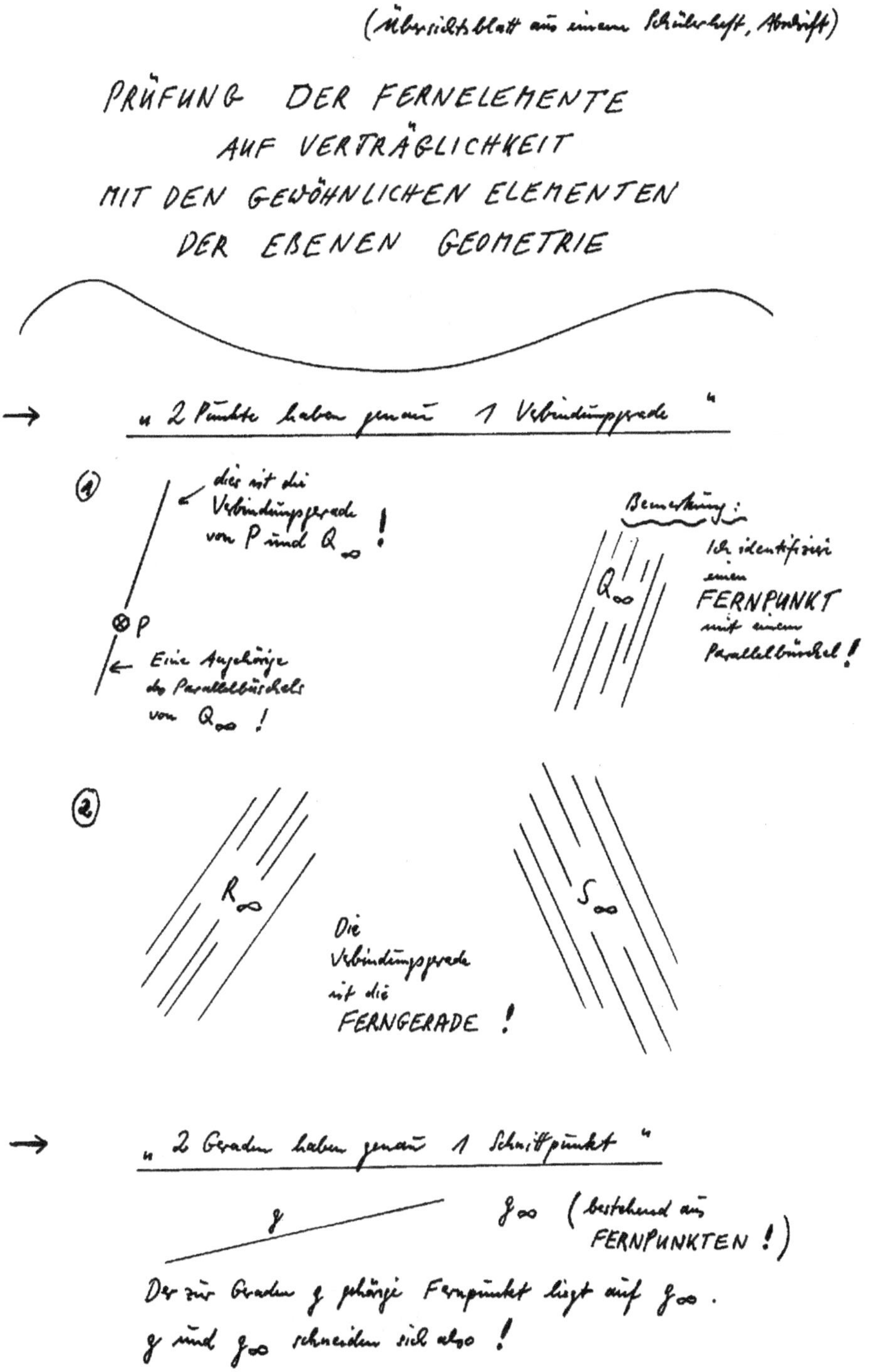

(Übersichtsblatt aus einem Schülerheft, Abschrift)

PRÜFUNG DER FERNELEMENTE AUF VERTRÄGLICHKEIT MIT DEN GEWÖHNLICHEN ELEMENTEN DER EBENEN GEOMETRIE

→ „2 Punkte haben genau 1 Verbindungsgerade"

① dies ist die Verbindungsgerade von P und Q_∞ !

⊗ P

Eine Angehörige des Parallelbüschels von Q_∞ !

Bemerkung: Ich identifiziere einen FERNPUNKT mit einem Parallelbüschel !

Q_∞

② R_∞ S_∞

Die Verbindungsgerade ist die FERNGERADE !

→ „2 Geraden haben genau 1 Schnittpunkt"

g g_∞ (bestehend aus FERNPUNKTEN !)

Der zur Geraden g gehörige Fernpunkt liegt auf g_∞. g und g_∞ schneiden sich also !

Theorem of Pappos(-Pascal):

(Schülerheft S.1)

Der Satz von Pappos(-Pascal):

Liegen die Ecken eines Sechsecks $P_1 Q_2 P_3 Q_1 P_2 Q_3$ abwechselnd auf zwei Geraden, so liegen die Schnittpunkte der Gegenseiten $P_1 Q_2, P_2 Q_1$ bzw. $P_1 Q_3, P_3 Q_1$ bzw. $P_2 Q_3, P_3 Q_2$ auf einer Geraden.

Der Satz von Pappos(-Pascal) duale Form:

Gehen die Seiten eines Sechsseits $p_1 q_2 p_3 q_1 p_2 q_3$ abwechselnd durch zwei Punkte, so gehen die Verbindungsgeraden der gegenüberliegenden Ecken $p_1 q_2, p_2 q_1$ bzw. $p_1 q_3, p_3 q_1$ bzw. $p_2 q_3, p_3 q_2$ durch einen Punkt.

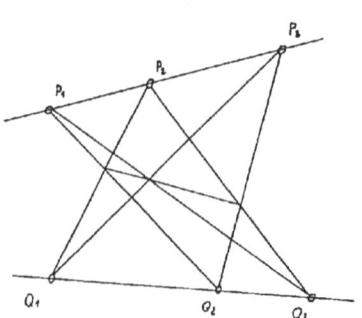

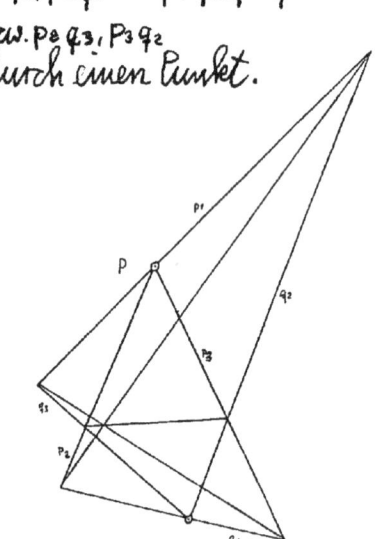

Entstehung von

Hüllkurven 2. Ordnung

durch fortgesetztes Verbinden und Schneiden nach dem Satz von Pappos:

Man findet die Verbindungsgeraden gleichbenannter Punkte. Diese sind die Tangenten des Kegelschnitts.

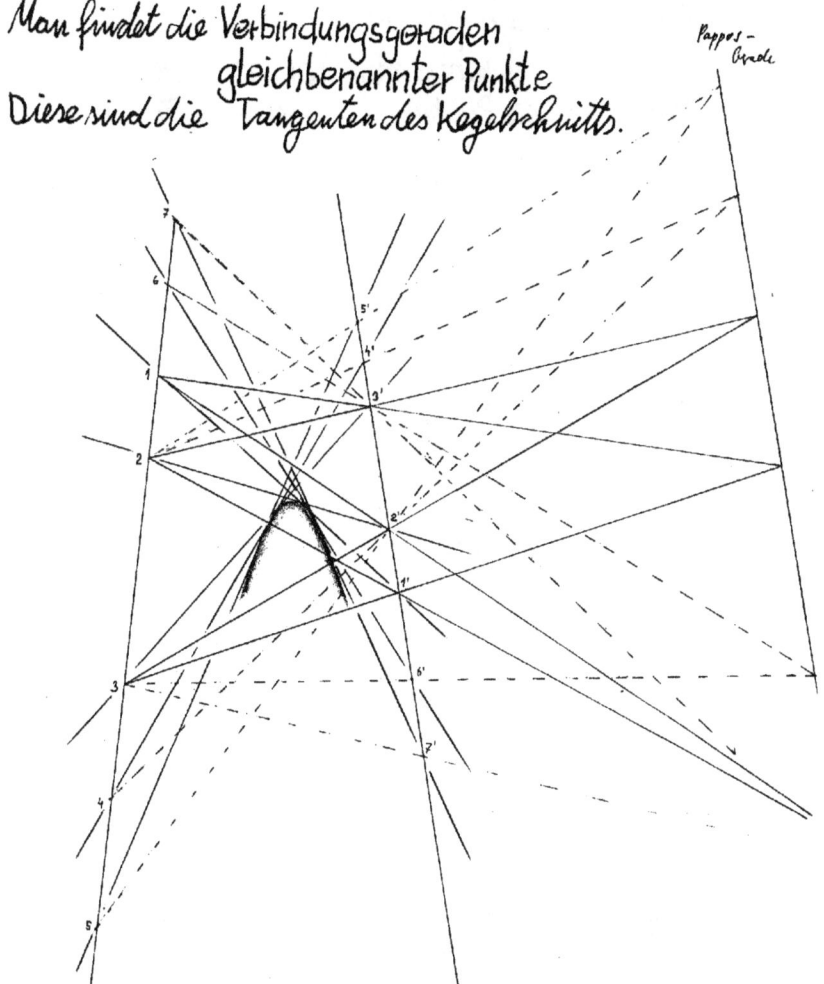

Curves of the second order

Through continous joining and intersecting according to the theorem of Pappos:

One finds the joining lines of like-named points. These are the tangents of the conic section.

Entstehung von

Punktkurven 2. Ordnung

durch fortgesetztes Schneiden und Verbinden nach dem Satz von Pappos:

Man findet Schnittpunkte gleichbenannter Geraden. Diese sind die Punkte des Kegelschnitts.

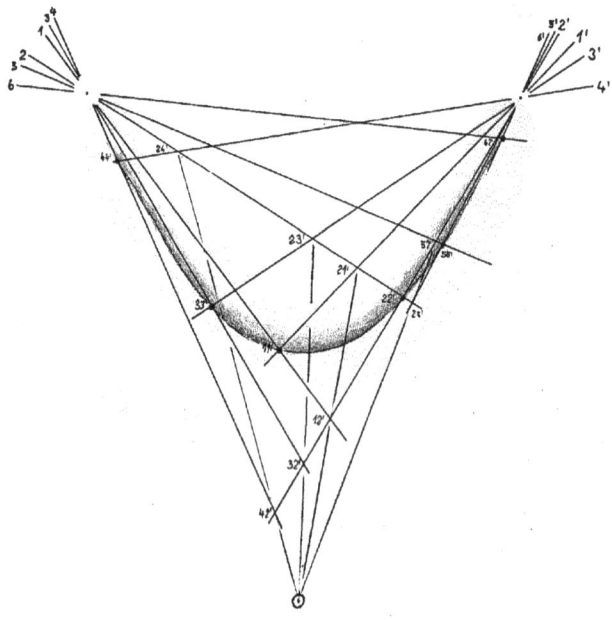

Through continued intersecting and joining according to the theorem of Pappos:
One finds intersecting points of like-named lines. These are points of the conic section.

From Ratio to Cross-Ratio

UWE HANSEN

For the developing student, it is an important and liberating experience to rediscover the familiar and trusted laws of Euclidean geometry in the general laws of projective geometry. Then laws which seemingly have no connection appear as special cases of a comprehensive relationship. This will be illustrated with an example.

The midpoints of the four sides of a square form another square. If we form further midpoints the result is Figure 1. This sequence of squares can be continued without limit inward and outward.

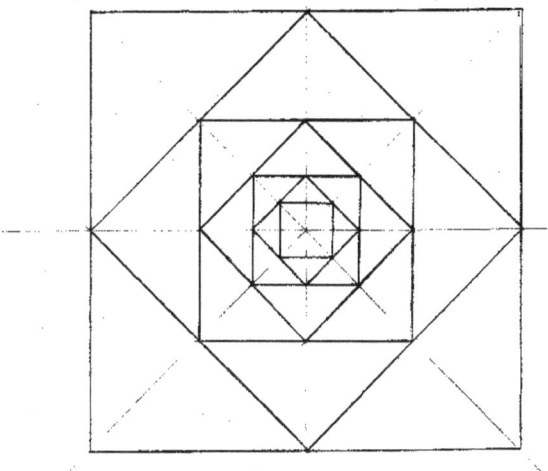

Figure 1

We take a look at the distances of the corner points of the squares to the common central point. Since the corner points lie on a line of the central point, the distances form a geometric sequence with common ratio $q = 2$.

We shall now investigate how Figure 1 changes when the original square is turned into an isosceles trapezoid, all the incidences of Figure 1 remaining unchanged in the process.

In Figure 1, the diagonals of a square are parallel to the sides of the next surrounding square and the converse is true as well. Because of the incidence requirements, in Figure 2 the trapezoid diagonals meet pairs of opposite sides of the surrounding quadrangle, and pairs of the opposite sides of the trapezoid meet the diagonals of the surrounding quadrangle, all in one line, which in Figure 1 was the infinitely distant line. This line must go through S and it must also be parallel to A_0B_0, since A_0B_0 is parallel to C_0D_0. It follows that the surrounding quadrangle is a kite whose sides intersect the diagonals of the trapezoid at the points T_1 and T_2. One diagonal of the kite goes through S and the other is parallel to A_0B_0. Since the trapezoid was assumed to be isosceles, the diagonals of the kite intersect at a right angle.

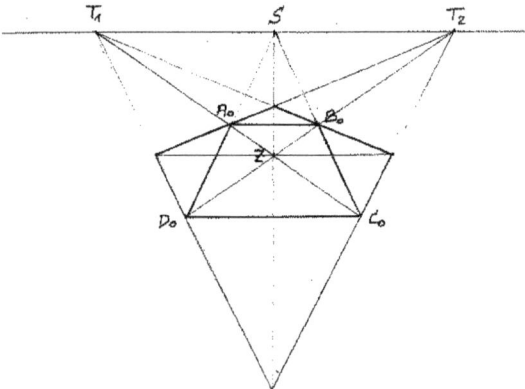

Figure 2

The trapezoid $A_0B_0C_0D_0$ was chosen so that A_0 is the midpoint of the segment T_1C_0. From this it follows that A_0B_0 is half as long as C_0D_0. Thus Z divides the distance A_0C_0 in the ratio of $1:2$. Therefore $ZA_0 : A_0T_1 = 1:3$. In other words A_0 divides the distance ZT_1 in the ratio $1:3$. This is also true of point C_0.

Equally, through repeated determination of side ratios of similar triangles we can show that

$$ZA_1 : A_1T_1 = 2:3$$
$$ZA_2 : A_2T_1 = 4:3$$

and generally:

$$ZA_n : A_nT_1 = 2^n : 3$$

(see Figure 3, in which further trapezoids and kites are drawn, whose sides must intersect in S or T_1 and T_2). This means that the ratios $ZA_n : A_nT_1$ form a geometric sequence with common ratio $q = 2$.

We thus have the following cross-ratios (anharmonic ratios):

$$(1) \quad \frac{ZA_{n+1}}{A_{n+1}T_1} : \frac{ZA_n}{A_nT_1} = 2.$$

We come to the astonishing conclusion that the constant ratio $q = 2$ from Figure 1 is transformed into the constant cross-ratio $D = 2$ in Figure 3. This result is independent of the chosen shape of the trapezoid $A_0B_0C_0D_0$.

On all lines going through Z, the corners of these metamorphosed quadrangles produce sequences of points for which the cross-ratio is equal to 2 – with the exception of the point sequence E_n. The points E_n lie on a line which is parallel to the line T_1T_2. For this sequence of points the following applies: The distances ZE_n form a geometric sequence with common ratio $q = 2$.

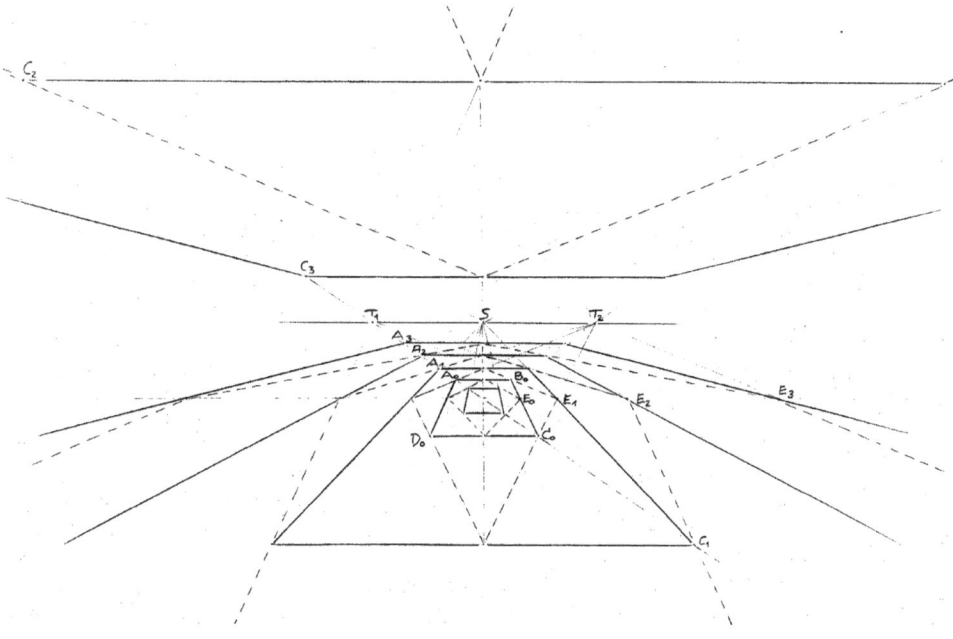

Figure 3

In Figure 3, the quadrangles approach on the one hand the center Z, on the other they surround the «limit line» $T_1 T_2$. In the limit the quadrangle is thus a point or a double line.

If we transform equation (1) into

$$\frac{ZA_{n+1}}{ZA_n} : \frac{A_{n+1}T_1}{A_n T_1} = 2$$

we see that if T_1 becomes an infinitely distant point, the second fraction converges to 1. The distances ZA_n then form a geometric sequence.

In a second step, the trapezoid is transformed into a quite general quadrilateral. If we draw in additional quadrangles, we get Figure 4. Here also the line $z = T_1 T_2$ has taken on the function of the «infinitely distant» line. The intersection points of opposite sides of the quadrangle lie on z. The point Z and the line z are the centers of this quadrangle transformation.

Here too we can ascertain the cross-ratio. To do this, we again look at the line ZT_1. It is an extra side of the complete quadrilateral $ZS_1, ZS_2, A_1S_1, A_1S_2$. Thus the four points $ZA_1; A_0T_1$ separate each other harmonically (see the contributions of Georg and Hünig).

From Ratio to Cross-Ratio — Uwe Hansen

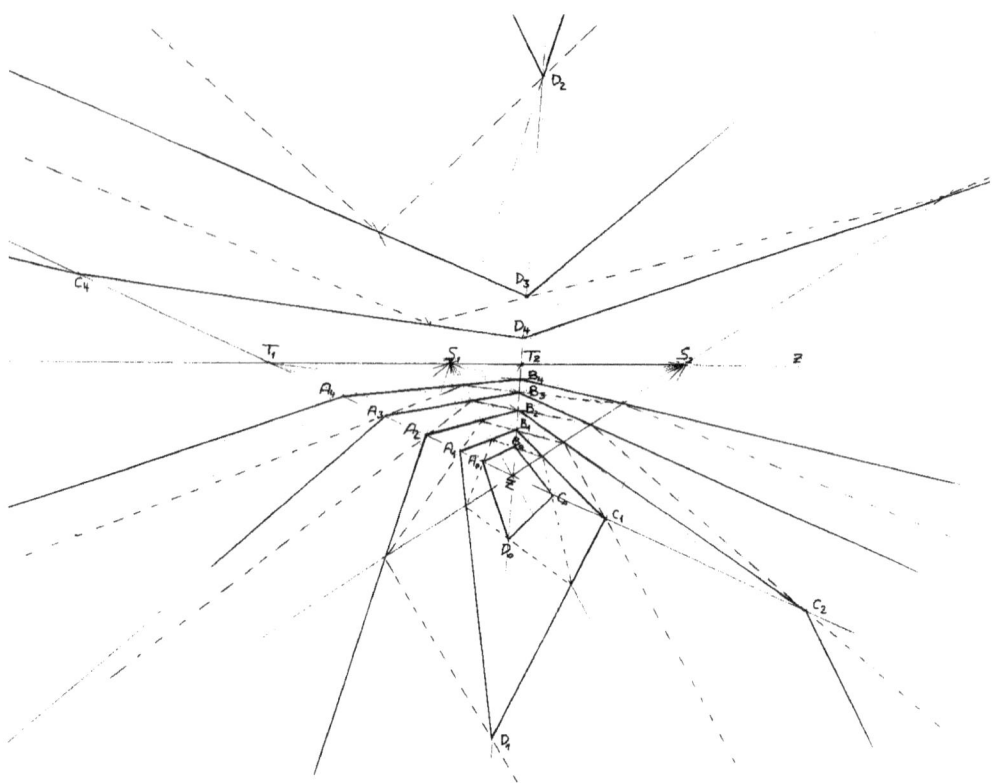

Figure 4

Thus we have:

$$(2) \quad \frac{ZA_0}{A_0A_1} = -\frac{ZT_1}{T_1A_1}.$$

We now let $ZA_0 = a$, $A_0A_1 = b$, $A_1T_1 = c$.

Hence:

$$\frac{a}{b} = -\frac{a+b+c}{-c}$$
$$ac = ab + b^2 + bc$$
$$2ac = ab + ac + b^2 + bc$$
$$2ac = (a+b)(b+c)$$
$$2\frac{a}{b+c} = \frac{a+b}{c}$$

or

$$2 \cdot \frac{ZA_0}{A_0T_1} = \frac{ZA_1}{A_1T_1}$$

or

$$(3) \qquad \frac{ZA_1}{A_1T_1} : \frac{ZA_0}{A_0T_1} = 2.$$

Starting from another quadrilateral, in the same way we can show the following:

$$\frac{ZA_2}{A_2T_1} : \frac{ZA_1}{A_1T_1} = 2$$

or generally

$$(4) \qquad \frac{ZA_{n+1}}{A_{n+1}T_1} : \frac{ZA_n}{A_nT_1} = 2.$$

We see that equation (1) applies generally for all quadrilaterals. So this constant cross-ratio 2 is an expression of the inner construction principle of this quadrangle metamorphosis, a sequence of quadrangles arising from the complete quadrilateral.

The complete quadrilateral (the fundamental harmonic configuration) shows a mysterious interweaving of triad and tetrad (see Figure 5): The four corner points P_1, P_2, P_3, P_4 are the «middle points» of the four three-sided areas and the three points A, B, C (they form the extra triangle) are the «middle points» of the three four-sided areas. The inner harmony of the triangle mediates between the tetrads of the four points P_1, P_2, P_3, P_4 and the four lines g_1, g_2, g_3, g_4.

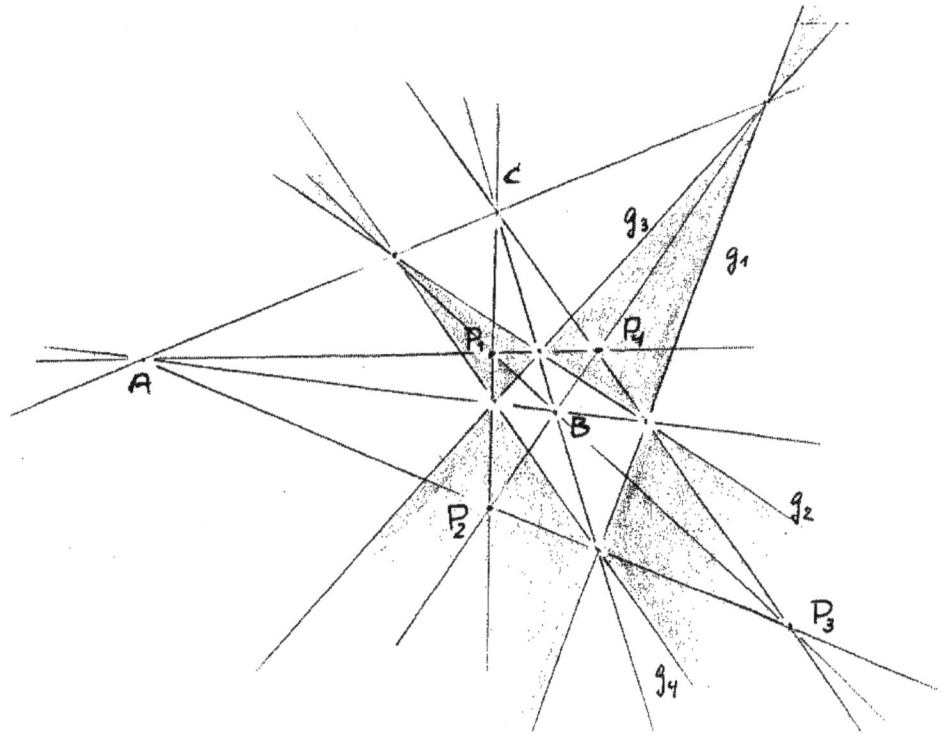

Figure 5

An extra point such as B can be seen as the center Z of a metamorphosis of the quadrangle – for instance $P_1P_2P_3P_4$ is one quadrangle. The line AC would then be the reference line z. The inner balance of the three with the four also suggests viewing the center of a three-sided area as the center of a triangle metamorphosis. For instance, if P_1 is the center, then the triangle ABC is part of this metamorphosis. The line g_1 is then the reference line.

First we'll look at the special case in which similar triangles arise (Figure 6). In this case, the distances ZA_0, ZA_1, ZA_2,... form a geometric sequence with common ratio $q = -2$.

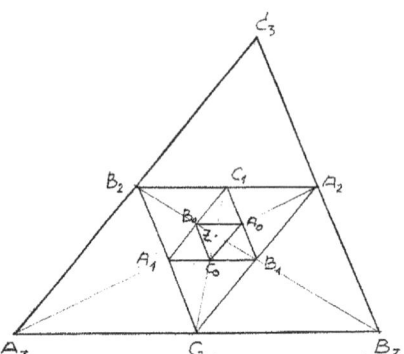

Figure 6

In the case of a general triangle, the cross-ratio $D = -2$ results. The following consideration shows this (Figure 7).

In the quadrilateral A_2B_1, B_1Z, ZC_1, C_1A_2, the line A_2Z is an extra side. Thus the four points A_1A_0; A_2Z are harmonic. Hence

$$(5) \quad \frac{A_1A_2}{A_2A_0} : \frac{A_1Z}{ZA_0} = 1.$$

A_2Z is also an extra side of the quadrilateral A_2B_1, B_1A_1, A_1C_1, C_1A_2. Thus the four points A_1A_2; T_1A_0 are harmonic, so that:

$$(6) \quad \frac{A_1T_1}{T_1A_2} = -\frac{A_1A_0}{A_0A_2}.$$

This equation (6) results from equation (2) when we replace the letters Z, A_0, A_1, T by A_1, T_1, A_2, A_0. If we make the same replacements in equation (3), then equation (6) implies:

$$(7) \quad \frac{A_1A_2}{A_2A_0} : \frac{A_1T_1}{T_1A_0} = 2.$$

Dividing equation (7) by equation (5) gives

$$\frac{A_1Z}{ZA_0} : \frac{A_1T_1}{T_1A_0} = -2$$

or

$$(8) \quad \frac{ZA_1}{A_1T_1} : \frac{ZA_0}{A_0T_1} = -2.$$

By a suitable choice of other quadrilaterals, it can be proven in general that

$$(9) \qquad \frac{ZA_{n+1}}{A_{n+1}T_1} : \frac{ZA_n}{A_n T_1} = -2.$$

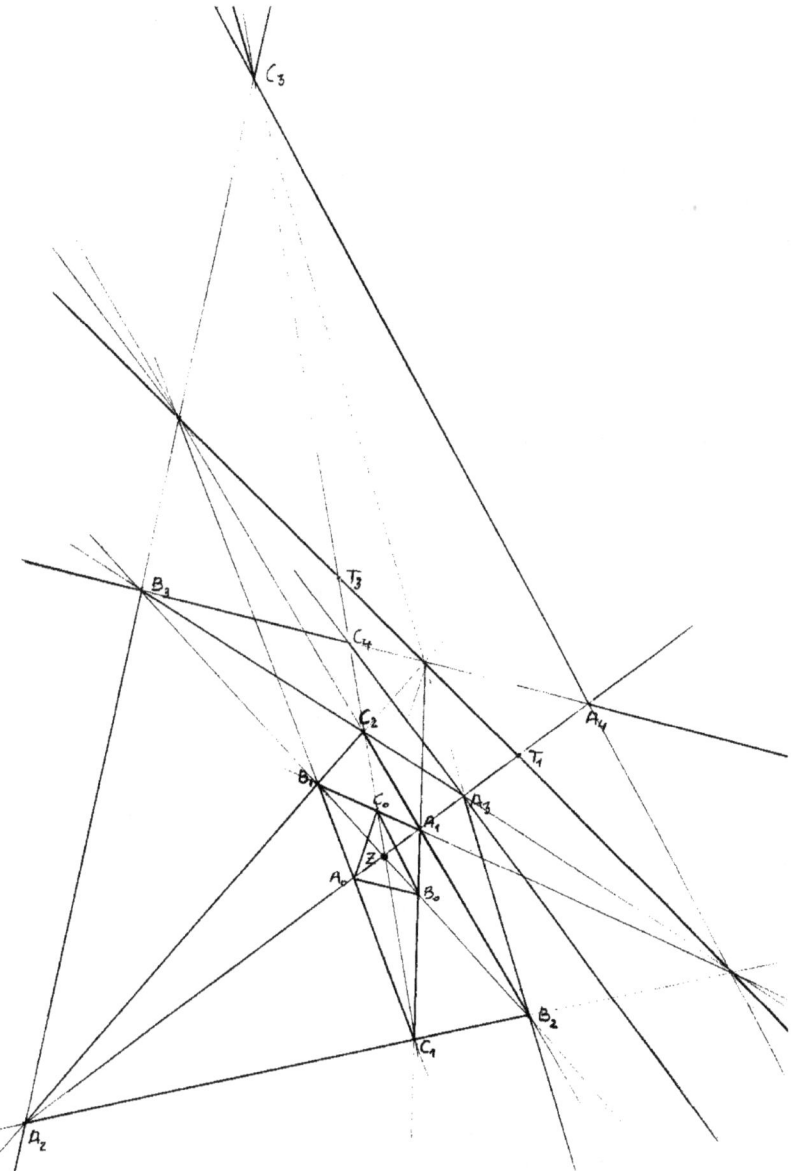

Figure 7

These statements have shown that the fundamental harmonic configuration (Figure 5) can be expanded into the quadrangle transformation (Figure 4) and into the triangular transformation (Figure 7) – Figures 1 and 6 show special cases. This reveals how projective geometry unites very different laws, here the laws to which these transformations conform. The quadrangle transformation is determined by the cross-ratio $D = 2$, the triangle metamorphosis is determined by the cross-ratio $D = -2$. Moreover, it became clear that the cross-ratio becomes a simple ratio whenever certain points become limit points of the plane. This is also shown by Figure 8 where the distances ZR_n form a geometric sequence with common ratio $q = 2$.

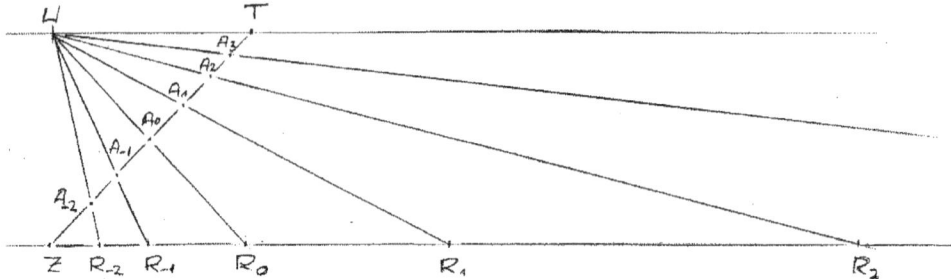

Figure 8

The point sequence A_n is a result of projection. Here T is the image of the point at infinity of ZR_0.

Now

$$\frac{ZA_n}{ZT} = \frac{2^n}{2^n + 1} \quad \text{(the distances } ZR_0 \text{ and } WT \text{ are the same).}$$

$$\frac{ZA_n}{A_n T} = 2^n \quad \text{so that} \quad \frac{ZA_{n+1}}{A_{n+1}T} : \frac{ZA_n}{A_n T} = 2.$$

We can understand ratios because our feelings resonate, for instance when we compare two distances. However, grasping an cross-ratio demands a stronger engagement of the will.

Figure 9 shows a pentagon transformation, which is characterized by the cross-ratio $8:5$. This cross-ratio occurs with all point sequences on lines going out from Z.

For instance we have

$$\frac{ZA_{n+1}}{A_{n+1}T} : \frac{ZA_n}{A_n T} = 8:5.$$

It is natural to think of the pentagon transformation as proceeding from the center Z, the distances from the center to the five corner points getting larger or smaller. It is characteristic of projective geometry also to think of this in a polar way – that is, as proceeding from the line z, the five pentagon sides turning in the five points of intersection with the line z. The angles of rotation correspond to the distances such as ZA_n. The pentagon is thus enveloped from outside, and narrowed or expanded.

This grasp of forms from outside meets the demand of our time to understand an individual in terms of the greater context, to think from the perspective of the whole.

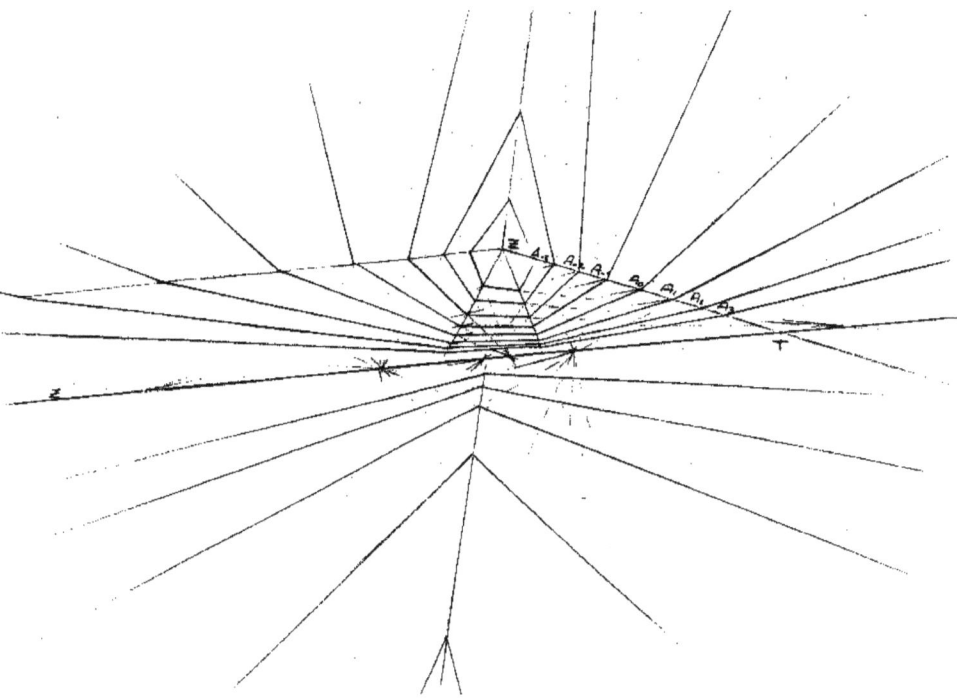

Figure 9

This is also related to Rudolf Steiner's call to comprehend the etheric by means of a coordinate system. This system has the infinitely distant plane of space as reference plane, rather than a central reference point.

Spherical Geometry

KLAUS LABUDDE

In working with spherical geometry, the students are entering new geometrical territory. Until now, the plane or space were the location of the action. This was so obvious that – generally – they were not even aware of it. Now this «place» is quite different, namely the surface of a sphere. This gives cause for some basic questions. The straight line – next to the point the most simple basic element of geometry known to the students – does not exist on the surface of a sphere. Whatever movement of a point we imagine on a sphere, it cannot be a line. If we want to force a line, we must either leave the sphere (for instance, along a tangent) or we must penetrate the inside – for instance, to the midpoint. But these are not movements on the surface. In this way, the question of a sensible replacement for the line results.

Students know that mathematics plays an important role in regard to shipping, air travel and satellites. And, as far as geometric questions are concerned, this all has to do with the surface of a sphere.

What should we imagine a triangle on such a surface to be? What kind of lines are the sides of the triangle? Nowadays, some students are familiar with the experience of a flight to the west coast of North America, such as from Frankfurt to San Francisco. In comparison to the departure airport, the destination lies further south. But at first, the plane takes a northward course and then flies over the south point of Greenland.

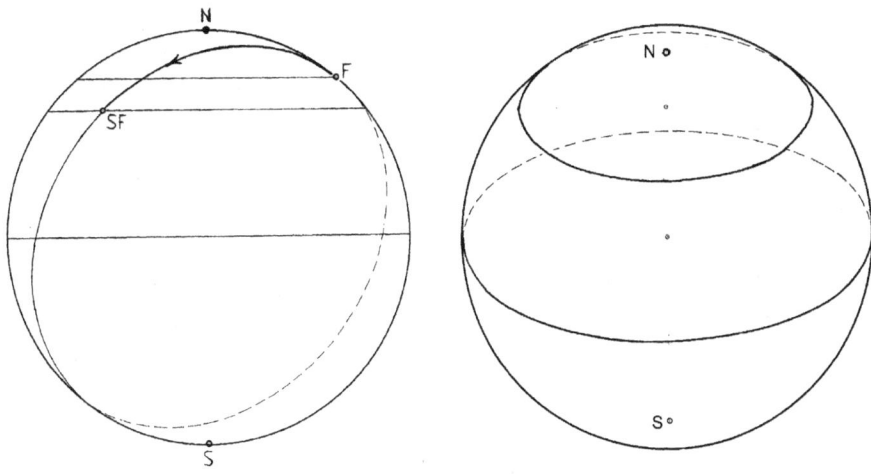

Figure 1   Figure 2

What is going on here? Is it not shorter to «directly» approach the destination with a definite somewhat southern course?

So the question arises of the shortest connecting path between two points on the upper surface of the sphere. Let's assume we are standing on a sphere at a point A and want to reach point B, which we can see, on the shortest route possible. The sphere is so large that – on the way from A to B, we do not slip and fall into the depths (Both A and B are lying in the higher part of the upper surface). But it's also so small that we feel we are standing on a sphere – that is, on a curved surface. We can thus experience that the shortest path to B does indeed exist. We simply have to watch that we have point B before us as we move. In other words: We may not deviate to the side. Such movement is possible and it comes the closest to going straight in the plane. To this extent, the path we found is the best possible substitution for the line and can take over the role which the line plays in the plane.

If we continue this path beyond the destination, we finally get back to the departure point A. This complete path is a circle, comparable to the equator on the globe. There are no larger circles on the upper surface of a sphere. Thus we call them great circles. They cut the upper surface of the sphere in half. All other circles on a sphere, called small circles, play the same role in spherical geometry as the circles in a plane. Examples of this on the globe are latitudes (sometimes called parallels), with the exception of the equator (figure 2).

Visually speaking, all spherical circles have two midpoints. These are the endpoints of the sphere's diameter which stands vertical on the plane of the relevant spherical circle. By comparison: On the globe, the north and south pole are the two midpoints of every line of latitude. In this regard, there is a significant difference between large and small circles. We can clearly assign a midpoint to the latter. It is that point from which all circular points have a distance which is smaller than a fourth of the circumference of the sphere. This distinction is not possible with the large circles. All large circle points have the same distance from both midpoints – namely, exactly one fourth of the circle's circumference.

There is yet a further difference between great and small circles. Two small circles can intersect in two points – they can touch each other or have no points in common. We know this about the circles in a plane. Two great circles always intersect, at two diametrically opposite spherical points (counterpoints, antipodes). A great circle and a small circle can have the same position relationship as a circle and a line in the plane. It cannot be determined by this view what is supposed to be inside and outside in the case of the great circle. Equivalent to this in the plane is that it is divided by a line into two half planes, which are to be viewed as «equal».

In summary we can say: There is an extensive correspondence between point, line and circle in plane geometry, as for point, great circle and small circle in spherical geometry. But this correspondence is not completely perfect. This is connected to some surprising peculiarities of spherical geometry.

Now let's move to the investigation of spherical triangles. In a plane, we can determine a triangle by three points, which do not lie on a line. This is not so easy with the sphere. Accordingly, we must demand that the three points do not lie on a great circle (no two of these points can be antipodes, because this condition can no longer be fulfilled with any position of the third point.) There is always exactly one great circle through each two points that are not antipodes and this circle is divided by these points into two dissimilar arcs. So we must determine which of these arcs should be the triangle's side. This should always be the shorter of the two arcs. (Euler triangles)

Now we can begin calculating spherical triangles. What statements can be made about circumference, area and angle-sum? Without limitation, a point can move on a sphere, as in a plane; but the sphere's upper surface has a finite content, in contrast to the plane. This must have consequences for circumference and area of a spherical triangle. Apparently they must be limited. But how do we find the limits?

One fundamental law for plane triangles also applies for spherical ones. Two sides together are longer than the third. The reason is the same for both types of triangles. If, for instance, AB is a side and thus the shortest path from A to B, we can view $AC+CB$ as another path from A over C to B; thus, this is a longer path. The same applies for the distances BC and CA and the attendant detours.

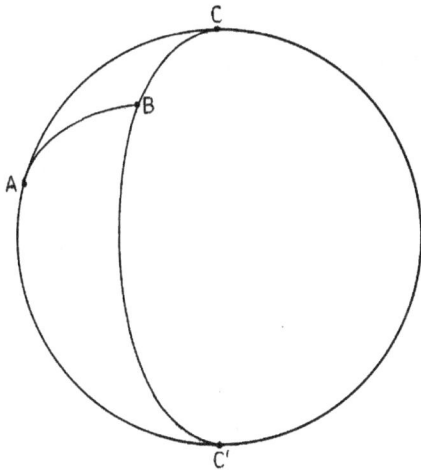

Figure 3

Now ABC and ABC' are two triangles with C and C' as antipodes (figure 3). Together they form the biangle (digon) CC'. According to the law above, the following applies for the triangle ABC'.

$$AB < AC' + C'B$$

Because C and C' are antipodes, the folling holds:

$$AC' = CC' - AC$$

and

$$BC' = CC' - BC.$$

It follows

$$AB < (CC' - AC) + (CC' - BC)$$

thus

$$AB + BC + AC < 2 \cdot CC'$$

To the left is the circumference of the triangle and the circumference of a great circle is to the right. This represents the upper limit for the circumference of the triangle. – At least instinctively we can approach this law with the help of the imagination. Without limiting the general conception, we can – on the basis of the globe – transfer the side AB to the equator, and the corner C to the northern half-sphere. If we want to obtain a triangle with the largest possible circumference, we'll have to put C «opposite» AB very near the equator. Then the triangular sides AC and BC must run very close to the equator. Moreover, AB lies exactly on the equator. The circumference line of the triangle comes very close to the equator; the closer, the less the distance of the corner C is from the equator. So it might be clear that the triangle's circumference approaches the circumference of a great circle, but cannot reach it.

The idea developed here suggests the presumption that the area of the half sphere is the upper limit for the area of a spherical triangle.

Finally, all three angles of such a triangle must be obtuse (the triangle almost completely covers the northern half-sphere).[1] In regard to the sum of the angles, we must figure on a law which deviates from that for plane triangles. If we discover that there are very unusual triangles on a sphere, then the problem of the angle-sum is even more exciting. For instance, if A and B lie on the equator and C at the North Pole, α and γ are right angles while γ is arbitrary (in certain circumstances, even a right angle). – These are examples with varying sums of the angles and all greater than 180°!

But how can we find a law? To progress here, we can first work out the concept of the polar triangle $A'B'C'$? of a triangle ABC. We show that the polar triangle of $A'B'C'$ is again the original triangle ABC.

If one runs through a great circle in one direction it possesses a «left» and a «right» pole.

This can be clarified with the example of the equator: If one runs in an easterly direction, the north pole is the left pole and the south pole the right pole. It is the reverse with opposing direction. If a point runs through the triangle ABC in the sequence $A\ B\ C\ A$, then, for every line traversed this way, there is a clearly determined left pole. Then these three poles A', B', C' determine a new triangle. (We could also choose the three right poles.) $A'B'C'$ is the polar triangle of ABC. It can be shown that ABC is again the polar triangle of $A'B'C'$. With the help of descriptive geometry, it can be shown that the sides of a triangle and the corresponding angles of the polar triangle add up to 180°.

Here we must point out that it is useful to select an angle as measure for the side of a spherical triangle. It should be that one which arises when we connect the endpoints of the sides to the sphere's midpoint.

If we form the triangle ABC with the side $c = AB$ at the equator and the corner C on the northern half-sphere, without loss of generality through vertical parallel projection on the equator's plane, so the pole C of the side $c = AB$ comes to lie at the midpoint of the equator (figure 4). There

---

[1] The angle between two great circles refers to the angle between the two circle tangents form at the angular point.

the angle appears as a measure for the side c in its true size, as well as the angle γ' of the polar triangle $A'B'C'$. We don't need to investigate exactly their corners A' and B' in the projection. It is enough to determine that A' must lie on a radius at a right angle to the diameter belonging to B.

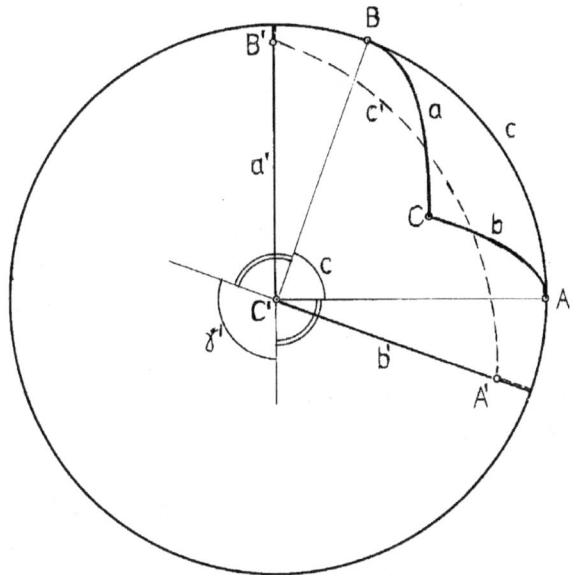

Figure 4

Accordingly, B' must lie on the radius perpendicular to the diameter belonging to A. So c, γ' and two right angles together yield the whole angle 360°. Now, in a generalized way, we have the law mentioned, in the form of equations:

$$\boxed{a + \alpha' = b + \beta' = c + \gamma' = a' + \alpha = b' + \beta = c' + \gamma = 180°}$$

Now, if we apply the law on the perimeter («side-sum») of spherical triangles to the triangle $A'B'C'$,

$$0° < a' < a' + b' + c' < 360°$$

and if we introduce the relationship found between the angles of ABC and the sides of $A'B'C'$, the following results:

$$0° < (180° - \alpha) + (180° - \beta) + (180° - \gamma) \quad \Rightarrow \quad \boxed{\alpha + \beta + \gamma < 540°}$$

and on the other hand:

$$360° > (180° - \alpha) + (180° - \beta) + (180° - \gamma) \quad \Rightarrow \quad \boxed{\alpha + \beta + \gamma > 180°}$$

The geometric preparations for the proof of this perimeter law are not exactly easy. But they are understandable for the students when taken step by step. This is if – in the tenth grade – the foundation was established through appropriate treatment of descriptive geometry. The continuation of the proof with equations and inequalities and transformations is of a different quality. The students dependent on looking and those tending toward numbers and calculation or algebra get what they want in different ways. The purely geometric observations on the globe indicate that the angular-sum is limited upward by $3 \cdot 180° = 540°$. The examples sighted suggest that it must always be greater than 180°. Moreover, we can get the feeling that a part of a spherical upper surface is the more flat, the smaller it is in relation to the entire surface. This feeling is supported by the experience that we have with a flat landscape or at the beach. We experience the surface in the surroundings seen as even, although we know that it is a part of an equally curved spherical surface. (Here we can omit the deviation of the geoid from the spherical form). So the justified opinion sets in, that the ratios on a spherical triangular surface come all the closer to those on a plane triangle, the more «flat» its spherical surface is in relation to the whole spherical surface. The consequence is that the angle-sum comes increasingly closer to the value of 180°.

This way of viewing or proceeding is not exact in the strict sense. Experience shows, though, it can be more easily structured in this way and many students need this. In the face of the reasoning based more on arithmetic, algebra and logical thought, one feels correctly that this is all strict and exact. But it is not so accessible for students strongly dependent on sight.

Also the calculation of surface area for a spherical triangle brings astonishing things to light. Let's say we have any spherical triangle ABC with the surface area F. The antipodes of its corner points form its polar triangle $A'B'C'$, which is congruent to ABC in the contrary sense. Six further triangles are formed by the great circles through A, B and C:

The three adjacent triangles ABC', BCA' and CAB' of ABC,

Which border on this triangle along its sides and

The three apex triangles $AB'C'$, $BC'A'$ and $CA'B'$ of ABC

Which touch against the corners of this triangle.

Figure 5

The first are apex triangles of $A'B'C'$ and the latter are side triangles of $A'B'C'$.

Finally, ABC' and $CA'B'$, BCA' and $AB'C'$, CAB' and $BC'A'$ are pairs of opposite triangles, also congruent in the contrary sense.

If we look at the structure which is composed of ABC and its three adjacent triangles (Figure 5), it follows that it takes in half of the sphere's surface area. Moreover, we can think of it having come about through combining 3 «spherical digons» with the digon angles α, β and γ – these overlap three times in the triangle ABC.

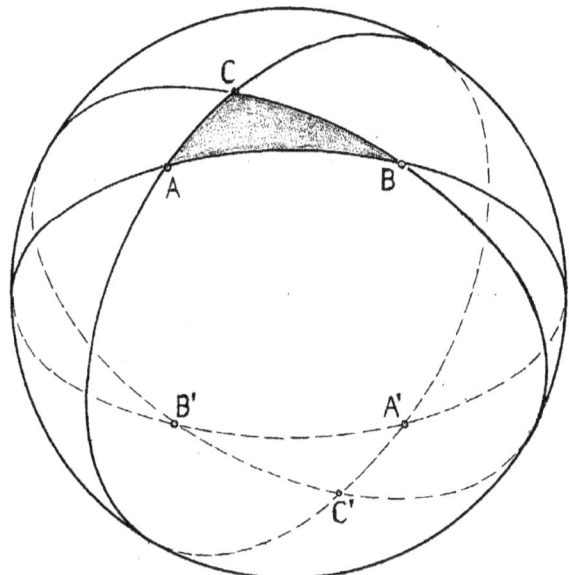

Figure 5

Their surface areas $4\pi R^2 \cdot \frac{\alpha}{360°}$, $4\pi R^2 \cdot \frac{\beta}{360°}$ and $4\pi R^2 \cdot \frac{\gamma}{360°}$ added have the same area as half the spheres area ($2\pi R^2$) plus twice the amount of F. So the following equation results

$$2\pi R^2 = 4\pi R^2 \cdot \frac{\alpha+\beta+\gamma}{360°} - 2F$$

it follows:

$$\boxed{F = \pi R^2 \cdot \frac{\alpha+\beta+\gamma-180°}{180°}}$$

In the numerator of the fraction is that angle, by which the angle sum of the relevant spherical triangle is greater than that of a plane triangle. We call it the spherical excess of the triangle ABC. What can be read from this result?

- It confirms that the angle sum is $\alpha+\beta+\gamma > 180°$. Otherwise, the formula would not yield a positive result for F.

- It also confirms that F must be smaller than half the sphere's surface area. This holds because $\alpha+\beta+\gamma < 540°$.

- For calculating the area of the triangle, there isn't any need for knowledge of a triangle's side. Besides the size of the sphere, which is determined by R, the content depends on the spherical excess alone. This also means that we don't need to know the three angles individually. It is enough to know their sum.

- If two triangles have the same angles, they have the same size. With plane triangles, this is generally not the case. That is, they only have the same form and not necessarily the same size. We can suppose that there are no similar spherical triangles (lying on the same sphere). In other words, triangles which have the same angles must be congruent.

It becomes clear that geometry on the surface of a sphere is fundamentally different from plane geometry. This raises further questions, such as that of constructive geometry. What corresponds to the construction on the plane with compass and ruler? Do we just solve construction problems by fitting the solutions for corresponding problems in the plane to those for the sphere? This would have to mean that the role of the lines as construction lines would be taken over by the great circles. Finally, there is the question of whether there are theorems in plane geometry which are transferable to the sphere. As we know, this does not apply for the theorem of the angle sum in the triangle. Let's pursue these questions with some examples.

The spherical compass can serve as the drawing instrument. With it we can draw great and small circles on the sphere.

The problem begins with connecting two points through a specified great circle. With the corresponding problem in the plane, we just put the ruler's edge to the points and draw the line. This is a construction challenge on the sphere. Around the two points A and B we put great circles. The distance measure of their intersecting points is 90° from A and B – this corresponds to one fourth of a great circle. If we draw the great circle around one of the intersecting points, it has to go through A and B. So it is the connecting great circle we are looking for. This rather lenghty process corresponds to a simple construction with a ruler in the plane.

Does the known construction of the mediator line of a distance AB (in the plane) work in a similar way on the sphere? Then we would have to draw two small intersecting circles of equal size around A and B. Then we would connect the intersecting points with a great circle, according to the construction above. This is determined by the construction and represents the «mediator line» being sought. Of course, the question is whether the two small circles can be replaced by the great circles. Their intersecting points are antipodes and this constrains the unambigous continuation of the construction.

Also the dropping of the perpendicular line from a point P to a great circle g succeeds analogously to the known construction in the plane. But here it is possible in another way as well. If we draw the great circle through P, this intersects g at two antipodes. If we draw a further great circle through one of these two points, this is the one we're looking for. It must go through the point given and intersect the given great circle at a right angle – since its midpoint lies on this great circle. It can be done, then, «with the ruler alone».

One can try cutting an angle between two great circles in half by a third one. Specifically, one could test whether the small circles inserted in the construction can be replaced by great circles.

Now to some theorems from classical school geometry!

It is known that, for every plane triangle, there are four special points: the circumcenter U, the incenter I, the orthocenter H and the center of gravity (S). What these have in common is that they are intersecting points of three triangular transversals. The question is whether the corresponding transversals of a spherical triangle also intersect at a point.

Two of the four questions are singled out and will be treated in detail. The rest is left to the reader as an incentive for further study. – We will first concern ourselves with the bisectors of the interior angles of a spherical triangle. It is a matter of uniquely determined great circles, which can be easily constructed (mentioned above). Every point of such a great circle has equal distances from the triangular arms of the angle, which it bisects. So one can draw a small circle around it, which touches both arms[2] of the triangle. Now let's take two of the three great circles bisecting the angles. They have two points of intersection, of which one lies inside the triangle. The other is inside its opposite triangle. The former has equal distances from the arms of two angles of our triangle – that is, especially from the arms of the third angle. So it must also lie on the angle bisector of this angle. It is the only possible point as midpoint of a small circle, which touches all sides of the triangle.

The theorem of the circumcenter of a plane triangle applies accordingly to the sphere. The proof can be done accordingly.

Now we'll turn to the question of whether the three altitudes of a spherical triangle intersect in a point. First we must determine that this altitude can be constructed as perpendicular of a corner on the side lying opposite. A proof for the theorem of the orthocenter frequently used in plane geometry uses the fact that the three mediators meet in a point. The problem of the altitude is then taken back to the problem of the mediators already solved. Now it can be shown that, with a spherical triangle, the three mediators intersect in a point. But we cannot succeed in producing the connection between altitudes and mediators on the sphere the same way as in the plane. We would have to put the great circle parallel to the opposite side through every corner of the triangle. Because there are no parallel circles on a sphere, this is, in principle, impossible. Either another proof yet to be found leads to the goal and the three altitudes intersect at a point. Or the opposite is the case and every attempt at a proof must fail.

How do we deal with the theorem of Thales? If it is transferrable to the sphere, the following must apply: AB is a great circle's arc which is, at the same time, diameter of a small circle (the smallest circle possible through A and B). C is a point different from A and B on the small circle. The spherical triangle ABC is completed in that we join C with A and with B through the great circle's arcs. We want to find out whether the great circle arcs AC and BC meet at a right angle at C.

An attempt will be undertaken with the help of descriptive geometry. To carry out the construction, we will use the globe as a sphere easily understood and place the arc AB on a meridian circle so that the midpoint of the arc's distance comes to lie on the North Pole (Figure 6).

---

[2] In this case, the arms of the triangle are not to be understand as spherical tangents but as triangle-sides.

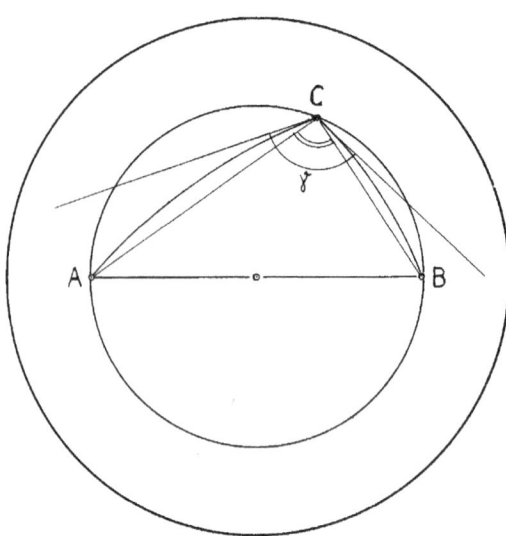

Figure 6

The small circle, which has *AB* as diameter, is then the common circle of latitude of *A* and *B*, on which *C* also lies. Now we will form the spherical triangle *ABC* and the circle of latitude through vertical parallel projection on a plane parallel to the latitude-plane.

In the projection, the image of the spherical triangle *ABC* appears as a structure bordered by a straight line side *AB* and two ellipse arcs, *AC* and *BC*. These meet at *C* at an obtuse angle. Why?

If we join *A* and *B* in the projection, with *C* with a straight line, then the plane triangle *ABC* is right-angled, with the right angle at *C*. This is because the circle of latitude – which is mapped in its true form – is a Thales circle of this plane triangle. Naturally, *AB* is meant to be a straight line distance. The angle field of the right angle lies completely inside the angular field, which is spanned by both ellipse tangents in *C*. So these enclose an obtuse angle. This angle is the projection of the angle γ of our spherical triangle *ABC*, formed from the tangents to the great circles through *A* and *C* or *B* and *C*. The tangential plane to the sphere in *C*, in which both tangents lie, is inclined toward the projection plane. Thus, the true angle γ must be smaller than its obtuse angled projection. Whether it is a right angle, that remains the question.

We can further pursue this question through a deeper investigation of the means of descriptive geometry (determination of the true size of the spherical angle γ, including the question of whether or not it can or must be a right angle). This can be done as well in conjunction with vector-geometry. If the coordinate system is set convenient according to our geometric observation, then the calculation is neither too long nor especially difficult.

Now we will pursue the question of whether the theorem of Pythagoras can be transferred to the sphere. In short: it is not possible. But this is not because the known relationship among the three squares of the plane right angled triangle does not apply to the sphere. The reason goes deeper and is elementary: there are no squares on a sphere!

Experience has shown that students mostly approach the question of squares constructively, with the unconscious assumption that squares exist. One idea they like to form proceeds from the globe with two meridian circles – these are bordered to the north and south by two latitudinal lines which have an equal distance from the equator. So a quadrilateral arises with four right angles. Moreover, it is possible to arrange things such that the two latitudinal arcs are as long as the meridian arcs. These have a minimum measure of 0° and a maximum of 180°. This grows with increasing geographical width of the latitudinal arcs. At the same time, the length of the latitudinal arcs, proceeding from a maximum, decreases toward the minimum of 0°. (In the extreme case, they lie on the equator). This is when they have arrived at the poles and have contracted to a point. So, for the latitudinal circles, there must be a certain position where all four sides of the square are equally long.

So far, so good. Unfortunately, however, two of the square sides are not great circle arcs. This is easily overlooked in the eagerness of construction. Also overlooked is the fact that two great circle arcs – sufficiently lengthened – always intersect, in fact, two times. It is also possible to form a square bordered by four great circle arcs. It has four sides of equal length and four angles of equal size. But here the opposite sides are not parallel and the four equal angles must be obtuse. If it were right angles, a great circle arc running diagonally would divide the square into two isosceles, right angled triangles with the angular sum of 180°. This is in contradiction to the angular sum of spherical triangles.

Finally, a feeling for form suggests that a square of the type described has sides curved outwardly, on the basis of its surface arch- - these cause obtuse angles at the corners.

Our series of examples is complete with this observation on the theorem of Pythagoras. Not all laws of plane geometry maintain their validity when transferred to the sphere. Moreover, some questions must remain unanswered.

If we concern ourselves with spherical geometry in the way described, then we determine that very different types of doing geometry are possible. As far as drawing is concerned, the free sketch can be considered as a mean for envisioning. This may not be exact in the strict sense, but is suited to pointing out what's important. Descriptive geometry is applied when an exact image should appear by means of parallel vertical projection. Also constructive considerations, which use the laws of the applied projection, can be drawn in for the purpose of demonstration. Elementary constructive geometry, which middle school students have learned, can be repeated in the comparison of spherical with plane geometry.

The spatial imagination, which is trained chiefly in the ninth and tenth grade, can be deepened through unusual questioning.

Rightly, we can assign spherical geometry to the mathematical areas which students experience as new in comparison to what they've learned so far. Since this is so, classroom discussion can lead to fundamentals, such as the difference between axiom, postulate and theorem (in the sense of Euclid). Also involved is the necessity for posing questions correctly. When the question is whether the Pythagorean theorem is valid on a sphere, the problem is not how we find the squares by the sides of a right-angled triangle, in order to compare size. Rather, it is whether there are squares on a sphere at all. Here we are suggesting that the treatment of spherical geometry also offers the opportunity to learn something in examples from mathematics not just of significance for mathematical thought – but also for that in other areas. I see this to be a pedagogical task overlapping different subjects in the instruction of upper classes.

The diversity of geometric activities in such a main lesson allows us to shape the lesson in different ways. This is according to the strengths and weaknesses of the students and what we want to emphasize in view of the particular class. In any case, we should begin with questions which count more on the practical understanding of students. I view the treatment of basic questions as a goal and not a departure point. When we get to this point, then we can attach the description of an area of the newer geometry: some basic thoughts of non-Euclidean geometry; this would include the dramatic history of solving the parallel problem.[3]

I consider two things important in this connection:

1. We experience that the gaining of mathematical knowledge doesn't need to be just a matter of sober reason schooled in logic. Rather, it can challenge the inner mobility and fantasy of a math student, leading him through highs and lows and even to the point of «life crises».

2. If we succeed in portraying the essence of an idea for dealing with the axiom of parallelism clearly and simply, then we've led the student to an important experience for the first time: Man can acquire the capacity to develop thought independent of the world experienced through the senses.

My hope was to approach this pedagogical goal. This was my motivation for providing a block on spherical geometry in the math instruction for the eleventh grade. With a concentrated approach, two weeks will be sufficient.

---

[3] See «Die beiden Bolyai» in: supplement to the magazine «Elemente der Mathematik», supplement nr. 11, May 1951; Birkhaeuser Publishing, Basel (out of print)

The Inner Symmetry of Spherical Geometry

UWE HANSEN

The inner symmetry of spherical geometry rests on the fact that the relationship of pole and polar arises quite naturally. The circle with radius $\rho = 90°$ and center the point P – which is a great circle, that is to say a spherical «line» – is the polar p of P. Since every spherical line can be seen as a circle with radius $90°$ for which two antipodal (diametrically opposite) points can be centers, it follows that to each polar there are two antipodal poles, which can therefore be identified.

Two points A and B on the sphere determine an arc AB. The polar m of the mid-point M of this arc (Figure 1) intersects the line $g = AB$ in another point M_1 at a distance of $90°$ from M. This point M_1 we shall call the *conjugate mid-point* of the arc AB. It follows that the polar m_1 of M_1 goes through M. m and m_1 intersect in the pole G of the line g. They are thus perpendicular to g; they are the two conjugate perpendicular bisectors of AB.

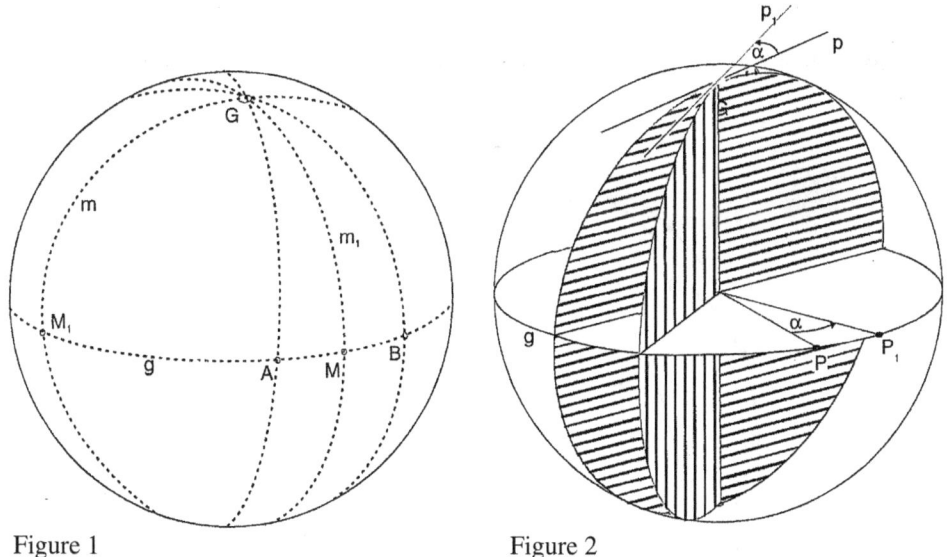

Figure 1 Figure 2

These two perpendicular bisectors halve the angle between the lines AG and BG. They are thus angle bisectors at the same time. The truth of this is shown by the following argument (Figure 2).

If a point P moves on a line g through angle α to P_1, then the polar p of P rotates in the pole G of g through the same angle α to p_1. This follows because the segment M_0P – where M_0 is the center of the sphere – is always perpendicular to the plane of p as a great circle. If P only moves through half the angle α, then its polar in G also moves through half the angle. Thus polars of mid-points are angle bisectors.

The fact that a perpendicular bisector of an arc is simultaneously an angle bisector in the pole of the segment reveals a wonderful relationship between a spherical triangle and its polar triangle.

223

If *ABC* is any spherical triangle then the polars of the triangle's vertices are the sides of the polar triangle, whose vertices $A_1B_1C_1$ are then the poles of the sides of *ABC*.

Since a perpendicular bisector of the triangle *ABC* is at the same time an angle bisector of the polar triangle $A_1B_1C_1$, it follows that the center of the circumcircle of triangle *ABC* is also the center of the incircle of triangle $A_1B_1C_1$.

Since a spherical triangle has an incircle and three excircles – which are incircles of the neighboring triangles – it follows that every triangle has four circumcircles. These go through the vertices $A\,B\,C$, $\bar{A}\,B\,C$, $A\,\bar{B}\,C$ and $A\,B\,\bar{C}$ respectively, where $\bar{A},\bar{B},\bar{C}$ are the vertices antipodal to A,B,C.

This occurrence of the number four in the triangle shows the connection to projective geometry: compare for example the extra 3-point in the complete 4-point. A spherical triangle also has for example four centers of gravity, and polar to them four «axes of levity».

Now the spherical line going through a triangle's vertex and through the corresponding vertex of the polar triangle must intersect the triangle sides which are polar to these two vertices at right angles; for example the line CC_1 is perpendicular to the sides AB and A_1B_1 (Figure 3). This means that the triangles *ABC* and $A_1B_1C_1$ have the same altitudes. Triangle and polar triangle are perspective with respect to the orthocenter (point of intersection of the three altitudes) *H* and its polar *h*.

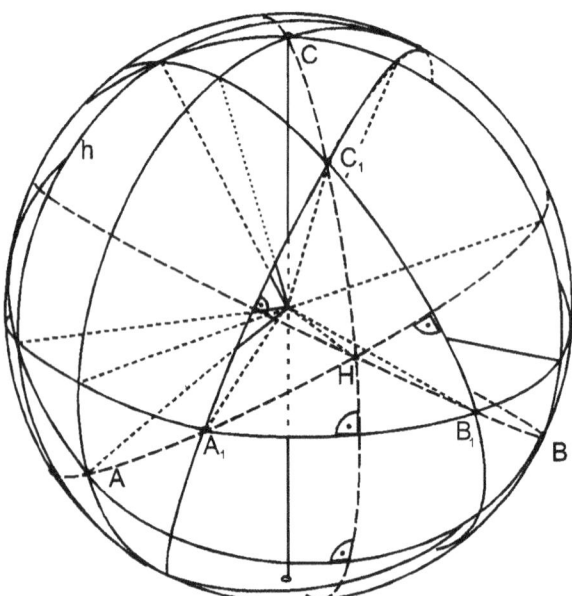

Figure 3

If we project the surface of the sphere from a point *N* of the sphere onto the tangent plane in the antipodal point $\bar{N}$, we obtain a picture of the spherical surface which preserves circles and angles (stereographic projection). If the image of the polar of *N* (and of $\bar{N}$) is the "base circle", great circles are then the circles intersecting the base circle in diametrically opposite points.

Figure 4 on the next page shows the laws of Figure 3 in a stereographic projection. Note that the polar h of H contains the three points of intersection of corresponding sides of the triangles (shown as filled points).

Some example will show how consistently the law of polarity can be applied in spherical geometry.

1. *Example:* The line joining a triangle vertex to the mid-point of the opposite side goes through the triangle's center of gravity.
   Polar to this, the points of intersection of the triangle sides and the angle bisectors in the opposite vertices lie in a line one could call the «axis of levity» of the polar triangle.

2. *Example:* A point P traverses the circumcircle of a triangle.
   Polar to this, a line sweeps through the tangent envelope of the incircle of the polar triangle.

3. *Example:* All points of the circumcircle of a triangle are the same distance from its circumcenter M.
   Polar to this, all tangents of the incircle of the polar triangle intersect the polar of M at the same angle. This polar is the central line of the incircle considered counterspatially.

4. *Example:* The perpendicular bisector of an arc halves this arc in its mid-point M and is at right-angles to it.
   Polar to this, the conjugate mid-point M_1 of the arc forms with the pole G of the line AB a «right arc», that is to say $M_1G = 90°$. Furthermore M_1G bisects the angle between AG and BG.

5. *Example:* The three perpendicular bisectors of a triangle meet in a point.
   Polar to this, the three conjugate mid-points of the triangle's sides lie in a line.

6. *Example:* Drop a perpendicular from P to the line g, in other words determine the line ℓ through P perpendicular to g, that is to say, determine the line joining P and the pole of g.
   Polar to this, suppose a line p and a point G are given. Which point of p forms a right arc with G? Determine the point of intersection of p with the polar of G.

7. *Example:* Erect the perpendicular to a line g in a point P of g, that is to say, join P to the pole G of the line g.
   Polar to this, consider a line p of a pencil G of lines. Intersect p with the polar g of G; the result is a right arc.

The Inner Symmetry of Spherical Geometry — Uwe Hansen

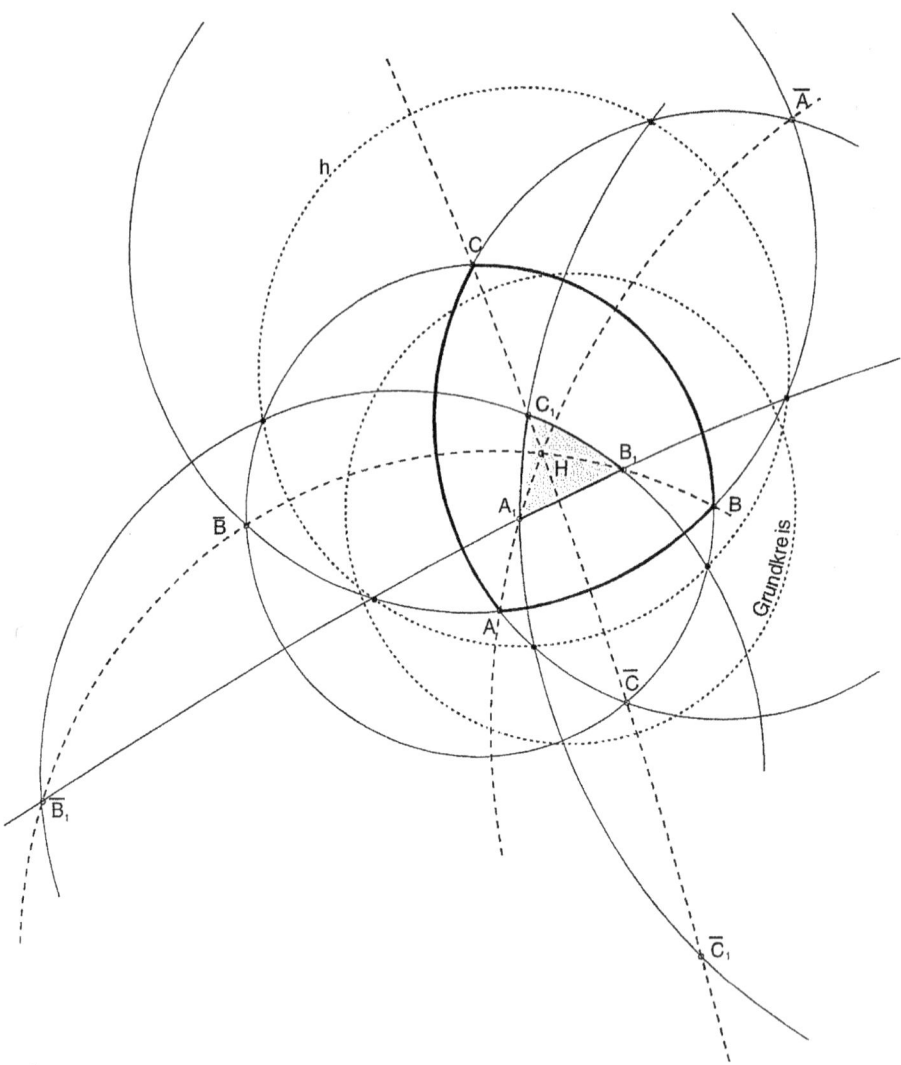

Figure 4

In spherical geometry there is no Euler line: center of gravity, orthocenter and circumcenter of a spherical triangle do not generally lie on a great circle. (Grundkreis = circle of reference)

Basic Spherical Trigonometry

PETER BAUM

In the following we are going to derive the basic formulas of spherical trigonometry using vectors. Let A, B, C be three points on a sphere with center $O\,(0,0,0)$ and radius $r = 1$. Let their position vectors be the unit vectors $\vec{a} = \begin{pmatrix} a_1 \\ a_2 \\ a_3 \end{pmatrix}$, $\vec{b} = \begin{pmatrix} b_1 \\ b_2 \\ b_3 \end{pmatrix}$, $\vec{c} = \begin{pmatrix} c_1 \\ c_2 \\ c_3 \end{pmatrix}$. The radian measures of the three angles $a = (\vec{bc})$, $b = (\vec{ca})$, $c = (\vec{ab})$ between the vectors are thus equal to the sides of the spherical triangle and are assumed to be greater than $0°$ and smaller than $180°$ (such a spherical triangle is called an Eulerian triangle).

The angles of the spherical triangle are the angles between the planes of the trihedral angle:

$$\alpha = (OAB)(OCA), \quad \beta = (OBC)(OAB), \quad \gamma = (OCA)(OBC).$$

They are also equal to the angles between the normals to these planes. The normal vectors of the planes are got from the three vector products of the position vectors $\vec{a}, \vec{b}, \vec{c}$:

$$\vec{n_a} = \vec{b} \times \vec{c}, \quad \vec{n_b} = \vec{c} \times \vec{a}, \quad \vec{n_c} = \vec{a} \times \vec{b}.$$

For the magnitudes of the normal vectors we have

$$|\vec{n_a}| = |\vec{b} \times \vec{c}| = |\vec{b}| \cdot |\vec{c}| \cdot \sin(\vec{bc}) = \sin a$$

and similarly $|\vec{n_b}| = \sin b$, $|\vec{n_c}| = \sin c$. Hence the scalar or dot product[1]

$$\langle \vec{n_b}, \vec{n_c} \rangle = \cos \alpha \cdot |\vec{n_b}| \cdot |\vec{n_c}| = \cos \alpha \cdot \sin b \cdot \sin c.$$

But equally

$$\langle \vec{n_b}, \vec{n_c} \rangle = \langle (\vec{c} \times \vec{a}), (\vec{a} \times \vec{b}) \rangle = \langle \vec{c}, \vec{a} \rangle \cdot \langle \vec{a}, \vec{b} \rangle - \langle \vec{c}, \vec{b} \rangle \cdot \langle \vec{a}, \vec{a} \rangle = \cos b \cdot \cos c - \cos a.$$

Thus

$$\cos \alpha \cdot \sin b \cdot \sin c = \cos b \cdot \cos c - \cos a$$

Solving for $\cos a$ we obtain the **side cosine rule**

$$\boxed{\cos a = \cos b \cdot \cos c - \sin b \cdot \sin c \cdot \cos \alpha}$$

---

[1] For an English speaker, the use of both a dot and juxtaposition (for example $a \cdot b$ and ab) both for scalar (inner) products and for multiplication in the field of scalars is very likely to be confusing. For this reason the ab and the $a \cdot b$ notation in the german book has been changed to $\langle a, b \rangle$ where a scalar products is meant.

Further, on the one hand $|\vec{n_b} \times \vec{n_c}| = \sin\alpha \cdot \sin b \cdot \sin c$ and on the other

$$\begin{aligned} |\vec{n_b} \times \vec{n_c}| &= \left|(\vec{c} \times \vec{a}) \times (\vec{a} \times \vec{b})\right| = \left|\langle(\vec{c} \times \vec{a}), \vec{b}\rangle \vec{a} - \langle(\vec{c} \times \vec{a}), \vec{a}\rangle \vec{b}\right| \\ &= \left|\langle(\vec{c} \times \vec{a}), \vec{b}\rangle \vec{a}\right| = \left|\langle(\vec{c} \times \vec{a}), \vec{b}\rangle\right| = \left|\langle \vec{n_b}, \vec{b}\rangle\right| = \sin b \cdot \cos\left(\vec{n_b}\vec{b}\right). \end{aligned}$$

Thus

$$\cos\left(\vec{n_b}\vec{b}\right) = \sin\alpha \cdot \sin c.$$

Likewise it follows on the one hand that $|\vec{n_b} \times \vec{n_a}| = \sin\gamma \cdot \sin b \cdot \sin a$ and on the other that

$$\begin{aligned} |\vec{n_b} \times \vec{n_a}| &= \left|(\vec{c} \times \vec{a}) \times (\vec{b} \times \vec{c})\right| = \left|\langle(\vec{c} \times \vec{a}), \vec{c}\rangle \vec{b} - \langle(\vec{c} \times \vec{a}), \vec{b}\rangle \vec{c}\right| \\ &= \left|\langle(\vec{c} \times \vec{a}), \vec{b}\rangle \vec{c}\right| = \left|\langle(\vec{c} \times \vec{a}), \vec{b}\rangle\right| = \left|\langle \vec{n_b}, \vec{b}\rangle\right| = \sin b \cdot \cos\left(\vec{n_b}\vec{b}\right). \end{aligned}$$

Thus

$$\cos\left(\vec{n_b}\vec{b}\right) = \sin\gamma \cdot \sin a$$

and hence the **sine rule** follows:

$$\boxed{\sin\alpha \cdot \sin c = \sin\gamma \cdot \sin a}$$

The Angle Cosine Rule of Spherical Trigonometry
derived by means of stereographic projection

PETER BAUM

Suppose we are given a sphere and a spherical triangle A, B, C with angles α, β, γ and sides a, b, c on it. The sides lie on great circles. Let's call the great circle through A, B, the equator, and the hemisphere on which C is, the Southern hemisphere. We then centrally project the sphere from the North Pole as center of projection onto the equatorial plane. This mapping is called stereographic projection. Meridians are mapped onto lines through the center, while all other circles on the sphere are mapped onto circles. The equator and its image are identical, its points being fixed points. Thus the points A and B of the sphere are identical with their image points. All points of the Southern hemisphere are mapped onto the interior of the equator, all points of the Northern hemisphere have their image points outside the equator.

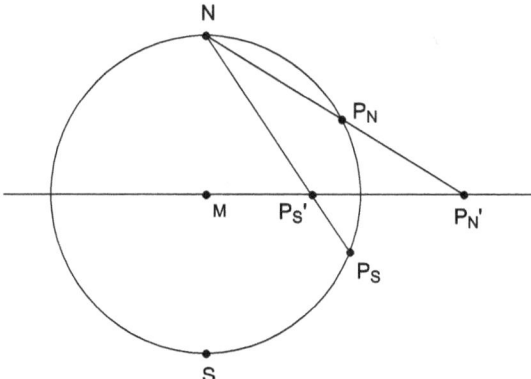

The next Figure represents the view from above onto the sphere and the equatorial plane. The outline of the sphere coincides with the equator; on it lie A and B as well as their diametrically opposite points A' and B'.

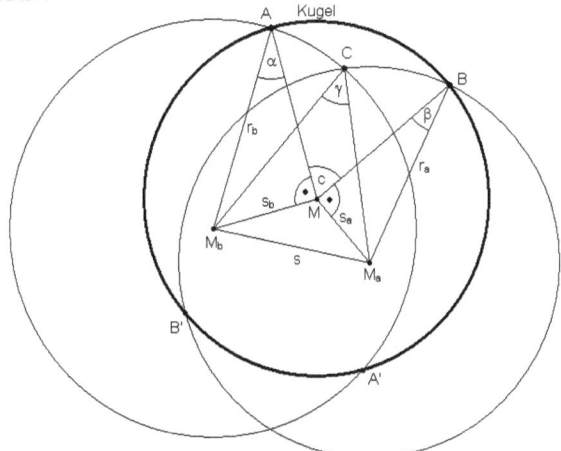

In the drawing the point C is the stereographically projected image inside the equator of the third sphere point. The side a of the spherical triangle lies on the great circle going through B, C and the diametrically opposite point B' of B. So its image must lie on the circumcircle of the triangle BCB'. Likewise the image of the side b lies on the circumcircle of the triangle ACA'.

Since stereographic projection preserves angles, the angles α, β, γ reappear in the projection plane between the tangents in the points A, B, C to the images of the great circles, hence also between the radii of the circles. Thus $\angle MAM_b = \alpha$, $\angle MBM_a = \beta$ and $\angle M_a C M_b = \gamma' = 180° - \gamma$. Likewise side c appears in its true length, so that $\angle M_a M M_b = c' = 180° - c$.

If we make the sphere's radius $= 1$, we have

$$r_a = \frac{1}{\cos\beta}, \quad r_b = \frac{1}{\cos\alpha}, \quad s_a = \tan\beta, \quad s_b = \tan\alpha.$$

Applying the cosine rule in triangle $M_a C M_b$, we thus have

$$s^2 = \left(\frac{1}{\cos\alpha}\right)^2 + \left(\frac{1}{\cos\beta}\right)^2 - 2\frac{1}{\cos\alpha}\frac{1}{\cos\beta}\cos(180°-\gamma)$$

$$s^2 = \left(\frac{1}{\cos\alpha}\right)^2 + \left(\frac{1}{\cos\beta}\right)^2 + 2\frac{1}{\cos\alpha}\frac{1}{\cos\beta}\cos\gamma$$

$$\cos\alpha \cdot \cos\beta \cdot s^2 = \frac{\cos\beta}{\cos\alpha} + \frac{\cos\alpha}{\cos\beta} + 2\cos\gamma.$$

Using the cosine rule in triangle $M_a M M_b$ we have

$$s^2 = (\tan\alpha)^2 + (\tan\beta)^2 - 2\tan\alpha\tan\beta\cos(180°-c)$$
$$s^2 = (\tan\alpha)^2 + (\tan\beta)^2 + 2\tan\alpha\tan\beta\cos c$$
$$\cos\alpha\cos\beta \cdot s^2 = (\sin\alpha)^2\frac{\cos\beta}{\cos\alpha} + (\sin\beta)^2\frac{\cos\alpha}{\cos\beta} + 2\sin\alpha\sin\beta\cos c.$$

Equating the two right hand sides, we thus have

$$2\cos\gamma = (\sin^2\alpha - 1)\frac{\cos\beta}{\cos\alpha} + (\sin^2\beta - 1)\frac{\cos\alpha}{\cos\beta} + 2\sin\alpha\sin\beta\cos c$$

$$2\cos\gamma = -2\cos\alpha\cos\beta + 2\sin\alpha\sin\beta\cos c$$

and finally the **angle cosine rule**

$$\boxed{\cos\gamma = -\cos\alpha\cos\beta + \sin\alpha\sin\beta\cos c}$$

Constructing and Solving Spherical Triangles

PETER BAUM

Spherical trigonometry has to a large extent disappeared from national curricula in Germany. In view of the (space and time) expenditure of logarithmic calculations this was understandable. But in the age of the calculator the cost of calculation is small. If spherical geometry is pursued already in school, and spherical triangles are constructed and the common problems of mathematical geography and astronomy solved graphically, then it is but a step to solving these problems by calculation. This article will show how this step can be taken.

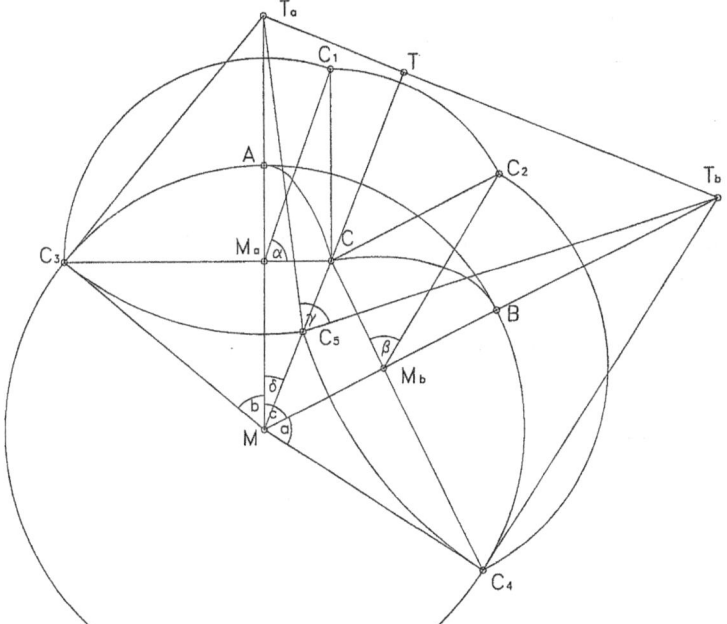

Suppose the (orthogonal) projection of a spherical triangle ABC with sides a,b,c and angles α, β, γ is given. Suppose the sphere has unit radius.

By folding down the great circles ACA' and BCB' along the axes AM and BM respectively into the plane of the drawing we obtain the sides $b = AC_3$ and $a = BC_4$ in their true lengths.

By folding down the small-circle planes through C perpendicular to AM and BM respectively we obtain the angles α and β in their true dimensions. The perpendicular from the sphere point C to the plane of the drawing is then folded onto CC_1 and CC_2 respectively. Therefore $CC_1 = CC_2$ and using basic trigonometric functions in the right-angled triangles MM_aC_3, M_aCC_1, MM_bC_4, M_bCC_2, together with the fact that $M_aC_3 = M_aC_1$ and $M_bC_4 = M_bC_2$ ... we have the **sine rule**

$$\sin b \cdot \sin \alpha = \sin a \cdot \sin \beta,$$

hence

$$\frac{\sin \alpha}{\sin a} = \frac{\sin \beta}{\sin b} = \frac{\sin \gamma}{\sin c}. \qquad (7)$$

Using basic trigonometric functions in right-angled triangles, and letting $MC = d$ we have

$$\triangle M_a CC_1 : \quad \overline{CM_a} = \sin b \cdot \cos \alpha$$
$$\triangle CMM_a : \quad \overline{CM_a} = d \cdot \sin \delta$$
$$\cos b = d \cdot \cos \delta$$
$$\triangle CMM_b : \quad \cos a = d \cdot \cos(c - \delta).$$

Using the angle sum formula for cosine: $\cos(c - \delta) = \cos c \cdot \cos \delta + \sin c \cdot \sin \delta$ we have

$$\cos a = d \cdot \cos(c - \delta) = \cos c \cdot d \cdot \cos \delta + \sin c \cdot d \cdot \sin \delta$$

and finally the **side cosine rule**

$$\cos a = \cos b \cdot \cos c + \sin b \cdot \sin c \cdot \cos \alpha \tag{8a}$$

By substituting $a = 180° - \alpha$, $b = 180° - \beta$, $c = 180° - \gamma$, $\alpha = 180° - a$ in the side cosine rule we get the **angle cosine rule**

$$\cos \alpha = -\cos \beta \cdot \cos \gamma + \sin \beta \cdot \sin \gamma \cdot \cos a \tag{9a}$$

The other equations (2b), (2c), (3b), (3c) are obtained by cyclic permutation.

Substituting in the side cosine rule the expression for $\cos \alpha$ given by the angle cosine rule, we have

$$\cos a = \cos b \cdot \cos c + \sin b \cdot \sin c \cdot (-\cos \beta \cdot \cos \gamma + \sin \beta \cdot \sin \gamma \cdot \cos a)$$
$$\cos a = \cos b \cdot \cos c - \sin b \cdot \sin c \cdot \cos \beta \cdot \cos \gamma + \sin b \cdot \sin c \cdot \sin \beta \cdot \sin \gamma \cdot \cos a$$

Rearranging and factoring out leads to:

$$\cos a \cdot (1 - \sin b \cdot \sin c \cdot \sin \beta \cdot \sin \gamma) = \cos b \cdot \cos c - \sin b \cdot \sin c \cdot \cos \beta \cdot \cos \gamma$$

and since $\sin c \cdot \sin \beta = \sin b \cdot \sin \gamma$ it follows that

$$\cos a = \frac{\cos b \cdot \cos c - \sin b \cdot \sin c \cdot \cos \beta \cdot \cos \gamma}{1 - \sin^2 b \cdot \sin^2 \gamma} \tag{10}$$

Helmut Rixecker (*Mathematisches Unterrichtswerk* Book 3, 1984) called this formula the **side cos cos rule**.

We obtain the corresponding **angle cos cos rule** by substituting in the angle cosine rule the expression for $\cos a$ given by the side cosine rule:

$$\cos\alpha = \frac{-\cos\beta \cdot \cos\gamma + \sin\beta \cdot \sin\gamma \cdot \cos b \cdot \cos c}{1 - \sin^2\beta \cdot \sin^2 c} \tag{11}$$

With these five rules, any spherical triangle can be solved given three of its quantities (sides or angles).

We can also derive the side cosine rule by way of the angle γ. This angle is constructed in the drawing above. The tangents which touch the great circles AC and BC in point C intersect the drawing plane in the points T_a and T_b on lines MA and MB. The tangents folded onto the drawing plane touch the great circle AB in the points C_3 and C_4 respectively. Thus all sides of the triangle CT_aT_b are present in their true lengths; this triangle can be constructed and provides the angle γ in point C_5.

The side $T_aT_b = x$ can be constructed both from triangle T_aT_bM and from triangle $T_aT_bC_5$ using the cosine rule. Thus

$$x^2 = (MT_a)^2 + (MT_b)^2 - 2(MT_a)(MT_b)\cos c = (C_5T_a)^2 + (C_5T_b)^2 - 2(C_5T_a)(C_5T_b)\cos\gamma$$

With $\quad MT_a = \frac{1}{\cos b}, \quad MT_b = \frac{1}{\cos a}, \quad \overline{C_5T_a} = \tan b, \quad \overline{C_5T_b} = \tan a \quad$ we have

$$\frac{1}{\cos^2 b} + \frac{1}{\cos^2 a} - 2 \cdot \frac{\cos c}{\cos a \cdot \cos b} = \left(\frac{\sin b}{\cos b}\right)^2 + \left(\frac{\sin a}{\cos a}\right)^2 - 2 \cdot \left(\frac{\sin b}{\cos b}\right) \cdot \left(\frac{\sin a}{\cos a}\right) \cdot \cos\gamma$$

$$2 - 2 \cdot \frac{\cos c}{\cos a \cdot \cos b} = -2 \cdot \frac{\sin b}{\cos b} \cdot \frac{\sin a}{\cos a} \cdot \cos\gamma$$

$$\cos a \cdot \cos b - \cos c = -\sin b \cdot \sin a \cdot \cos\gamma$$

and finally

$$\cos a \cdot \cos b + \sin b \cdot \sin a \cdot \cos\gamma = \cos c.$$

We shall now investigate how, given three sides/angles of a spherical triangle, the other three sides/angles can be calculated. In doing so we shall assume that all the given quantities are $< 180°$ (the conditions for an Eulerian triangle, which lies entirely on one hemisphere). Moreover we note that in a spherical triangle $a > b > c$ if and only if $\alpha > \beta > \gamma$.

1. (SSS) and (AAA)

    Suppose three sides a, b, c are given. A triangle exists only if
    $a+b+c < 360°$ and $a+b > c, \ b+c > a, \ c+a > b$.
    All three angles are calculated uniquely by means of (2). The polarly corresponding result applies for the polar case (in which three angles are given and which is solved by (3)).

2. (SAS) and (ASA)

   Suppose two sides b, c and the included angle α are given. The third side a can always be uniquely calculated using (2). Then see I(SSS). The polarly corresponding result applies for the polar case (ASA; the third angle is found using (3)).

3. (SSA)

   Suppose two sides a, b and one opposite angle, say α, are given. In this case there are either two solutions or just one solution or no solutions. First the second angle β is found with the sine rule (1). We examine the following cases:

   a) $\sin a < \sin b \cdot \sin \alpha \Rightarrow \sin \beta = \frac{\sin b \cdot \sin \alpha}{\sin a} > 1$, which means there is no solution.
   b) $\sin a = \sin b \cdot \sin \alpha \Rightarrow \sin \beta = \frac{\sin b \cdot \sin \alpha}{\sin a} = 1$, that is, $\beta = 90°$.

   From (2b) we deduce $\quad \cos c = \dfrac{\cos b}{\cos a}$

   and from (3c) we have $\quad \cos \gamma = \sin \alpha \cdot \cos c = \sin \alpha \cdot \dfrac{\cos b}{\cos a}$.

   Since $\sin a = \sin b \cdot \sin \alpha \Rightarrow \sin a \leqslant \sin b$ and $a \leqslant b$, it follows that

   $$|\cos b| \leqslant |\cos a| \quad \text{and thus} \quad |\cos c| = \left|\frac{\cos b}{\cos a}\right| \leqslant 1$$

   so there is just one solution.

   c) $\sin a > \sin b \cdot \sin \alpha \Rightarrow \sin \beta = \frac{\sin b \cdot \sin \alpha}{\sin a} < 1$, which means first that there are two solutions for the angle β. Substitution in (4b) and (5b) gives us c and γ, possibly for both solutions of β.

The following drawing gives us a summary of the possible solutions in the case SSA.

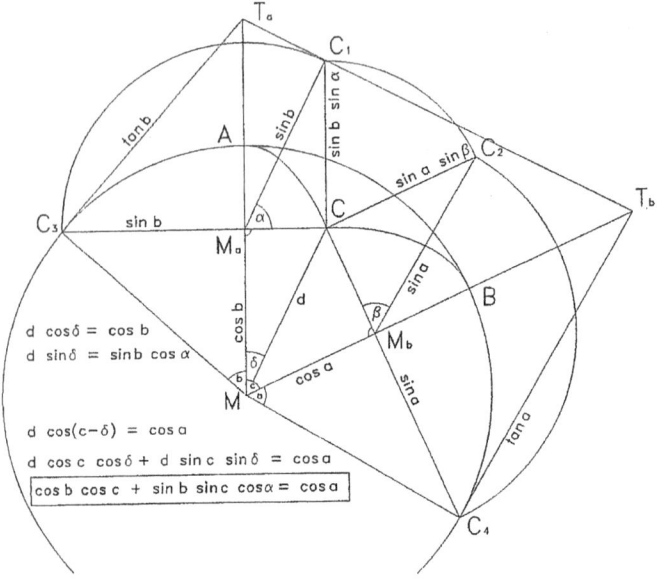

Given a, b and α, the construction can be done by means of M, A, C_3, M_a, C_1, C. Now an angle a drawn anywhere in point M provides the radius $r = \cos a$ of a circle about M, to which the tangents from C are constructed. This is only possible if $\cos a < MC$, that is, if $\sin a > CC_1 = CC_2$. The contact points with the circle of the two tangents are M_b And M'_b. The line MM_b intersects the sphere's equator on the side of M_b in B and on the other side in the opposite point B'. Similarly the line MM'_b (see Fig. 3) intersects the equator in the diametrically opposite points B'' and B'''. If $\cos a > \cos b$ (Fig. 3), then B and B'' lie on the right semicircle AA' and provide one side $c < 90°$, and B' and B''' lie on the left semicircle and provide one side $c > 90°$. Then B and B'' are two solutions if α and a are acute angles, and B'' and B''' are two solutions if α and a are obtuse angles. If α is acute and a obtuse, or the other way round, and if $\cos a > \cos b$, the problem has no solution.

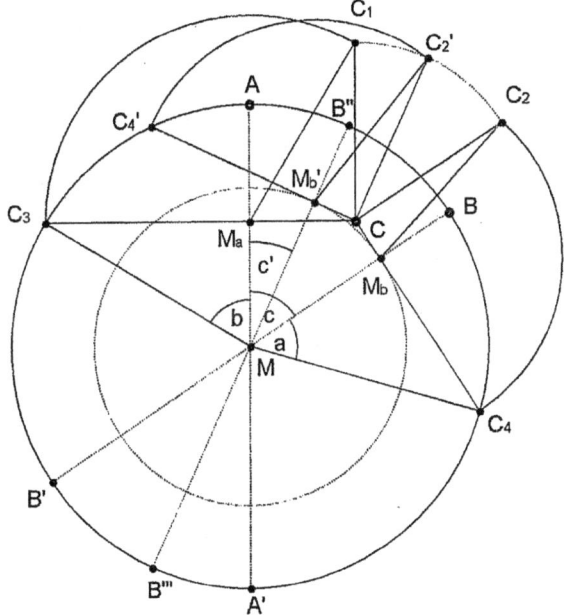

Fig. 3

If $\cos a < \cos b$ (Fig. 4), there are the following solutions:

B	if α acute and a acute
B''	if α obtuse and a acute
B'	if α obtuse and a obtuse
B'''	if α acute and a obtuse.

$\cos a = 0$ implies $M_b = M'_b = M$, $a = 90°$, and $B = B'''$ is a solution if α acute, $B' = B''$ is a solution if α obtuse.

235

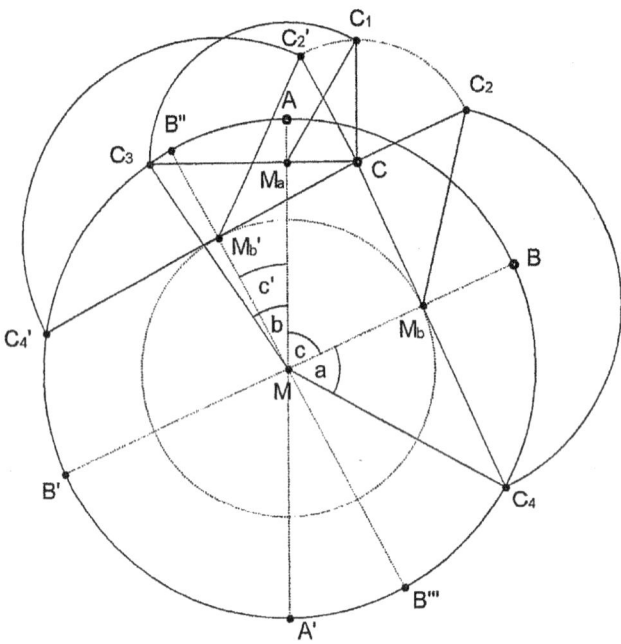

Fig. 4:

Formula summary

1. Sine rule

$$\frac{\sin\alpha}{\sin a} = \frac{\sin\beta}{\sin b} = \frac{\sin\gamma}{\sin c} \tag{1}$$

2. Side cosine rule

$$\cos a = \cos b \cdot \cos c + \sin b \cdot \sin c \cdot \cos\alpha \tag{2a}$$

$$\cos b = \cos c \cdot \cos a + \sin c \cdot \sin a \cdot \cos\beta \tag{2b}$$

$$\cos c = \cos a \cdot \cos b + \sin a \cdot \sin b \cdot \cos\gamma \tag{2c}$$

3. Angle cosine rule

$$\cos\alpha = -\cos\beta \cdot \cos\gamma + \sin\beta \cdot \sin\gamma \cdot \cos a \tag{3a}$$

$$\cos\beta = -\cos\gamma \cdot \cos\alpha + \sin\gamma \cdot \sin\alpha \cdot \cos b \tag{3b}$$

$$\cos\gamma = -\cos\alpha \cdot \cos\beta + \sin\alpha \cdot \sin\beta \cdot \cos c \tag{3c}$$

4. Side cos cos rule

$$\cos a = \frac{\cos b \cdot \cos c - \sin b \cdot \sin c \cdot \cos\beta \cdot \cos\gamma}{1 - \sin^2 b \cdot \sin^2 \gamma} \tag{4a}$$

$$\cos b = \frac{\cos c \cdot \cos a - \sin c \cdot \sin a \cdot \cos\gamma \cdot \cos\alpha}{1 - \sin^2 c \cdot \sin^2 \alpha} \tag{4b}$$

$$\cos c = \frac{\cos a \cdot \cos b - \sin a \cdot \sin b \cdot \cos \alpha \cdot \cos \beta}{1 - \sin^2 a \cdot \sin^2 \beta} \qquad (4c)$$

5. Angle cos cos rule

$$\cos \alpha = \frac{-\cos \beta \cdot \cos \gamma + \sin \beta \cdot \sin \gamma \cdot \cos b \cdot \cos c}{1 - \sin^2 \beta \cdot \sin^2 c} \qquad (5a)$$

$$\cos \beta = \frac{-\cos \gamma \cdot \cos \alpha + \sin \gamma \cdot \sin \alpha \cdot \cos c \cdot \cos a}{1 - \sin^2 \gamma \cdot \sin^2 a} \qquad (5b)$$

$$\cos \gamma = \frac{-\cos \alpha \cdot \cos \beta + \sin \alpha \cdot \sin \beta \cdot \cos a \cdot \cos b}{1 - \sin^2 \alpha \cdot \sin^2 b} \qquad (5c)$$

The nautical triangle

If A = CNP is the celestial north pole, $B = Z$ the zenith of the observer and C a star, we call the triangle ABC on the celestial sphere a nautical triangle. Suppose the star's altitude is h, the azimuth from the south a, the declination δ, the hour angle τ and the observer's geographical latitude φ. Then, if we let the triangle ABC have sides a', b', c', we have
$a' = BC = 90° - h$ (zenith distance), $b' = AC = 90° - \delta$, $c' = AB = 90° - \varphi$, $\alpha = \tau$ and $\beta = 180° - a$.

Substituting in (1)

$$\frac{\sin \alpha}{\sin a'} = \frac{\sin \beta}{\sin b'} = \frac{\sin \gamma}{\sin c'}$$

then gives

$$\sin \tau \cdot \cos \delta = \sin a \cdot \cos(h)$$

Substituting in (2)

$$\cos a' = \cos b' \cdot \cos c' + \sin b' \cdot \sin c' \cdot \cos \alpha$$

$$\cos b' = \cos c' \cdot \cos a' + \sin c' \cdot \sin a' \cdot \cos \beta$$

gives

$$\boxed{\begin{aligned}\sin(h) &= \sin \delta \cdot \sin \varphi + \cos \delta \cdot \cos \varphi \cdot \cos \tau \\ \sin \delta &= \sin \varphi \cdot \sin(h) - \cos \varphi \cdot \cos(h) \cdot \cos a\end{aligned}}$$

Substituting in (4)

$$\cos c' = \frac{\cos a' \cdot \cos b' - \sin a' \cdot \sin b' \cdot \cos \alpha \cdot \cos \beta}{1 - \sin^2 a' \cdot \sin^2 \beta}$$

gives

$$\sin \varphi = \frac{\sin(h) \cdot \sin \delta + \cos(h) \cdot \cos \delta \cdot \cos \tau \cdot \cos a}{1 - \cos^2(h) \cdot \sin^2 a}$$

The Conic Section

PETER BAUM

In the usual construction of a conic section as the locus of a point at an equal distance from a point and a line or circle, the connection with a cone is not immediately obvious. For the ellipse construction using a loop of string and two pins, one generally uses the so-called Dandelin spheres to show that the ellipse is the section of a cone.

In the following we derive a unified construction of the ellipse, parabola and hyperbola from the section of a plane with a cone. This construction was even used for teaching the conic section. Students find a certain satisfaction in seeing the construction's link with the cone. The construction also affords a simple derivation of the conic section's polar equation.

A cone has vertex $S(0,0,1)$ and it has the z-axis as a generator (line in its surface). Its semi-vertical angle is α.

It is intersected by the (x,y)-plane in a curve. As is well-known, this curve is an ellipse for $\alpha < 90°$, a parabola for $\alpha = 90°$ and a hyperbola for $\alpha > 90°$. Figure 1 below is the section of the cone in the (x,z)-plane.

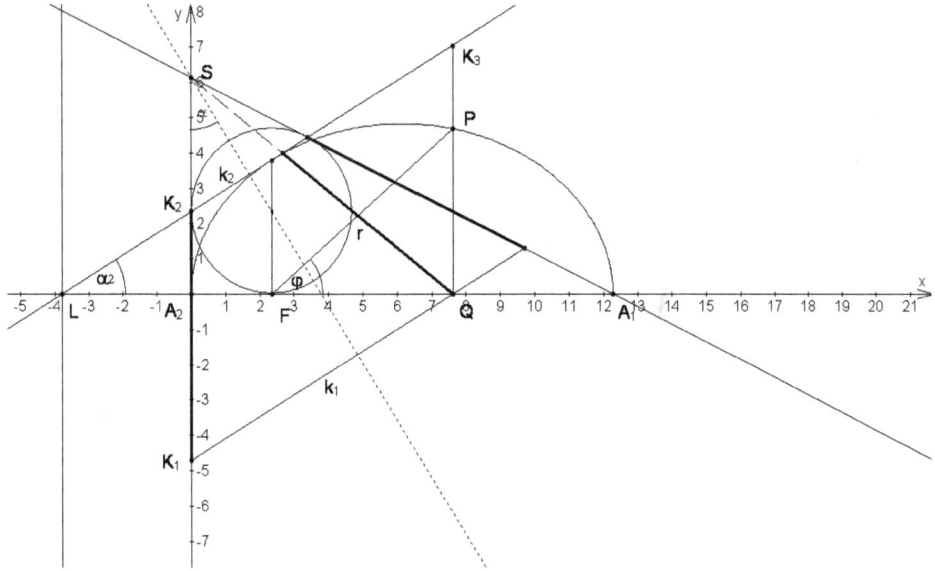

Fig. 1

Let Q' be any point of the curve of intersection of the (x,y)-plane and the cone and Q its projection onto the (x,z)-plane. The plane through Q perpendicular to the cone's axis intersects the cone in a circle k_1, touching the z-axis in K_1. The insphere between the cone and the (x,y)-plane touches the cone in a circle k_2 parallel to k_1, it touches the (x,y)-plane in F and the z-axis in K_2. The plane of k_2 intersects the (x,y)-plane in the directrix and the x-axis in L.

All generators, in particular the one through Q', touch the two circles k_1 and k_2 in two points always the same distance apart. This distance is that of K_1K_2 and is the same length as all tangent segments from Q' to the insphere, in particular the tangent segment $Q'F$. Hence $Q'F = K_1K_2$. From the triangle QK_1K_2 we construct a parallelogram and obtain K_3. Then $Q'F = QK_3$. If we rotate the (x,y)-plane about the x-axis into the drawing plane (the (x,z)-plane), then the y-axis rotates into the z-axis and Q' moves through a quarter-circle into the point P of the conic section. This gives us the following construction: A line parallel to the y-axis through an arbitrary point Q of the x-axis intersects the projection of the plane of k_2 in K_3. The circle about F with radius $r = QK_3$ intersects this parallel in two points P and P' of the conic section.

To derive the polar equation we set (see Figure 1) $\tan\alpha = \varepsilon$, $p = \varepsilon \cdot LF$ and $FP = r$. Then

$$r = QK_3 = \varepsilon \cdot LQ = \varepsilon \cdot (LF + FQ).$$

Since $FQ = r \cdot \cos\varphi$ we have $r = p + \varepsilon \cdot r \cdot \cos\varphi$, and therefore

$$\boxed{r = \frac{p}{1 - \varepsilon \cdot \cos\varphi}}$$

This is the conic section's equation in polar coordinates with the left focus as pole. It is

an ellipse if $\varepsilon < 1$

a parabola if $\varepsilon = 1$

a hyperbola if $\varepsilon > 1$.

If we rotate the conic section through $180°$ about F, F becomes the right focus and since $\cos(\varphi + 180°) = \cos\varphi$ we have

$$r = \frac{p}{1 + \varepsilon \cdot \cos\varphi} \tag{6}$$

Putting $\varphi = 90°$ we obtain the ordinate $y = p$ of the point of the curve vertically above the focus, the parameter p of the conic section.

If the conic section is the elliptical orbit of a planet with perihelion A_1, aphelion A_2 and center M, then the angle $E = \angle A_1MK$ is called the eccentric anomaly and the angle $\varphi = \angle A_1FP$ the true anomaly (see the next Figure). The conic section's equation can be expressed in terms of these quantities.

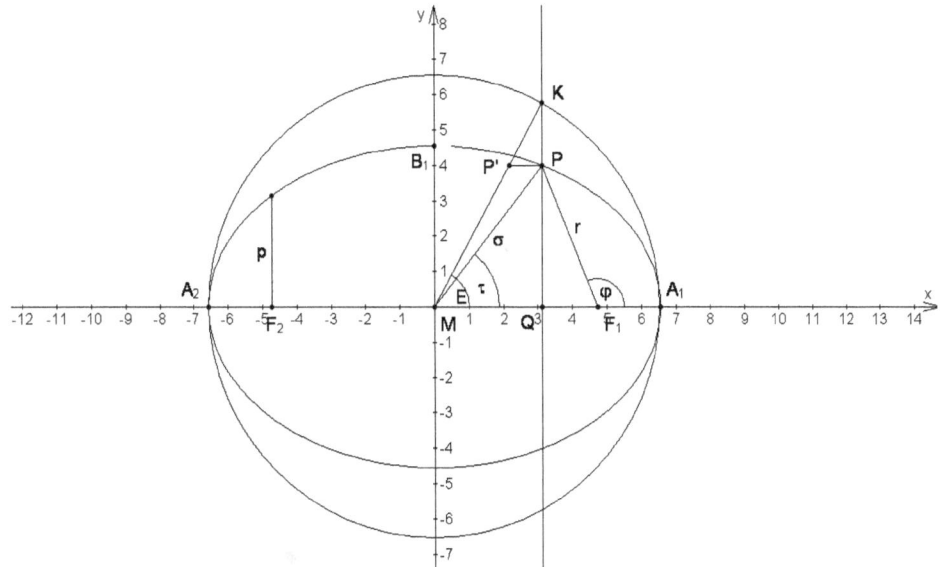

The following equations connect the constants $MA = a$, $MB = b$, $MF = e$, the parameter p and the numerical eccentricity ε:

$$a^2 = b^2 + e^2$$
$$e = \varepsilon \cdot a$$
$$b^2 = a \cdot p$$
$$a^2 = a \cdot p + e \cdot \varepsilon \cdot a$$
$$a = p + e \cdot \varepsilon$$

Now $FQ = r \cdot \cos \varphi$ and $MQ = a \cdot \cos E = MF + FQ$ which together imply $a \cdot \cos E = e + r \cdot \cos \varphi$.

(1) implies $r + \varepsilon \cdot r \cdot \cos \varphi = p$ and thus $r + \varepsilon \cdot (a \cdot \cos E - e) = p$.

Since $\varepsilon \cdot a = e$ and $p + \varepsilon \cdot e = a$ we thus have

$$r = a - e \cdot \cos E \qquad (7)$$

To derive the conic section's polar equation with respect to a central pole we proceed as follows. If $\sigma = MP$ then $e \cdot \cos E = \varepsilon \cdot a \cdot \cos E = \varepsilon \cdot \sigma \cdot \cos \tau$ and

$$r = a - \varepsilon \cdot \sigma \cdot \cos \tau. \qquad (8)$$

From

$$F_1 Q = r \cdot \cos \varphi = \sigma \cdot \cos \tau - e \qquad (9)$$

and
$$QP = r \cdot \sin\varphi = \sigma \cdot \sin\tau \tag{10}$$

we have, after squaring and adding, the following:
$$r^2 = \sigma^2 + e^2 - 2 \cdot e \cdot \sigma \cdot \cos\tau. \tag{11}$$

From (3) it follows that
$$\begin{aligned}r^2 &= a^2 - 2 \cdot a \cdot \varepsilon \cdot \sigma \cdot \cos\tau + \varepsilon^2 \cdot \sigma^2 \cdot \cos^2\tau \\ &= a^2 - 2 \cdot e \cdot \sigma \cdot \cos\tau + \varepsilon^2 \cdot \sigma^2 \cdot \cos^2\tau.\end{aligned} \tag{12}$$

Eliminating r from (6) and (7) finally gives
$$\sigma^2 \cdot (1 - \varepsilon^2 \cdot \cos^2\tau) = a^2 - e^2 = b^2$$

and hence the equation with respect to a central pole

$$\boxed{\sigma = \frac{b}{\sqrt{1 - \varepsilon^2 \cdot \cos^2\tau}}}$$

The Projective Construction of the Conic Section

PETER BAUM

Famously, at the age of 16 the philosopher and mathematician Blaise Pascal (1623 - 1662) discovered the following theorem:

> *If 6 points are distributed arbitrarily on a circle and numbered 1, 2, 3, 4, 5, 6 in any order, then the three points of intersection $X = (12)(45)$, $Y = (23)(56)$, $Z = (34)(61)$ of opposite sides of the hexagon lie in a line.*

This has come to be called the *Pascal line*. For a particular distribution of points (a particular hexagon) there are at most 60 different Pascal lines to be found by re-numbering the points. Of the total of $6! = 720$ different permutations of the numbers, the 6 cyclic permutations $1 \to 2 \to 3 \to 4 \to 5 \to 6 \to 1$ always lead to the same points X, Y, Z, as the following table shows:

123456	(12)(45)	(23)(56)	(34)(61)
234561	(23)(56)	(34)(61)	(45)(12)
345612	(34)(61)	(45)(12)	(56)(23)
456123	(45)(12)	(56)(23)	(61)(34)
561234	(56)(23)	(61)(34)	(12)(45)
612345	(61)(34)	(12)(45)	(23)(56)

As a result the number of distinct Pascal lines is reduced to $720 : 6 = 120$. But the same points also arise by effecting the following (non-cyclic) permutation: $1 \leftrightarrow 2$, $3 \leftrightarrow 6$, $4 \leftrightarrow 5$.

Thus

$$X = (12)(45) = (21)(54)$$
$$Y = (23)(56) \leftrightarrow Z = (16)(43)$$

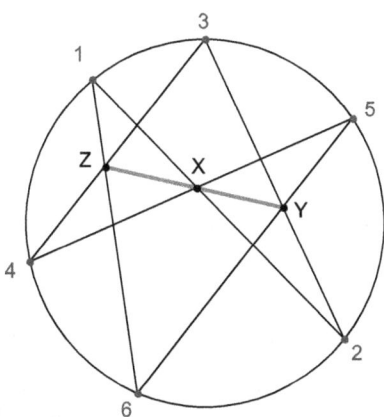

Figure 1

As a result the number of distinct Pascal lines of a particular hexagon is further reduced to $120 \div 2 = 60$.

In the case of a regular hexagon the 60 Pascal lines coincide five at a time for reasons of symmetry. We are then left with just 12 distinct Pascal lines.

Pascal knew that that this property of the circle applies to all conic sections. His work relating to this is lost, but Leibniz had held it in his hands and in a letter to Pascal's nephew dated 1676 gave the titles of the six sections of which it consisted.[1] From these titles it emerged that Pascal saw the circle as plane section of a cone with vertex S. Thus exactly one plane goes through each side of the hexagon and the cone's vertex S. The six planes intersect each other in the generators through the six points of the circle and the cone's vertex; they also intersect each other in the three lines XS, YS, ZS, which obviously lie in a plane through the Pascal line and S. If this spatial figure is intersected by any plane not containing S, the result is a hexagon inscribed in the conic section, which likewise leads to three collinear points of intersection of opposite sides.

The duality principle in the plane states that a geometric proposition remains valid if the concepts point and line are interchanged. In 1810 Brianchon availed himself of this and by dualizing Pascal's theorem discovered the following one:

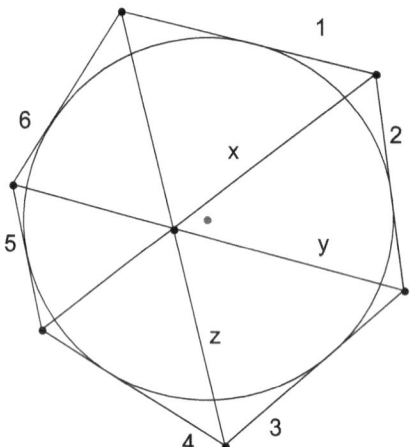

Figure 2

If six tangents 1,2,3,4,5,6 are distributed arbitrarily on a circle, then the three lines $x = (12)(45)$, $y = (23)(56)$, $z = (34)(61)$ connecting opposite points of intersection go through a point.

We come to the projective generation of the conic section as follows. In the Pascal figure we hold the circle and the first five points fixed and move point 6 on the circle. Thus the point $X = (12)(45)$ also remains fixed, but side (16) turns about point 1, side (56) turns about point 5, point Y moves on side (23), point Z moves on side (34) and the Pascal line rotates about point X.

---

[1] See M. Chasles *Geschichte der Geometrie*, translated into German by L.A. Sohncke 1839, Reprint Wiesbaden 1968, p. 67 ff or Moritz Cantor *Vorlesungen über Geschichte der Mathematik*, Leipzig 1913, Vol. II, p. 680 ff

If in this way point 6 moves round the entire circle (or conic section), then side (16) goes through the line pencil in point 1. Furthermore Z goes through the point range (34), the Pascal line goes through the line pencil in point X, point Y goes through the point range (23) and side (56) goes through the line pencil in point 5. To each line of point 1 we can construct the corresponding line of point 5 and thus the point of intersection 6.

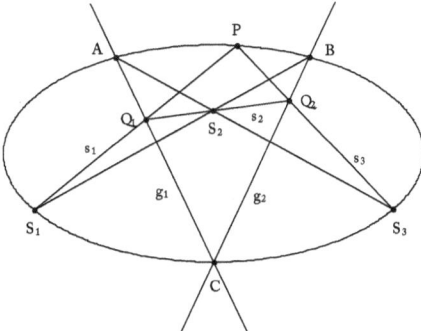

Figure 3

From now on the we shall always call the points bearing the line pencils S_1, S_2, S_3, and the lines bearing the two point ranges g_1 and g_2. These can be chosen arbitrarily. The assigning of lines of S_3 with lines of S_1 works as follows. s_1 intersects g_1 in Q_1, the connecting line Q_1S_2 intersects g_2 in Q_2, the connecting line Q_2S_3 is the line s_3 assigned to s_1 and intersects it in the point P of the curve.

A result of the construction is that the points S_1 and S_3 as well as the intersection point $C = g_1g_2$ are points of the curve. Two further curve points are $A = (S_3S_2)g_1$ and $B = (S_1S_2)g_2$. If we decide on *these* five curve points, this gives us the two point ranges $g_1 = AC$ and $g_2 = BC$ and the point of intersection $S_2 = (AS_3)(BS_1)$. For all further considerations, knowledge of this construction from five elements (3 line pencils and 2 point ranges, or five curve points) is assumed, as is this naming of points and lines.

The following question now arises. How we can we discern from the positioning of the five basic forms (the three line pencils and two point ranges) which generate the curve, whether that curve will be an ellipse, a parabola or a hyperbola, including the «degenerate» cases of point, line and double line?[2]

Before we turn to this question in Section IV, we consider some specializations of Figure 3 which are possible.

I. We can allow A to coincide with S_3, and B with S_1 (Figure 4)

This means the lines AS_3 and BS_1 become tangents, and the point ranges g_1 and g_2 go through S_3 and S_1 respectively. And the conic section is uniquely determined by two points with their tangents and one other point C. A further specialization consists in arranging the three points and

---
[2] Investigation of the degenerate cases is left to the reader.

the two tangents symmetrically. As a result the perpendicular bisector of the segment S_1S_3 goes through C and S_2 and the mid-point S. The point C is a vertex of the ellipse. We obtain the other vertex D by means of the line through S_2 parallel to the line S_1S_3. It intersects g_1 and g_2 in the symmetrical points Q and Q', through which go the related lines s_1 and s_3 which intersect in D.

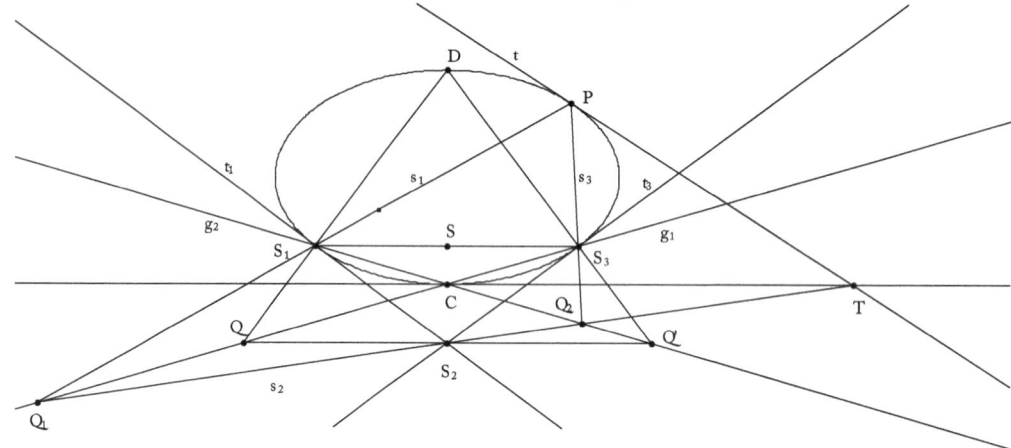

Figure 4

The point of intersection T of Q_1Q_2 with the tangent in C provides the tangent in P. This follows from Pascal's theorem applied to the hexagon $P = 1$ and 2, $S_1 = 3, C = 4$ and 5, $S_3 = 6$ with points of intersection $(12)(45) = T$, $(23)(56) = Q_1$, $(34)(61) = Q_2$ and with the Pascal line TQ_1Q_2.

Starting from this symmetrical layout we merely vary the center S_2 of the pencil in a vertical direction and observe the changes in the curve and the segment QQ'. The following cases arise:

1. $\overline{S_1S_3} < \overline{QQ'}$. This means $\overline{SC} < \overline{CS_2}$ and the curve is an ellipse (see Figure 4. Proof?)

2. $\overline{S_1S_3} = \overline{QQ'}$. This means $\overline{SC} = \overline{CS_2}$ and QS_1 is parallel to $Q'S_3$. D is thus a point at infinity and the curve is a parabola (Figure 5). Why is there not a second point at infinity?

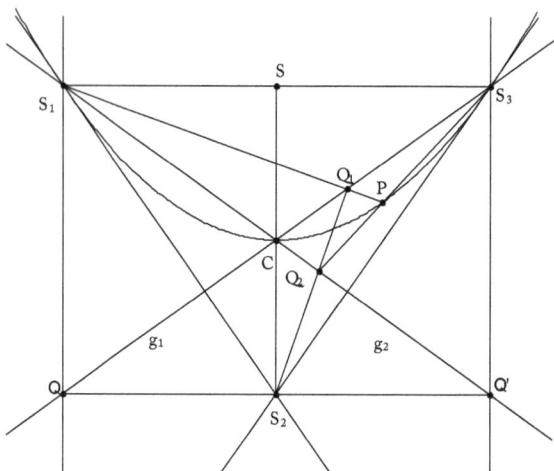

Figure 5

3. $\overline{S_1S_3} > \overline{QQ'}$. This implies $\overline{SC} > \overline{CS_2}$ and the curve is a hyperbola with vertices C and D (Figure 6).

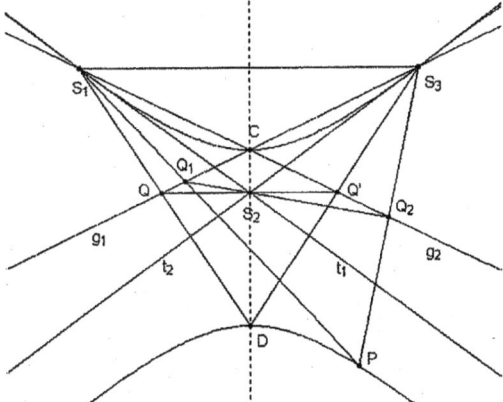

Figure 6

II. Further specializations

Still greater specializations in the choice of the five basic forms can be made as follows.

1. Ellipse

We choose two of its vertices for S_1 and S_3. This means that the tangents are parallel and S_2 is a point at infinity. The construction we obtain is shown in Figure 7.

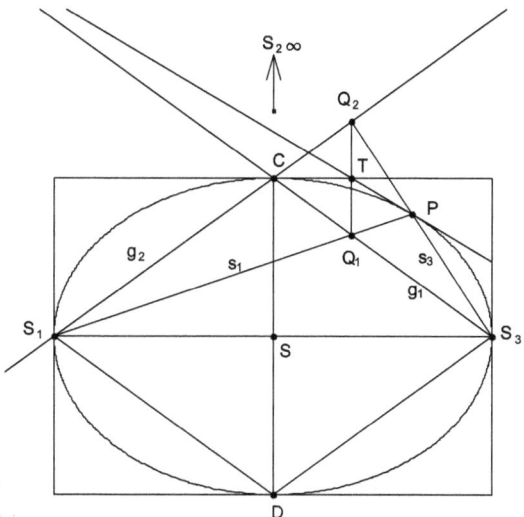

Figure 7

2. Parabola

The parabola is a conic section with just one point at infinity. One of the four points S_1, S_3, C, D can be this point at infinity. In Figure 5 it is the point D. If we choose C as point at infinity then the point ranges g_1 and g_2 are parallel and the result is the construction in Figure 8.

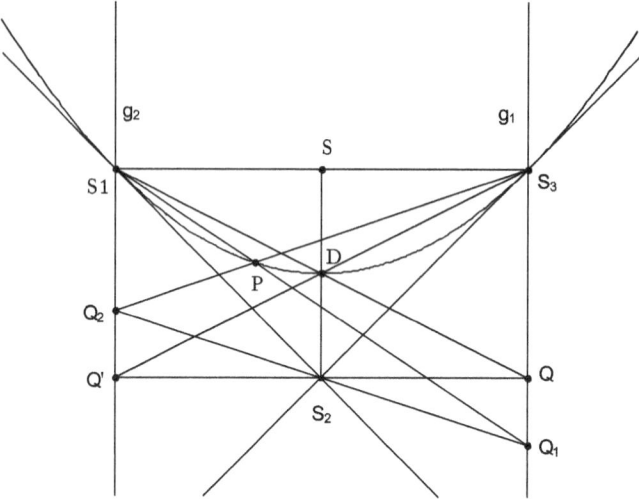

Figure 8

If S_1 is chosen as vertex and S_3 as point at infinity then C and D are symmetric points of the parabola and we have Figure 9. There cannot be another point at infinity because the lines going through S_3 can only take one direction.

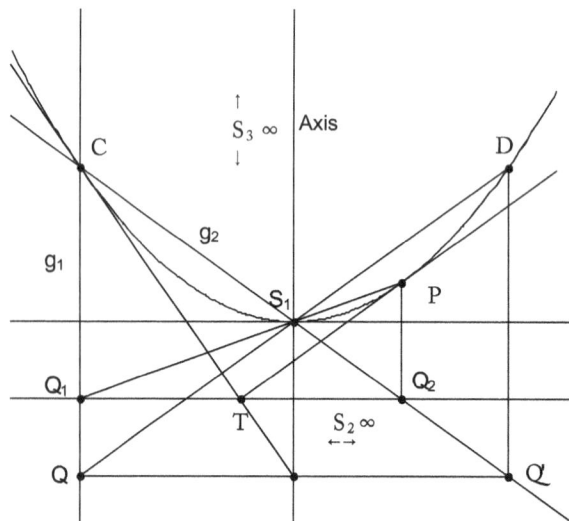

Figure 9

The point of intersection T of the tangent in C with $s_2 = Q_1Q_2$ is also the mid-point of the segment Q_1Q_2 since it's the fourth harmonic point to Q_1Q_2 with the external dividing point S_2 as point at infinity. The Pascal hexagon $P = 1$ and 2, $C = 4$ and 5, $S_1 = 3$, $S_3 = 6$ leads to the Pascal line $T = (12)(45)$, $Q_1 = (23)(56)$, $Q_2 = (34)(61)$, so that T provides the tangent in P.

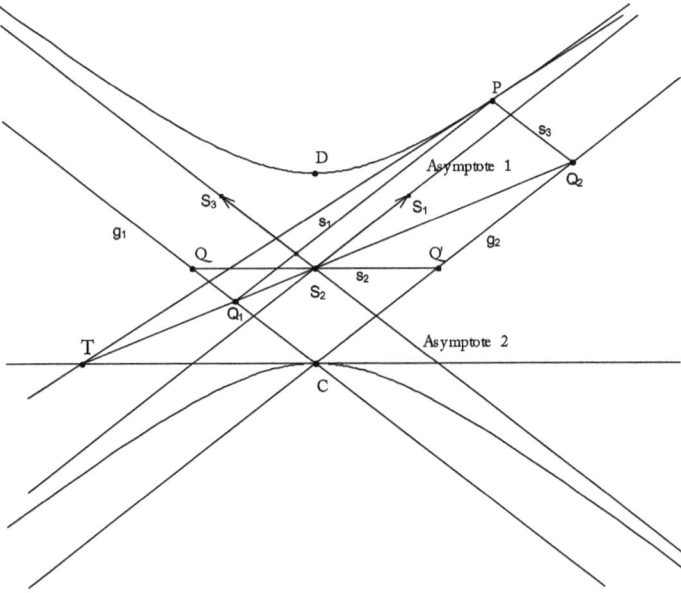

Figure 10

3. Hyperbola

The hyperbola has two points at infinity. In Figure 6 none of the five chosen points was a point at infinity.

S_1 and S_3 are obvious choices to be points at infinity. Their tangents are then asymptotes of the hyperbola. Point C is a convenient choice for vertex (Figure 10).

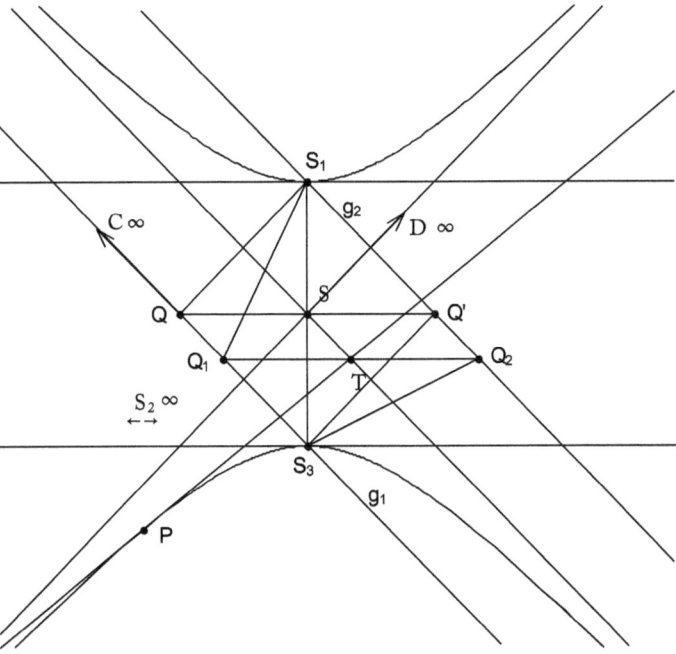

Figure 11

We could also choose C as point at infinity and S_1 and S_3 as vertices. D is then the other point at infinity of the hyperbola, and S_2 is the point at infinity of the two vertex tangents. The two point ranges g_1 and g_2 go through S_3 and S_1 and give the direction of the first asymptote. This goes through the mid-point S of the segment S_1S_2. The connecting line SS_2 intersects the point ranges g_1 and g_2 in Q and Q', providing the direction D_∞ of the second asymptote (Figure 11).

III. The equations of the ellipse, parabola and hyperbola

1. Ellipse

Suppose the vertices $S_1(-a,0)$, $S_3(a,0)$, $C(0,b)$ are given and S_2 is the point at infinity of the y-axis (Figure 7). Then s_2 is parallel to the y-axis, so Q_1 and Q_2 are (x_1,y_1) and (x_2,y_2) respectively, say, with $x_2 = x_1$.

$$Q_1 \text{ lies on } g_1 \text{ giving } y_1 = -\frac{b}{a}(x_1 - a) \tag{1}$$

$$Q_2 \text{ lies on } g_2 \text{ giving } y_2 = \frac{b}{a}(x_1 + a) \tag{2}$$

$P(x \mid y)$ lies on S_1Q_1, so $\dfrac{y}{x+a} = \dfrac{y_1}{x_1+a}$ and on S_3Q_2, so $\dfrac{y}{x-a} = \dfrac{y_2}{x_1-a}$.

Multiplying these last two equations, and also equations (1) and (2), gives

$$\frac{y^2}{x^2 - a^2} = \frac{y_1 \cdot y_2}{x_1^2 - a^2} \quad \text{and} \quad \frac{y_1 \cdot y_2}{x_1^2 - a^2} = -\frac{b^2}{a^2}$$

from which follows the ellipse equation:

$$\boxed{\frac{x^2}{a^2} + \frac{y^2}{b^2} = 1}$$

2. Parabola

In the construction in Figure 8 let D be the origin of coordinates, $S_1(-a,b)$, $S_3(a,b)$, and $S_2(0,-b)$. Then Q_1 is (a,y_1), Q_2 is $(-a,y_2)$, and S_2 being the mid-point of the segment Q_1Q_2 means that $y_1 + y_2 = -2b$.

$P(x \mid y)$ lies on S_1Q_1 so that $\dfrac{y-b}{x+a} = \dfrac{y_1-b}{a+a} = \dfrac{y_1-b}{2a}$ (two point form)

and on S_3Q_2 so that $\dfrac{y-b}{x-a} = \dfrac{y_2-b}{-a-a} = -\dfrac{y_2-b}{2a}$.

By subtraction we have

$$\frac{y-b}{x+a} - \frac{y-b}{x-a} = \frac{y_1+y_2-2b}{2a} = -2\frac{b}{a}$$

$$\frac{y-b}{x^2-a^2} \cdot (-2a) = -2\frac{b}{a}$$

$$y - b = \frac{b}{a^2}(x^2 - a^2) = \frac{b}{a^2}x^2 - b$$

and hence

$$y = \frac{b}{a^2}x^2$$

For the construction in Figure 9, S_1 is $(0,0)$, $C(-a,b)$, and $Q_1(-a,y_1)$.

$Q_2(x\mid y_1)$ lies on CS_1, so $\quad \dfrac{y_1}{x} = \dfrac{b}{-a}$

$P(x\mid y)$ lies on S_1Q_1, so $\quad \dfrac{y}{x} = \dfrac{y_1}{-a}$.

This implies
$$y = y_1 \cdot \frac{x}{-a} = \frac{b}{-a} \cdot x \cdot \frac{x}{-a} = \frac{b}{a^2}x^2$$

thus
$$y = \frac{b}{a^2}x^2$$

3. Hyperbola

The derivation of the hyperbola's equation from Figure 12 is very simple. With the usual notation, we have, by similarity of triangles, the following ratio forms:

$$\frac{y}{x+a} = \frac{y_1}{x_1+a}, \qquad \frac{y}{x-a} = \frac{y_1+2b}{x_1-a}$$

and
$$\frac{y_1}{x_1-a} = \frac{y_1+2b}{x_1+a} = \frac{b}{a}$$

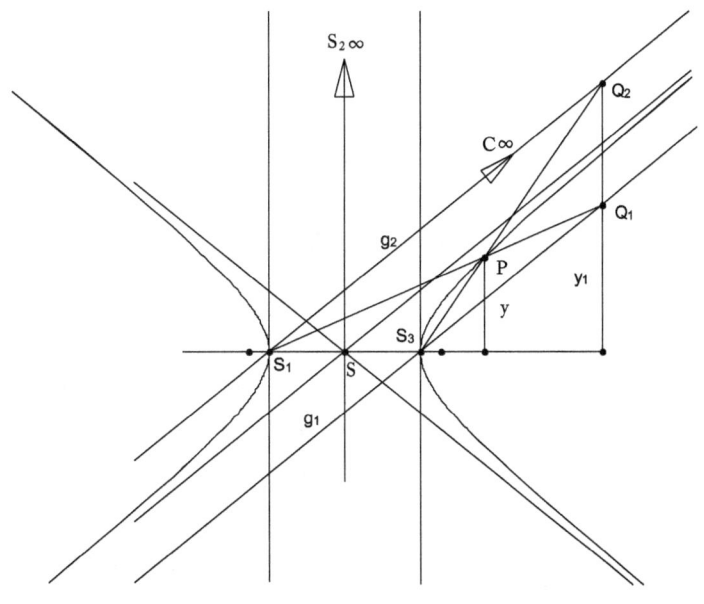

Figure 12

Multiplying the first two equations gives

$$\frac{y^2}{x^2-a^2} = \frac{y_1}{x_1+a} \cdot \frac{y_1+2b}{x_1-a} = \frac{y_1}{x_1-a} \cdot \frac{y_1+2b}{x_1+a} = \frac{b^2}{a^2}$$

so
$$\frac{y^2}{b^2} = \frac{x^2-a^2}{a^2} = \frac{x^2}{a^2} - 1$$

$$\boxed{\frac{x^2}{a^2} - \frac{y^2}{b^2} = 1}$$

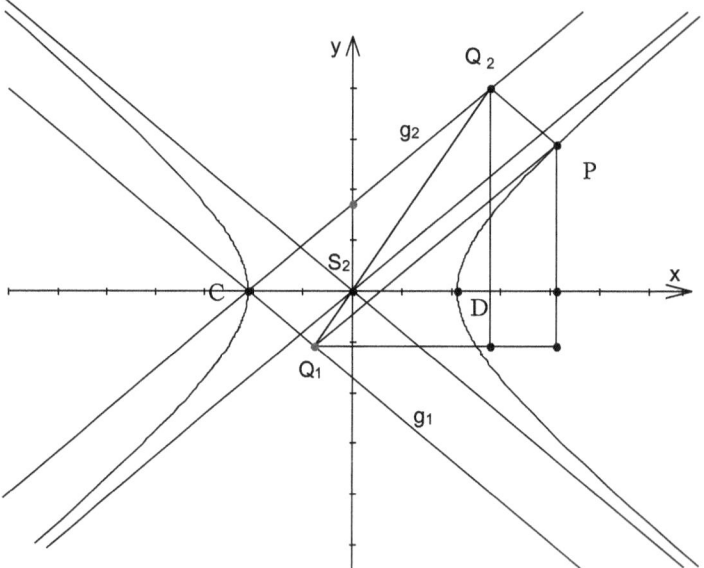

Figure 13

For the construction in Figure 13 we get the hyperbola's equation as follows:

The line PQ_1 has gradient $\frac{b}{a}$, thus $\qquad y - \frac{b}{a}x = y_1 - \frac{b}{a}x_1$ \hfill (1)

The line PQ_2 has gradient $-\frac{b}{a}$, thus $\qquad y + \frac{b}{a}x = y_2 + \frac{b}{a}x_2$ \hfill (2)

Q_1 lies on g_1, so $\qquad \dfrac{x_1}{-a} + \dfrac{y_1}{-b} = 1 \qquad$ (intercept form) \hfill (3)

Q_2 lies on g_2, so $\qquad \dfrac{x_2}{-a} + \dfrac{y_2}{b} = 1 \qquad$ (intercept form) \hfill (4)

The line Q_1Q_2 goes through the origin, thus $\dfrac{y_2}{x_2} = \dfrac{y_1}{x_1}$ or $y_1x_2 - y_2x_1 = 0$.

Multiplying (1) and (2) gives
$$y^2 - \frac{b^2}{a^2}x^2 = y_1y_2 + \frac{b}{a}(y_1x_2 - y_2x_1) - \frac{b^2}{a^2}x_1x_2$$

and thus
$$\frac{y^2}{b^2} - \frac{x^2}{a^2} = \frac{y_1y_2}{b^2} - \frac{x_1x_2}{a^2}.$$

Multiplying (3) and (4) gives $\dfrac{y_1y_2}{b^2} - \dfrac{x_1x_2}{a^2} = -1$.

Substituting in the preceding equation gives the hyperbola's equation

$$\boxed{\dfrac{x^2}{a^2} - \dfrac{y^2}{b^2} = 1}$$

IV. The limit hyperbola

Three arbitrary points S_1, S_3 and C of a conic section are given, hence also the point ranges $g_1 = CS_3$ and $g_2 = CS_1$. Suppose the center of the pencil S_2 is variable; it provides the tangents $t_1 = S_1S_2$, $t_3 = S_3S_2$ and thus determines the conic section uniquely.

We'll now investigate the three domains of points in which S_2 must lie such that we get an ellipse, a parabola and a hyperbola respectively.

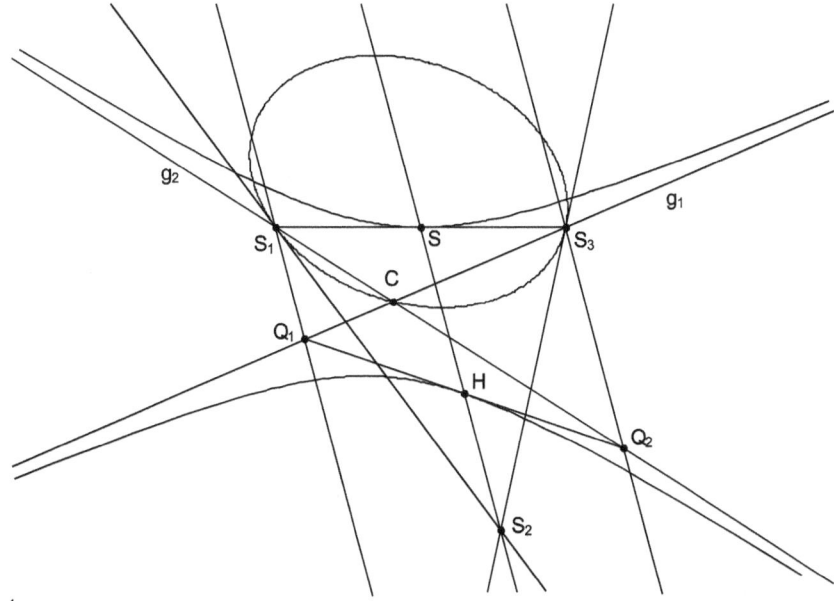

Figure 14

First for arbitrary S_2, we consider the diameter $d = SS_2$. Holding the diameter fixed we ask: In which point H of d must S_2 lie so that we obtain a parabola?

When we do, the point at infinity of d must be a point of the curve. We join it, by means of parallels to d, with S_1 and S_3 and obtain the points Q_1 and Q_2 on g_1 and g_2 respectively. The point of intersection of Q_1Q_2 with d is the required point H.

H is obviously the mid-point of Q_1Q_2. If d turns round S, then Q_1 moves on g_1, Q_2 on g_2, and H moves on a hyperbola, the *limit hyperbola*. Its asymptotes are g_1 and g_2 and it goes through S.

If the pencil center S_2 lies in the interior point domain of this hyperbola (those points through which none of its tangents go) the result is an ellipse (Figure 14). If the pencil center S_2 lies in the hyperbola's exterior point domain, the result is a hyperbola (Figure 15).

Orthogonal Pencils of Circles

PETER BAUM

In the following we describe a fact that could be made into a central theme from the 11th grade on. At this time, in analytic geometry, students calculate the points of intersection of two circles. To do this, first the equation of the common secant of the two circles is obtained by subtracting the circle's equations in normal form. But doing this we always obtain the equation of a line, even if the circles do not intersect or touch each other. In this case, continuing to calculate the points of intersection of the line (the *radical axis* or *power line* of the two circles) with one of the circles is well known to lead to negative determinants of second order equations and thus to square roots of negative numbers, that is, to complex solutions. Our considerations will eventually show that these complex numbers are directly related to the positions of circle and line, and how.

Trying to interpret imaginary geometry has preoccupied many mathematicians since the 16th century. Gauss' complex plane is well known. Less well known is C. von Staudt's theory of the imaginary in which imaginary elements are represented by geometric movements. Felix Klein devoted a chapter in his lectures *Elementarmathematik vom höheren Standpunkte aus*[1] (Berlin 1925, Vol. II p. 126) to this theory. L. Locher-Ernst gives a description of it in his book *Geometrische Metamorphosen* (Dornach 1970) in the Chapter «Das Imaginäre in der Geometrie» where he explains the arrow representation. In Chapter 27 «Der Kreis als Stauprodukt einer Bewegungsgestalt»[2] of his book *Projektive Geometrie* (Stuttgart, 1984) Arnold Bernhard describes involutions in a line and in the Appendix makes some remarks about analytic solutions leading to imaginary numbers. I shall try to represent the same facts as a sequence suitable for teaching.

1 The radical axis or power line of two circles

Starting from two circles that lie outside each other, one can have the students calculate the radical axis and draw it using the equation. *But how can we construct it?*

The students can attempt to answer this question using several drawn examples. Fundamental properties of the radical axis are soon discovered:

- it is perpendicular to the line-segment joining the centers of the circles
- it bisects this segment whenever the circles' radii are equal
- it is closer to the larger circle (Fig. 2).

The teacher can easily feel tempted to give further help too quickly. It does no harm to allow a problem to stand a day or two if no-one can solve it. How one cautiously proceeds if no student strikes gold depends very much on the class and the material handled up to now.

---

[1] *Elementary mathematics from an advanced standpoint*
[2] "The circle as the damming-up of a movement form"

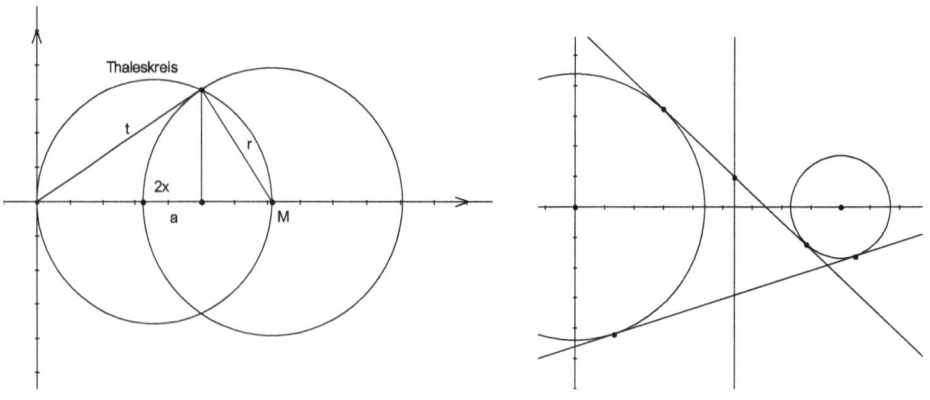

Figure 1   Figure 2

Various approaches are possible:

- extreme cases could be investigated, one circle becoming a point, say
- the common tangents could be drawn
- the general solution could be calculated.

Briefly, the last one goes like this:

Suppose the circle equations

$$x^2 + y^2 = s^2 \quad \text{and} \quad (x-a)^2 + y^2 = r^2.$$

are given. Subtraction leads to the line equation

$$2ax - a^2 = s^2 - r^2, \quad \text{or} \quad 2ax = s^2 + a^2 - r^2.$$

In the extreme case $s = 0$ and we obtain $2ax = a^2 - r^2$. The problem of interpreting the quantities in an equation now arises, often a fruitful process toward discovering constructions.

The difference of two squares can be interpreted as the square on a «leg» (one of the shorter sides of a right triangle). Thus, by Thales' theorem, we come to the circle with the hypotenuse a as diameter and to the tangent segment (the leg) of length t from the origin to the circle of radius r, that is, to the relationship: $t^2 = a^2 - r^2$. The equation $2ax = t^2$ relates to Euclid's proof of the Pythagorean theorem (the so-called «Bride's Chair» figure) and the segment $2x$ is the subtangent[3] (Fig. 1).

Thus the radical axis bisects the subtangent and the tangent segment of length t. If $s > 0$, the radical axis bisects the segments between the points of contact of the four common tangents.

---

[3] The projection of the tangent segment onto the x-axis.

This the students now see in their drawings. For the proof, the concept of the *power of a point with respect to a circle* is needed, which one can take this opportunity to introduce.

Suppose P is a point outside a circle k. Suppose also an arbitrary secant through P of the circle intersects k in A and B, and a second such secant intersects k in C and D. Then by the intersecting secant theorem[4] the product of the directed lengths of the segments formed is the same for both secants:

$$\vec{PA} \cdot \vec{PB} = \vec{PC} \cdot \vec{PD} = p(P)$$

and depends only on k and the position of P in relation to k. This product $p(P)$ is called *the power of P with respect to k*. In the limiting case when $C = D = T$ the secant is a tangent through P with point of contact T and $p(P) = \vec{PT}^2 = t^2$.

The power is positive since both segments directed from P have the same direction. If P lies on the circle then $p(P) = 0$. If P is inside the circle then the two segments of the secant have different directions and the power $p(P)$ is negative.

The name «power» comes from Jakob Steiner[5], who used it by analogy with the «power of a hyperbola» (the constant area of the parallelogram enclosed between a hyperbola and its asymptotes). The intersecting secant theorem is in Euclid (*Elements*, Book 3, Proposition 36).

2 Orthogonal pencils of circles

Suppose two fixed points A and B on the x-axis are given (Fig. 3) and the perpendicular bisector of AB is the y-axis. All the circles which go through A and B, together form what is called a pencil of circles. Their centers lie on the y-axis. The line AB is common secant of all the circles; it's called the radical axis or power line of these circles, since a point P of AB has the same power $p(P)$ with respect to every circle of the pencil:

$$p(P) = PA \cdot PB = t^2.$$

If T is the point of contact of any tangent through P to any circle of the pencil, then $PT = t$.

From this it follows that the circle with center P and radius $t = \sqrt{p(P)}$ intersects all the circles of the pencil in right angles (orthogonally). If P moves on the power line AB together with this circle, the result is a second pencil of circles with the property that every circle of the second pencil is orthogonal to every circle of the first pencil.

From this it follows in turn that the center M of a circle of the first pencil has the same power with respect to every circle of the orthogonal pencil, since every radius belonging to M is also the segment of a tangent to a circle of the second pencil. Therefore the perpendicular bisector of AB

---
[4] Also called the intersecting chord theorem.
[5] Jacob Steiner *Allgemeine Theorie über das Berühren und Schneiden der Kreise und der Kugeln* [*General theory of the contact and intersection of circles and spheres*], Zürich 1931.

(the y-axis) is the power line of the second pencil. While all circles of the first pencil intersect in A and B, no two circles of the second, orthogonal pencil have a point in common.

Moreover we can see that both pencils are determined by any two circles of the same pencil, since two circles determine exactly one power line and thus all other circles possessing the same power line as these two.

Each of the two power lines can be regarded as a limit circle, having the point at infinity of the other power line as center. While every point of the perpendicular bisector of AB is the center of a circle, the second pencil has no circle centers in the interior of the segment AB.

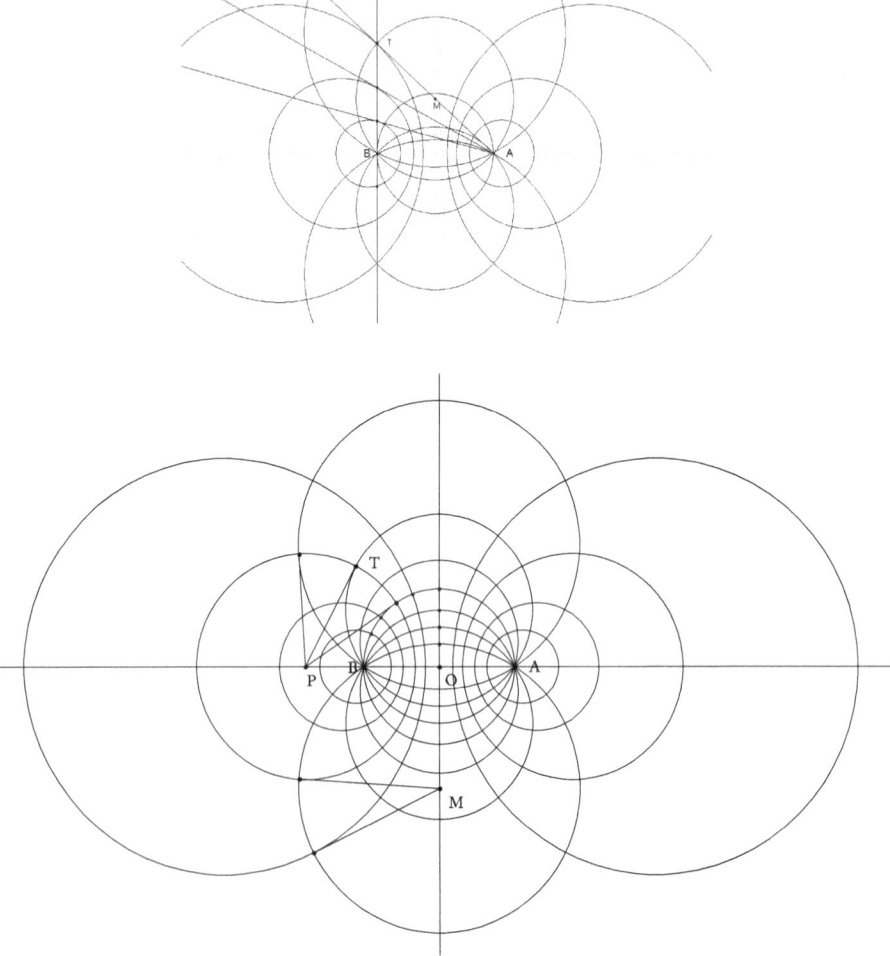

Figure 3

Another property of the second pencil of circles is noteworthy. Let a be the line parallel to the y-axis through B and b the parallel to the y-axis through A. Then (A,a) and (B,b) are pole and polar with respect to every circle of the second pencil. For suppose k is an arbitrary circle of the second pencil such that A lies outside k. The tangent to k through A touches k in T say, and intersects the y-axis in M say. So the circle of the first pencil with M as center has this tangent through its center and goes through the points A, B, T, which form a right triangle with diameter AT as hypotenuse (Thales' theorem). Thus the line BT is perpendicular to AB, and therefore the polar a of A. (Fig. 3)

3 Involution in a line

For what follows we need briefly to explain the concept of the *involution in a line g*.

Suppose k is a circle and g a line. To each point P of the line g we can assign a definite point P' lying in g as follows. P' is the point of intersection with the line g of the polar p of P with respect to the circle k. This relationship we call an involution in the line g. Now to the point P' we can equally well assign a point P''. But by the main proposition of polar theory, the polar of P' goes through P itself, since P' lies on the polar of P. Thus $P'' = P$. The mutually assigned points P and P' are called conjugate points.

We notice immediately that if the line g is a secant then the two points of intersection S_1 and S_2 of g with the circle k are self-conjugate: $S'_1 = S_1$ and $S'_2 = S_2$. We call them the double points of the involution. If P moves on the secant g then its conjugate point P' moves on g in the opposite direction. This involution is called *opposite* or *hyperbolic*. On the other hand the involution induced on a *passant line* (a line interior to the circle's tangent envelope) is *direct*, the conjugate points move in the same direction one after the other, and there are no real double points (a so-called *elliptic* involution). If g is a tangent, the involution is degenerate, because the point of contact is conjugate to every point of the tangent (a so-called *parabolic* involution).

Returning to the two orthogonal pencils of circles, the following fact is true:

Every circle k' of the second pencil generates *the same* elliptic involution on the y-axis, and every circle k of the first pencil generates *the same* hyperbolic involution on the x-axis. The points of intersection of k with the y-axis and the points of intersection of k' with the x-axis are pairs of conjugate points of the respective involutions.

To see this we must show that if P is an arbitrary point of the y-axis then all the polars of P with respect to the circles k' meet each other *in one point* P' on the y-axis, and P' lies on the circumcircle k^* of ABP (Fig. 4).

Suppose k be an arbitrary circle of the first pencil; it thus goes through A and B. Let the center of k be P. Suppose k' is an arbitrary circle of the second pencil with center M, and T and T' are the points of intersection of k and k'. Then, because of the orthogonality of the circles k and k', the common secant TT' is the polar of P with respect to k', *and* the polar of M with respect to k. This polar intersects the y-axis in a point P'. Since M lies on the line AB, by the main proposition of polar theory the polar TT' of M must go through the pole P^* of AB with respect to k. But this pole P^* lies on the y-axis, and so $P' = P^*$. The lines $P'A$ and $P'B$ are therefore tangents to k and are perpendicular to the radii PA and PB. Therefore the points P, A, P', B lie on a circle (by Thales' theorem), which belongs to the first pencil, and are independent of the choice of k'.

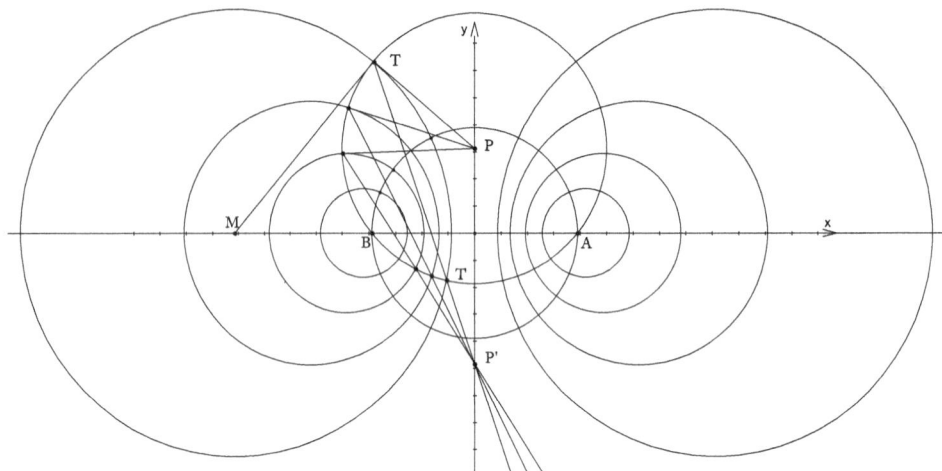

Figure 4

P and P' are thus conjugate points of an involution on the y-axis. Each circle k' of the second pencil therefore induces *the same involution* on the y-axis. Each circle k of the first pencil intersects the y-axis in conjugate points of this involution.

We can show in exactly the same way that every circle of the first pencil generates *the same involution* on the x-axis. Each circle k' of the second pencil intersects the x-axis in conjugate points of this involution. The involution on the x-axis is opposite (hyperbolic), with real double points A and B, whereas on the y-axis a direct (elliptic) involution is induced.

The latter involution possesses two imaginary double points which are characterized by the *strait* or *amplitude EE'*, the points of intersection of the smallest circle k_0 of the first pencil with the y-axis, as we shall see.

We add, without proving it, that a rectangular hyperbola is associated with each circle k' of the second pencil, a hyperbola which touches the circle in its vertices on the x-axis. Thus the second pencil of circles induces a set of rectangular hyperbolas. It turns out that the hyperbolas all meet each other in the points E and E' of the y-axis (Fig. 5).

It is a good idea to have the students describe how the circle changes as it goes through its pencil. In the second pencil, the disappearance of the circle in point A and its emergence in point B is of interest. The figure of the two orthogonal pencils of circles lends itself to an abundance of beautiful picture exercises.

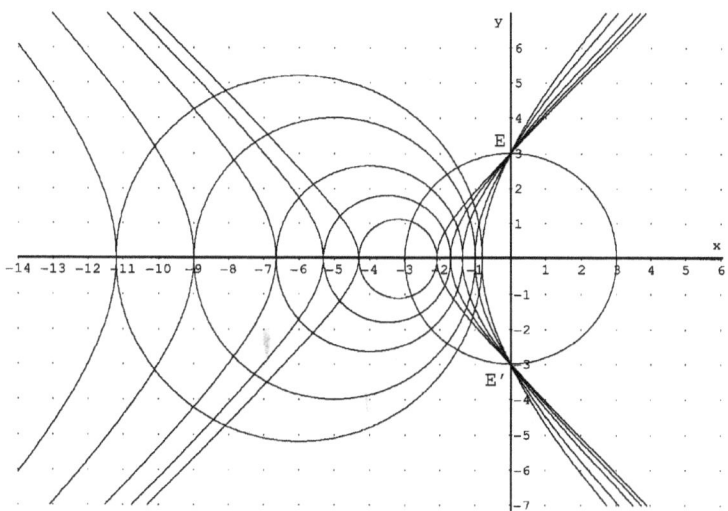

Figure 5

4 A geometric interpretation of complex solutions

If we calculate the coordinates of the points of intersection of any two circles of the first pencil we of course always obtain the same pairs of real solutions $A(x_A, y_A)$, $B(x_B, y_B)$.
If $A = (a, 0)$ and $B = (-a, 0)$, the parametric equation of the first pencil is

$$x^2 + (y-t)^2 = a^2 + t^2.$$

For the parametric equation of the second pencil we obtain:

$$(x-s)^2 + y^2 = s^2 - a^2.$$

If we calculate the points of intersection of any two circles of the second pencil, we obtain first always the same radical axis $x = 0$ and then the imaginary solutions $y = \pm i \cdot a$. The points $E(0, a)$ and $E'(0, -a)$ are the points of intersection of the radical axis with the circle about O with radius a, the smallest circle of the first pencil. Arnold Bernhard calls the segment EE' the *strait*[6] of the elliptic involution. Wherever we place the pencil of circles in the coordinate system, we obtain two conjugate complex solutions both for the x- and for the y-values. We conjecture that *the complex solutions always lead to the characteristic points E and E'*!

To see this we confine ourselves in the calculation to the power line (as special circle of the pencil) and another circle of the pencil, and calculate their points of intersection. Furthermore we

---

[6] Enge

choose a general passant line for the power line and put the center of the circle at the origin of the Cartesian coordinate system. The foot of the perpendicular from the circle's center to the passant determines the passant's position completely. The result is Figure 6:

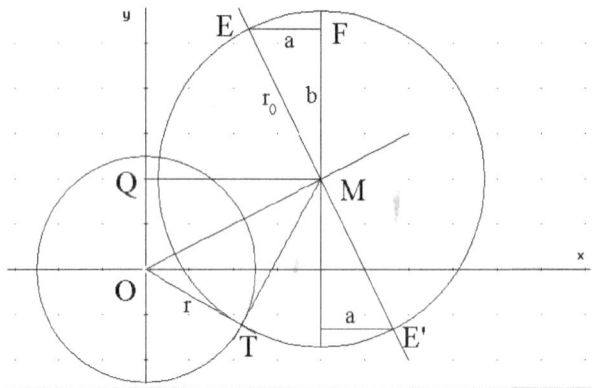

Figure 6

Suppose the circle about O has equation $x^2 + y^2 = r^2$.

And the coordinates of the foot M of the perpendicular from the origin O to the passant g are (x_M, y_M). Then the line g has equation

$$\frac{y - y_M}{x - x_M} = -\frac{x_M}{y_M}$$

Let $E(x_M - a, y_M + b)$ and $E'(x_M + a, y_M - b)$ be the points of intersection of the passant g with the circle k_0 about $M(x_M, y_M)$, circle k_0 intersecting the given circle about O orthogonally in T. Then by the similarity of the triangles MEF and OMQ (Fig. 6)

$$\frac{a}{y_M} = \frac{b}{x_M}, \quad \text{and thus} \quad a \cdot x_M = b \cdot y_M. \tag{1}$$

The theorem of Pythagoras applied to triangles MEF and OMT produces the equation

$$a^2 + b^2 = x_M^2 + y_M^2 - r^2 = r_0^2. \tag{2}$$

For the complex coordinates of the common imaginary points of circle and passant we make the following guess:

$$S_1(x_M - i \cdot a, y_M + i \cdot b) \quad \text{and} \quad S_2(x_M + i \cdot a, y_M - i \cdot b)$$

If this is correct, the coordinates must satisfy the equations of circle and passant. Substitution in the passant's equation gives:

$$\frac{y - y_M}{x - x_M} = \frac{i \cdot b}{-i \cdot a} = -\frac{b}{a} = -\frac{x_M}{y_M}, \quad \text{since} \quad a \cdot x_M = b \cdot y_M,$$

and so the passant's equation is satisfied.

Substitution in the circle equation gives

$$(x_M - i \cdot a)^2 + (y_M + i \cdot b)^2 = r^2$$
$$x_M^2 - 2 \cdot x_M \cdot i \cdot a - a^2 + y_M^2 + 2 \cdot y_M \cdot i \cdot b - b^2 = r^2$$
$$-2 \cdot i \cdot (a \cdot x_M - b \cdot y_M) = a^2 + b^2 + r^2 - (x_M^2 + y_M^2).$$

Therefore, because of equations (1) and (2), we have

$$0 = 0.$$

By the same token the second pair of complex solutions also satisfies the line and circle equations.

We must not of course identify the real points E and E' with the imaginary points S_1 and S_2. Yet for students it is satisfying that the real coordinates of the characteristic points E and E' are identical with the real and imaginary parts of the complex solutions if we omit the imaginary unit i.

At this point one can go directly into the representation of a complex x-coordinate as an arrow on the x-axis and the complex y-coordinate as an arrow on the y-axis. Translating the arrows to the point M and adding them in the usual way then leads to the arrows $\overrightarrow{ME}$ and $\overrightarrow{ME'}$ by which the involution on g is normally represented.

A note in conclusion about the terms hyperbolic and elliptic. We explained the concept of involution by means of the pole-polar relation with respect to a circle. With the orthogonal pencils of circles we have seen that the involution on the power line is determined by the two double points A and B and is independent of the choice of a particular circle: every circle through A and B generates the same involution.

It can be shown that every ellipse, parabola and hyperbola through A and B also creates, with the pole-polar relation, the same involution on the line AB.

In the projective plane there's a special line, the line at infinity. Every conic section generates an involution on the line at infinity as well. Since every hyperbola intersects the line at infinity in two real points, it generates on it an opposite involution with two real double elements, which explains the name «hyperbolic».

The line at infinity is a passant line to every ellipse, thus generating on it a direct involution with two imaginary double elements, hence the name «elliptic».

Creating Regular Solids from the Tetrahedron

UWE HANSEN

By comparing two polar opposite solids (polyhedra) we can enable the student to get to know the polar elements of space and the relationships between them. The student can then go on to study the connections and correspondences between polar processes such as the following.

If a point of a solid approaches the solid's center, then the polarly corresponding plane of the polar-opposite solid recedes from *its* center proportionately. If a point moves along the edge of a solid, the plane polar to that point rotates about the corresponding edge of the polar-opposite solid.

If a line turns in the vertex of a solid then the polar line moves correspondingly in that plane of the polar-opposite solid which is polar to the vertex. If a line actually moves in a flat pencil, the polar line also moves in a flat pencil.

By means of such movement processes the polarity between a range of points and a sheaf of planes, and the self-polarity of the flat pencil, become especially clear. Through exercises in spatial imagination these polar relationships can be experienced even more strongly than through the corresponding exercises in the geometry of the plane.

Particularly important is the contrast of «inner» and «outer», of kernel and surround. If two solids penetrate each other, we can ask: What points do they have in common? We then arrive at the *kernel* of the interpenetrating solids. The planes surrounding both solids form the *surround* of the interpenetration. With kernels we are thinking point-wise from inside to outside; with surrounds the center is the plane point at infinity, while with kernels we are thinking with respect to the solid's central point. This comparison begins to develop a feeling for counterspace.

Here the solids are still considered entirely in the sense of Euclidean geometry. But the law of polarity paves the way for the essential elements of projective geometry.

The following shows how starting from the tetrahedron we can then go on to develop other regular and semi-regular solids. This way of developing solid geometry can provide a direction for the lessons.

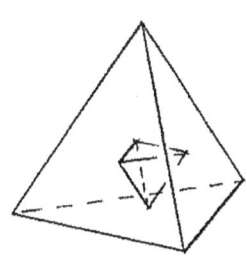
Figure 1

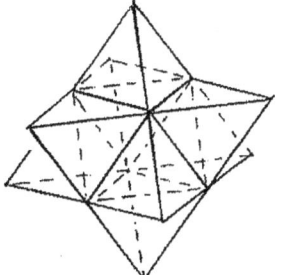
Figure 2

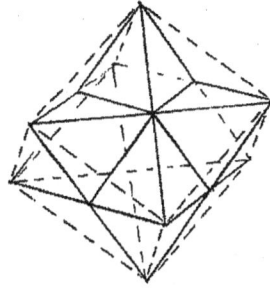
Figure 2a

Creating Regular Solids from the Tetrahedron   Uwe Hansen

The tetrahedron is the only one of the five Platonic solids that is self-polar. The centers of the tetrahedron's faces thus form another tetrahedron (figure 1).

If we expand the small, inner tetrahedron from the two tetrahedra's common center until both tetrahedra are the same size we get the double tetrahedron (figure 2). The edges of the two tetrahedra bisect each other; they also intersect at right angles.

These two tetrahedra penetrate each other in such a way that the points lying inside both – including the boundary points – form the interior points of an octahedron. The kernel of the interpenetrating solids is thus an octahedron. At the same time all the planes surrounding both tetrahedra surround the cube whose eight vertices are those of the two tetrahedra, just as the eight octahedron faces are also faces of the two tetrahedra. The plane-surround of the double tetrahedron is thus the plane-surround of a cube (figure 2a). We can also see this in figure 3 where the tetrahedra are standing on edge.

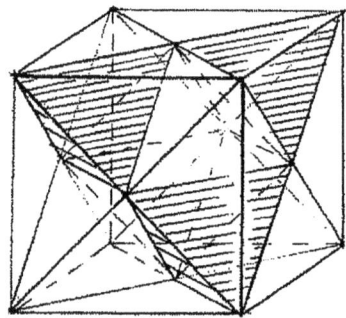

Figure 3

Cube and octahedron are polar-oposite solids. The centers of the cube faces are the octahedron's vertices. Each three-edged cube vertex stands opposite a three-sided octahedron face. Equally each four-edged octahedron vertex lies in a four-sided cube face. Corresponding cube and octahedron edges are in perpendicular directions.

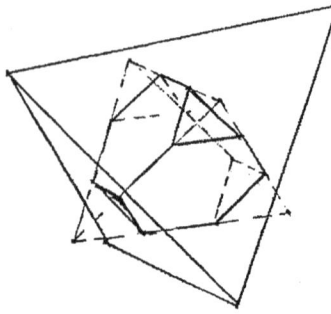

Figure 4

In figure 1 the smaller tetrahedron has edge-length one third that of the larger tetrahedron. If the smaller tetrahedron is enlarged so that the ratio of its edge-length to that of the larger becomes 3 : 5 then in the transition to figure 2 an important intermediate position occurs. The faces of the larger tetrahedron now cut off the vertices of the smaller in such a way that the triangular faces of the smaller tetrahedron become regular hexagons. What results is the truncated tetrahedron, an Archimedian solid, that is, a solid with edges of equal length and whose faces are regular polygons (figure 4). The truncated tetrahedron has 12 vertices, 18 edges and 8 faces: 4 triangular faces and 4 hexagonal faces.

The vertices of the truncated tetrahedron are the points of intersection of the larger tetrahedron's faces and the smaller tetrahedron's edges. At the same time a polar process takes place as the planes joining the little tetrahedron's vertices with the big tetrahedron's edges create the faces of a pyramidal tetrahedron. This is the polar-Archimedian solid corresponding to the truncated tetrahedron. The truncated and pyramidal tetrahedra arise simultaneously – they determine each other. In the vertices of the larger tetrahedron regular 6-faces (hexahedral angles) arise which are polar to the hexagons of the truncated tetrahedron (figure 5).

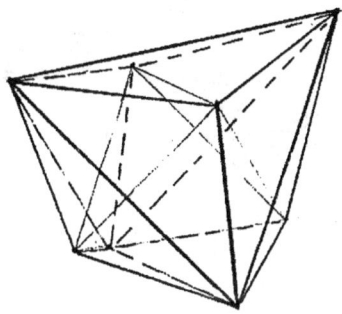

Figure 5

The vertices of the smaller tetrahedron intrude into the plane-space surrounding the larger one, and this space is reduced as a result. The planes of the larger tetrahedron correspondingly diminish the point-space of the smaller one.

In a polar-Archimedian solid the angle between any two neighboring faces is always the same; all vertices are regular n-faces (polyhedral angles).

The pyramidal tetrahedron has 12 faces, 18 edges and 8 vertices: 4 three-edged vertices and 4 six-edged vertices. The laws of polarity in space can be introduced by comparing the cube and the octahedron; this could be done for example at the beginning of a main lesson block.

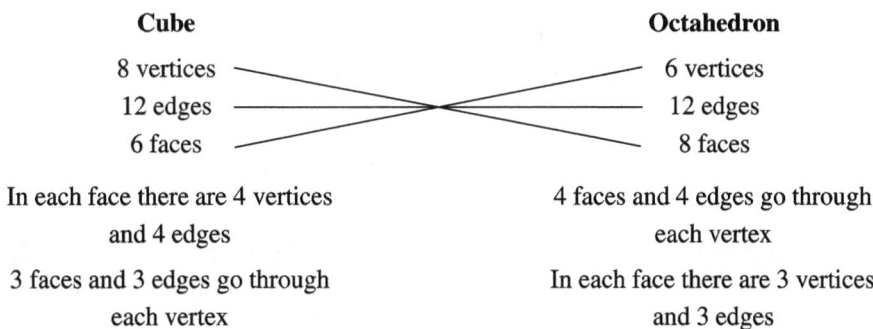

This comparison shows that Vertex (Point) and Face (Plane) are polar elements of space. The line is self-polar, mediating between Point and Plane.

These relationships are particularly well shown by the solid formed when cube and octahedron penetrate each other (figure 6).

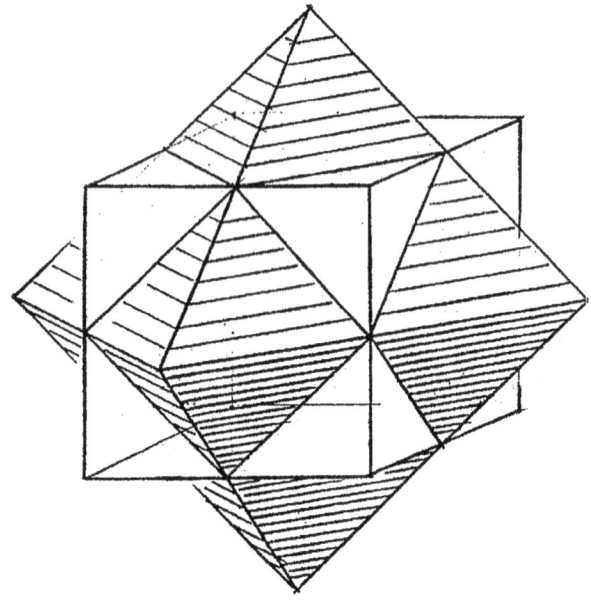

Figure 6

Cube edges and octahedron edges bisect each other. They are also perpendicular to one another. Each vertex of one solid is opposite a face of the other (polar) solid:

| three-edged vertex of the cube | — | three-sided face of the octahedron |
| four-edged vertex of the octahedron | — | four-sided face of the cube |

Mutually polar are:

4-edge	—	4-side
4-face	—	4-point
3-edge	—	3-side
3-face	—	3-point
Line joining two points	—	Meeting-line of two planes
A point moves along a line	—	A plane rotates in a line
(Range of points)	—	(Sheaf of planes)

A point moves along the three sides of a face of the octahedron.
  Polarly: a plane rotates about the three edges of a vertex of the cube. Since the octahedron's face lies entirely in the finite, the sense of this rotation must be chosen in such a way that the plane does not go through the center of the cube.

If a plane rotates about an edge in such a way that it passes through the central point then the polar point goes through the limit point (point at infinity) of the polar edge.

If a line sweeps though a flat pencil then the polar line sweeps though a flat pencil as well. If for example a line turns in an octahedron vertex in such a way that it sweeps over a face of the octahedron, then the polar line turns in a cube face in such a way that it remains in the cube vertex polar to the octahedron face, and also covers the cube's face.

If a line goes through the center, the polar opposite line is a limit line (line at infinity).

The concepts «limit point» and «limit line» must be developed in a meaningful way. This too can be done using figure 6, by first realizing that if two faces of a solid are parallel then the line joining the two polar vertices goes through the center. If two edges of a solid are parallel then the plane joining their polar edges goes through the center.

There is something else we can see in figure 6, namely that the kernel of these interpenetrating solids, that is to say the largest solid lying in both cube and octahedron, is the cuboctahedron (figure 7). The vertices of the cuboctahedron are the points of intersection of the cube edges and the polarly corresponding octahedron edges. Hence the solid polar to the cuboctahedron is formed by the planes connecting the cube edges and the polarly corresponding octahedron edges. This solid is the rhombic dodecahedron (figure 8).

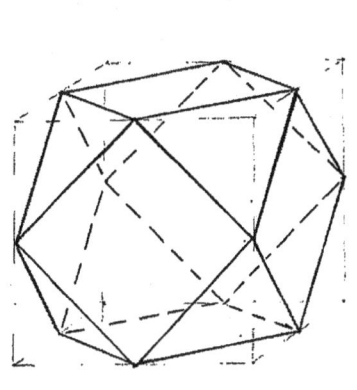
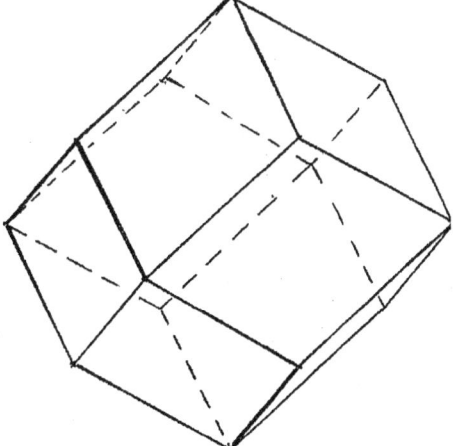

Figure 7

Figure 8

Cuboctahedron

12 vertices

24 edges

14 faces (8 triangular, 6 square)

Rhombic Dodecahedron

12 faces

24 edges

14 vertices (8 three-edged, 6 four-edged)

The cuboctahedron is an Archimedian solid; the rhombic dodecahedron is the corresponding polar-Archimedian one. Since the cuboctahedron, like all Archimedian solids, has no *insphere* (sphere touching every face) the centers of the cuboctahedron's faces do not form the rhombic dodecahedron.

All points lying inside both the cube and the octahedron (see figure 6) form the cuboctahedron. All planes surrounding the cube and the octahedron surround the rhombic dodecahedron.

Four more semi-regular solids can be formed from the interpenetration of cube and octahedron.

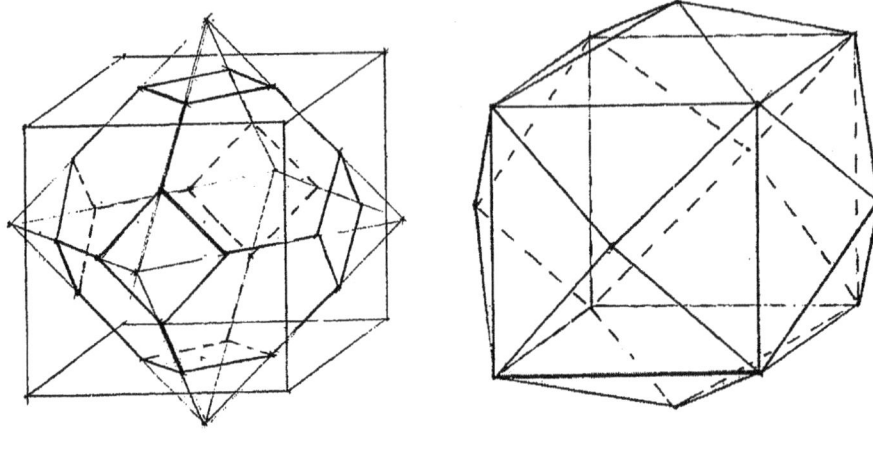

Figure 9   Figure 10

In figure 9 the octahedron penetrates the cube in such a way that the octahedron's axis is 1.5 times as long as the edge of the cube. The result of this is the truncated octahedron, an Archimedian solid, and the pyramidal cube, a polar-Archimedian solid, which arise simultaneously (figures 9 and 10). The ratio 1.5 is chosen so that the octahedron's faces become regular hexagons, and regular 6-faces arise in the vertices of the cube.

Truncated octahedron	**Pyramidal cube**
24 vertices	24 faces
36 edges	36 edges
14 faces	14 vertices
(6 squares, 8 regular hexagons)	(6 four-edged, 8 six-edged)

The truncated octahedron is produced from the octahedron by cutting off square pyramids from its six vertices. «Plane-wise» pyramids are also cut off in the pyramidal cube. This is because the cube's surround of planes is reduced by six regions of planes, each region bounded by a vertex of the octahedron and by the four vertices of the polar face of the cube (figure 11).

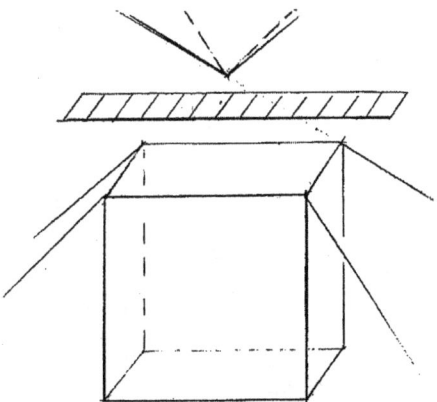

Figure 11

The «opposite» penetration is obtained if a cube vertex pushes through the polar face of the octahedron. This again results in two semi-regular solids provided the cube's half-diagonal is greater by a factor of $3 : (1+\sqrt{2}) = 1.2426\ldots$ than the distance from the cube's center to the center of an octahedron face. The result now is the truncated cube (figure 12) – an Archimedian solid – and the pyramidal octahedron (figure 13) – a polar-Archimedian solid.

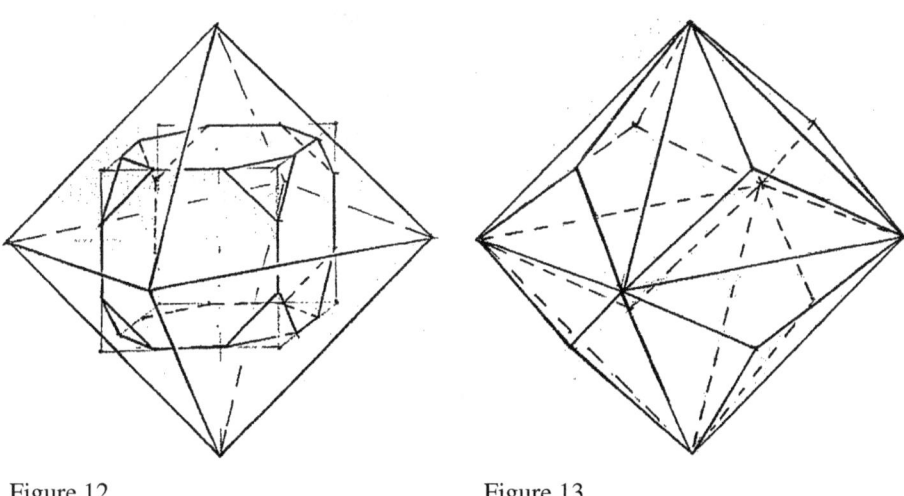

Figure 12   Figure 13

Truncated cube
24 vertices
36 edges
14 faces
(6 regular octagons,
8 equilateral triangles)

Pyramidal Octahedron
24 faces
36 edges
14 vertices
(6 eight-edged and
8 three-edged vertices)

The vertices of the truncated cube are the points of intersection of the faces of the octahedron and the edges of the cube. The faces of the pyramidal octahedron are the planes connecting the vertices of the cube with the edges of the octahedron.

Cube and octahedron intersect in such a way that the cube faces become regular octagons, and that regular 8-faces are produced at the octahedron's vertices.

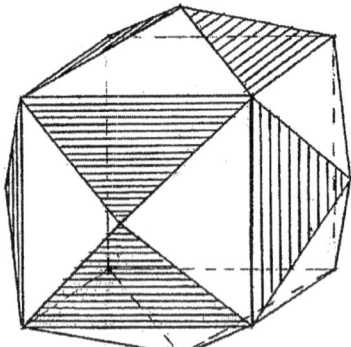

Figure 14

There is an interesting connection between the truncated cube and the truncated octahedron: they have the same number of vertices, edges and faces. Thus a superficial consideration could lead us to suppose that the truncated cube is polar to the pyramidal cube. Yet this is not the case because the solid which is polar to the latter must exhibit regular hexagons like the truncated octahedron, whereas regular octagons are not allowed to occur.

The pyramidal cube can be understood as the kernel of two interpenetrating dodecahedra. For if we take every other face of the pyramidal cube (figure 14) and let these intersect, the result is a solid bounded by twelve symmetrical pentagons which are not equal-sided however (figure 15).

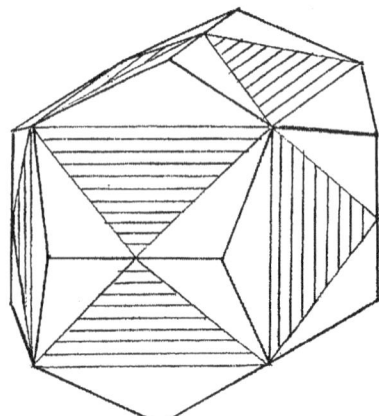

Figure 15

The pyramidal cube was produced when an octahedron penetrated a cube, the length of the octahedron's axis being 1.5 times the length of the cube's edge.

If the octahedron's axis is now increased in length to $\frac{1}{2}(1+\sqrt{5})$ times the cube edge ($\frac{1}{2}(1+\sqrt{5})$ = 1.618...), then the pentagons of figure 15 turn into regular ones and the result is the pentagon dodecahedron.

Thus we obtain this pentagon dodecahedron by having the octahedron and cube penetrate each other in the ratio of the golden section. The faces of the pentagon dodecahedron arise if each vertex of the octahedron is connected to two opposite edges of the cube-face polar to that vertex (figure 16).

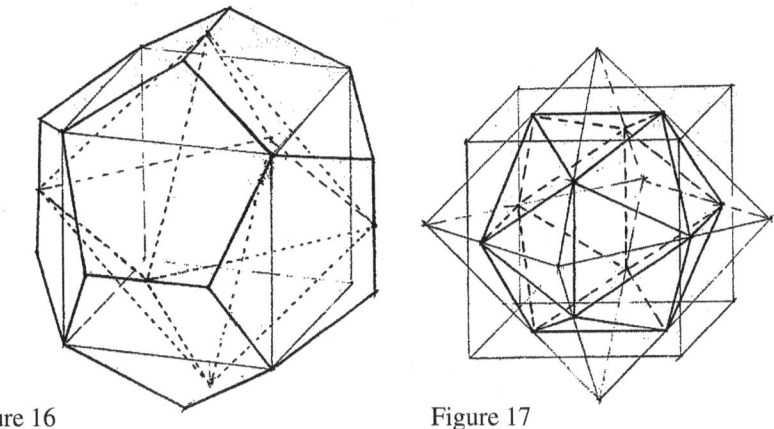

Figure 16   Figure 17

The polar process is as follows. The vertices of an icosahedron arise if each cube face is intersected by two opposite edges of the octahedron vertex polar to that face (figure 17). Again these two polar opposite solids arise simultaneously.

What we have seen so far can be summarized in the following schema:

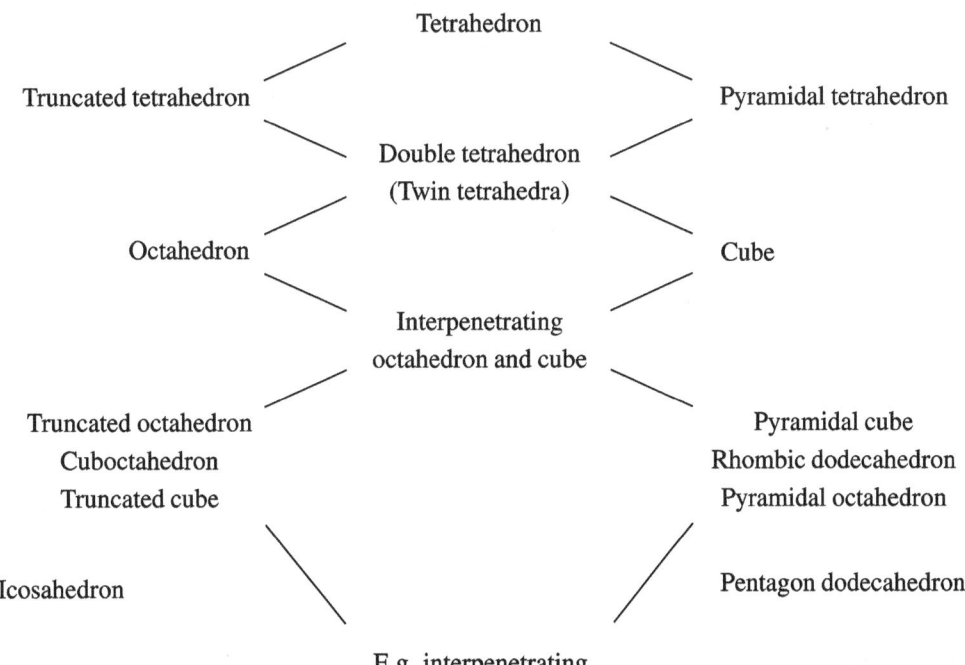

This process of generating further solids by forming kernels and surrounds of two interpenetrating solids can be continued. Here are some examples in which the interpenetrating solids meet each other in their edges.

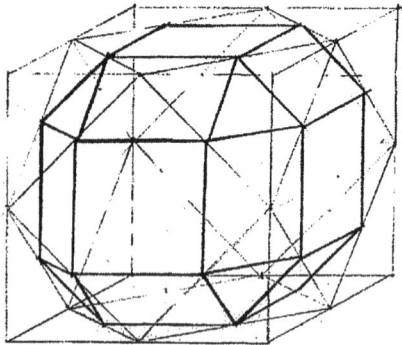

Figure 18

Figure 18 depicts the solid which is the kernel of the interpenetration of a cuboctahedron and a rhombic dodecahedron. This solid is not Archimedian since rectangles arise (with sides in the ratio $1 : \sqrt{2}$). However it does have a circumsphere (sphere through all its vertices).

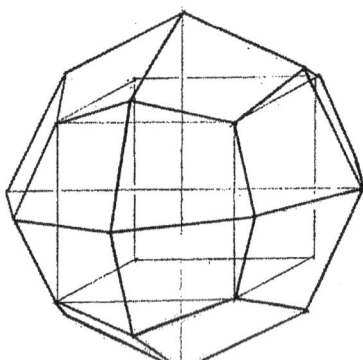

Figure 19

Figure 19 shows the polar opposite solid. It is the surround of the interpenetration of a cuboctahedron and a rhombic dodecahedron. It is not an Archimedian solid yet does have an insphere.

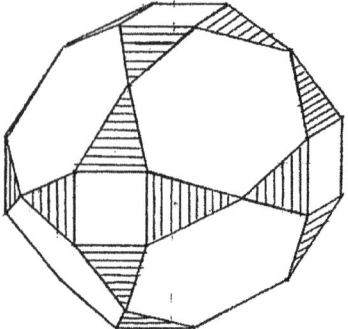

Figure 20

Figure 20 shows the kernel of the interpenetration of pyramidal cube and truncated octahedron. Again this solid is not Archimedian but does have a circumsphere.

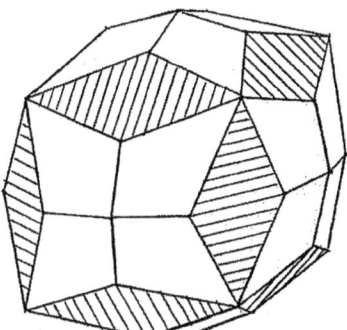

Figure 21

Figure 21 shows the surround of the interpenetration of pyramidal cube and truncated octahedron. It has an insphere but is not a polar-Archimedian solid.

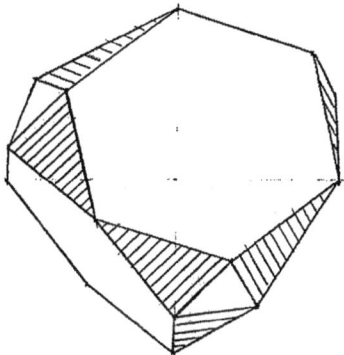

Figure 22

Figure 22 shows the kernel of the interpenetration of truncated tetrahedron and pyramidal tetrahedron – a non-Archimedian solid which possesses a circumsphere.

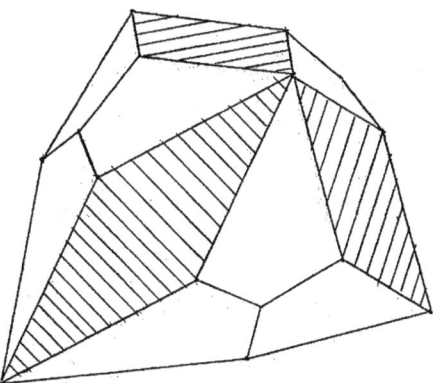

Figure 23

Figure 23 is the solid which is its polar opposite. There are many solids formed by interpenetrations whose kernels and surrounds exhibit neither circumsphere nor insphere nor *edge-sphere* (sphere touching all the edges), for example the interpenetrations of octahedron and pyramidal cube, or of tetrahedron and pyramidal tetrahedron.

A Note about Limits

UWE HANSEN

In the 11th grade greater demands are made on the intellect of the student, because the penetration by Will and Imagination characteristic of mathematics can only be sustained by particular kinds of thinking activity.

The student must experience how the active will is brought into the the intellect to spark the power of imagination there. This is necessary for example when defining limits or when statements about infinite sets are made.

It is in this developmental phase of the approximately-seventeen-year-old that a marked inwardness, an increasing psychological and intellectual sophistication appears. And it is in this phase that, by dealing with mathematical contradictions and paradoxes, the human «I» is specially fostered and strengthened as it separates and frees itself from the soul.

The contradictions arising in our day in connection with set theory appeared basically already in the time of ancient Greece. *Zeno* of Elea, for instance, attempted in his famous paradox to show that truth lies not in multiplicity, in the mutability of things, but in the whole, in the eternal grasped by thought: true being is One. Therefore, he said, an arrow in flight is at each moment in one particular place, and so cannot be moving! This completely logical conclusion Aristotle tried to refute (Book 6, Chapter 9 of his «Physics»), by declaring that, on the contrary, time does not consist in the indivisible Now. In taking limits too – here we restrict ourselves mainly to limiting values of sequences – we have on the one hand the multiplicity of of the members of the sequence, and on the other the law –the One – by which they are determined. First we shall consider some examples.

Example 1
A whole is divided into three equal parts. The middle third (see Figure 1) is again divided into three equal parts, and this process is repeated successively. The middle sequence of fractions tends to zero. Thus if we add together all the numbers on the left, or equally all those on the right, both sums approach the same limit of 1; the 2 total sum must be 1 after all. This statement can also be justified by Figure 2 ...

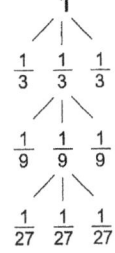
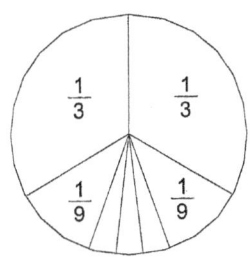

Figure 1   Figure 2

... or by the following equations:

$$1 = \frac{1}{3} + \frac{1}{3} + \frac{1}{3}$$
$$= \frac{1}{3} + \frac{1}{9} + \frac{1}{9} + \frac{1}{9} + \frac{1}{3}$$
$$= \frac{1}{3} + \frac{1}{9} + \frac{1}{27} + \frac{1}{27} + \frac{1}{27} + \frac{1}{9} + \frac{1}{3}$$
$$= \ldots$$

From this it follows that:

$$\frac{1}{3} + \frac{1}{9} + \frac{1}{27} + \cdots = \frac{1}{2}$$

The essence of this proof is that we systematically divide up a whole into summands (parts which are summed), and consider one of the summands which forms a sequence tending to zero.

This result is also obtained from a simple geometrical consideration (see Figure 3).

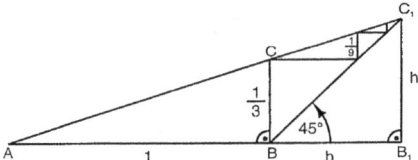

Figure 3

Because of the similarity of triangles ABC and AB_1C_1, $1+h$ must be three times h. Therefore $h = \frac{1}{2}$. Thus we have a legitimate division of the height:

$$\frac{1}{2} = \frac{1}{3} + \frac{1}{9} + \frac{1}{27} + \cdots$$

Here too a whole is divided up, and in the actual making of a judgment about the limit, *certainty* arises in the student.

This example can be generalized to an arbitrary sequence x_n in the middle which tends to zero and equal sequences a_n on right and left. Then the series formed by summing the sequence a_n converges to $\frac{1}{2}$. For $x_n = \frac{1}{5^n}$ and $x_n = \frac{1}{7^n}$ the scheme of Figure 1 becomes:

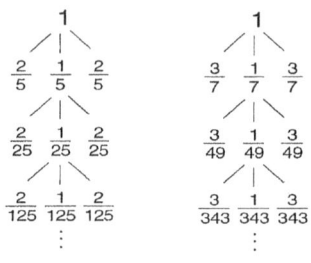

Figure 4　　　　Figure 5

respectively. Thus $\frac{2}{5}+\frac{2}{25}+\frac{2}{125}+\cdots+\frac{2}{5^n}$ must converge to $\frac{1}{2}$

hence $\frac{1}{5}+\frac{1}{25}+\frac{1}{125}+\cdots+\frac{1}{5^n}$ converges to $\frac{1}{4}$

and $\frac{3}{7}+\frac{3}{49}+\frac{3}{343}+\cdots+\frac{3}{7^n}$ must converge to $\frac{1}{2}$

hence $\frac{1}{7}+\frac{1}{49}+\frac{1}{343}+\cdots+\frac{1}{7^n}$ must converge to $\frac{1}{6}$.

This result leads us to suppose that

$$\frac{1}{k}+\frac{1}{k^2}+\frac{1}{k^3}+\ldots \quad \text{converges to} \quad \frac{1}{k-1}.$$

If we add 1 on both sides and set $\frac{1}{k}=q$, we get the well-known formula for the infinite series.

A further example is when for example the members of the sequence on the left are multiples of those on the right, say twice:

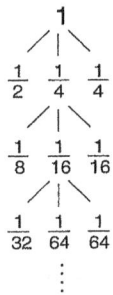

Figure 6

Here the middle number is always divided in the ratio 2 : 1 : 1. Since the sequence of middle terms again tends to zero, it follows that the series on the right converges to $\frac{1}{3}$, that on the left to $\frac{2}{3}$, because the sum total of 1 must be divided in the ratio 1 : 2.

Thus we have $\frac{1}{4}+\frac{1}{16}+\frac{1}{64}+\cdots=\frac{1}{3}$.

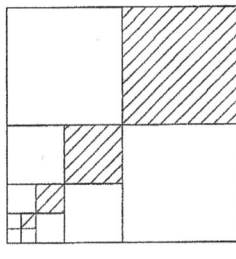
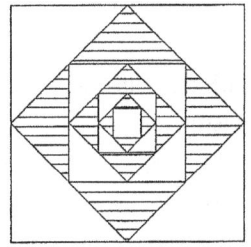

Figure 7   Figure 8

The same kind of argument works for Figures 7 and 8. For each shaded area there are two equal areas which are not shaded; hence in both squares the proportion of shading is one third.

Figure 8 can lead us to conclude that these squares «eventually» contract to a point. This is substantiated by the fact that there cannot be two distinct points lying in all the squares.

This must be countered with the fact that every square formed by the mid-points of the sides of a given square *is* another square; therefore to think of contraction to a point is impermissible.

However, the following should be stressed: this common point is determined by the ever-repeated step of the construction. So it is determined by the law present here, not by the infinitely multiplying squares. The «One» is decisive here and not the «Many».

Such arguments demand the whole of the student's inner strength. The student must act with his or her I to make a proper judgment. That way the I frees itself from the soul envelope. This is one of the goals of the teaching done in the 11th Grade.

Example 2

We consider the series

$$1 - \frac{1}{2} + \frac{1}{4} - \frac{1}{8} + - \ldots$$

This series determines the following partial sums

$$0; \; 1; \; \frac{1}{2}; \; \frac{3}{4}; \; \frac{5}{8}; \; \frac{11}{16}; \; \ldots$$

Regarding these values as co-ordinates, we have the picture shown in Figure 9. The points are labeled alternately A_n and B_n.

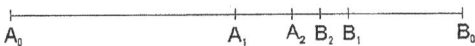

Figure 9

In this sequence of points $A_0 B_0 A_1 B_1 A_2 B_2 \ldots$ we get the next point by halving the last step $A_n B_n$ or $B_n A_{n+1}$ and making it in the opposite direction. This means that the segments $A_n A_{n+1}$ are always twice as long as the segments $B_n B_{n+1}$. Hence the point G which divides the segment $A_0 B_0$ in the ratio $2 : 1$ must be an upper bound of all point A and a lower bound of all points B. This means the series has limit $\frac{2}{3}$.

This way of arguing, which deliberately forgoes algebra, shows that the limiting value is directly determined by the construction law for the points A_n and B_n, and not by a complicated infinite sequence of intervals. In Zeno's sense, the reality is in the concept, the conformity to law, in the One and not in the Many.

The line of reasoning of Example 2 can be applied in the following series:

$$1 - \frac{1}{3} + \frac{1}{9} - \frac{1}{27} + - \ldots$$

In this case the current step is always one third of the preceding step in the opposite direction. Hence in this case the limit point G must divide the whole interval $A_0 B_0$ in the ratio $3 : 1$, so that the limit of the series given above is $\frac{3}{4}$.

Generalizing this argument we arrive at the conjecture:

$$1 - \frac{1}{k} + \frac{1}{k^2} - \frac{1}{k^3} + - \ldots \text{ has limit } \frac{k}{k+1}.$$

Here also, by setting $q = -\frac{1}{k}$, that is $k = -\frac{1}{q}$, we obtain the limiting value $s = \frac{1}{1-q}$.

Example 3

Consider the series

$$1 + \frac{2}{3} + \frac{4}{9} + \frac{8}{27} + \ldots$$

Let the limit of this series be s. Since each member of the sequence arises from the preceding one by the same law, the following ratios must be equal:

$$s : 1 = (s-1) : \frac{2}{3}$$

Because if we begin the series with $\frac{2}{3}$, the limiting value we get must be reduced by 1. Since the common ratio remains the same and 1 is replaced by $\frac{2}{3}$, so $s - 1$ must be $\frac{1}{3}$ smaller than s. Hence 1 must be one third of s, in other words $s = 3$. We arrive at the same result by solving the above equation of course. But the 3 is easier to understand if we don't – if we refrain from solving equations!

The following observation is intended to augment these thoughts.

A unit segment is halved. Each half is then halved again and this is repeated indefinitely. The letters L and R will be used to indicate whether the left or right half-segment is chosen after each bisection.

Thus for example the sequence $LRLR \cdots = \overline{LR}$ means that left and right halves are considered alternately. This choice determines the point with co-ordinate $\frac{1}{3}$. Because by writing $\overline{LR}$ as a binary fraction we obtain

$$\overline{LR} = 0.\overline{01} = \frac{1}{4} + \frac{1}{16} + \frac{1}{64} + \ldots$$

$\overline{RL}$ determines the point with co-ordinate $\frac{2}{3}$. The point with co-ordinate $\frac{2}{3}$ is represented by $\overline{LRRL}$.

In each case a point is identified that lies in every segment of a sequence of segments. This point is determined in advance by the law. In the absence of such a law, the sequence of intervals is not determined. It is the «law of what is given» that produces something infinite.

A consequence of this is that a random number generator giving an infinite sequence of zeros and ones that would produce a nested sequence of intervals cannot exist. Putting it somewhat more generally, it is unthinkable that a sequence as a ready-made whole could arise by arbitrarily choosing its individual members.

The next example, too, shows us that thinking can have limits to which we should pay heed.

Example 4

Starting with an infinite sequence of sequences, *Cantor*'s diagonal procedure enables us to determine a new sequence.

E.g. consider the arithmetic sequences

$$\underline{1}\ 2\ 3\ 4\ 5\ \ldots\ a_n^{(1)} = n$$
$$1\ \underline{3}\ 5\ 7\ 9\ \ldots\ a_n^{(2)} = 2n - 1$$
$$1\ 4\ \underline{7}\ 10\ 13\ \ldots\ a_n^{(3)} = 3n - 2$$

and so on, thus in general $a_n^{(k)} = (n-1)k + 1$. In this array the diagonal terms

$$a_n^{(n)} = n^2 - n + 1$$

form a second-order arithmetic sequence. Thus a new sequence arises.

Consider the sequence of fractions

$$\frac{1}{2}\ \frac{1}{4}\ \frac{3}{4}\ \frac{1}{8}\ \frac{3}{8}\ \frac{5}{8}\ \frac{7}{8}\ \frac{1}{16}\ \frac{3}{16}\ \frac{5}{16}\ \ldots$$

that is to say fractions of the form $\frac{m}{2^n}$ in which m is an odd integer, and which are less than 1. These can be expressed in the ternary number system as infinite periodic «3-ary fractions», e.g.

$$\frac{3}{4} = 0.\overline{20}, \quad \frac{5}{8} = 0.\overline{12}, \quad \frac{7}{12} = 0.1\overline{1022}.$$

Taking the first place after the decimal point from the first fraction, the second place after the decimal point from the second fraction, and so on, we obtain the non-periodic fraction

$$0.122112220220211\ldots$$

This is also true if we move on to the anti-diagonal sequence, e.g. by cyclically permuting the three digits 0, 1, 2. Here too we obtain from the diagonal sequence a number that does not occur in the sequence.

It was with such an anti-diagonal sequence that Cantor sought in 1874 to prove the uncountability of the decimal fractions between 0 and 1.

Yet the question arises as to whether, in considering the totality of these decimal fractions as something given, we over-step the limit of what is thinkable.

Example 5

An arbitrary segment is divided into three equal parts. The middle third is removed, and the other two thirds are likewise divided into three equal parts and the middle third – that is to say one ninth of the original segment – again removed. This process is continued.

Figure 10

If we draw this «perforated» segment reduced to one third of its size then – provided we imagine the dividing process continued without limit – it will fit exactly twice into itself. It is therefore self-similar.

For this reason we give this «limit object» dimension D, where

$$2 \cdot \left(\frac{1}{3}\right)^D = 1 \quad \text{or} \quad D = \log_3 2$$

This characterization, that is to say the property of having a dimension, awakens the impression that such a «limit object» exists. Yet all the quantity D does is characterize the following process: From three parts make two parts – the middle third being removed each time. This process is the only real thing here. Regarding D as property of a limit object is objectionable because this limit object is a pure fiction.

The characterization R. Steiner has given is especially important in this connection. In the lecture of 18.3.1921 (GA 324, «Anthroposophy and science» [*Mathematik, wissenschaftliches Experiment*]) he stressed that what is mathematical lives in

> the constructive activity of the soul, and is thus experienced in the continuous activity itself and in the soul's perception of its own activity.

The soul's throwing light on its own activity, its having become picture of its own activity, can therefore be seen as so to speak the archetypal gesture of the mathematical. In mathematical activity the two polar soul activities of the human being – Will and Imagination – are really very closely bound up with each other.

In Example 4 given above – the limit object looked at is called «Cantor dust» – we leave the realm where we perceive our own activity. This is because we imagine that the infinitely many steps of the construction which are *possible* are already carried out. But we should not leap to the conclusion here that *we necessarily remain in the process.*

Example 6

Let ABC be a right-angled isosceles triangle with $AC = CB = 1$ and $AB = \sqrt{2}$ (Figure 11). Let A_1, B_1 be the mid-points of the segments AC, BC respectively, C_1 the mid-point of AB. Then the chain of segments $AA_1C_1B_1B$ has the same length as the chain ACB, namely 2. Points A_2, B_2, C_2, A_3, B_3, C_3 are likewise mid-points of the relevant segments. The chain of segments $AA_2C_2A_3C_1B_3C_3B_2B$ in turn has length 2. This process can be repeated indefinitely; the resulting segment-chains always have length 2.

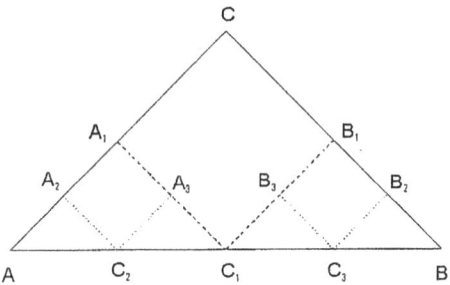

Figure 11

Is there a «limiting segment-chain»? Since the maximum distance from the segment AB of all points of the chain after the n-th step is $\frac{\sqrt{2}}{2^{n+1}}$, it is natural to regard the segment AB as the limiting line. But this cannot be the case, since segment AB has length $\sqrt{2}$ only.

If we regard the segment chains as graphs of functions f_n and consider the sequence of function values $f_n(x)$, where x is the x-co-ordinate of a point of the segment AB, then we always have $\lim_{n \to \infty} f_n(x) = 0$. What holds for the individual points x, does not hold for the whole segment-chain. In other words, we cannot characterize the whole by the properties of the parts.

It is surely desirable to acquaint the adolescent student with the ideas of Georg Cantor (1845-1918). Here one can point to the contradictions arising from Cantor's definition of a set:

> By a set we understand the bringing together to form a whole M of particular well-distinguished objects m of our perception or thought, called the elements of M. (*Contributions to the founding of the theory of transfinite numbers*, 1895 – the quotations are taken from «G. Cantor, Mathematical and philosophical treatises [Abhandlungen mathematischen und philosophischen Inhalts]», edited by E. Zermelo, 1932.)

In this definition it is required on the one hand that a set is formed by any collection of elements – hence the parts determine the whole – and on the other hand it is stipulated that this multiplicity is a whole, something fixed, a «constant» as Cantor says.

Cantor himself saw that his definition of a set is full of contradictions. The gross arbitrariness of the choice of elements contradicts the unity of the whole. In a letter to R. Dedekind of 28.7.1899 he writes:

> ... a multiplicity can be obtained in such a way that the assumption of a «gathering together» of all its elements leads to a contradiction, so that it is impossible to grasp the multiplicity as a unity, as a «finished object». Such multiplicities I call absolutely infinite or inconsistent multiplicities. It is not hard to convince oneself that, for example, the sum total of everything we can conceive is such a multiplicity (page 443 of the work mentioned).

The idea of the «sum total of everything we can conceive» shows that Cantor imagined that there is nothing that has not been thought – everything has already been thought. This inability to discriminate has often led to the so-called paradoxes of set theory.

This passage also shows how plausible abstract thinking can lead to self-contradictory thought structures without content. Yet by granting properties to these inconsistent multiplicities, Cantor showed that he regarded them as «things». The concept is reminiscent of the concept of «a circle with three corners».

Cantor imagined these absolute infinite multiplicities are only realized «in God»; he differentiated between them and the abstract «actual infinity» (pages 372 and 378 of the work mentioned above).

In a letter of 28.8.1899 Cantor poses the question to himself even: Are sets such as for example the set of all real numbers («Aleph 1») not perhaps inconsistent? He demanded the consistency of these multiplicities as an axiom of an extended transfinite arithmetic (which does not solve the problems either).

For Cantor, for every infinite set M there also exists the set M_1 of all subsets of M, the so-called power set of M, which always has a greater cardinality than M. Assuming this we can construct, by continued formation of power sets, a countably infinite sequence of sets of ever greater cardinality. Cantor was convinced that by means of this unbroken ascent of cardinalities, which he called Aleph 0, Aleph 1, Aleph 2, ..., every conceivable cardinality is accounted for.

In a letter of 31 August 1899 to Dedekind, Cantor went on to consider the system of all sets. For each cardinality a he took a set M_a of this cardinality and combined these sets into an overall set T. T itself possess a definite cardinality a_0. The power set of T then has a higher cardinality a'_0. But since all cardinalities appear in the sets that are united to form T, the cardinality a_0 of T must be at least a'_0. Hence we must have both $a_0 < a'_0$ and $a'_0 \leqslant a_0$.

This argument of Cantor's we have outlined can be summarized briefly as follows:

The set of all sets is a meaningless concept since the cardinality of its power set is greater than its cardinality, even though as set of all sets it must contain its own power set.

Here the problematic nature of considering infinite sets as given totalities, as was demanded by Cantor, reappears at a higher level.

To require that the set of all sets exists corresponds to asking for the greatest whole number, the formation of the power set corresponding to the transition from n to $n+1$.

Today one tries to get round this contradiction by means of an axiomatic structure. Whether such contradictions reappear just the same, only time will tell.

The last observation above points to the fact that considering limits within set theory calls for particular attentiveness. Moreover it should show that the ideas represented by Zeno about the relation between the One and the Many have their justification today as well.

Index

4-line, 166
4-point, 166

altitude theorem, 39
analytical geometry, 21
angle bisector, 9, 41, 223
angle cos cos rule, 233
angle cosine rule, 230, 232
angle of intersection, 8
anharmonic ratio, 88
antipode, 213
Archimedian solid, 270
arithmetic sequence, 282

basic elements, 104
bearer, 79
Brianchon Theorem, 142, 187
bundle of lines, 104, 153
bundle of planes, 104, 153

cassinian curves, 26
center of rotation, 7
central projection, 58, 72
circle, 44, 52
circle equation, 43
commutative, 8
complete 4-point, 90
complete 4-side, 93
complete hexahedron, 124
complete octahedron, 128
complete quadrangle, 90
complete quadrilateral, 93, 205
conchoid, 29, 31
conic section, 137, 239
coordinate system, 22, 38, 50
cosine rule, 230

cross-ratio, 201
cube, 108, 267
cuboctahedron, 109
curriculum indications, 49
curves of position, 21

Desargues configuration, 98, 160
Desargues Theorem, 70, 75, 116, 161, 181
digon, 216
double ratio, 88

ellipse, 44, 52, 240, 250
elliptic involution, 261
Envelope, 69
Euler line, 226

field of lines, 81
field of points, 81
fundamental structure, 131

great circle, 212, 223, 229, 231

harmonic configuration, 95, 205
harmonic division, 88
harmonic lines, 93, 169
harmonic partial ratio, 170
harmonic points, 167
hexagon, 244
homology, 75
hyperbola, 39, 44, 52, 240, 249, 260

identity, 8
image triangle, 60
improper point, 150
involution, 259

latitude, 212

Index

law of polarity, 108
limit, 277
limit hyperbola, 253
limit points, 14
line, 44
line at infinity, 80
line field, 152
Locus, 69

mapping, 7
meridian, 229
Moebius band, 82

nautical triangle, 237

octahedron, 108, 266
orthogonal pencil, 257

Pappos Theorem, 198
parabola, 43, 44, 52, 240, 248
Pascal line, 244
Pascal Theorem, 142, 177, 244
pencil of lines, 79, 104, 152
perpendicular bisector, 37, 223
perspective collineation, 75
perspective cube, 119
perspective map, 79
plane at infinity, 81
plane pencil, 153
platonic solids, 112
point at infinity, 61, 79, 246
point field, 104, 152
point range, 79, 104, 152
pole, 214
principle of duality, 97
projection, 89
projective plane, 69
pyramid, 114
pyramidal cube, 270

pyramidal octahedron, 271

radical axis, 255
reflection, 9, 10
rhombic dodecahedron, 109, 269
rotation, 7, 10

secant tangent theorem, 40
sequence, 278
sheaf of planes, 104, 153
side cos cos rule, 232
side cosine rule, 227, 232
sine rule, 228, 231
small circle, 212
special linear complex, 154
sperical triangle, 231
spherical geometry, 211
spherical triangle, 213
spherical trigonometry, 227
strophoid, 27
synthetic projective geometry, 49

tetrahedron, 113, 123, 265
Thales Theorem, 219
topology, 49
transformation, 8
transformations, 85
translation, 10
trapezoid, 201
truncated cube, 271
truncated octahedron, 270

unreal bearers, 154

vanishing lines, 151
vanishing plane, 151
vanishing point, 60, 149

www.ingramcontent.com/pod-product-compliance
Lightning Source LLC
Chambersburg PA
CBHW081203170426
43197CB00018B/2904